The Spirit of Umunna and the Development of small Christian Communities in Igboland

European University Studies

Europäische Hochschulschriften

Publications Universitaires Européennes

Series XXIII

Theology

Reihe XXIII Série XXIII

Theologie

Théologie

Vol./Bd. 544

PETER LANG

Frankfurt am Main · Berlin · Bern · New York · Paris · Wien

Peter Osuchukwu

The Spirit of Umunna and the Development of small Christian Communities in Igboland

PETER LANG
Europäischer Verlag der Wissenschaften

Die Deutsche Bibliothek - CIP-Einheitsaufnahme

Osuchukwu, Peter:

The spirit of Umunna and the development of small Christian communities in Igboland / Peter Osuchukwu. - Frankfurt am Main ; Berlin ; Bern ; New York ; Paris ; Wien : Lang, 1995
(European university studies : Ser. 23, Theology ; Vol. 544)
Zugl.: Frankfurt (Main), Philos.-Theol. Hochsch. St. Georgen, Diss., 1995
ISBN 3-631-49301-0

NE: Europäische Hochschulschriften / 23

F 42
ISSN 0721-3409
ISBN 3-631-49301-0
US-ISBN 0-8204-2933-3

Satz: Unitext, Frankfurt a.M.

Printed in Germany 1 2 3 4 5 7

Dedication

to:

Akudo Victoria Ukaji (Nee Osuchukwu);

Alexander Bukuts (U.S.A.);

Nze (Chief) Osuchukwu Chigere (my Late Father).

Contents

Acknowledgements

I am filled with deep reverence and gratitude to God, who despite my failings called me to share in the ministerial priesthood of His Son and gave me the courage to pursue this study. Many persons were involved in the inception and development of this study, and I wish there were enough space to mention them all. Special thanks goes to my lovely mother who was the first person to introduce me to Christianity and Catholicity.

I wish to express my gratitude to my Bishop, Rt. Rev. Dr. M. Eneja, who punctuated my pastoral work with this study in Europe. My special and unalloyed thanks go to my academic adviser Father, Prof. Dr. Ludwig Bertsch SJ, whose concern gave me the most effective tools with which to fight my academic battles. Words cannot express the extent of my gratitude to the respected professors of the *Phil.- Theologische Hochschule Sankt Georgen, Theologische Fakultät*, Frankfurt; especially Prof. Dr., Michael Sievernich SJ, who with patience and kindness not only helped me in this work, but allowed me to draw from his profound wisdom of personal experience in Latin America. The final composition of this work is due to the incisive suggestions of Prof. DDr. Anicletus Odoemene. I owe him my respect and gratitude.

Professor Leo Karrer's method of teaching and conducting seminars in pastoral theology inspired me to pursue the study. Also in the Staff of the University of Fribourg in Switzerland with Karrer is my respected Professor Dr. Christoph von Schönborn OP (Auxilary bishop of Vienna) whose humility and erudition inspired and brought about significant and positive changes in my life.

Were it not for the Diocese of Basel (Switzerland) that assisted me financially, and the fatherly care of Rt. Rev. Dr. Msgr. Anton Cadotsch (Vicar General), both the study and this work would not have seen the light of day. To him, I am very grateful. Thanks go to the Institute of Missiology Missio for financing my trip to Kenya for this research. Special thanks also go to the Diocese of Limburg (Germany) that gave me a home in Hochheim. Here I met wonderful people and families:- Karlheinz Wagner, Michael and Birgit Bukuts, Klaus Wagner, H. Lepka, Josef Bock, Klaus and Annette Zwaack, J.K. Koschnitzki, Walter Pankala, M. Bourgeon, A. Barysch, Hans-W. Bauing Schäfer, Pfarrer W. Pfaff, R. Rupert, Christian Pönitz; Frau Linden, Rita Büdel, Theresia Hück, A. Lauer; Christine Wodarz, Nadine Cyranka, Katharina Schröck, Peter Wagner and members of Kolping familie Hochheim.

As the Igbo saying goes: "there is sometimes a relation in a strange land"; so I found a home in the family of Metzler of Bad Homburg. Thanks to Mama Katharina Metzler, for her love and care. She was instrumental in my coming to Germany. Thanks also to the family of Josefine and Erich Schäfer (Darmstadt) and the caring Dominican sisters in Marien Krankenhaus Flörsheim. I am grateful to these families, Aebischer, B. Hollinger, F. Hofstetter, and Rev. Fr. F. Hobi OP (all from Switzerland), for their concerns and help. My special thanks goes to Mrs. Ann Breckenridge for reading and correcting the first draft of this work and thanks to her husband and their children for allowing her the needed time. Thanks also go to Mr. David Blaz and Frau Hunter Schoefert (Hochheim) who read the final script.

A work like this attracts a lot of help by way of materials, suggestions and criticisms; for these, I am grateful to the Rev. Frs. Chikodi.J. Ike, G. Ohaeri, Austin Echema, H. Okeke, T. Anyanwu, J. Aguwa, C. Nwosu, C. Ehiem, R. Madu, C. Ushi, G. Nwachukwu, and a host of others, including Rev. Prof. N.N. Iwe. Thanks to the students and staff of CIWA, Port Harcourt, for caring and allowing me to use their resources for this work. Those who feel that their names should have appeared here, I did not forget you, but for want of space, I simply say thanks and God bless you all.

Abbreviations

A.M.C.	Annual Mission Collection
AAS	Acta Apostolicae Sedis (Roma)
Acts	Acts of Apostles
ADS	AMECEA Documentation Service
AFER	African Ecclesial Review
AG	Ad Gentes
AMECEA	Association of Member Episcopal Conferences in Eastern Africa
Apg	Apostelgeschichte
APS	Acta philologica Scandinavica (Kopenhagen)
Art	Article
BCC/BCCs	Basic Christian Community/ties
Bd/e	Band/Bände
BECs/ECBs	Basic Ecclesial Community/ies
C.I.C.	Codex Juris Canonici
C.M.S.	Church Missionary Society
Cf	Confer
CFO	Catholic Fathers Organization
Co.	Company
CONV	Convergencia (Journal of Brazilian Conference of Religious)
Cor	Corinthians
Corp.	Corporation
CTS	Catholic Truth Society
CWO	Catholic Women's Organization
DC	District of Columbia
Dec.	December
Deut	Deuteronomy
ed/s	Editor/s
EN	Evangelii Nuntiandi
Eng.trans	English translation
Eph	Ephesians
Exd/Ex	Exodus
Ezek	Ezekiel
Ezr	Ezra

Feb.	February
ff.	following/s
Gal	Galatians
Gen.	Genesis
GS	Gaudium et Spes
i.e.,	id est (that ist)
Ibid	Ibidem (the same reference)
Idem	Same author
JBL	Journal of Biblical Literature
Jer	Jeremiah
JHSN	Journal of Historical Society of Nigeria
Jn	John
JTS	Journal of Theological studies
LG	Lumen Gentium
Liv	Leviticus
Lk	Luke
Ltd	Limited
Mk	Mark
Mtt/Matt	Matthew
MTZ	Münchener Theologische Zeitschrift
n.d.	No date
Neh	Nehemiah
Nr./s	Number/s
NT	New Testament
NTS	New Testament Studies
OT	Old Testament
p/pp	page/s
Phil	Philippians
Ps	Psalm
Publ./s	Publication/s
Rev. Fr.	Reverend Father
rev.ed.	Reversed edition
Rom/RM	Romans
Sam	Samuel
SBS	Stuttgarter Bibelstudien
SC	Sacrosanctum Concilium
SCC/SCCs	Small Christian Community/ties
SECAM	Symposium of Episcopal Conference of Africa and Madagascar
St	Saint
TDNT	Theological Dictionary of New Testament

ThW	Theologisches Wörterbuch
UK	United Kingdom
v.	Verse
Vol.	Volume

General Introduction

The rapidity of population growth and migration to urban areas in Igboland today is alarming. The Igbo traditional community faces the harzards of modernization brought about by the impact of urbanization with its concomitants of materialism and secularism. Before Nigerian independence, the Igbo had less than three urban areas, but today they are numbered in tens. Urbanization has become the most important social reality in Igboland. This development poses a pastoral problem to the Church.

Important Igbo morals and values are eroding away due to the ills that are associated with modernization. Some of these values include respect for authorities and old people, reverence for sacred things and places, concern for the less privileged, hard work for all etc. These are the bedrock for community life. The secretariat for Promoting Christian Unity confirms the above view when it notes:

> A breakdown of traditional social structures, cultural patterns, and traditional sets of values, caused by industrialization, urbanization, migration, rapid development of communication systems, all-rational technocratic systems etc., leave many individuals confused, uprooted, insecure, and therefore vulnerable.[1]

Another effect of urbanization is also seen in the division being created between dwellers in the cities and those in the hinterland. This is giving rise to instability within the framework of the Igbo community. The Igbo have different social and political settings. One of these is *Umunna*[2] community. *Umunna* -'kinship' or 'patrilineage', is the social group or unit common to the Igbo. This refers to the agnate who are capable of tracing their links to a common ancestor. One may rightly say that this hereditary unit is the proper and fundamental social, religious and political unit in Igboland. This unit is so important that care is taken not to incur its wrath, for to be cut off or excluded from it is considered a real tragedy. Ekechukwu, an Igbo theologian, expresses it thus:

---

1 **Vatican Secretariat for Promoting Christian Unity, Sects or New Religious Movements in the World: Pastoral challenges, (United States Catholic Conference, May 3, 1986), p 12.**

2 Umunna - literally meaning "**children of the same father**". The explanation and etymology of the term will be given later.

That one should be in good relationship with one's patrikin is accentuated by the fact that the ancestors are the heads of the lineage who look after the welfare of the living and to be cut off from the patrilineage means losing the protection of the living and the dead.[3]

The *umunna* pattern of living is based on three basic principles of traditional life. The first of these is 'respect', which entails a recognition of mutual involvement with one another – Love. Each member of the *umunna* unit recognizes the place and rights of the other members. It is a concept of mutual relationship in the community. No one ever thinks of himself as complete in himself and independent from the rest of the community. The concern for one another is intrinsically embedded in the psyche of the people. Although the rights within *umunna* vary according to sex, age, ability and character, care is always taken to see that there is a minimum below which no one can exist without disgracing the whole *umunna*.

The second principle is related to property. The basic goods are held in common and shared among members, who are descended from a common ancestor, who is believed to be the owner of these goods. This principle expresses also that whatever one person has in the way of basic necessities, belongs to all. No one goes hungry while others hoard food. And no one is denied shelter while others have space to spare. Inequalities exist, but they are tempered by comparable family or social responsibilities. The inequalities are never allowed to grow in such a way that they threaten the basis of *umunna* community life.

The third and final principle is the obligation to work. Different tasks are done by different people, but each must do something. Rights and obligations are commonly distributed to all. This last principle is basic for the smooth running of the *umunna* and for the continuation of the other two principles.

In Igboland, *umunna* ensemble serves to stabilize the Igbo community. This can be done through its value systems, one of which is the family. Family and community ties are strong, in spite of the new technical civilization. Other important values include community life, leadership, self-regulation etc. *Umunna* serves as a base for education and awareness of Igbo and Christian values in

---

3 A. Ekechukwu, "**The problem of suffering in Igbo traditional Religion**"; in: **AFER** (African Ecclesiastical Review), vol. 24, 2(1982), p. 160. Simon Ottenberg writing on the organizational structure of Afikpo (a town in Igboland), says: "The organizational structure of the village group is complex, being characterized by double descent group structure under the leadership of senior age groupings and priests of special shrines." "**Personal Shrines at Afikpo**", in: **Ethnology: An International Journal of Culture and social Anthropology**, vol. ix, (University of Pittsburgh, U.S.A., 1970), p. 27. Ottenberg was trying to describe the workings of ***Umunna***; instead of looking at the formation he only saw the functionaries.

the face of modernization. The Igbo favour small groupings that are quite personal and caring.

The threat from the ills of urbanization does not affect the Igbo society alone, but also the Church. A notable development in this is increasing secularization. The Church's value systems are not only questioned but radically criticized. A community-oriented Church is giving way to individualistic tendencies. Religion and religious matters are shelved to the realm of the private. Following the example of a worldly division of labour and its spirit of specialization, religious matters are left to the few active Christians, termed specialists. And participation in the life of the Church is left to these specialists. Such Church participation is reduced to mere Sunday services.

Since the distortion of man's life due to the ills of urbanization, there has been the quest for belonging or the sense of community, the search for answers, for cultural identity, for wholeness, for transcendence, and the need for spiritual guidance, vision, participation, and involvement. There is a breakdown of traditional values and feelings of frustration common in our world today that cause people to look for fulfillment and belonging. The Church has not been able to deal with these problems adequately.

The result has been the birth of numerous sects and religious movements. Such sects seem to supply the answers. Those who are not patient with the Church tend to look for sects. The problem of sects prompted the Vatican Secretariat for promoting Christian unity in 1986 to publish the document, "Sects or New Religious Movements in the World". This document addressed a serious concern expressed by episcopal conferences around the world, which calls for;

> a rethinking... of the traditional parish community system; a search for community patterns which will be more fraternal, more adapted to people's life situation; more basic ecclesial communities: caring communities of lively faith, love (warmth, acceptance, understanding, reconciliation, fellowship), and hope; celebrating communities; praying communities; missionary communities: outgoing and witnessing; communities open to and supporting people who have special problems: the divorced and remarried, the marginalized.[4]

The traditional parish structure was introduced into Igboland with the coming of the missionaries. They evangelized the people and set up the parish structures which were familiar to them. They did not take into consideration the people's socio-religious and political set-up. The parishes were too large and consequently encouraged anonymity among Christians, who as a people were used to small social units.

---

4 Vatican Secretariat for Promoting Christian Unity, op.cit., (1986), p.13

They transported the Western parish structure, where parishes are seen as a territorial unit or geographical district, rather than as a community. Moreover, the central concerns of early missionaries in Igboland lay in intra-Church activities, such as the teaching of religious doctrine, the dispensing of sacraments and other means of spiritual sanctification, and the ordering of the Christian body through ecclesiastical discipline and legislation. Though moral conduct was part of pastoral concerns, this morality was conceived of in terms of the person's own conscience. The people's cultural setting were neglected. The Igbo still look at the Church and its structure as imported, because they do not fit into the parish structure.

This is a system where a mission or parish is considered, for pastoral purposes, as consisting of a certain number of outstations, i.e., territorial subsections of the mission. The consideration here is primarily geographical, organizational, and administrative. Some of these subsections are now parishes, but the system still remains the official policy of the Church in Igboland. The Church in Igboland is still wearing the European garment of modern society.

Despite these European trappings, we still experience great numbers of people trooping into the churches on Sundays. Such attendance may give the impression that the Church has come to stay. The parish structure as described above is not very apt in building a Christian community. Whereas this structure can cope with large groups, with numbers of people whom the few priests can serve only when they assemble in crowds, the fear is that we may have achieved numbers, while members are few. Can the Church at this rate survive and take root in Igboland?

Some critics hold, and sometimes correctly, that faith has not found a home in Igboland and that most Igbo Christians live in two worlds: the world of their traditional culture, religion and social groupings; and the prestigious life of Sunday-Sunday Christians. There should be an emphasis today on the need to revitalize the parish structure and to develop a spirit of personal and communal responsibility among all Christians for the mission of the Church. Naturally, the best means to this is to create structures based on a caring community. A local community like the *umunna* has the ability for such a structure. Our thanks goes out to the Vatican II Fathers, who on the dogmatic constitution on the Church stressed the importance and role of the local community:

> This Church of Christ is really present in all legitimately organized local groups of the faithful, which, in so far as they are united to their pastors, are also quite appropriately called Churches in the New Testament... In these communities, though they may often be small and poor, or existing in the diaspora, Christ is present...(LG 26, cf. 28).

We deduce from the document that the local community of the faithful should be above all a Church of communion and community, a sharing

Church, a Church which respects its members and consults them seriously, a missionary and evangelizing Church, a caring and serving Church. Both the Church and *umunna* communities have a lot to offer each other. The *umunna* can and should use her values, roles, community or social structure and its participatory-oriented governance for the incarnation of the Church; while the Church will elevate the profane nature of *umunna* to a sacred level and offer *umunna* the real trinitarian concept of God, as will be seen later in this work.

For sometime now there has been a movement towards a more practical and community oriented Church. Vatican II highlighted this and it was reiterated by the Synod of Bishops in 1985, when they clearly said:

> The ecclesiology of communion is a central and fundamental idea in the documents of the Council. *Koinonia*/Communion, based on Sacred Scripture, was held in great honour in the ancient Church and is so held in the Eastern Churches right up to our time. Since Vatican II much has been done to make the Church, as communion, more clearly understood and more concretely translated into living reality.[5]

They stressed the Church as **communio**. This has given rise to many Christian communities. In Latin America, for example, the formation of Basic Ecclesial Communities is associated with the people's struggle for liberation. But in East Africa, the Small Christian communities are a pastoral option of the hierarchy. *Umunna,* being a cultural setting, will equally serve as a Christian community.

The mention of *umunna* as a Christian community is capable of eliciting varied opinions. Some will see *umunna* as a very satisfying and exhilarating experience to be employed. Others may see it as a dangerous phenomenon, where people might become insulated, capsuled and complacent, and the outcome may be a privatized faith. *Umunna* Christian Communities are not seen as Churches of themselves, but as part of the larger parish, indeed of the universal Catholic Church, the people of God.

Umunna here will be seen as a help to deepen the Church's tradition, teaching, leadership and guidance[6]; in this way, the working of the parish will be made more meaningful for the Igbo. The parish at this point will be an umbrella shading all *umunna* communities, thus "becoming Community made up

---

5 **SYNOD REPORT**: **The Final Report and Message to the People of God** ***of the Extraordinary General Assembly of the Synod of Bishops*** Rome, 24 Nov. - 8 Dec., 1985, on the theme: **The Second Vatican Council** ***A celebration, reaffirmation and a carrying forward of its work;*** (Catholic Truth Society, London, 1986), **Do 571**, p.15.

6 Cf. Kleissler, T.A., et alia, **Small Christian Communities: A Vision of Hope**; (Paulist Press, New York/Mahwah, 1991), p. 3.

of many small communities"[7] According to this pastoral vision, the parish consists of communities rather than the geographical units of outstations. The primary consideration is given to local communities (*umunna*) rather than the administrative convenience of the pastor.

It will be a radical view to equate *Umunna* with the Church community, as it was in Europe to speak of the Catholic Church as a community (*Gemeinde*, in Germany) years before the Second Vatican Council.[8] But looking at the theology of the community as an ethical pastoral idea for the pastoral care after the Vatican II, we have no hindrance in employing this idea into the Igbo *umunna* set-up. When one understands the theology of community, that we need a living community, and going through the basic tasks of the Christian community, which includes the proclaiming of the Good News, liturgy and service to the community, the temptation will be more on studying the *umunna* set up in Igboland as a fertile ground for the formation of Small Christian Communities (SCCs).

We envisage reactions to the use of or option for *umunna*. Some may regard it as a passing fad. Others may think that it is subdivision of the outstation which they claim to be a full-fledged Christian community. It does not mean that there are no problems or difficulties.

One may ask: How can the peculiar situation and context of Igbo Christians be integrated in the organization of their Christian life? How can the Igbo, while sharing in the One, Holy, Catholic and Apostolic Church express their faith in their cultural situation without being forced into a monolithic or uniform structured catholic Church?[9] How can our parishes in Igboland be structured using the *umunna* set-up? Can the parish be divided into *umunna* communities, where all Christians know each other and collaborate to form a true unity in their Christian life and endeavours?

---

7 Bernardin, J., "**Evangelizing the Active Catholic**", in: **Pentecost '87 Supplement; A national Satellite celebration of Catholic Evangelisation, Sunday, June 6, 1987;** (Paulist National Catholic Evangelization Association, Washington, D.C., 1987), p.17

8 Wilhelm Zauner clearly says: "Im Bereich der Katholischen Kirche redet man noch nicht sehr lange von Gemeinde. Wer es vor etwa vierzig Jahren schon getan hat, konnte damit rechnen, des Protestantismus geziehen zu werden". "**Prinzip Gemeinde?**" **Diakonia** - Heft 6(1980), p.361. "*For a longtime, no one could speak of the Church as a 'community' in the Catholic world. Any one who did that about forty years ago would have been termed a protestant*".

9 Experience shows that the Catholicity of the Church consists in the richness of its two thousand year tradition; a tradition extended not only in time but also in space. For more on the Catholicity of the Church see A. Dulles, **The Catholicity of the Church**, (Clarendon Press, Oxford, 1985).

How can the Igbo Christians express their own values of community, harmony, and solidarity in the context of their Christian faith? Can the *umunna* community be used as a base for the establishment of Small Christian Communities in Igboland? Is it possible to have *Umunna* as Christian Community? Is the *umunna* we are proposing problem free?

Does *umunna* belong to the State structure or is it a merely religious set-up? Will *umunna* help the Church to evangelize profane society, or does it help profane society to derive the full benefits of the Church's life as represented by the parish structure? Is *umunna* a catalyst for grace and full participation of the laity in the life of the Church? What will be the role of the laity within the *umunna* ensemble? Will the use of *umunna* give rise to a powerful lay authority in the Church? Does obedience to the parish priest reduce the role of the laity? What will be the role of the priest in such a set-up?

These problems and questions constitute the scope of this work. In order to achieve a community-oriented Church from the Igbo perspective, we shall make an in-depth study of community in Igbo context. This will form the first chapter of our work. We shall start by discussing *umunna* as being a system of patrilineal organization which not only determines one's rights and duties accruing from such membership, but gives one the base for social, religious, political and economic life. In the attempt to describe *umunna* we shall see its scope, whether strangers can be admitted. Since *umunna* is also the minimal polity in Igboland, time will be taken to discourse its administrative make-up, after which we shall have a sociological survey of community in Igboland, its people and how it views the world.

There is an awareness that the greatest source of hope in the Church today lies in Small Christian Communities. Over the course of the Church's history, small communities have played a significant role in proclaiming and developing the love of God for his people. The efforts of these small communities is our focus in the second chapter as we consider Christianity as a community religion. This will entail a survey of community life expressed in the Bible. In the Old Testament we shall see how God's will was expressed in small communities. The community life of Jesus and his disciples will be described in our survey of New Testament writings. Here we shall consider the early Christian communities and the development of the house Church.

The quest for a relevant structure for the Church has always preoccupied Church officials and theologians. We shall take account of the development of the Church, from the house church to parish structures. Then the history of the Church structure in Igboland will be explored to see if we need a relevant structure for the Church in Igboland. All these will be handled in Chapter Three. In Chapter Four, we shall look at the Basic Christian Communities and evangelisation. A survey of BCCs and SCCs in both Latin America and Africa will be made.

The question on how the Church should exist and function using the people's cultural set-up will preoccupy us in the fifth chapter, as we explore *umunna* traditional and the natural groups found in Igboland for a better understanding and structuring of the Church. There will be a proposal for the *umunna* unit as an ecclesiological order or structure. This is really en route to a *Umunna* Christian Community. There is no doubt that objectives and methods of ministry are determined ultimately by how those in the ministry understand the Church. Here we shall look at structural, theological and ecclesiological significance of Umunna Christian Communities.

We are not giving a detailed blueprint of how to build a Christian community. To do so would be to return to the old structures. We are giving pastoral hints which may help to overhaul the traditional parish system. These hints will enable the parish to move away and to develop into a communion of communities.[10] Our ultimate aim is to contribute something to a more authentically African Christianity. Problems shall be raised, suggestions made, but the actual solution must be worked out in practice.

---

10 Cf. Hetsen, J. and Holmes-Siedle, J., "**Aspects of Christian Community Building in Africa**", in: **SPEARHEAD**, **Nr. 75**, (Gaba Publications, Kenya, 1983), p.19.

Chapter One: Umunna – A basic Igbo community

1.0. Introduction

In pre-colonial times, many African societies were stateless. Groups of families who claim descent from a common ancestor form a community that can be said to be basic to every other community, an exogamous and important unit of a tribe. In such societies, to one of which the *Igbo* belong, political, social and religious functions are carried out on a primary level, a little above that of the family to accommodate other families, forming what the Igbo call *umunna*. This monogenetic entity determines and shapes the political, social, military and religious life of a tribe, and today, even nations, and can therefore never be overlooked, especially by the evangelizing Church.

This basic community is the most intense form of community. It is a small group of people who feel related because of common ancestry. At this level, everybody knows everybody else. This basic community is on the level of what is called the *primary group*. The level is characterized by affective (as opposed to merely utilitarian) motives, and by direct, intimate, and face-to-face contact, because of its blood relationship and its small size. It is also called a primary group because it is the first place where a child is socialized. This is a group that influences the whole life of an individual.

In such basic groups, people meet to discuss their problems, to share what they have and to bring about reconciliation among those members whose inter-personal relationships leave much to be desired. Such groups in Igboland normally have common ancestors. There are other settlements which can equally give rise to a basic community, where common ancestor or linage may not be the purpose of the community, such as settlement in an area due to urbanization, or agricultural, political and social reasons.

In the case of the Igbo people, we shall be considering the traditional basic community called *umunna*. In *umunna*, there exists a common spirit of belonging, solidarity and communal life. This spirit affords its members union and a sharing of ideas, thoughts and sentiments, which requires living together intimately, sharing goods, sharing responsibilities and tasks, and also requires participation at the level of resources and responsibilities. The spirit in *umunna*, as we shall see later, calls for the recognition of the society as an extension of the basic family unit. This spirit is life-embracing, a vehicle for social integration, the spirit of communion and of compassion. When aware of the above facts concerning the spirit within *umunna*, one notices that an *Igbo,* wherever he finds himself, tries to form a community where he can express some of these qualities.

In this first chapter, we intend to study the phenomenon (history, nature and functions) of the *umunna*-community in Igboland, to see how this community and its spirit could be used as a platform for the formation of Basic Christian communities. This basic community in Igboland, *umunna*, as we shall see later, promotes morally unobjectionable objectives that are meant to improve human conditions. We shall view *umunna* communities through an historical approach. We shall explore some of the sociological factors which shape our contemporary *umunna* communities.

1.1. Igbo People and community life

The term *Igbo or Ibo*[11] stands for both the people and their language. A lot has been written concerning the origin, use and etymology of the term Igbo.[12] We shall limit ourselves to certain facts that have relevance to our work and as far as possible the term Igbo will be preferred to Ibo; since *Ibo* is an anglicized form of the term *Igbo*.[13]

One important conceptual category which seems to have developed in the era of the slave trade was the distinction between **Igbo** and ***Olu/Oru***, inland and river-bank.[14] Actually the use of the words Igbo and Oru/Olu can be used

11 The word **Igbo** or **Ibo** has been very controversial. Some say that the word **Igbo** is the language, while **Ibo** are or is the People, and vise-versa. Cf. **Agu, C.C.,** Secularization in **Igboland: Socio-religious change and its challenges to the church among the Igbo**, Verlag Peter Lang, Frankfurt, 1989**.** Here he writes that "the anthropologists and the white man in general to circumvent the difficulty in pronouncing the letter '**gb**'. **Eboe, Hebos, Ebus,** and **Hebus** are also met in the very earliest records. Indigenous writers (some of them though, have even fallen prey to the anglicized form **Ibo**) prefer **Igbo.** The **Igbo** never addressed himself as **Ibo**. Cf. Azorji, E.E. **Some recurrent problems of Christian inculturation in Nigeria with special reference to the Igbo people;** (Roma, 1988), p. 155.

12 .The word **Igbo** has attracted a lot of questions, explanations, controversies regarding its origin, its derivation and meaning. See, Meek, C.K., **Law and Authority in a Nigerian Tribe;** (Oxford University Press, London, 1950), p. 1. "It may be suggested that the term **Ibo** means, like so many tribal titles in Nigeria, '**The Men**' or **The People".**

13 Agu, C.C., **Secularization in Igboland...**op. cit., 1989, pp.215f.

14 Isichei, E., **A History of the Igbo People:** (Macmillan London, 1976), p. 19. Cf. I. Nzimiro, **Studies in Ibo Political System:** (Frank Cass., London, 1972), p.3.; E. Isichei, **The Ibo People and the Europeans;** (Faber and Faber , London, 1964), p. 71; G.T. Basden, **Niger Ibos**, (Frank Cass., London, 1966), p. 121; M.A. Onwuejeogwu, **An Igbo**

to illustrate how the Igbo see the universe. The Igbo say: "*Agalam Igbo, gaa Oru ahubehum ihe di-otua*"(I have gone to Igboland and gone to Oruland, never have I seen a thing like that).[15] It can also mean people of the inland and riverbank respectively. There is also a saying that *jom maka azu, esim oru* (ask me anything about fish because I am from Oru). This goes to suggest that the Oru have a lot to do with water and fish. Both the Igbo and Oru are called *Ndi Igbo*, though those who are called or referred as Oru sometimes claim to be non-Igbo. These use the term Igbo in a derogatory way to mean the uncivilized.

> The Olu/Oru, with their well-watered farms and protein-rich diet, despised the Igbo, for their food and water shortages, and their role as slave suppliers.[16]

The Igbo language is generally spoken by everyone with little dialectical differences. The Igbo, generally speaking, are loving , caring but cunning. They are intelligent, business-like and very enterprising.

Geographically, *Igboland* is located in Southeastern Nigeria, approximately between Latitudes 5° and 7° north of the Equator and Longitudes 6° and 8° east of Greenwich. Apart from the large group of *Igbo* of the East, there are other *Igbo* settlements on the west bank of the River Niger.

Today the *Igbo* occupy the whole of the territory belonging to the states of *Abia*, *Anambra, Enugu*, and *Imo* of Nigeria and a good part of the *Delta* and *River states* as well. The *Igbo* as a group is surrounded by different ethnic groups which influence or are influenced by the *Igbo* race. In the South are the *Ijaws* and *Ogonis*; in the East, the *Ibibios*; and in the North are the *Igala; Idoma* and *Tiv* live to the Northeast; and the *Urhobo* and *Edo* live in the West beyond the Niger.[17] Talbot gave his own description of the *Igbo* by compart-

---

Civilization, *Nri* Kingdom and Hegemony; (Ethiope Publ. Corp., London, 1981), p. 8. Cf. S.N. Chinwuba Obi, **The Ibo Law of Property:** (Butterworths, London, 1963), p. 1; For the problem of terminology see P.O. Nsugbe, **OHAFFIA : A Matrilineal Ibo People:** (Clarenden Press, Oxford, 1974), p. 33.

15 **Oru** here means any faraway place or people of the other side of the world. When one goes to some distant place and spends some time, he is always said to have gone to **Oru.** And for the **Igbo** it is only **Igbo** and **Oru** that exist. The origin of the word is not yet known. For an **Igbo** to travel all over the world is to have gone to **Igboland** and **Oruland**. In the thinking of the **Igbo** the earth/world is made up of land and water. Those living on the land are called **Igbo** while those on the water-side are called **oru**.

16 Isichei, E., **A History of the Igbo People**, (1976), p. 19; See also C.C. Agu, **Secularization in Igboland**..., (1989), pp. 216-217.

17 Cf. Onwuejiogwu, M.A., **"The Igbo Culture Area" in: F.C.Ogbalu, and E.N.Emenanjo**, eds., **Igbo Language and Culture**; (Ibadan, 1975), pp. 1-3; C.K. Meek, **Law and Authority in a Nigerian Tribe**; (1965), p. 1.

menting them into subtribes and clans, basing his facts from the census of 1921.[18]

The *Igbo* are commonly estimated to make up 17% of the total population of Nigeria.[19] If we will accept the latest population estimate by the united Nations, the *Igbo* must now be over 15 million people, out of the 89.02 million population of Nigeria.[20] Culturally speaking, the delimited territory in which the one *Igbo* language is spoken in its diverse but mutually comprehensible dialects share typical and significant common culture traits and patterns. Such traits include living in basic units, title taking, love of freedom, caring for the family, the institution of age-grade and secret societies for law and order; their religiosity, ancestor worship, enterprising, equality of all and hospitality. Some of these traits help to form their world-view.

The ordinary person in Igboland does not merely talk about community. Community for the Igbo is lived and experienced by everyone, every day. Generally speaking, community as the Igbo understand it is a conscious commitment to give and share one and the same life with a limited number of people in a defined geographical area.

The sense of community is also a conscious commitment, where constant inter-action and inter-relationship among people are expected, working for the benefit of all. The Igbo see the community from the point of view of those relationships that are found between individuals, because of any of the shared

---

18 Cf. Talbot, P.A., **The People of Southern Nigeria,** Vol. iv, (Oxford University Press, 1926), pp. 39f.; Meek is of the opinion that the **Igbo** should be described as a tribe, "...because they speak a common language, occupy a common territory, and on the whole share a common culture and common out-look on life." With this type of argument, to qualify a people as a tribe attracted a comment from S.N. Chinwuba Obi: "But surely if these be the criteria of a 'tribe', then Wales and Eire no less than England and Scotland would be good examples of tribes." **The Igbo Law of Property** (1963), p. 5. The problem, I suppose, stemmed from the term "tribe" which the concise Oxford Dictionary defines as a "group of barbarous clans under recognized chiefs." One wonders, says Obi, whether the **Ibo** of 1937 when Meek wrote his book were really barbarians. The **Igbo** can be more qualified as a nation rather than a tribe.

19 Cf. **NIGERIA: Die Kirche im Volksreichten Land Afrikas,** in: **IFD**, Nr. 3240 (3.Februar, 1982), ND 58; Seng C., **"Gescheitertes Experiment mit der Demokratie",** in: **Herkorr**, 38(1984) 580. See also **New Nigerian: Census Figures Released,** Nr.8,073, (20.3.1992).

20 Cf. **United Nations Demographic Year-Book**; 1983, (N.Y., 1985), p. 163. But with the latest census of 1991 this estimate has been mate. See **New Nigerian** of Friday, March 20, 1992, Nr.8073 for census figures.

common factors, a family, a village community.[21] The principle underlying such relationships is expressed by Delespesse thus:

> The underlying principle may assert itself as given data: for example, children belong to a family without having chosen it; or it may be the result of a choice and a deliberate option, as when one freely embraces some religion. But in both cases, the bonds uniting the members are shown by love; without that a community might exist externally for a time, but would never be more than a body without a soul.[22]

The family is very important in Igboland, for it forms the basis of every community. A family is not a wholly patrilineal group. In Igboland it is focussed on an agnatic core of a man and his children, with his wife/wives and mother, whose patrilineal affiliations lie elsewhere. In patrilineal descent, members are all geographically dispersed groups of autonomous men, while a family is a domestic group whose members occupy a single homestead. The Igbo family is founded in and continues to be concerned mainly with domestic affairs. Patrilineal-descent groups are primarily associations of heads of families and therefore, indirectly, of the families themselves.

A family is characterized by a unity stemming from the authority of the family head, the husband and father; in contrast, a lineage group is known by the equality of its members and an absence of authoritarian control. There are two major phases in any family: that of the nuclear family, i.e., a man, his wives and their young children; and that of the compound family, when the original nucleus is augmented by heteronomous units, each comprising a married son with his wife and children.[23]

These two phases grow and merely identify the two main periods of the total process of a family's development. When the head of the family dies, the family breaks apart – giving rise to a number of successor nuclear families, each of which is headed by a son (usually the first son called *okpara*), and which now becomes an autonomous family. The first son of the man who is the *okpara* assumes the leadership role.

---

21 Cf. Mutiso Mbinda, J., *"Pastoral Anthropology and the Church"*,in **SPEARHEAD**, Nr. 60, Gaba Publications, Kenya, (1979), p. 46. A Community among other things is a union of human persons held together by an underlying principle, or by sharing the same values. This underlying principle unites the members in their very persons and makes them come to know and love each other. This knowledge acquired from the community is concretely expressed in sharing at various levels, both spiritual and material, in mutual support and in certain common life.

22 Delespesse, M., **The Church Community**, Ave Maria Press, New York, (1973), p. 10.

23 Gulliver, P.H., **Social control in an African society: A study of the Arusha - agricultural Masai of Northern Tanganyika**, Routledge and Kegan Paul, London, (1963), pp.70ff.

The father in a family, or *okpara* in case of the death of the father, holds the family together. The framework of the family expands, as we shall see later, from nuclear to compound, and finally, to town-state. These are mostly units of co-activity in a wide range of social situations. In their activities, the Igbo illustrate clearly the preoccupation with egalitarian individualism, tempered by the value of reciprocal assistance. This value helps to form and keep people together in a caring community.

One can rightly say that the community is the bedrock of Igbo existence. The Igbo person sees himself in relation to his community. Community is so important to the Igbo that death does not stand on its way. Igbo humanity is defined in the context of the community and the role each individual plays in this community for its growth and continuity. What G.H.Muzorewa says about Africans applies directly in a special way to the Igbo:

> So we find that African Humanity is primarily defined by a sense of belonging, serving one's own folk, and kinship. For the African, it is not enough to be a human being; unless one shares a sense of community.[24]

Solidarity and humanization find clear expression in the context of the community. Even in the Igbo traditional religion, humanity is conceived as "being" in relationship to others, just as Oduyoye says concerning Africans:

> Africans recognize life as life-in-community. We can truly know ourselves if we remain true to our community, past and present. The concept of individual success or failure is secondary. The ethnic group, the village, the locality, are crucial in one's estimation of oneself. Our nature as beings-in-relation is a two-way relation: with God and with our fellow human beings.[25]

An Igbo is defined within his/her own social context – community. For an Igbo not to be identified with or belong to a community is equivalent to death without the right of ancestorship. Igbo proper names illustrate these views. *Igbokwe* (if the Igbo as a community permits), *Igbojiokwu*, (The Igbo has to say), *Ohakwe* (If the clan agrees). This type of name can apply not only to Igbo as a race but also to the names of villages, town, kindred etc.viz *Mbakwe*, *Amauzarikwe*, *Madukwe*, *Ibekwe* (if the Town, village, man,others permit). There are names like *Okoronweike*, *umunnanweike*, *Igwebuike*(the kindred has the power, to be or belong to the community is power);*Nwaozuzu/Nwaoha*

---

24 Muzorewa, G.H., **The Origin and Development of African Theology;** (Obis books, Maryknoll, N.Y., 1985), p. 17.

25 Oduyoye, M.A., "The value of African Religious Beliefs and Practices for Christian Theology", in: **African Theology en Route**, eds., Kofi Appiah-Kubi and Sergio Torres, Maryknoll, Obis Books, New York, (1979), pp. 110-111.

(the child of the all, community), *Adaoha* (the daughter of the community), *Ohanyeaka* (community help); *Ihediohamma* (the child which has pleased the community).

Names such as these indicate the Igboman's view of both community and its growth and continuity, and also of children. It is through such names that the value of community solidarity is transmitted to the people.[26] Igbo beliefs, mentality, historical and social circumstances are revealed in the names given to their children.[27]

Mankind is a combination of male and female, a community of persons, a concept eloquently lived out in Igbo society. For an Igbo without community, life is rootless, homeless and anchorless. The concept of community is so paramount in Igbo thinking that a person is seen rather in relation to his community than as an individual. *Ebee ka osi* (where does he come from); *Kedu onumara osi* (to which community does he belong?): these are Igbo common questions. They are so wrapped up in community thinking that sin in Igboland has a more communal effect than on the individual who commited the sin. Community is not simply a place that can be identified by street names or village sign-posts, neither is it a town-hall where meetings are held on certain occasions, nor is it shopping centers or restaurants. It is persons, individuals engaged in the activities of living and dying, believing and hoping, searching for meaning in this world and beyond it. Song puts it thus;

> Community is a matter of the spirit. It has to do with the future, and it has to do with faith that transcends the limitations of the present.[28]

All these tend to illustrate the Igbo ideas of community. The Igbo look at existence in relation to others and the community in which they belong. It is the community that defines the individual. Onwu in his contribution on the Igbo notion of community says;

> From the concept of man, a concept necessary for the understanding of the nature of Igbo community , man is not only by name born into a community, he is also a man because of other men. Since man's existence mcans co-existence with others, a community is

---

26 The giving of names in **Igboland** is both circumstantial and historical. The **Igbo** history to a large extent can be derived from names. Circumstances are expressed in names.

27 Cf. Odigbo, G., **Eucharistie im Afrikanishcen Kontext: Ein theologisch-pastoralliturgischer Beitrag zur Neugestaltung der Messfeier bei den Igbo**. Als Lizentiatsarbeit vorgelegt dem Fachbereich katholische Theologie der Johannes Gutenberg-Universitaet, Mainz, (1987), p. 6.

28 Song, C.S., **Theology from the Womb of Asia;** (Obis books, Maryknoll, New York, 1986), p. 124.

a communal and spiritual environment and every individual is to manifest the spirit of community by sharing collective responsibilities, rewards and sacrifices.[29]

In this situation, offenses are seen not as affecting only the individual person, but the community as a whole. Every community tries to guide itself against disgrace arising from misdeeds. Those who go contrary to the norms of the community are ostracized or punished severely.

That the Igbo cannot think of existence without community is true, but for an Igbo, the smaller the community the better. They do not believe in large communities that cannot be effectively managed or controlled. In an interview with a journalist in Switzerland, Osuchukwu describes beautifully the Igbo idea of community as a place of care, love, and solidarity.[30]Such life can only be lived in a small community. It is not enough to talk about community, all the members of a given community are known to each other and every one is prepared to help and work with each other. Suffice it to say, that the Igbo community is an accepting community, an ideal place to recognize the worth and dignity of every person. Emeka Ojukwu, one-time leader of the Igbo in their struggle for self-determination, in his book describing the make-up of Nigerian Nation says;

This nation-state included an effectively blended mix of *Hausas* and Muslim *Fulanis* in the north, a highly structured group in the West called the *Yorubas* and in the East, the *Igbos* – a highly decentralized confederation of clans held together by a common language and a common culture.[31]

It will be unthinkable to fashion Igbo community on a large scale. That the Igbo loved and cherished small communities rather than unmanageable large ones can be seen in this well-thought-out philosophy by Ojukwu;

Centuries before the advent of the white man, the Igbos had first dominated their forest environment. Then they began and successfully established their own indigenous life support system. As they made progress in the forest region, they conceived of, developed and established, a rather unique political philosophy. This philosophy opposed all forms of hegemonistic tendencies. It was a philosophy that declared that large is bad and small is

29 Onwu, N., "**Igbo Religion: Its Present Situation**", in: **African Marburgensia**, Rome, xviii, 2(1985), p. 21.

30 Osuchukwu, P., "Innerhalb einer solchen sollte jeder merken, was der andere braucht, wo diesen der Schuh drückt. Jeder fühlt sich für jeden, für die Alten, die Kinder, die Gebrechlichen, verantwortlich. Solche Solidarität muss aktiv sein, darf sich nicht mit Sprüchen begnügen". **In diesen Tagen im Entlebuch getroffen**, in: **Entlebucher Anzeiger; (24.8.90)**, p. 3.

31 Ojukwu, E.O., **Because I am involved**; (Spectrum books, Nigeria, 1989), p. 15.

good. This wisdom dictated to the Igbos that wherever anything threatened to grow large it had to be fragmented.[32]

There is even a saying which goes thus: *Nkita muru asaa, amukala, ma ya amuzila ozo* (a dog that gives birth to seven puppies, has done well but should not try that again). During family prayers it is customary to hear *otu otu ulo eju* (one by one fills the house); this is taken in connection with child bearing, since twins were then regarded as an abomination. It may not be out of place to suggest that the rejection of twins may have originated from this philosophy of "the smaller the better". The Igbo have a way and means of organizing themselves in order to achieve the desired community.

1.2. Umunna Community

What cannot be deciphered in man's or a group's nature "becomes clear and understandable only if we read it in the larger letters of man's political life",[33] for a man's history depends primarily on how much of his community's standards he accommodates. Naturally, a culture that shores up most of its norms of life with oral tradition and strong family ties, as is true in Igboland, has the upper hand in seeing this through. The traditional Igbo culture is community oriented. Nwoga explains that "to a large extent, the individual in Igboland is subsumed within the requirements of the community."[34]

---

32 ibid., p. 129. Immediately after the Nigerian civil war, the missionaries in the East were expelled by the Nigerian Government, and the running of the Church was placed at the hands of the indigenous clergy. Every town started agitating for their own parishes. There were complaints but all stemmed from the fact that parish structures never took into consideration the **Igbo** community make-up and really never cared for their needs. C.C. Agu has this to say of the **Igbo:** "I know of no wars between them and other tribes around. This is not surprising either, since there was no political unit in their tribe that was larger than a village group and no influential leader had a large number of people under his command". **Secularization in Igboland...** Op.cit., p. 242. As the **Igbo** started to migrate to live in the lager cities in the other parts of the country, they never ceased to get back home periodically. But more significantly than that is the fact that urban centers began to develop in **Igboland** and at a remarkable rapidity, whereas the complete absence of cities was the hall mark of the **Igbo** country before the advent of the white man.

33 Cassier, E., **Myth of the State**, (Yale University Press, London, 1946), p. 61.

34 Nwoga, D.I., **1984 Ahiajoku Lecture**, Owerri, p. 28. Nzimiro says; " For the Igbo as for many Africans, to exist is to live in the group (**umunna**), to see things with the group (**umunna**). Life is not an individual venture. "**A study of Mobility among the Igbo of Southern Nigeria", in: Kinship and geographical Mobility**", ed. by Ralph Paddington, (Leiden, E.J.Brill, London, 1965), p. 754; words in bracket are mine.

The term ***umunna*** is both exclusive and inclusive. It depends on the context in which the term is used. Etymologically speaking, the term is a combination of two different words:-*umu* – meaning children and *nna* – meaning father. *Umunna* literally means children of the same father and can refer to the children of a particular father. But the most common application of the term refers to the descendants of an ancestor or for a major lineage.[35] Green gives the simplest understanding of the terms, but the real meaning goes beyond his explanation. The people who appear to be called *umunna* can in a given situation be called *umunne*, and people who are called or supposed to be *umunne*, in a given situation can be called *umunna.* Meek seems to understand the term more than Green as he clearly writes;

> And the term *umunna* may be used loosely to include, not merely the speakers own consanguineous relatives, but all the members of his village or even of his village-group or clan.[36]

These terms are, as it were, overextended in their use; usually they can only be comprehensible within the context of their application. Members of the group can live together in one territory. But this does not constitute a significant item in the definition of the group. What is important is that the group should trace their unity to a single ancestor and validate their unity by sharing things together. They can also worship together as a means of assessing their

35 Green, M.M., says that "the original ancestor of the village (Agbaja) had two wives and that the children of one, form half,'nce', known as *Umueke*-Owerre, while the children of the other are called Umueke-ama. Thus, while all the people born in Umueke are *umunna* - children of the same father - those born in Umueke-owerre are *Umunne* - children of the same mother, as are those born in Umueke-Ama". **Igbo Village Affairs:** (Frank Cass and Co. Ltd., London, 1964), pp. 15-16. Cf. Ardener, **Lineage and Locality Among the Mba-ise Ibo**, in: Africa xxix (1959), pp. 117-119.; O.P. Nsughe, **OHAFFIA: A Matrilineal Ibo People**, (Oxford University Press, London, 1974), pp. 33f; The two terms **Owerre** and **Ama** can only be understood from the point of view of how the **Igbo** looks at his community. For the **Igbo**, as has been expressed in the terms `**Igbo**' and `**Oru**', there is always `**Ama**'-meaning those living at the place of entrance or contact with other communities. Usually the eldest or strongest is stationed at **ama** as against any attack by enemies. Then **Owerre** signify the back-yard or the security zone from where people, especially women and children can take to their heels at the attack of a stronger enemy.

36 Meek, C.K., **Law and Authority in a Nigerian Tribe**; (OUI, London, 1950), p. 89. This looseness of terminology is really a reflection of the dynamic condition of society. Villages are constantly breaking away from the parent stock and kindred growing into clans. Cf. S.N. Chinwuba Obi, **The Igbo Law of Property**; (Butterworths, London, 1963), p. 15.

membership.[37] The Igbo wants to be identified with a community he can call his own.

Some families may grow to the size of a kindred or even a village and still they remain *umunna*. This term *umunna* is widely used in Igboland. It is the nucleus of the Igbo community existence. It is the political, social and religious life-wire of any given community in Igboland. When an Igbo speaks of *umunna*, he thinks of people who can trace their origin to the same father or ancestor, strictly speaking. *Umunna* is a group of families with a common ancestor, usually represented by a common **ofor** (a household, official and ritual symbol object)[38] normally called **ofor-ukwu** – differentiating it from the rest of the *ofor* held by different families.

Other terms used by some writers to describe *umunna* are "lineage" and kindred. Chinwuba Obi, in trying to look for a compromise between these two terms, accepted the term 'patrilineage'. It is an improvement on the two terms, since it restricts membership to one lineage only, i.e. descendants of a common father. But it does not necessarily exclude break-away groups now independent of the parent group.[39]

This compromise is ambiguous, since there is no limit to the size or area of the *umunna*. Forde and Jones in their work '*The Ibo and Ibibio-speaking people of South-Eastern Nigeria*', made use of the term 'localized patrilineage' which actually will suit our purpose, since it includes the idea of all such descendants residing in, or at least belonging to, the same locality as their progenitor, which Chinwuba Obi calls the original founder of the *umunna*. Chinwuba Obi also explains *umunna* thus:

> The unit known as *umunna* cannot properly be described as a family, however 'extended'... Like the village of which it is a part, it consists of all the descendants of a given ancestor who belong together, occupy the same territory and recognize the same immediate authority, plus their wives and less their daughters given away in marriage.[40]

It is difficult and unpracticable to fix the number of families that make-up an *umunna*. The population of *umunna* varies, some run up a hundred, and others less. *Umunna* is invariably exogamous. So, *umunna* can be seen in re-

---

37 Anigbo, O.A.C., **Commensality and Human Relationship among the Igbo**, (University of Nigeria Press, Nsukka, 1987), p. 62.

38 Cf. EJIZU, C.I., **Ofo: Igbo Ritual Symbol**, (Fourth Dimension Publishers, Enugu, 1986) Idem. "The Taxonomy, Provenance and Functions of OFO, a dominant Igbo Ritual and Political Symbol", in: **Anthropos**, 82(1987), pp.457-467.

39 Obi, S.N.C., **The Igbo Law of Property**; (Butterworths, London, 1963), p. 15.

40 ibid., p. 16. When a daughter gets married, she gets, as they say, "a second god". She is enclosed into the husbands linage and gods. Her role in her former family becomes consultative and mainly is seen in settling of cases.

lationship to kinship and lineage structure. This structure is similar to other patrilineal societies such as the **Nuer.**[41]

We have the kin of the father as well as the kin of the mother. But one can not be called *umunna* in the kin of the mother, rather he is called *nwanwa* (son of the child) or *nwadiani.* This is because the Igbo is patrilocal. This bilateral nature of the kinship is very important, but since Igbo is a patrilineal society, with the exception of the *Ohaffia* people that are matrilineal, the system persists. Raymond Firth sees the growth of *umunna* thus:

> keeping its essential individuality within the society, losing members but gaining others.[42]

As they gain and lose members, there is no difficulty in knowing who is who.

Umunna – children of the father – differs from *umunne* – children of the mother – in some important respects. *Umunna* is a corporate group: membership to it is by birth and is permanent, unless one is ostracized for having committed acts contrary to the values vital for the survival of the group. Death does not end the membership, especially where one attains the status of an ancestor. On the other hand, *umunne* cannot be referred to as a corporate group.[43]

In the traditional Igbo community, everybody within a given locality is a brother or sister depending on where he or she comes from; if a stranger, the situation is different. One is never confused regarding the real consanguinity as Ardner clearly says;

---

41 Evans-Pritchard, E.E., says: "A man`s kin are persons with whom he is genealogically connected through father and mother. This does not mean that kin relationships are merely extensions of relations within the same family. The kinship system exists in its own rights, and a child is born into a kinship system. But it does not mean that the kin relationships are the same order as family relations. They are not, certainly not to a **Nuer**. To him, his father and mother and brothers and sisters are not **mar** and he does not speak of them as such. They are members of his **gol**, his family, the intimate circle which he sees as something quite distinct from him, just as we do when we say that some one is a relative and not a member of the family or that another is almost one of the family." **The Nuer,** (Oxford University Press, London, 1960), p. 152. From the above quotation, we can see that also in **Igboland** the kin relationship is not the same as family relationship. Father, mother, brothers and sisters can not be addressed as ***umunna***, rather they are **Nna, Nne,** and **Nwanne** respectively - equivalent to **gol** in **Nuer**.

42 Firth, R., **Human Types,** (London, 1958), p.121.

43 Cf. Anigbo, O.A.C., **Commensality and Human relationship**, p.63.

Every Ibo is conversant with kinship terms within and often far beyond the radius in which he may seek his wife, just as he is aware of dialectical variations in any other field of terminology.[44]

Ardner tries to explain the life of the Igbo regarding kinship, though within this nation, there exist different linguistic variations. There are alot of kinship terminologies which are reflected in dialects, but all mean the same thing.

The motivating factor in an Igbo is the spirit of belonging which one imbibes from belonging to an *umunna*. This spirit is above all transcendent. The Igbo tries to be identified with a group. The Igbo finds fulfillment within a community. This is the reason for an Igbo to recall the spirit of *umunna* whenever he finds himself outside the natural *umunna*, by forming another community.

First he tries to identify himself with those who speak his language, even if they don't come from the same area. In the midst of those who do not speak his language, those who do, form a sort of *umunna* ensemble and address themselves as such. In its loosest sense, *umunna* can be applied to the village, town, local government area, or even to the whole Igbo people living in an area like Lagos.

This spirit of identifying with a group is life embracing, a vehicle for social integration and brotherhood, and also qualifies for communion. This spirit, inherent in the Igbo psyche, becomes apparent when the Igbo is threatened or when a common good is at stake. It is such a spirit that gave birth to what is called the *Igbo Union* – a strong political union within the Nigerian body politic.

There was of course no sense of pan-Ibo identity -invariably the Iboman felt a strong local patriotism; a sense of pan-Ibo came only when its people left Iboland or to put it succinctly, the pan-Ibo idea came when they were confronted by their hosts in the North, the Cameroons, the Cross River, the Rivers and Lagos.[45]

This spirit reminds an Igbo that the person living next to him or her is a neighbour, a brother or sister, hence they say: *Agbata onye bu nwanne ya* (one's neighbour is his brother or kin).

Umunna, as we mentioned above, belongs to the primary group level, in contrast to the secondary group level. The difference is found in the type of social contact and the degree of organization. The latter is larger and more formal. Its contact group is known for its social organization, which implies an

44 Ardner, E.W., "**Lineage and Locality among the Mba-Ise Igbo**", **AFRICA**, Vol. xxiv, Nr.2, (London, April, 1954), p. 85.

45 Ojukwu, E.O., **Because I am involved**, Nigeria, Spectrum Books, (1989), p. 96.

order of rules and regulations for its stability. Invariably, hierarchical structure characterizes its relationship. At this level, it is not possible for people to know everyone else. It is a sort of military community with its formal orders, ranks and discipline; a large business firm is another example; and most of our parishes fall under this secondary category. The primary level is more caring and personal.

We are making this distinction between the primary and secondary levels of community, because we intend to base our model of a basic Christian community on *umunna*, which is on a primary group level, on the concept of a truly fraternal community where affection, love, care and solidarity are vital elements. Here the life and communion we have in Christ will undoubtedly be deeper, more personal and more intensely shared.

Communities are characterized by the values they embody; the individual and collective motivations they encourage; the incentives and sanctions they inspire; the ideals by which belief, attitude, and behaviour are established.[46] In traditional Igbo society, informal education is the order of the day. During an ***umunna*** gathering, the children and youths are educated concerning norms and morals. Talbot, writing about the Igbo and their attachment to *umunna*, says:

> The negro is perhaps the most gregarious of all men; his great joy is to be found in amusing himself with companions in dances, plays etc.; and perhaps his greatest grief is solitude, unpopularity and ridicule of his town men.[47]

Talbot only saw the aspect of amusement in the gathering and lost sight of the communitarian and spiritual aspect. It is during such a gathering that morals and community spirit are inculcated in the youths. There is no documented legal regulation or laws governing the Igbo people. But the norms of the land are known by everyone and are transmitted through an oral tradition called *omenala*[48]. When some one behaves in a manner unexpected from an Igboman, the question that arises is: *itokwere n'ulo*? (did you at all grow up here?). So it is believed that every member of the *umunna* knows the custom of the land.

---

46 Capps, W.H., "Society and Religion", in: **Encyclopedia of Religion**, M. Eliade ed., vol. 13, New York, (1987), p. 375.

47 Talbot, P.A., **The People of Southern Nigeria**, (1962), p. 754.

48 **Omena Ala** or **Omena ani** - means happenings in the land or behaviour patterns according to the tradition of the land. This is the uncodefied system of living approved and passed on by the ancestors. Anigbo says that: "It is the interpretation of **ome na ala** that guides the Igbo in his attempt to harmonize himself with his social experience". O.A.C. Anigbo, **Commensality and Human Relationship among the Igbo**, (University of Nigeria Press, Nsukka, 1987), p. 51.

Moral education is a household duty and the various *umunna* meetings stress the conduct of its members as being of paramount importance. In *umunna*, there are office-holders without office, who carry their office with them. Their persons and position in the *umunna* demonstrate their office. There are certain basic elements on which *umunn*a communitarian life is built. Such basic elements include: kinship, marriage, ancestorship, leadership, language, religious beliefs etc.

Igbo kinship is different from the Western definition of G.A Allan;[49] the later lacks the basic communitarian elements that mark the richness of kinship. While the description of western kinship centers around a relationship from a sexual point of view, the Igbo sees man from a communitarian perspective. Kinship, though founded on a biological or blood relationship known as consanguinity, extends in Igbo thought to include some affinitive relations like domestic groups, peer age relations, neighbourhood affiliations and bonds of secret societies (*Mmanwu*); as well as friendly relationships among others.[50] The reality of the kinship is rooted in the extended family. The kinship system in the traditional Igbo communities creates in the members a single soul, a high ideal of solidarity which is religiously guided. In matters of kinship, marriage and sexuality come to mind, since it is through them that kinship is extended. Marriage from the point of view of the Igbo is an extension of the community. No wonder Igbo marriage is more of a community affair, an *umunn*a thing as opposed to the Western conjugal individual system.[51]

Marriage plays an important role in the extension of the *umunn*a communities. In the traditional Igbo community, marriages are arranged between two families with or without the consent of the two individuals who are getting married. Members of the same *umunn*a are forbidden to marry. Wives are initiated into the families of their husbands and automatically become members of the husbands' families. In such cases divorces are rare, since it is the whole *umunn*a community that has the right to send the woman away, for instance, when there is a case of witchcraft or proven case of poisoning brought against her.

In the traditional Igbo community, the wife is "our" wife, the child "our" child; everyone is taken care of, both in life and in death. No wonder that the dead are respected and those who qualify by their good life and old age are

---

49 Allan, G.A., "A sociology of Friendship and Kinship", in: **Studies in Sociology**, 10 (G.Allen, and Unwin ltd, London, 1979, p.93).

50 Kalem'Imana, J.B., **Christianity and Socialism in Tanzania**: A Dissertation submitted to the graduate school of Drew University in partial fulfillment of the requirements for the degree, Doctor of Philosophy; Madison, New Jersey, (1986), p.3.

51 Ivan, N.F., and F.M. Bernardo, **The Family: Its structure and interaction;** Mary Knoll, New York, (1973), p.40.

recognized as ancestors. A rootless Igbo, that is, one who is unable to link oneself to a particular ancestry, is hard to find. The position and reverence of the ancestors help to bring the *umunn*a together, make them share their love and sufferings. The idea of communal sharing and belongingness is rooted in the person of the ancestor, who is looked upon as a model and father both for the living and the dead in a given family or *umunn*a ensemble. Using this definition of *umunna*, how can one limit the members of a given *umunna*?

1.2.1. Scope of Umunna

The question may arise, if *umunna* literally means children of the same father or in actuality, people who have the same ancestor, how can it be of help in the formation of Small Christian Communities? The *umunn*a spirit is transcendental. It is the spirit that rallies people together and constitutes the community. This is a spirit of solidarity, belongingness, care and compassion which is also ecclesial in nature. This spirit always extends beyond a blood or ancestor relationship. *Nwa-ạfo* or *Nwa amuru n'obi* (the child from the stock or the child from **obi**) are normally words used to describe citizens of the *umunna*. Strangers not yet initiated into the *umunna*, bondsmen and slaves are excluded. The *umunna* is for its citizens. Every person takes the activities of the unit seriously as his own and actively participates.

Wherever the Igbo are found, this spirit is always exhibited. They gather together and form a non-blood or non-ancestor-related *umunna*. In this case language plays an important role. Language binds them together, just as the Word of God binds Christians. Professions, settlements, common interest and the like can serve as a unifying factor, but the core of this unity is that motivating factor in *umunna* that brings Igbo people together, no matter where they find themselves. This *umunna* spirit, which is transcendental, is always used to form *umunna* communities that are not *umunna* qua *umunna*. The Igbo by so doing looks forward to a unified world with a God that acts like a father and all men his children. When all people acknowledge the fatherhood of God, then we are all *umunna*.

*Umunn*a may help us to understand the common Fatherhood of God. Even the concept of *umunn*a in its entirety makes room for those who are not related by blood to be accepted, since the *umunna* spirit is transcendental. In Igboland, one of the things that helps to create community feeling is obedience to the *Okwara* (the first born). Those outside the ancestral descent could be assimilated into a given *umunna* after some conditions are met and they are ready to obey the **okwara**.[52]

Strangers have the opportunity of belonging to an *umunna*, with which he or she has no blood relation. Nzimiro mentioned those strangers who can be admitted and the conditions required:

> A stranger might be attached to a ward, and after years of settlement acquires some degree of citizenship and the right attached thereto. He is permitted to marry in the town, observing the rules of exogamy of the group (he should not marry into the ward in which he is accepted as a member), to participate in some of the ritual ceremonies and be initiated in some of the traditional titles.[53]

The word "attached" is of importance, since in Igboland, almost everybody is his brother's keeper. Before one is granted rights as a citizen, enquiries are conducted to find out his social status in his original *umunna*. Nzimiro, in a work treating the social structure, contributed immensely to what may be of help in the formation of the Small Christian Community in Igboland using the existing structures. Nzimiro in his treatment on *umunna*, looking at its transcendent nature and its constituent units, says;

> The corporate nature of all *ebo* and *ogbe* is expressed in most social contexts and most notably in political and ritual matters. Membership is primarily defined in terms of agnatic descent but is also determined by common residence..., strangers and original inhabitants are either incorporated as small lineages into the ogbe of the dominant element, or, if they are sufficiently numerous and cohesive they may form separate ogbe or, in the case of Osomari, separate ebo.[54]

Chinwuba Obi, after examining the word *umunna* as used loosely- "*children of the same father*" and as it is more technically used, which has a precise and essentially political connotation, went on to say:

> The unit known as *umunna* cannot properly be described as a family, however 'extended',at this stage in the history of Ibo society. Like the village of which it is a part, it

---

52 Nzimiro, F.I., showed how a man can belong to a ward outside his own in Oguta area, as he says; "Oguta men could be allocated land in the farming hamlets of their wives or mother '*Ikwunne*' , and in some cases, a man may be asked to migrate to any ward where other kinsmen from maternal side reside. This might be possible through the advice of a native doctor, who may forecast that certain misfortune to the man and his family can be avoided if he migrates elsewhere". **Family and Kinship in Iboland...**, (1962), pp.102-103. Cf. G. Homans, **Human Group,** (Routledge and Kegan Paul, London, 1958), p. 198.

53 Nzimiro, F.I., **Family and Kinship in Igboland...**, (1962) p.103.

54 Nzimiro, I., **Studies in Ibo Political Systems: Chieftaincy and Politics in Four Niger States**. (Frank Cass and Co. LTD., London, 1972), p. 22.

consists of all the descendants of a given ancestor who belong together, occupy the same territory and recognize the same immediate authority, plus their wives and less their daughters given away in marriage. The group is known by the name of this ancestor. (there is often, however, an immigrant element in the Umunna-group, who have been sufficiently integrated into the socio-political fabric as to cease to be treated as strangers).[55]

This elaborate connotation of *umunna* in the present Igbo set-up is of great help to us for the formation of Small Christian Communities using Chinwuba Obi's description. The stress will be more on the descendants of a given ancestors who belong together, occupy the same territory and recognize the same immediate authority, plus their wives and immigrant elements sharing the same vicinity.

The attraction of strangers to a given *umunna* may be due to land, prosperity or even strength, as explained by Philip Nsugbe in his narration of the make-up of the Ohafia group and concerning those who enjoy the right to *Umuaka* – (which I may call the original descendants), in their various villages:

A possible explanation is that the Ohaffia villages not represented were daughter villages. It is likely, however, that they were not all derived from the eight, but that some of them were attracted to settle by the power of the eight and in the Ibo manner are now regarded as Ohaffia.[56]

We must stress here that though the ancestral descent is still strong, among the present Igbo such alliances and assimilation of people of different descent are quite common and they are not always based upon descent, but often upon territory.[57] Such openness is a credit and provides fertile soil for the formation of the Small Christian Community, using the *umunna* set-up in Igboland. Green, in one of her works, recorded interesting ways in which people of different ancestral origin were accepted in a given *umunna* or village:

These alien elements in the population, however, modify little if at all the fact that village consists of a kindred and their wives. They are, in fact, assimilated to the kinship group in the matter of exogamy, having to find their wives outside the village and send their daughters outside for husbands. They do not, therefore, disturb the significant pattern of the village as both a kinship and a local group.[58]

---

55 Obi, S.C.N., **The Ibo Law of Property,** (1963), p.16.

56 Nsugbe, O.P., **OHAFFIA: A Matrilineal Ibo People,** (1974), p.35.

57 Cf. G.I. Jones, "**Dual Organization in Igbo Social Structure**" in: **Africa**, vol. xix (1949), p. 152; cf. M.M. Green, **Igbo Village Affairs, Chiefly with Reference to the Village of Umueke Agbaja**, (1964), pp. 16-17.

58 Green, M.M., **Ibo Village Affairs...**, (1964), p. 25. The stress on marriage pattern is to enforce morality which is taken seriously in Igboland. Since incest is an abomination

This spirit of the *umunna* community helps in enriching the Church in Igboland, focussing on a group of families, several of which make up *umunna*, composed of *kindred* who happen to live within a territory, who are generally descended from a common ancestor, and in many cases, where strangers have settled who are regarded as belonging to this *umunna*. This is a group where everyone knows everyone by name.[59] For such a group to function well, it must have clear-cut polity.

1.2.1. The Social and Political Character of Umunna

Three sets of social structures are easily spotted out in traditional Igbo society. These are the family (*Ezi n'ulo*), which is the prime unit; the *umunna* ensemble; and the village. There are other sets of social structures within the Igbo society, but these three are the most important. In the Igbo social organization, the basic social unit is the group of patrilineal relatives who live together in close association and constitute what is known as *umunna*.[60]

*Umunn*a is made up of any number of *onumara*, as shown in Fig.**1** and Fig.4. The reason for calling this unit *umunna* (children of the same father) is actually to rally them together. It is the state of *onye aghala nwanne ya* (where no kin is left out). This term has an immense psychological and unifying force and inspires a strong attachment and togetherness from its members whenever used. There is no fixed number of *onumara* to make up an *umunn*a, but care is always taken that number will not be so much that will constitute a problem in administration. The rate of birth of *umunn*a or other social units in Igboland is amoebic. The amoebic nature makes it split and retains the old, gives birth to new one without disruption of events. Meek puts it thus;

> Villages are constantly breaking away from the parent stock and kindred growing into clans.[61]

---

against the land and the ancestors, any sexual relation within a given *umunna* or village is disallowed.

59 Cf. P.A. Talbot, **The People of Southern Nigeria;** vol.111, (London, 1926), p. 538; P. Osuchukwu, **"Interview", "In diesen Tagen im Entlebuch getroffen", in: Entlebucher Einzeiger**, (Schweiz, 24.8.1990).

60 Onwuejeogwu, M.A., notes that; "The *umunna* concept is a system of patrilineal organization which not only determines one's right and duties accruing from such membership". **"The Igbo Culture Areas"**, in: **Igbo language and Culture**, F.C. Ogbalu, and E.N. Emenanjo, eds., p.5.

61 Meek, C.K., **Law and Authority in a Nigerian Tribe**, (1950), p.90. Green in her study of Igbo village affairs, noticed also this phenomenon as she reports that: "The two op-

But Nzimiro also does not see the breaking away as an obstacle to the smooth running of the entire society when he expresses;

> Thus, segmentation starts and as the population increases, the different families grow and become their own lineage. As they break, the sons of the same father and different mothers continue to perform collectively their religious and other sacrificial ceremonies. They do this generally during their life time.[62]

There are ceremonies or feasts that help to bring people of the same ancestral lineage together. This helps to keep the lineage alive as long as it is not out of control, as Anigbo remarks:

> Meeting for religious services, especially those connected with ancestors, can be organized to take place in the territory regarded as the original home of the ancestor of the group. The meeting is kept alive as long as it serves the interest of the group. But where a section of a major lineage residing in a separate territory finds itself large and strong enough to look after its own interest, it may gradually relinquish the ties with the members of the group in other territories. One can therefore conceive an Igbo country linked together by a net-work of major lineages.[63]

Every member of a given *umunna* knows every other person by name, that would become difficult if the *umunna* is too large. The number constituting an *umunna* may not be allowed to be too small, hence a unit reduced by death may join another *umunna* to strengthen its bargaining position in all social activities. Politically, the structural and functional features of the *umunna* are enlarged and maintained as the dynamic political units unfold. They shift and adjust themselves as the population increases. The most remarkable feature of the *umunna* is the principle of collective responsibility for the conduct of its

---

posite processes of fission and accretion are constantly at work as slow forces of change in the village kinship, and hence local, structure. Kindred which increase in size ultimately split into smaller units, as tradition recorded..." M.M. Green, **Igbo Village Affairs ...** (1964), p. 21

62 Nzimiro, F.I., **Family and Kinship in Igboland...**, (1962), p.94. Ejiofor in trying to describe *umunna* and its rate of expansion says; "It is a group of related extended families which have a common grand ancestral descent and which becomes a separate social entity, not because the warmth of relationship has given way to strained co-existence but because, if the original *Idumu*(*onumara*) was allowed to expand indefinitely, it would become unwieldy as a family cluster. It is difficult to place a dividing line at any particular point of expansion between one group and another. There is no break in genealogy between the *Idumu*(*onumara*) and the quarter". L.U. Ejiofor, **Igbo Kingdoms, Power and Control;** (African Publications Ltd., Nigeria, 1982), p. 90.

63 Anigbo, O.A.C., **Commensality and Human Relationship**, p. 63.

members. This makes it the political organ that exercises the greatest intrusion into the personal behaviour of the individual.[64]

The description of *umunna* as an existing political and social structure has been accredited to different authors, who give this unit different names: *quarter*,[65] *Localized lineage*,[66] *Localized patrilineage*,[67] *Kindred*.[68] From the above terminologies, one may be left with a lot of interpretations regarding *umunna*. Meek, the great colonial anthropologist, described the characteristic feature of the Igbo traditional society as;

> almost complete absence of any higher political or social unit than the commune or small group of contiguous villages whose customs and cults are identical and whose sense of solidarity is so strong that they regard themselves as descendants of a common ancestor.[69]

Meek did not actually understand the working of Igbo parademocracy and its linkage to other units. The *umunna* group in Igboland can hold formal meetings and decide on how to improve their lot. *Umunna* meetings are generally where the features of community development plans for the community are tabled. Every *umunna* unit is headed by the *okwara* or *okpara*, who is the eldest or represents the eldest in the community.

1.2.2.1. Okwara/Opara Umunna

In the Igbo set-up, every *umunna* has an *Obi* (meeting hut or reception hall), sometimes called *obi nnanyi (a hall belonging to our father)* or *obi-ukwu* (the big hall). This *obi* acts as a palace, normally built in the *ngwuru* of the *okwara* of the senior extended family unit, or *onumara*.[70]

---

64 Njaka, E.N., **Igbo Political Culture**; (1974), p. 86. Cf. E. Isichei, **Igbo Worlds: An Anthropology of oral Histories and Historical Descriptions**, (1978), pp. 72-73.

65 Okafor, D.O., **A Nigerian Village in Two Worlds;** Faber and Faber Ltd., London, (1962), p. 32.

66 Anene, J.C., **Southern Nigeria in Transition, 1885-1906**, Cambridge University Press, London, (1966), p. 12.

67 .Gailey, H.A., **The Road to Aba**: University Press, London, (1971), p. 22.

68 Olisa, M.S.O., **"Political Culture and Stability in Igbo Society"**, in: **Conch**, Vol.111, Nr.2 (1971), pp. 16-27.

69 Meek, C.K., **Law and Authority...**, (1950), p. 3; cf. M.M. Green, **Igbo Village Affairs...**, (1947), pp. 3-5.

70 The **obi** is an assembly hall for all the members of the same **umunna**. The **obi** can and should serve as the place of meeting for the Small Christian Community gatherings. No one is exempt from the meeting of the ***umunna*** without adequate reason.

The *okwara* holds the *ofo*[71] of the *umunna* as his staff of office and authority, justice as well as status symbol. The *okwara* of any given *umunna* is very important both in authority and in the mediation process, for he is the symbol of the *umunna* and coordinates affairs of the umunna, of cause with the approval of the *oha*. This authority held by the *okwara* is not noticeable by an outsider, since the whole authority is so diffused among the *okwara* of each *onumara* and the rest of the people.

Complaints, messages, duties and other responsibilities involving an *umunn*a go to the *okwara*, since he represents his unit in any gathering unless otherwise indicated by the unit or *oha*. The *Okwara* is a link between one social group and another. The *okwara* may initiate new ideas, projects, ceremonies and also the admission of strangers into the *umunna*; these must be according to the *omeneal*a (custom) with the support of the *oha*. So doing, brings the checks and balances in Igbo society.

Offices in *umunn*a are transparent ones, and goes with the saying "do as I do" as opposed to "do as I say". The functioning of *umunna* will be handled regarding different positions occupied by some people and responses by the whole members of the *umunna* in the affairs concerning them.

1.2.2.2. The Umunna Executive Council

As already shown in the set up of *obodo*, different *ama* make up *ngwuru* and different *ngwuru* make up *onumara*; thus different *onumara* make up *umunna*. Each unit has an *okwara* and the executive council of the *umunna*, which is made up of the *okwara* of its respective *onumara* or those called *oji ofo* (holders of ofo). These are leaders of each *onumara*, since each has the big **ofo** of the *onumara*.

Because of the democratic or para-democratic nature of the **Igbo**, any elder, or a wealthy person, or intelligent adult may be co-opted to serve on the executive council. Normally the *okwara* of the *umunna* presides over such a meeting and often summons meetings. The task of the council is to carry out any urgent matter concerning the *umunna*.

The executive council plays an important role in dealing with confidential matters and often handles cases that could not be solved by the *umunna* council, (which will be discussed below). The *umunna* executive has the right to legislate and can also order the death penalty to any member for the good of the community. Serious cases handled by *umunna* executive include incest,

71 **Ofo/ofor** - is a piece of wood from **"detarium elastica"**. The opara being the head of the **umunna**, represents the ancestors and his symbol of office is due to his having the **Ofo-ukwu** (the big **ofo**).

treachery, grand theft and murder. Such cases are handled very early in the morning or late at night to exclude children, sometimes women, and more importantly, to allow the presence of the ancestors, who are believed to be attentive during these periods. The *umunna* executive acts as a check to the *okwara* of the *umunna* and controls his excesses.

The *umunna* executive council's decision is taken as final, and even if one does not agree with it, obedience to such decision is called for before one can complain. Since the plaintiff has a representative at the executive, his complain should be directed to his representative. Njaka clearly says;

> Each member of the onumara is thereby automatically bound to whatever decision his okwara onumara has supported. If he has discovered an error, it is his duty to obey first and complain within his onumara unit later, but he must never betray the *umunna* leadership.[72]

Such allegiance belongs only to the *umunna*. That is why the idea of *umunna* as a contribution to the formation of Small Christian Communities in Igboland will go a long way in incarnating Christianity in Igboland and will also help to administrate the church.

1.2.2.3. The Umunna Council

All the male adults in a given *umunna* belong to the *umunna* council. During meetings, children are not excluded, but they may only observe. The admission of the young ones into such gathering is meant to help them acquire the art of governing and the art of addressing people and speaking in public. It is a sort of educational forum for the young.

The Igbo use a lot of anecdotes, parables and idioms while speaking or addressing a public, which Igbo orators refer to as the 'oil' with which words are "eaten". This art is most easily learnt by the young in the *umunna* council meetings. For an elder to tell a young one to think well, he will only say *were iregi guo ezegi* (use your tongue to count your teeth).

In the *umunna* council there is always an equal participation inherent in it that promotes the customary healthy atmosphere. Everyone is given the opportunity to air his view, for "*uka anaghi ano na onu ajonjo*" (one can not judge an unspoken word). Whatever real regulatory powers that existed among the Igbo

---

72 Njaka, E.N., **Igbo Political Culture** (1974), p. 89. Cf. E. Isichei, who also says; "After taking the decision at the village level, we then retired to the lineage or ***umunna*** level... and because people saw themselves as very intimate relations that must accept the opinions of the **okenye umu-nna**. see **Igbo Worlds...**, (1978), pp. 72-73.

was exercised mainly by a loosely constituted council, whose personnel included kin-group heads, elders, other notables and in some places members of title societies.[73]

Most of the problems concerning the *umunna* as a whole are discussed in the council meetings. This differentiates it from the *umunna* executive council. Such problems include incest, theft, immigration and emigration, trade and industry, farming, land disputes, obligations towards higher units, the constitution, festivals, burials, marriages, and juvenile delinquency.[74]

The council, among other things, acts as checks also to the *okwara*, its executive and its citizens. Problems affecting individuals, *ama, ngwuru* or *onumara* are mainly handled by the *umunna* council. Every member of the *umunna* keeps a watchful eye on his neighbour – both for protection and correction. When two *onumara* or *umunna* have a dispute, the rest will encourage them to settle but will never intervene unless called to do so. Such a political or social attitude of non-intervention Njaka calls *parademocratic* or *ohacratic* individualism.

The *umunna* council is described by Afigbo as the village-group council, and with a similar function. He went on to say;

The core of the village-group council comprised the sublineage-heads popularly known among most Ibo as *ndi ama ala* or *ndi isi ofo* – the *ofo* being among this people the supreme ancestral symbol, the staff of traditional authority and influence as well as the symbol of justice, truth and right living.[75]

Having seen different groups within *umunna*, the question then is, how does one relate to the whole *umunna* ensemble. Every adult has a say in the community and normally shares in the authority and powers within the umunna. Knowledge is normally transmitted from the elders to the young. The duty of an old man or woman is to show a good example to the young ones, and correction is the duty of all. Njaka puts it thus:

Each older person is responsible for those younger than he and to those older than he. Nobody stands by while something goes wrong. Hence the proverb that 'an old man does not allow a goat to die entangled in a rope while he is at home'.[76]

---

73 Brown, P., "**Patterns of Authority in West Africa**", in: **AFRICA**, vol. 21, 4(1951), p. 267.

74 ibid., p. 91.

75 Afigbo, A.E., **The Warrant Chief's Indirect Rule in Southern Nigeria 1891 - 1927;** (OUI, London, 1972), p. 21.

76 Njaka, E.N., **Igbo Political Culture**; (1974), p. 93.

Children are organized into age-grades, where they learn how to manage affairs, be it political or social. Every member of the *umunna* is his brothers' keeper and failure to listen to the pleas of a fellow member is a grievous offence which is punishable by the *umunna* Council. The importance of *umunna* cannot be overemphasized. A citizen who constantly exposes his *umunna* to public ridicule is in danger of losing his citizenship, by being put to death, or by being sold into slavery.[77] The guilt of any member is the guilt of the *umunna*, he belongs to the *umunna* as the *umunna* belongs to him. An *umunna* has the right to banish its citizen, since it is *umunna* who has the right to question his where-about. Care is always taken by citizens not to drag their *umunna* into dispute.

Sometimes members of an *umunna* are forced to take steps like suicide or running away, if they commit an offence that may drag the reputation of *umunna* to the dust, knowing fully well that what awaits him will either be hanging or banishment.

> An *umunna* citizen knows clearly what will be involved if he should drag his unit into disrepute. Therefore he realizes when it is necessary for him to hang himself, run away, or surrender in order to save his immediate and extended families or *umunna* and return honor and prestige to them. If he does not accept his appropriate fate, the *umunna* must act at once, disposing of him to redeem itself from public ignominy.[78]

The citizen has also the right to be defended by the whole *umunna* if he happens to be accused falsely or threatened by an external power. It is the function of the *okwara*, or *onyeisi*, as he is sometimes called, to notify the whole *umunna*, who will deliberate on the line of action to be taken.

1.3. Various Structures in Igbo Social Set-Up

An understanding of the Igbo presupposes a real study of their social, political and religious structures. These structures are so interwoven that to study them separately will not only be difficult but involve a repetition of terms and concepts. The Igbo is wrapped up in holistic thinking rather than dualism. Social life, politics and religion are taken as one entity – focussed on feelings regarding a three-dimensional world of ancestors, the living and the unborn, on the

---

77 ibid., p. 94.
78 ibid.

one hand, and a world of *Chukwu*, *Chi*, and Spirits, on the other, in response to human behaviour and its contradictions.[79]

This holistic approach goes even deeper in language patterns, where thought patterns are not constructed on *Aristotelian* roots but on African roots, conditioned by the language's own environment and logic. This goes to support the saying that a man's physical environment influences not only his economic activity but also his social and political activity. In the study of the structure of Igbo community, we shall be dealing with concepts which are peculiar to the Igbo culture. One of the important terms or concepts is *Oha* (literally meaning assembly of the whole community), which has a broader meaning that can be extended to mean the people, a gathering of the people, a sovereign body, government and a way of life, affecting a community. Sometimes the term *Oha* is used synonymously with *Obodo* (the State). *Oha* in the real Igbo sense represents what Leopold Sedar Senghor calls *community-society*; or *communocracy,* according to Sekou Toure; Njaka prefers to call it *Ohacracy*. All these terms are used to express a form of government or social administration found in some part of Africa.

These terms which are used by these eminent sons of Africa try to show how the individual is related to the community and the importance Africans attach to the sovereignty of the people. Another important concept in our treatment is *Ikwu na Ibe*.[80] It is the term used to differentiate a close kin from a distant one, as will be explained. After the concept *Ikwu na Ibe* we have the *Ofo* (a religious symbol and staff of office for the holder), which is the central system of Igbo religion and in the social and political structure gives the holder the sense of authority. Ejizu has done one of the most comprehensive studies on the subject of the *Ofo*, tracing its spread, types and functions in Igbo traditional society. He defines *Ofo* as "a male symbol that primarily represents ancestral power and authority and the key values of truth and justice".[81]

---

79 Cf. E.N. Njaka, **Igbo Political Culture;** (Northwestern University Press, Evanston, 1974), p. 10.

80 **Ikwu-** are members of one's family while **Ibe** becomes the next kin where competition is expected to strive.

81 EJIZU, C.I., "The Taxonomy, Provenance and Function of *Ofo*, a Dominant Igbo Ritual and Political Symbol", in: *Anthropos*, 82(1987), 457-467; see also E. Ilogu, "Christianity and Culture", NOK Publishers, New York, 1974, and M.A. Onwuejeogwu, "An Igbo Civilization, Nri Kingdom and Hegemony", Ethiope Publishing Cooperation, London, 1981. E.N.Njaka contributing says; " *Ofo*, the embodiment of the Igbo Religion, allows each person to be his own priest on possessing it, assures its holder of a great measure of individualism within the concept of *'Oha' (sovereignty of the sovereign people*), and yields to him a share of authority". E.N. Njaka, **Igbo Political Culture,** (1974), p. 14.

The basic and dominant social structure among the Igbo, as it is among several other ethnic groups in West Africa, is lineage. This lineage structure is "a system of patrilineal organization which not only determines one's membership of a patrilineage but also determines one's rights and duties accruing from such membership".[82] Families normally joined to form a lineage; thus a lineage group was constituted by the social accretion brought about by the common habitation of kinsmen. This means that all in a lineage are related to one another through direct descent from a common ancestor.[83]

The formation of the maximal lineage, a village or Town consists in the enlargement of the minimal lineage segment of a few families, and the union of the resulting major lineages. This is actually the social structural process in Igboland. The highest social and political unit in Igboland is the town-state. Within this town-state are various levels of social-political structures which can be illustrated with the following figures (see Figs. 1-3 in index). An individual with a family has an *ama* (block H). As the sons grow, they establish their own *ama* and a combination of some *ama*, will turn to be *ngwuru* (block G). Any number of *ngwuru* arising from a common ancestral origin, make up an *onumara*. This growth continues and *umunn*a is formed, comprised of any number of *onumara*. *Onumara* provides a legal admission to the *umunna*, including those who may not share a common ancestral origin.

Strangers can form their own *onumara* and apply for inclusion to a given *umunna*, mostly through association. *Umunn*a is very important in the social and political life of the Igbo people. Looking at the political structure of the Igbo, Njaka says;

> The *umunna* polity, (**E**), is the backbone of the Igbo political system. It is where political actions begin and it is what makes and unmake the Igbo- the strength and weakness of the Igbo. The *umunna* is the minimal political unit of the Igbo, the *agbata ebe* (the place beyond which man cannot run for protection),the orientation system that characterizes the Igbo. The umunna, though minimal, is autonomous in the matter of admitting immigrant to a city-state. While the city-state can give protection to an outsider, the final decision about his admission goes to the umunna**.** It is here that individualism and ***Ohacracy*** gain or lose their strongest influence on the Igbo.[84]

Such a strong structure should form the backbone of Small Christian Community, if Christianity is to find a home in Igbo nation.

---

82 OGBALU, F.C. and EMENANJO, E.N. (eds.), "Igbo Language and Culture", Oxford University Press, Ibadan, 1975, p.5.

83 ONYISI, E., **An Introduction to the Study of African Culture**, Heinemann, London, 1977, p.17.

84 ibid., p. 27; cf. M.A. Onwuejeoqwu, **An Igbo Civilization: Nri Kingdom and Hegemony.** (London, 1981), p. 12.

The *mkpuru* (D) constitutes many *umunna*; this strata does not play a major role politically or otherwise. The combination continues, as any number of *mkpuru* whose members are descended from a common ancestor constitutes an *Ogbe* **(C);** then a number of *ogbe* make up an *ebe* **(B).** *Ebe* and *Ogbe* constitute important units in the **Igbo** political and social system. Any number of *ebe* make an *Obodo* or *Mba* (the town-state).[85]

After going through all these set-ups, it is important to point out that the *oha* (the people) decide what happens in any of the structures. Because the Igbo society is a place where men live a covenant life with spirits as well as with *Chukwu*, the spirits play a vital part in a whole series of human relationships. Law and order are seen as coming from the gods through the ancestors, who should be obeyed – since "*madu anaghi aba chi ya ogu*" (no one fights with his God). For the Igbo, Law and Order are maintained because the ancestors so desire and **oha** so commands. And the ancestors desire law and order because **Chukwu** must have approved them.[86]

The ethical justice and political responsibility which are not separable in Igbo life or kinship (*Umunna, mkpuru, Ogbe* in the concept of *Ikwu na Ibe*), include responsibility to the laws of both *Chukwu* and man. It follows that it is the *Oha* and not the rulers who posses the sovereign rights of the state; no wonder some refer to it as **ohacracy**. Ozoemenam Mbachu,[87] seeing the type of social and political administration which exists in Igboland as opposed to the western democracy, clearly states;

> One would only say that the type of democracy that existed in traditional Igbo society is not exactly the same thing as the parliamentary or representative democracy of the western world. The Igbo form of democracy (Ohacracy) is a direct democracy which knows of no limitations... Thus, modern democracy is representative, indirect; the people govern through representatives periodically elected by them. The ordinary citizens part in government is limited. On the other hand Ohacracy was direct, primary. The Oha constitute the assembly, in which every citizen could take part. In other words, the Oha is the sovereign body in the state to decide national affairs, great and small. The citizens have a considerable amount of opportunity to take part in the executive and judicial administration.[88]

---

85 cf. ibid.

86 ibid., p. 46.

87 Ozoemenam, M., **Ohacracy as a system of Government in Igbo culture area of Nigeria;** A paper presented at the first annual conference of the center for **Igbo** Studies, (**Imo** State University, **Okigwe**, July 11 - 13, 1991), p. 3.

88 ibid., p. 11-12.

The traditional Igbo society had no central political authority "that welded the entire Iboland into a political whole".[89] The basis for political organization in Igboland is the lineage structure, as Nzewunwa explains:

> It is at the lineage or village level that political organization proper can be said to begin. Each village was independent in every sense of the word, maintaining its territorial integrity, tolerating no interference in its internal affairs and recognizing no other authority except that within its territorial framework.[90]

This set-up contributed to Horton's conviction in 1868 that the Igbo is a Land "governed by independent kings and chiefs whose extent of domination varies greatly. Some exercised authority over large and extensive districts, others rule over a town or village".[91] Here Horton was really describing the different structural strata in Igboland.

In traditional Igbo society, it is possible to notice five types of political organization. The first type of political organization is found among the Southern Igbo, such as those in Owerri, Okigwe and Mbaise. *Ezeji* and *Duru* are Igbo traditional titles which existed in these areas, but their holders played an insignificant political role. The second political organization, essentially democratic, consists of a non-hierarchical power base which at the same time admits other components. Besides family or lineage representation, the role of age grades and societies are prominent. This organization is more pronounced around the Eastern Igbo such as those living in the Abriba, Ohafia and Arochukwu areas.

In the Southern Igbo area, such as in Ngwa, Bende, Ohuhu and Ibeku, we have the third type, which is also basically democratic. It consists of a power base constituted by family or lineage head representations along with secret cult society. There is a tremendous political power exercised by the secret cult called *okonko.* The fourth type existed in parts of Northern Igbo, Nri and Nsukka ares, where political democracy had witnessed the emergence of an elite group, known as *Ozo or Eze*. "Traditionally the whole of Nri is under *Eze Nri* who is regarded as a SACRED KING. He governs Nri with his multiple of twelve councilors called Nzemabua".[92] However in the Nsukka area, the

---

89 GREEN, M.M., **Ibo Village AFFairs**, Sidgwick, London, 1947, pp. 5-7.

90 NZEWUNWA, N., "Pre-colonial Nigeria East of the Niger", in: R. Olaniyan ed., **Nigerian History and Culture,** Longman, Lagos, 1985, p. 25.

91 SHEPPERSON, G., ed., ***Horton James Africanus 1886,*** **African Countries and Peoples**, Edinburgh University Press, Edinburgh, 1969, p. 25.

92 ONWUEJEOGWU, M.A., "An outline account of the dawn of Igbo Civilization in the Igbo cultural area", in: **Odinani**, vol. 1, 1(March 1972), p. 47. Here, one should notice the use of twelve councilors in relation of the twelve tribes of Israel and the twelve Apostles.

situation is different. Here, the *eze* did not command so much authority or embody great symbolism. In both cases the democratic principle of consultation and consensus abound.

On both the East and West banks of the Niger, there exists a fifth type which consists of Igbo kingdoms. This area include Onitsha, Oguta, Aboh, Ogwashi. These were elaborate title systems which were hierarchically structured, but strict monarchies never existed. They remained republican. Each king (in Onitsha *Obi*) ruled along with a political elite composed of titled men known as *ndiche ume, okwa and ndiche okwaraeze*. Every lineage was represented by the title member and their function as the decision-making body eliminated every form of autocracy. To this Isichei says that the "kings were regarded as sacred, and lived in ritual seclusion. But they were not absolute and took decisions in conjunction with titled men, and representatives of groups. Their decisions could be challenged, and their persons deposed."[93] We may here mention John Whitford's description in the 1870s of an audience given to him and his group by Obi Akazua (d.1872) the *Obi* (King) of Onitsha, concerning permission to establish an European trading firm as an example of democracy within the monarch.

> The King consulted his chiefs on one hand and the commons on the other. Committees of each left for private consultation in another part of the palace. Speeches were made, some of which were very loud and angry in tone. One old woman came forward, and kneeling before the king, stated her views. At length, in a few brief, but effective sentences, a very ugly little man... spoke out, and he was cheered loudly by sudden burst of acclamation at each period. So that it was settled to allow trade with white man."[94]

These types of political organization demonstrated how democratic the Igbo are. In all cases, consensus was required in the exercise of authority. Freedom and equality were basic assumptions in social and political interactions. Democratic values were part of the peoples' life, as Horton says:

> The Egboes (Igbo) cannot be driven to act, they become most stubborn and bull-headed; but with kindness they could be made to do any thing, even to deny themselves of their conscience, by coercion, to the performance of any act, whether good or bad, when they have not the inclination to do so; hence there is not that unity among them that is found among tribes, in fact every one likes to be his own master.[95]

---

93 ISICHEI, E., **A History of the Igbo People**, Macmillan, 1972, p.23.

94 WHITEFORD, J., "Trading life in Western and Central Africa", in: E. Isichei, **Igbo World, An Anthropology of Oral Histories and Historical Descriptions**, Macmillan, London, 1977, p. 259.

95 SHEPPERSON, G., ed., **Horton James Africanus**..., op.,cit., pp. 163-164.

Igbo democratic spirit was so widespread that women, both as individuals and as groups, exercised rights of self determination. This aspect is also appreciated by Horton that "among the Egboes (Igbo), women hold a very superior rank in the social scale; they are not regarded as among other heathen tribes, as an inferior creation and doomed to perpetual degradation, but occupy their rightful status in society".[96]

The study of the social structure and organization of the Igbo is thus important for us in order to see how *umunn*a as a social unit can help the Church in Igboland in the form of Small Christian Communities. Since social organization and social structure molds men's impulses[97], the effect of *umunna* as a social structure has on the people is of paramount importance. It is pertinent to point out that social structure and organization are just two of the forces which mould human behaviour.

The understanding of the social structure and the organization of the Igbo community will be of great help in the identification of power structure and participation of individuals and groups in the system. They help to shape the individual's early concept of himself in society.

They also have a significant contribution to the configuration of power in that society. There is a classification of power in the community, between the individual and the social power-center. The linkage of power can be direct, as in classical democracy, or indirect, as is expected in hierarchical power structures, and depends upon what agencies act as buffers to possible absolutism from the center.[98] Here the individual understands society from the point of view of his participation in the system, which leads us finally to the individual seeing his participation in the system as being shaped according to his perception of self in that system.[99] When all these reasons are present in any society, be it social or political, the Igbo is at home and his identity guaranteed, and he can then give his helping hand to the smooth running of the community.[100] The community becomes our community. Igbo towns can be referred to as confederated villages. Nzimiro clearly says;

---

96 Ibid., p. 156.

97 Cf. B. Russell, **Political Ideals** (Unwin Books, London, 1963), p. 15.

98 Cf. N. Berry, **Political Configurations: An Analysis of the Political System in Society.** (Good-year Publ. Co. Inc., N.Y. 1972), pp. 26ff.

99 .Milbrath, L.W., **Political Participation: How and Why do People get Involved in Politics**, (Rand McNally and company, London, 1965), pp. 110ff.

100 Cf. L.U. Ejiofor, **Igbo Kingdoms: Power and Control**, (1982), pp. 54-56.

A typical Ibo community, though it is often referred to as a town, consists of a federation of dispersed villages(Obodo or Ikoporo).[101]

Among these units, the most important include *obodo, ebe*, *ogbe* and *umunna*. Just as the family forms the basis for any social structure, the first of these political organization embodies maximally democratic elements and consists in the constitution of the power base on family or lineage representation. Lineage heads normally represent their lineages. By such an arrangement, all powers, whether political, legislative or judicial, are exercised by consensus. The representatives enjoy equal opportunity to deliberate and no one man can be so distinguished that he overrules the voices of the rest. Everyone listens to his representative and holds his unit sacred, so that other units may not ridicule them, hence the spirit of *ikwu na ibe*.

1.3.1. Ikwu na Ibe

Ikwu naturally means kin, while *Ibe* stands for one's neighbour. *Ikwu* begins with one's family and expands as the case may be to include other social structures, with the exclusion of the one that represents the *Ibe*. As soon as *Ikwu* expands to be the entire *nqwuru*, the *Ibe* shifts to the *Onumara*. And when *onumara* becomes *ikwu*, *umunn*a immediately takes the place of *ibe*, and so on, until the earth is again the limit. This concept is ready to include the world as *ikwu*, if any non-terrestial beings are known to threaten the earth.[102]

The term *ikwu na ibe* illustrates this spirit vividly. *Ikwu* always begins with a man's family, *ama* and automatically the *Nqwuru* becomes his *ibe* (see **Fig.1**). He looks at those within the *Nqwuru* as his rivals, and as soon as *ikwu* expands to be the entire *Nqwuru*, the *ibe* shifts to the *Onumara*, and so on. He tries to be superior to any one in the other social unit, for example, the *nqwuru*, *onumara* etc., and derives consolation from the saying *ibe awu chi* (Ibe is never the god), so with hard work he is confident that he will be better than those in a different or opposite camp. The sky is the limit of this *ikwu na ibe*.

No matter in which social unit the Igbo finds himself, he always runs to the *Ikwu* for protection, especially when challenged by the *ibe*. The defence of a member of the *ikwu* is a task that has to be done by every Igbo, whenever and wherever he is in trouble. At birth one is introduced or grows within his *ikwu* and later his *ibe*.

---

101 Nzimiro, I., **Studies in Ibo Political Systems: Chieftaincy and Politics in four Niger States**; (1972), p. 21.

102 ibid., p. 54.

The *ikwu* concept is lived more within the *umunna* level. This spirit is not limited to the Igbo, but to the whole of traditional Africans. It has its own negative aspect which has to be Christianized. Its monolithic worldview, drawn from its origin and historical development, is becoming more and more resistant to a pluralistic concept of the world and nation in particular. The Igbo in particular and Africans in general concentrate on this clannish mentality. This phenomenon is undoubtedly to a large extent responsible for political unrest in Africa today, e.g., in Somalia, Rwanda, Burundi, even in Nigeria, where ethnic politics reign supreme.

The traditional basic community (in the case of the Igbo Umunna) or clan is the only apparently safe political, economic, social and religious haven today in Africa. It can equally be described as the primary constituency for many African political, social, religious and economic activities. No wonder there is no single organized religious group in traditional Africa. To be accepted at this unit is the primary concern of many African leaders; their rise and fall depend upon this basic unit.

It is precisely because of its importance in African society as the basic community that people seem to live for, that it somehow manipulates and predetermines their actions in political and other public functions. There is a need, therefore, that religion, i.e., Christianity, should carry on a dialogue with this basic community, for a better Igboland, Nigeria, Africa and the Salvation of the individual, to accept the pluralistic world view and see the nation as well as the Church as the ultimate end of the basic community.

The concept of *ikwu* and *ibe* prepares an Igbo for this participation. No wonder that after a century of Catholicism in Igboland with its pyramidical parish structure, the Catholic church is still addressed as *uka fada* (the priest's church). There are stories of people walking out of the Church while priests were preaching, because they were not allowed to contradict the priests or challenge them as they speak.[103] This is why the church had its humble beginning in Igboland with slaves and those normally addressed as weak or as village never-do-wells.

It is imperative that the Igbo participates in the social activity of his people. Failure on his part to do so will make him lose not only his rights in the society, but his sense of belonging, his prestige, his ego and self-esteem. He learns this participation as he learns to walk. To participate is a religious duty. For

---

103 There is even a saying that **'ihia abughi okwu chukwu n'anaghi asasa'** (this is not a priest's sermon that requires no comment or interrogation). There is another interesting saying that illustrate the mind of the **Igbo** in this regard: **Obu onye gara uka ka fada na abaramba** (only those who go to church can afford to take the scolding from the priest). So to be a real **Igbo**, is to avoid going to the church.

the Igbo to participate early in life, for the good of the *ikwu*, the position of the *umunna* in Igbo society is stressed.

The Igbo are known for their concern and deep respect for the principle and practice of direct primitive democracy, called **ohacracy**. The village assembly meetings are the place where this is experienced and exemplified. No wonder a British administrative officer once complained that;

> Every male person had the right to attend a meeting... and to speak when he so desired. This was an indisputable privilege bestowed on each individual and handed down to posterity, and such was the conservative mind of the people that any suggested modification or diversion from this rule of government would have been regarded as bordering on the ridiculous. The members of the (village) council only began to operate administratively when the subject matter of the meeting had already been discussed.[104]

This part of Igbo life has been totally ignored by the Church, and in order to achieve meaningful participation of the Igbo in their local church, this aspect of their life ought to be revived.

1.3.2. Authority in Igbo society

We have expressed how important democracy is in Igbo society. In trying to express how authority in Igboland rests on the community and not on any one person, Ayandele recalls the experience of the colonial masters as was found in their diary;

> Moreover in the absence of traditional rulers of the states of *Yoruba Obas* among the Ibo the head of the Ibo village could not override majority opinion in the village which, as a rule, was in favour of inviting missionaries in a bid to have the village children inducted into the mystery of reading and writing.[105]

---

104 **Intelligence Report** No. **S.P.10411/12**, National Archives, **Enugu**, Eastern Nigeria, 28th.Feb. 1934; Such a report shows how the Igbo takes his affairs into his own hand. The Church never cared to realize this aspect of Igbo life. The Church by so doing did alienate the Igbo by not allowing them make decisions on things that concern them; cf. O.P. Nsugbe, **OHAFFIA...** op.cit., (1974), p. 67.

105 .Ayandele, E.A., "**The Missionary Impact on Modern Nigeria, 1842-1914: A Political and Social Analysis**", in: **Ibadan History Series**, (Nigeria, 1966), p. 171. Looking at the democratic nature of authority in Igboland Annene says: "Generally speaking, the Ibo communities were democracies in the sense that the government of the communities was the concern of all"; **Southern Nigerian in Transition 1885-1906**, p.14; cf. A.E. Afigbo, **The Warrant Chiefs's Indirect Rule in Southern Nigeria 1891-1929**, (1972), pp. 26-27.

Such is the position of the Igbo, when it comes to authority. The **oha** is supreme and no one person may take it upon himself to usurp the position of deciding for others. The head of any community consults the elders and presents his case to the *oha*. The elders are respected, and at times are influenced by their most able leaders, yet decision and ultimate authority rests in the hands of the group as a whole.[106] Although the Igbo say: *Onye nganga (ije) ka onye isiawo ihe ama* (literally- a traveller has more knowledge than one with gray hairs), the general conception is that wisdom comes with age. Nsugbe says;

> The prestige and influence of '*ndi Ichin*' derive from the fact that, among the Ibo generally, wisdom and knowledge of local traditions are associated with age.[107]

There are age grades which also participate in the smooth running of the Igbo society. The Igboman is perplexed by the understanding of authority in the Western thinking, just as the Western concept of power eludes the Igboman.[108]

The common expression in Igbo *Oha-lee* (let the whole community decide or look at the matter) illustrates how authority is vested on the community. Meek puts it this way;

> although certain personages were assigned special duties of a public character, these duties were primarily ceremonial, and did not usually carry with them any definite form of

---

106 .Ottenberg S., **Community and Change in African Culture,** in: Bavom and Herskovits edts. p.353.

107 Nsugbe O.P., **OHAFIA: A Matrilineal Ibo People**, (1974), p.66; **Ndi Ichin** is another name for the elders in a given community, especially in **Ohafia, Bende and Umuahia** areas, but most Igbo called them **Ndi Ichie.** The Igbo culture is traditionally handed on through sayings and folk stories, idioms and the like, since there is no written documentation. It is passed down from age to age through the oral traditions. The old people and their counsel are respected. This could be derived from the fact that the aged know more things by experience, since there was no means of recording events. Only those who have more years in age can tell the stories of past events. Knowledge of the events in the life of the people is through oral tradition, the elders have some degree of authority. Age plays a very important role in **Igboland** as regards authority.

108 Njaka, says; "An authority in which he (the Igbo) has no share is suspect and intolerable. When a Western speaks of the power of the State, the Igbo conceptualizes a State power or the **Oha** in which he participates in his traditional way". **Igbo Political Culture**, op.cit.,p.59.

personal authority. The community was governed by the whole body of the people represented by the heads of families.[109]

It is important to note that the elders of the people also play an additional, important role in the community. When cases seem impossible, the elders are asked to deliberate privately on it, called *igba-izu*. The community accords great respect to the elders, who are believed to be nearer to the ancestors and to possess enough traditional knowledge. Their presence helps to maintain the stability of the community. This does not mean that an ignorant elder takes precedence over an intelligent, knowledgeable younger person. The self-regulation in the Igbo set-up helps the ignorant elder to know when to remove himself from a position in favor of a younger person.

Social structure in Igboland has some outstanding determinant factors which characterize the uniqueness of its *Ohacratic* nature. These include individualism, self-regulation, recruitment, representation, achievement orientation and leadership, to mention but a few. We shall try to look at some of these determinant characteristics.

1.3.2.1. Individualism

The stress on community sometimes makes one overlook the individualistic aspect of the Igbo person. It is true that they emphasize a communion of persons more than an individual, but that does not deny the individualistic tendency in them. The individual sometimes claims an air of autonomy within the society and it is his sense of belonging to this group that helps to develop in him his potential, his initiative and drive for achievement, his originality, and his ability to ward off inordinately selfish ambitions which could remove him from the society's communion.[110] To maintain a correct perspective in the light of the rather aggressive individualism of Igbo man, conflicts are on the whole minimized by kinsmen's respect for each other's autonomy; they are ever ready to safeguard this autonomy. The Igbo derive their spirit of individualism from the structure and organization of the simple family or compound family units which encourage individual achievement within the communal context of the *umunna* units. In other words, Igbo individualism is based on the structure of *umunna*.[111] It is the **ikwu na ibe** spirit that portrays the Igbo individualism.

---

109 Meek C.K., **Law and Authority...**, (1950), p.138. In criticism of Meek C.K., cf. Ayandele E.A., **The Missionary Impact on Modern Nigeria 1842-1914:** (1966), p.330.

110 Njaka,E.N., **Igbo Political Culture:** (1974), p.60.

111 Ejiofor L.U. **Igbo Kingdoms: Power and Control**, (1982); cf. Ogbalu,F.C. and Emenanjo,E.N., eds.,**Igbo language and Culture**, (Oxford University Press, London, 1975), p.91.

The Igbo look at the *ibe* from their *ikwu* position; no wonder that names like *Ibekwem* (if *Ibe* allows me I will be great) *Ibezimako* (it is from *Ibe* that one gets the sense to fight and overcome) are common. It is with constant communion with persons in the *ibe* that the Igbo derive their pride, boldness and individualism.

Individualism is stressed in that no one can remain idle.[112] Just as no community will be associated with a lazy person, no one wishes to bring shame on his community by not struggling hard. A man's strength and pride are reserved in his community – this explains the saying in Igboland that a bee collects its stinging power from its hive before it stings.

This way of thinking and acting helps the Igbo to conceptualize government and other social organizational affairs with the basic community spirit; devoid of outside authority, that will guarantee a person's individuality in the group process and afford each person the opportunity of free action as a respected, responsible human being. This idea made the colonizers conclude that the Igbo were ungovernable, being without formal government, or a ruler etc.[113] Igbo individualism does not mean equality in the community, but instead, that everyone has his or her rights within the community, which must be respected by all. Igbo individualism concedes that, while all people are not equal, yet each person has that which distinguishes him from the rest or in which he excels. Consequently, each individual is entitled to a hearing in any gathering, for example, and should be given due respect, for whatever he is worth, at all times. People have equal rights but this does not make them equal.[114] The individualism of the **Igbo** gives rise to independence.

Every Igboman struggles in nature to be independent and this is achieved by having a family of his own, building a house and constructing his own *ama* (pathway).

> Thus housing is important to the Igbo, because adulthood has not been completely attained until a young man owns a house which may in time become the nucleus of an *umunna* or a strong arm of one.[115]

---

112 Cf. Okonjo,I.K., **The Role of Women in Social Change among the Igbo of Southern Nigeria living West of the River Niger,** (Boston, 1986), p.27; where she wrote:"The **Igbo** are highly individualistic and therefore also highly achievement-oriented and achievement-conscious. Because of these qualities of character they accord more respect to achieved than inherited status."

113 Cf. Basden G.T., **Niger Ibos**, (1966), pp.234f; Meek C.K., **Law and Authority...**; Green M.M., **Igbo Village Affairs...**, (1964),

114 ibid.,p.61.

115 ibid.; Ottenberg stated that the **Ibo**s are highly individualistic, but while a man is dependent on his family lineage, and residential grouping for support and backing, strong

This individualism can also be carried over to the social units. It is quite contrary to the Igbo way of life to think of a town or social unit dominating and ruling another. Thus, there are guidelines both for individuals and social units, preventing them from excesses.

1.3.2.2. Self-regulation

Though the individual acts alone, his or her action has a communal effect and no one is prepared to bring shame to the community. One acts alone, but the fate of the community is at the forefront in the decision before action is taken. Each person aspires, both as an individual and as a member of the unit, to achieve greatness for the community. Thus in an average **Igbo**, there are internalized checks and balances regulating behaviour. These are dynamic and formidable and influence his allocation of priorities. A failure in self-regulation means that the individual forfeits his share of the diffuse authority of his unit.[116]

Such self-regulation is lacking in the parish structure, where the Igbo is lost in the crowd. It would be a good step in the right direction to bring back this very important trait in the formation of small Christian community in Igboland, using its basic community. And this self-regulatory mechanism also preserves the spirit of individualism. It helps the Igbo to bear in mind that one is not alone but represents one's community.

1.3.2.3. Representation

The Igbo saying *Onye onyeya n'anoghi ngahu, ji ya huru n'agaoku* (when one has nobody caring for one's interest, one's yam is normally at the side of the fire), is the base for the Igbo spirit of representation. Such a saying expresses how important a representative governance is entrenched in Igbo culture.

Those appointed to represent the people in any social unit are subject to the people. The Igbo expect to have the opportunity to control them and not play the role of their servants. They demand the power to recall their representatives whenever they demonstrate bad faith or refuse to bow to public opinion.[117]

In summing up, we maintain that the aforementioned factors shape the social character of the Igbo. An Igboman dreads any outside authority that will

---

emphasis is placed on his ability to make his own way in the world." **Continuity and Change in African Culture:"** eds., Bavom and Herskovits, p. 137.

116 ibid., p. 62.

117 ibid., p. 64.

not afford him a breathing space for self-participation in the affairs affecting him and subsequently afford him the opportunity to negotiate. The social and political culture of the Igbo emphasize communal interests and individual achievements. One realizes one's individuality through participation in communal life. The participatory nature of the Igbo society is of great help to the people, in terms of both governance and communication. Njaka beautifully puts the whole thing as;

> adaptability, selectivity and mobility, group orientation, individualism and self-regulation, structural flexibility, high and low legitimacy conflicts compromised through functional self-regulation of segregated and diffused authority, and the uniqueness of republicanism working within the framework of politico-religious constitutional monarchy, are essentially the components of traditional Igbo culture.[118]

Njaka's assumptions play an important role in identifying the Igbo. They also help the Igbo to exhibit and live the community spirit that is transcendent. He (the Igbo) perceives life as participation and the source of this life is God; and those closest to God are the ancestors; hence the importance of ancestral worship. Participation in this life coming from the ancestors is the only way the individual in Africa shares the life of one's basic community. This basic community in Igbo land is called ***Umunna.***

1.4. Conclusion

From our treatment so far, we have seen that it is at the *umunna* community level that the Igbo life activities are expressed. The Igbo take human relations seriously because of the fulfillment and stability of the community. One is at home in one's community. The stability and fulfillment of the community is expressed in the seriousness with which the African in general and Igbo in particular handles the affairs of the community.

The *umunna* which is the focus of our research is headed by an *onye isi* (the head of the family) or *okwara* (first son), who because of his position as the okwara of all *onumara* (one of the social structure) within the *umunna* system that constitutes the executive council is the chairman. This body can and does act as legislative body for the *umunna.*

It is interesting to note that *onye-isi* (the head person) may not necessarily be the oldest in some particular Igbo communities, but happens to be the *okwara* in the *ama* where the *obi-ukwu* (small reception hall) is located. He serves both the living and the dead. An *umunna* council of elders is composed

118 ibid., p. 69.

of the *onye-isi* and the heads of all the *onumara*. The supreme authority of the *umunna* is in the *umunna* assembly (oha), which consists of the *okwara* of *ama* and *ngwuru* and every other eligible adult within the *umunna*. The *umunna* assembly normally gathers at the *obi-ukwu* which is located in the *okwara*'s compound.

Umunna, though low on the structural ladder as shown in the Figures 1 – 4 (see Appendix), is the most effective political, social and religious unit in the hierarchy of the Igbo traditional structure and the understanding of its importance will help us to appreciate its contribution in the formation of small Christian communities.

The traditional Igbo transcendent spirit of communalism has its root in their belief in God and their ancestors. These beliefs constitute a form of social control in the community. Communal participation in the affairs of the community is encouraged by the ancestral cults, thereby revitalizing, reconciling and regenerating a new sense of commitment to communitarian values. It is not only a sense of awe for the mysterious which makes the individual innerself believe in them, but 'springs from the individual's reaction to social facts, to common culture, historical and ecological context'.[119] The Igbo see community as a place in which life and work take place, as basic and manageable social groupings whose members can experience real interpersonal relationships and feel a sense of communal belonging. This is a gift from God which the Igbo treasure.

God endows people with gifts and communicates with them in various ways. And it is a known fact that God communicates with a people on a level which concerns their innermost core of existence. The core of existence for the Igbo as we have seen is the community – *umunna*. The spirit in which the Igbo live may not be clear or transparent to an outsider, but it does possess a meaning and give a direction to their decisions in the thousand trivialities of daily life. When the impression of the spirit as expressed in everyday life is unmasked, it gives the real essence of their existence – solidarity.

This spirit of grace becomes a rallying point that constitutes a community. In the Igbo community, the families combine to form an *umunna*, which have their ancestors as a focus and cannot help being communitarian; just as the person of Christ and the faith in his resurrection constitute the Christian community. Christianity's ecclesial character or spirit lies not only in the fact that man has a social nature, but even more because God addresses a people.

---

119 Shorter, A., **African Culture and Christian Church**. (Maryknoll, New York, 1973), p. 45; cf. Kalem'Imana, op. cit., p.30.

Christianity is a community religion.[120] This shows that a people can better reach Jesus and his teaching through the community. This community ought to be a caring and community full of faith, where solidarity, compassion and love abounds.

The Igbo who has the mystique of life – the spirit that compels him and what may be called a transcendent experience, the spirit of *umunna*, can also be a good Christian. This spirit is a gift from God. The meeting of the Christian and *umunna* spirits is called conversion. This is a culmination of the transcendent experience through which the Igboman goes out of himself to identify with others and in the process of this transcendence comes in contact with the spirit of Christianity.[121]

Building a community does not actually mean forming organizations; it means creating and deepening the spirit of love and service among people. It is a gift from God. Thus, for the fulfillment and stability of the community, and through the *umunna* ensemble, the Igbo take human relationships very seriously. The goal of the *umunna* unit is to provide for everyone and make everyone feel the sense of belonging. A community which provides a general experience of belonging and commitment is an essential element to any understanding of Church. *Umunna* will offer the promise of new vitality for the church and give an added impulse to people to live according to the gospel, since with it people will rediscover the values of community. Our next task is to see how this community spirit is expressed in the Christian Church. Does *umunna* community life run contrary to the Christian life? What has each of the two cultures to give one another?

---

120 Rahner affirms that: "Those who believe in Jesus cannot be individualistic in their religion, if only because of their common relationship to the Lord. Moreover faith in Jesus can only be awakened through active witness and therefore demands the social structure of a community of faith which is gathered around Jesus Christ... which means that the history of his freedom is worked out in the context of the community". K. Rahner, *Experience of the spirit source of theology,* in: **Theological Investigations**, XVI, London, Darton, Longman and Todd, (1979), p. 20

121 Rahner affirms that: "Like any other experience, the transcendent experience of the radical "nature" of the spirit is mediated through categorical objects, for the finite, spiritual essence of man only comes to self expression in relationship to what is other, and in the ultimate analysis this other must be personal". ibid., p.28.

Chapter Two: Christianity – A Community Religion

2.0. Introduction

Small communities are indispensable not only in the Igbo nation but also in Christianity, which assimilates, transmits and solidifies Christianity in the community, for the community, and by the community. In this chapter we shall attempt to have an insight into the essence, the nature and the mission of the Church as a community of believers.

We shall first study the idea of community in the Old Testament; secondly, the New Testament understanding of the Church as community. Then we shall examine the early Christian communities of the Constantine era and their famous house Churches.

2.1. Community in the Old Testament

There is some controversy concerning the historical existence of Israel as a people. Historical investigation has made it clear that Israel was a name given to the sacral alliance of tribes which was only constituted in Palestine after the settlement. We shall not involve ourselves into such controversy, which is also outside the scope of our work. The people of Israel came into being in Egypt (Ex.1:6f). From this period on, Israel proceeds through all the well-known events of history (oppression in Egypt, the Exodus, the Revelation at Sinai, the wandering in the wilderness) down to the migration into Canaan as a homogeneous entity.[1]

Modern society has shifted significantly from the relation of the individual man to the social group as seen in the Old Testament (OT) and in the rest of the ancient world. This shift has resulted in heated arguments and different stands without producing a consensus of opinion. The discussion has been polarized into collectivism and individualism. Some have attributed an exaggerated collectivism to the OT people. But a deep look at the reality will reveal that both the OT and primitive society hardly thought of collectivism or individualism, since the terms represent modern ideas. The idea of community in the OT is expressed in the covenant.

---

1 von Rad, G., **Old Testament Theology**, vol. 1, London, SCM Press, (1985), pp. 4-6.

2.1.1. Covenant People

The "Covenant" does not pertain only to things regarding God. Men were bound to each other by agreements and contracts which entailed rights and duties that were usually reciprocal.[2] In the Bible, there are covenants of brothers(Am.1:9); covenants of friendship (1 Sam.23:18), covenants of peace (Gen.14:13). "Covenant" stands for varying types of agreements or relationships. It is a sign of relationship.[3] The underlying factor of a covenant is that it is an interpersonal relationship. It is not an act of one person or one group but involves a second person or second group. For a covenant to be what it stands for, there should be involvement of all parties both as a relationship and as an act. Jacob Kavunkal summed it up by saying:

> It cannot usually come about unless all join in making it and it means nothing unless all are somehow involved in it, even tied to it.[4]

In nearly every religion, sharing a meal is recognized as a sign of covenant. Covenants are sealed by communion, as expressed in the Bible. A covenant can be seen as an expression of acceptance and belonging to a community. There are many different covenants, but one of the salvation covenant communities was sealed at Sinai, through the mediation of Moses.[5] This covenant spelt out the terms by which God became their God and Israel became the people of God – the **EL ELYON**. Every right has its obligation; in this case, Israel must obey Yahweh: "if you obey my voice and keep my covenant, you shall be my own possession among all peoples; for all the earth is mine, and you shall be to me a kingdom of priests" (Exd. 19: 31).

---

2 Cf. J. Gilbert, and P. Grelot, "**Covenant**", in: **Dictionary of Biblical Theology**, L. Dufour, ed., (London, 1982), p. 93.

3 Cf. P. Kalluveettil, **Declaration and Covenant**, (Rome, 1982), p. 25.

4 Kavunkal, J., **To Gather Them into One: -Evangelization in India today a Process of Building Community.** (Satprakashan Sanchar Kendra, India, 1985), p. 30.

5 "Moses, rising early the next day, erected at the foot of the mountain, where the tablets of the Law were given, an altar and twelve pillars for the twelve tribes of Israel. He sent out young men of the Israelites "to offer holocausts and sacrifice young bulls as peace offerings to the Lord"(Ex.24:5). From the sacrifice offered, Moses collected the blood of the victims in bowls. He splashed half of it on the altar and the rest he left in some bowls... Then Moses took the blood and sprinkled it on the people..." P. Osuchukwu, **Home-sick for Paradise Lost**...(1988), p.68. Such a rite involving blood in the covenant-sacrifice, Lyonnet and Sabourin in their write-up state that; "The blood joins or unites the two parties which are to contract a pact, as is the case in pacts of friendship, where the blood of the one is mixed with the blood of the other, so that one life, as it were, is produced". S. Lyonnet, and L. Sabourin, **Sin, Redemption and Sacrifice: A Biblical and Patristic Study**; (Biblical Institute Press, Rome, 1970), p. 172.

Israel at this point in time began to see herself as being a special people of God. "You are a people holy to the Lord your God; the Lord your God has chosen you to be a people for His own possession, out of all the people that are on the face of the earth" (Deut.7:6). Here we see the expression of Israel's self-understanding and her position as the elect of God. The Sinai covenant produced a new people, bound together into a religious and political community. The covenant served as the basis of their new identity. It is here that they entered into a covenant relationship with Yahweh, and their worship of Yahweh gave rise to a national religion. The two-fold spheres of a relationship are demonstrated here in the Sinai covenant: vertically – a relationship with God; and horizontally – a relationship with one's fellow men.

The sacrifices carried out at Sinai by Moses and the young men (Exd. 24: 3-8) are sacrifices of communion, that is, they effected a union between God and the people and so produced the relationship which is the object of all covenants.[6] The understanding of the place of blood in the thinking of the Hebrews as the seat and sign of life, helps us to see the role of blood in the sacrifice. The sprinkling of the blood both on the altar and on the people, as mentioned, shows a sharing of some sort between Yahweh and the people, of the same blood and hence the same life. McCarthy further says:

> The covenant meal means admission into the family circle of another but the blood rite is especially vivid. Yahweh somehow shared the same blood in the rite.[7]

From the features of Sinai-theophany which are expressed through sacrifice, blood rites, and sacred meal, we are provided with an example of a perfect communion, expressed in a community. There are two words employed by OT writers to describe Israel as the covenant people of God. These words are ***Qahal*** and ***Edah***. Berkhof describes *qahal* as a derivative from an absolute root ***qal*** which means 'to call', while *edah* comes from ***ya adh***, meaning 'to appoint', or 'to assemble at an appointed place'.[8] Another scholar who made some revelations in the meaning of *qahal*, Coenen, shows that in Deuteronomy the overall meaning is the covenant congregation at Sinai,(Deut.9:10; 10:4), which is linked with the name of Yahweh (Deut.23:2); this stands for the people summoned by God and bound by the ordinances He has given.[9] The

---

6 Cf. D.J. McCarthy, **Treaty and Covenant: A Study in Form in the Ancient Oriental Documents and in the Old Testament;** (New Edition, Rome, 1978), p. 255.

7 Ibid., p. 295.

8 Berkhof, L., **Systematic Theology**, (Banner of Truth, London, 1978), p. 554.

9 Cf. L. Coenen, **Church**: C. Brown, ed., **The New International Dictionary of New Testament Theology**, Vol.1, Exeter, (The Paternoster Press, N.Y., 1975), p. 291. There are other meanings to qahal such as summons to war of all capable men,(Gen.49:6;

OT meaning of *qahal* ranges from summons for military service, through assembly for political or civil meetings, to more solemn gatherings for worship. The term *Edah* is found more in the *Pentateuch* and passages in the Bible attributed to the priestly redactors. Coenen, quoting Rost, sees *edah* as coined by the priestly writers as:

> The announcement of a resolution or decision, the carrying out of which is so bound up with a particular place or an appointed time or a given situation, that any departure from the determining or conditioning factors is equivalent to a failure to carry out the command.[10]

With regards to this definition, the root is very closely related to the Deutronomistic use of *qahal*. For Berkhof, the two words *qahal* and *edah* are sometimes indiscriminately used, though they were not at first synonymous.[11]

He went on to agree with Coenen, that in the passages where both occur in the same context (Exd. 12:6; Num. 14:5; Jer. 26:17), as ***qahal edah***, the meanings are distinctly different. In my view, whereas *edah* is the unambiguous and permanent term for the covenant community as a whole or their representatives, assembled or not assembled, *qahal* stands for the actual meeting of the people for religious, secular, or communal interests. This shows that "the assembly of the congregation" becomes the nearest acceptable translation of *qahal edah*.[12]

It is also important to note that Berkhof and Coenen are in agreement that the Septuagint and the Targums are consistent in rendering *edah* as synagogue and *Kenista* while *qahal* is rendered *ekklesia* by Septuagint in the later books of the Bible. As we know, community involves persons. Experience has shown that this community involves both the human and divine. "From this you know that now..., you of all the nation shall be my very own for all the earth is mine. I will count you a kingdom of priests, a consecrated nation" (Exd. 19:5-6). A covenant, though kept by individuals, is not made with individuals, but instead with the whole people. The people as a community are the beneficiaries of God's covenant of love and saving action. Here, one can apply

---

Num.22:4), the representatives of the people or the whole people (Num.16:33); a special solemn assembly. Also in post-exilic period, it stands for the special general assembly of all the people which included women and children (Ezr. 10: 1; Neh. 8:2), and in Ezekiel a mustering of the Gentile troops (Ezek. 17:17, 27:27, 32:22).

10 ibid.

11 Berkhof, L., **Systematic Theology** (1978), p. 555; for more information cf., H. Kung "**The Church**" (1967), pp. 117-124.

12 Cf. A.O. Nkwoka, **New Testament Concept of Diakonia as a Paradigm for Interpreting Leadership Crisis in the Nigerian Churches;** (unpublished thesis, Ile-Ife, 1990), p. 36.

the old Latin saying that: "**unus Christianus nullus Christianus**" Therefore, the human relationship is important for the community. In this covenant community, the rallying point is God.

In the Book of Psalms, we see how important the covenant community is, that an Israelite found it almost unnatural to praise God alone. "I live in a desert like the pelican, in a ruin like the screech owl, I stay awake, lamenting like a lone bird on the roof" (Ps. 102: 6-7). Someone cut off from the covenant community always has a longing of returning to the community as we read from the Psalm about the lament of a Levite in exile (Ps. 42 – 43). Maly says;

> The close-knit community of tribes and of the patriarchal family helped to make this notion of covenant salvation intelligible and meaningful to ancient Israel. But long after Israel had adopted the ways of city life and after the ancient tribes had lost some of their cohesiveness, she remained a 'people of God' called by the Lord to covenant community.[13]

There are a lot of passages in the Old Testament which point to the fact that Israel had been called by Yahweh. The liberation from slavery in Egypt, the crossing of the Red sea, the desert episode and the encounter with God at Sinai, marked Israel out as God's people. Community in OT is theocentric, bound by a covenant with God, who in turn binds the people to one another as children of the same Father, with the same feeling as in a large family. They received from Yahweh a Community built neatly around their ancestors, their teachings and laws, which was a wonderful combination of reverence to ancestor and worship of God.

Israel should be seen as a microcosm within the macrocosm of the world community. Kavunkal also says;

> Israel's covenant is a typical example of what the Bible believes, is the basic relationship between God and mankind. By putting the covenant with mankind in the same context as the covenant with Israel, the Yahwist understood the relationship between Israel and humanity in the same sense.[14]

Even the covenant with Noah made no mention of Israel: "But I will establish my covenant with you, and you must go on board the ark... "(Gen. 6:18). In the new understanding, no one is excluded from the people of God. And this was the mission of Christ to bring all to the community of God's Children. Let us see how this community is expressed in the New Testament.

---

13 Maly, E., "**Still a Case for Infant Baptism?**" (1981), p. 97.

14 Ibid., p. 35.

2.2. Community in the New Testament

Jesus, being a Jew, conducted his mission with the background of OT thought. He saw that the old order was giving way to a new one, and also saw his mission as a continuation of God's dealings with his people. Not being nationalistic, he was essentially concerned with the "people of God" in a new and vital way. He came to make the Kingdom of God present to us – Immanuel.

2.2.1. Kingdom of God Realized and Yet to Come

The central concern and theme of the words and actions of Jesus was the proclamation of the Kingdom of God. According to Mk.1:15, it was his manifesto.[15] But how did the use of the term Kingdom of God come about, since it is rare in the Old Testament. The roots of the symbolic kingdom of God is perhaps derived from myths of the ancient Near East. Cultures borrow and lend; the culture of Israelites is not an exception. They did borrow a concept of the kingdom as Mowinckel clearly says;

> This was taken over by the Israelites from the Canaanites, who had received it from the great kingdoms on the Euphrates and Tigris and Nile, where it had been developed as early as ancient Sumerian times.[16]

The term Kingdom of God occurs about 90 times in the synoptic Gospels. One can argue that it was a way which Jesus chose to make his mission known to the people. Pope John Paul II says:

> The proclamation and establishment of God's kingdom are the purpose of his mission: (L.4:43, 14-21). Since the 'Good News' is Christ, there is an identity between the message and the messenger, between saying, doing, and being.[17]

The expression of the Kingdom of God can be identified with Jesus, "expressing his own particular consciousness of mission and his own personal

---

15 Cf. J. Gray, **The Biblical Doctrine of the Reign of God,** (T., and T. Clark, Edinburgh, 1979), p. 317.

16 Cf. Mowinckel, **The Psalms in Israel's Worship,** (N.Y. and Nashville, 1962), p. 114, quoted by N.Perrin, **Jesus and the Language of the Kingdom** , (London, 1976), p. 16; cf. J. Kavunkal, **To Gather Them into One:** Evangelization in India today A process of building community,(SSK Book, India, 1985), p. 44. It is the myth of a God King protecting his people that influenced Israel to learn to think of their God in terms of a God King.

17 John Paul II, **Redemtoris Missio,** (C.T.S., London, 1991), p.11.

experience of God."[18] There are two leading mythical elements in the thinking of the Jews: one is about a god who acted as a King in creating the world, and in the course of which he had overcome and slain the primeval monster. This god continued his role as King by annually renewing the fertility of the earth, and he showed himself to be the king of a particular people by sustaining them in their places.[19] From the so-called enthronement Psalms,(Ps.47, 93, 96, 97, 98, 99), Perrin concludes that Israel learnt to think of their God in this way.[20]

The second tradition is what Gerhard von Rad calls "*Heilgeschichte*",[21] where the activity of God on behalf of his people are expressed (Cf. Deut.26:5b-9; 6:20-24; Jos.24:2b-13). These two traditions might have influenced the Jews in their thinking, according to Kavunkal:

> The two traditions are brought together in various ways. The bringing together of the two, the myth of God as king with its emphasis on creation and renewal, and the myth of the salvation history with its emphasis on the activity of God on behalf of his people are key moments in their history prepared the way for the emergence of the symbol the kingdom of God. At the level of language, kingdom is derived from the kingship of God, for **Malkuth**- reign, kingdom – is an abstract noun formed from the root **M-L-K** which means reign, be king. At the level of immediate reference, however, the symbol evokes the features of the salvation history. Thus the kingdom of God refers to the active presence of the God who created the world, on behalf of his people in their history.[22]

From the two traditions, Israel as a people began to see the kingship of God as a deed and not just a title, as they experience his actions in their daily life. No wonder then Schnackenburg remarks that;

> This original meaning, namely, that Yahweh as king actively rules, must be kept in mind through the whole growth of the **basileia** theme.[23]

This kingdom of God for the Israelites is not removed from their psyche. God's sublime sovereignty always directs both the world and history. Jesus in his teaching preserved this holistic approach, expressing the far-ranging vision of cosmic kingship when he asked his listeners not to swear either by heaven or by earth. Yahweh administers the world and directs the history of salvation.

---

18 Soares-Prabhu, G.M., **The Kingdom of God: Jesus' vision of a New Society,** Amalorpavadass ed., quoted by J. Kavunkal, **To Gather them into One...** (191985), p. 44.

19 Cf. J.B. Pritchard, ed., **Ancient Near Eastern Texts Relating to the Old Testament,** (Princeton University Press, Princeton, 1950), pp. 60-72.

20 Cf. N. Perrin, **Jesus and the language of the Kingdom**, (SCM Press, London, 1976), p. 16.

21 Cf. G. von Rad, **The Problem of Hexateuch** , (New York, 1966).

22 Kavunkal, J., **To Gather them into One...** (1975), p. 45.

23 Schnackenburg, R., **God's Rule and Kingdom,**(New York, 2(1968), p. 13.

He will gather the scattered community (Cf. Jer. 31:8, Ps.19:44; 24:28; 45:1-6; Micah 2:12; Ez.34:15ff.). The mission of Jesus Christ was summed up in Mark's gospel in these words;

> After John had been arrested, Jesus went into Galilee. There he proclaimed the good News from God. 'The time has come' he said, 'and the kingdom of God is close at hand. Repent, and believe the Good News' (Mk.1:14 – 15).

We can see from the above statement that the kingdom of God was the nucleus of Jesus' message. Jorge Pixley put it thus:

> Essentially Jesus spoke of nothing else. The kingdom was the precious pearl for which the merchant sold all his possessions (Mtt.13:45-46), Jesus believed that the kingdom of God had become a present reality in his own healing ministry and that of his disciples (Lk.11:20; 17:20-21). And he affirmed that the coming of the kingdom of God in its fullness was so imminent that some members justice.[24]

This Kingdom is summed up in love as Kavunkal says;

> This radical love is the newness of the kingdom that Jesus preached. Everything he said, did and his own very being is the manifestation of the kingdom, in so far as it reveals the unconditional love of the Father for his people. It is this liberating love, which has its source in the fatherhood of God, that Jesus offers when he proclaimed the coming of God's kingdom.[25]

In Jesus, this definite foundation of the Kingdom of God is realized. It is the present eschatology. The church, which is the Body of Christ, is a realization of the Kingdom, but not identical with the Kingdom. Boff writes that;

> The church is not the kingdom but its sign (explicit symbol) and its instrument (mediation) in the world..., the church is the anticipatory and sacramental realization of the kingdom in the world, as well as the means whereby the kingdom is anticipated most concretely in the world.[26]

---

24 Boff, L., **Trinity and Society,** (Burns and Oates, Kent, 1988), p. 28. But the church is not simply a sign like a post that points to something else, only for earthly kingdom and struggle as Boff wants us to understand, but a sign that signifies what it is. It is a means or rather a growth which will reach its full-growth or fulfillment at the consummation of the kingdom. The consummation, when we "shall be like Him, for we shall see him as he really is", which will not usher in a disappearance of the church, rather a matured church will emerge.

25 Kavunkal, J., **To Gather them into One...** (1975), p. 47.

26 Boff, L., **Church Charism and Power: Liberation Theology and the Institutional Church,** (SCM., London,1985), p. 2. In this line of thought A. Dulles, wrote: ".., the

Christ is the kingdom of God objectified, which needs subjectification. Jesus sees himself as both proclaiming and bringing about this kingdom, as an essential part of it as he expressed: "If I cast..." (Lk.11:20). What Jesus practiced brings the kingdom about because it consists of fellowship with the poor, reconciliation with sinners, sharing his life with all, particularly with outcasts the marginalized and unlimited service to all who come his way without discrimination.[27] It is forming a caring community. Hence the call to this subjectivity gave rise to the actual gathering of the people of God for the futuristic eschatology. We can see that the great purpose of the Father is for the establishment of the kingdom. It is in the person of Jesus that this Kingdom community gathered. Contributing Boff says:

> The kingdom of the Father begins to be brought about in history and in human society. This is why Jesus, in his tender relationship with the Father revealed the Father also in creation, in the birds of the air that neither sow nor reap, but are fed by this Father in heaven (Matt.6:26). He also sees the Father as Providence.[28]

This present eschatology in Christ is to be shared and realized in man, hence the calling of the group to be named Christians, who are followers of Christ and are called to share the life of Christ. This gave rise to the actual gathering. Hans Küng saw this as being "called out" (**ek – kletoi**)[29], **ekklesia**, like congregation, meaning both the actual process of congregating and the congregated community itself. The former should not be overlooked. The New Testament Community is called to share the life of Christ, which is to internalize the kingdom of God. This actual gathering then gave rise to the house Church. Brown commenting on John's gospel says:

> Instead of writing of the rule or Kingdom of God, John centers all imagery on Jesus as the one in whom the reign of God has been perfectly realized, so that inhering in him replaces entrance into the kingdom. Sacraments are signs through which Jesu gives and

---

church is not simply a sign or pointer to the kingdom of God, nor is it a mere servant of the kingdom. The church is either identical with or at least central to the kingdom. Whatever contributes to the church by that very fact contributes to the kingdom, and whatever detracts from the church thereby diminishes the kingdom. To say that the goal of the church is the kingdom of God, therefore, is not to deny that the church is, in a certain sense, an end in itself." A. Dulles, **The Reshaping of Catholicism: Current challenges in the Theology of the Church**. (Harper and Row, San Francisco, 1988), p. 138. To make the Church only a mere sign, as Boff wants us to believe, will be depriving the church of its essence.

27 Cf. L. Boff, **Trinity and Society,** op. cit., pp. 28-29.

28 ibid., p. 167.

29 Cf. H. Küng, **The Church**, (1968), p. 84.

nourishes life. Church offices and even apostleship are of lesser importance when compared to discipleship, which is literally a question of (eternal) life and death.[30]

Stanley expressed that the Kingdom of God which Jesus proclaimed as coming was realized soon after his departure in the Christian Church.[31] Stanley seems to equate the Church or rather identify the church with the Kingdom. But this is not so, though the Church makes present the Kingdom, it is not identical with the Kingdom.

The Kingdom of God, in its plentitude, is identified with the new heaven and the new earth, in which the whole of creation will be gloriously transformed (**GS 39**). Since it is the future of the world as well as that of the church, the kingdom is in some sense wider than the church. But the heart and center of the new creation will be the company of the blessed as they praise and worship the triune God (**LG 51**).[32]

By so doing, Stanley suggests that Christ did not know that He is the Kingdom realized. We are aware that prior to all deliberate reflection on the Church, prior to any theology of the church, there existed in reality, the vitality of the community confessing Jesus Christ as the Lord. In other words, the reflection was on the words and actions of Jesus Christ and his followers. A community arose on account of the teaching of Christ to usher in the Kingdom of God. The Gospel message and Pentecost event necessitated a community. "Brethren what shall we do?" (Acts 2:37-38). Now we have to ponder and judge the New Testament documents themselves as an expression of the Church's life in the community and as speaking testimony to the way the church viewed itself.[33]

---

30 Brown, R.E., **The Churches Apostles left Behind**, (Paulist publishers, New York, 1984), p. 95.

31 Cf. D.M. Stanley, "**Kingdom to Church: The Structural Development of Christianity in the New Testament". Theological Studies** xvi, (1955), pp. 1 - 29.

32 Cf.A. Dulles, **The Reshaping of Catholicism:** op. cit., p.137. The goal of the Church is described by the Vatican II, as the Kingdom of God, in its eschatological completion (**LG 9**). When the fullness of the kingdom arrives, the Church will attain its full perfection (**LG 48**) and be everlastingly united to its King (**LG 5**). The teaching on the Kingdom appears to tend to confine itself to a geographical area, to a concrete territory. However, the presence of the Kingdom of God in Christ's words, in his person, in his activities, cannot be identified with the Church. Gods Kingdom is neither an organization, nor does it comprise of the just and sinners; it does not draw, or better still, depend on earthly and human factors. The Church, on the contrary, these elements are present and are characteristic of it. The Church can be referred as the object and place of divine activity and therefore organ and instrument of salvation, but not as the Kingdom of God.

33 Cf. R. Schnackenburg, **The Church in the New Testament,** (Burns and Oates, London, 1974), pp. 9 - 10.

2.2.2. Community in the Gospels

That Jesus gathered a group of men around him, his disciples, is undeniable. The followers of Jesus were addressed as **mathetes**. The selection of some people presupposes the intention of Jesus to form an ongoing community. In this community he makes it clear that authority should be that of service and that all his **mathetes** are brethren who have the same teacher, himself (Mtt 23:8) and one Father – God in heaven. The greatest in this community should be their **douloi** -servant.

In the teachings of Jesus, the word **ekklesia** occurs two times in Matthew. There has been much debate concerning the non-inclusion of the word **ekklesia** in Luke and Mark.[34] His upliftment will draw people to him (Jn 12:32). His death will not be for the salvation of Israel only but 'to gather into one the children of God who are scattered abroad' (Jn 11:52). John gave these references that can be attributed to the understanding of the NT community. For these two statements in John to come to fulfillment, there is need for the emergence of a Christian community based on the redemptive work of Christ (i.e., a redeemed community).

The disciples of Jesus saw themselves as an eschatological community called and chosen by God, hence the early Christians often referred to themselves as 'the elect' **eklektoi**, or as 'the Saints' **agioi**. When they speak of the new covenant of the Messiah, they use the singular **ekklesia tou theou**, an exact rendering of the **gahal Jisrael** in the Septuagint. They were the new Israel, the new '**qahal Jahweh**'- the community of God of the Old Testament. The term ecclesia has a lot of interpretations and usages in the NT.

What comes to a close understanding of this word is the Greek term **ekklesia**[35] (often rendered as **ekklesia tou theou** -Acts 20:28). This was the understanding, because Christ, by his death on the Cross brought forth, this new

---

34 For further discussion concerning the controversy see W.G. Kunnel's discussion and bibliography, **Promise and Fulfillment**, Eng., trans., SCM Press, London, 1957, pp.138ff; D.O. Via, **"The Church in the gospel of Matthew"**, **SJT** II, 1958, pp. 271-286; E. Schweizer's note on **"The 'Matthean' Church"**, **NTS** 20, 1974, p.215. Bultmann is of the opinion that Jesus never thought of founding a Church, since he spoke only of a coming kingdom (ThB 20, 1941, pp.265ff); O.Cullman, Peter: Disciple, Apostle, Martyr, (Eng. trans., 2(1962), pp.176ff.

35 The words church and ekklesia have their Germanic and latin origins. From the German **Kirche**, the Swedish **Kyrbe** and Slav **Carkov** the word **Church** was born. Church does not seem to have emanated from the word **Curia** as this word apart from being a fairly recent word, means more "a congregation" than an eschatological community. The word **ekklesia** on the other hand has much in common with the Latin **ecclesia**, the spanish **iglesia**, the French **eglise** and the Italian **Chiesa**. All these usages stem from the Greek **ekklesia**.

community. Cambron expressly declared in his work that the word 'church' cannot be found in the New Testament and he says that:

> It is a rendition of the word ecclesia, which means a called out company or assembly.[36]

For Barclay, the word *ekklesia* is the New Testament expression for Church, and he sees it as one of the most important words of the New Testament. Though it is a Greek word, it has a double background of both Hebrew and Greek.[37] To assume Cambron's view will be to take the position of some biblical fundamentalists who even want everything to be written in the Bible before it can be accepted. They say that one should allow the Bible to speak for itself. Hans Küng sees the origin of the church as not lying solely in the intention and message of Jesus in the pre-Easter period, (I should also add that, not in picking which word), but in the whole history of Jesus' life and ministry. He declared;

> It was not any particular words of Jesus, nor ultimately his teachings, but his person as the hidden Messiah and as the Risen Christ, which historically speaking constitutes the root of the Church.[38]

Whether it is a rendition of *ekklesia* or a translation, Cambron should have known that words have meaning only within the **sitz im Leben** of human communication and understanding. The New Testament background of *ekklesia* comes from the Septuagint, where the word occurs 100 times and represents exclusively the Hebrew **Qahal.**[39] The many or various interpretations of *qahal*, such as assembly or congregation, as we shall see later cannot be confused with *qahal Yahweh*, which is generally accepted to mean the chosen or elected people of God, which in the Old Testament context refers to Israel.

However, there is a warning from Mainer as he says that the semitic equivalent of *ekklesia*, is however, still disputed.[40] Schmidt [41] strongly supports the Aramaic *Kenista* while Cullmann [42] prefers the Hebrew *qahal*. Considering the evidence of the Qumran literature, Schnackenburg suggests the

---

36 Cambron, M.G., **Bible Doctrines: Beliefs that Matter**, (Baker Book House, Grand Rapids, 1974), p. 213.

37 Barclay, W., **New Testament Words,** (SCM Press, London, 1977), p.68.

38 Küng, H., **The Church,** (Image Books, New York, 1976), p. 110.

39 Coenen, L., **"The Church"**; (1975) p. 292.

40 Mainer, G., "**The Church in the Gospel of Matthew: Hermeneutical analysis of the current debate**"; in: **Biblical interpretation and the Church;** D.A. Carson, ed., (Thomas Nelson, Nashville, 1985), p. 60.

41 See K.L. Schmidt, in: **ThW III**, article **'Ekklesia',** pp. 502 - 539.

42 Cf. O. Cullmann, **Christ and Time** , (London, 1962).

equivalent *sod* and *edah*. Looking at the issue from the Greek background, *ekklesia* was a convened assembly of free citizens for political, social or religious issues that affect all. Barclay noted that all the meetings of the *ekklesia* began with prayer and sacrifice and it was a true democracy, where freedom and equality were upheld. In obedience to the law of the state, the *ekklesia* was the supreme authority in judicial, military, financial and in fact all matters, that concerns the state and her citizens.

In such a situation, the individual freedom and rights were so guided that serious punishments like ostracism or banishment could not be imposed when less than 6,000 citizens were present. And at this point, Barclay agrees with Deissmann's position, that looking at the church from the background of Greek ekklesia, it is God's assembly, God's muster, and the convener is God.[43] Coenen seems to be of the same opinion in his assertion that *ekklesia* is derived via **ek – kaleo**... from **kaleo**, to call and also of the fact that in Greek Lexica, *ekklesia* is treated under *kaleo*.[44] The two original words, *qahal* and *ekklesia*, when applied to the Christian community emphasize the initiative and action of God. So, the Church as *ekklesia* is, in essence, a body of people summoned by God to serve His purpose.[45] The concept of Church has root in Christian antiquity, but is surprising that the word *ekklesia* is absent in the Gospels with the exception of two instances in Matt.16:18 and 18:17.

The word *ekklesia* appeared in the other books of the New Testament 114 times, and out of this number, 33 are found in what are called "authentic" letters of Paul. With the exception of Acts of the Apostles where it occurred 23 times, 1 Cor. has the largest use, where it appeared 22 times. In Acts, Luke made use of *ekklesia* in its Greek common and secular sense as he referred even to a mob mustered by the aggrieved silver-smiths (Acts.19:32, 39,41). He also used this term earlier on, for a Jewish religious terminology, in reference to the company called out from Egypt, which became the covenant people of Yahweh at Sinai.

With different meanings of the term *ekklesia*, one may question whether the community is a divine institution as we try to portray. Such a question calls for historical and exegetical considerations. The exegetical treatment is beyond the scope of our work. The Apostles saw in Jesus the Anointed one of God. This concept of King implies in its very essence a people or nation, the messianic community of the redeemed. This notion of seeing Christ as King has taken over the position of the original historical Israel. As Israel through

---

43 Barclay, W., **New Testament Words** (1977), p. 69.
44 Coenen, L., **The CHURCH**, (1975), art. cit., p. 291.
45 Nkwoka, A.O., **New Testament Concept of Diakonia...** (1990), p.39.

their rulers refused to accept the Messiah, Jesus turned to the small circle of His disciples, who are taken as the "remnant of Israel".

They constituted his *ekklesia*, the insignificant *kenischtha, a* special Synagogue in which the best of Israel is saved (Mtt. 18: 18, 16: 19). Here the *ekklesia* is seen as belonging to the divine plan of salvation. The progress of this plan began with Adam, and passed through Isaac and Jacob to the twelve tribes of the covenant on Mount Sinai. Following Christ becomes the concrete fulfillment of this entire holy salvific evolution. Rahner says;

> The Church is in its deepest essence, the historical remaining-present of the Incarnate Word of God in the world. It is the historical apprehensibility of the salvific will of God which has taken place in Christ.[46]

At the very center of the Church is the Anointed one, ascended to heaven, whom we await to come again in His glorious *parousia*. This *Kyrios*, is ever present in the Church, through the Apostles, the prophets and the evangelists. His spirit directs the destiny of the Church, and whenever they gather, He is in their midst. Kahlefeld says this of the community;

> The *ekklesia* is a community the likes of which can be found nowhere else on earth: she is open to things above, ruled and nourished from there in the interchange of love and life between bridegroom and bride. And with this, the ancient truth of the Old Testament is continued and fulfilled; the marriage between God and His people becomes a reality.[47]

The community in the New Testament is seen both in the small group or in all groups gathered to worship in Christ and to break bread. Though many scholars agree that there is no single concept of the Church as presented by the

---

46 Rahner, R., "**Theology of the Parish**", in: Hugo Rahner, ed., **The Parish from Theology to Practice**, (The Newman Press, Maryland, 1958), p. 27.

47 Kahlefeld, H., "**Community Life in the New Testament**", in: Hugo Rahner ed., **The Parish from Theology to Practice**, (The Newman Press, Maryland, 1958), pp. 38-39. And *ekklesia* is not something that is formed and founded once and for all and remains unchanged; it becomes an *ekklesia* by the fact of a repeated concrete event, people coming together and congregating, for the purpose of worshipping God. The concrete congregation is the actual manifestation, the representation indeed the realization of the New Testament community. Cf. H. Küng, **The Church**, (Sheed and Ward, New York, 1968), p. 84. In his own contribution concerning the idea of community in the New Testament, Lehmann says; "Die Kirche ist für das Neue Testament keine ideale Größe, sondern die Gesamtkirche kommt in der Einzelgemeinde zur Erscheinung; selbst die konkrete Gemeindeversammlung wird "Ekklesia" genannt.... Jede Einzelgemeinde ist mit ihren sichtbaren und unsichtbaren Verflechtungen auf dieses Geheimnis der "Kirche" hin entworfen und lebt insgeheim von ihm"; K. Lehmann, "**Gemeinde**", in: **Christlicher Glaube in moderner Gesellschaft**, Bd. 29, Herder, Freiburg, (1982), pp. 16-17.

New Testament,[48] the expression is seen throughout as faith in the Risen Lord. It is only when we take the New Testament as a whole, with all its writings, its divergences and nuances, that we can avoid the heresy of selection and naivety of schematic harmonization. The New Testament should be taken as the positive witness of the Gospel of Jesus Christ, as Küng points out;

> Ecclesiological study of the New Testament, in other words, needs and it is no easy task, to combine catholicity, a breath and awareness of tensions, with evangelical concentration.[49]

From these ideas we can deduce that there is something paradoxical about the New Testament concept of the Community, and an attempt to explain the paradox may be unfruitful. The preaching and ministering of Jesus has given rise to the reality, existence, and the vitality of the community confessing Jesus, which is the basis of the post-Easter primitive Church.

There is no doubt that Jesus addressed his message of the coming Kingdom of God to all Israel, and whoever received that message, was welcomed, even the so-called societal out-casts, like the tax collectors and prostitutes. Jesus insisted that, if one wants to be his follower, one should deny himself, take up his cross and follow him. And it is this group that is the Church that Jesus envisaged, as Nkwoka rightly suggests;

> We, therefore, subscribe to the view that all along, Jesus was aware of the uniqueness of his ministry and the eventual emergence of a new Community (which happened to be the church) when the time was fully ripe.[50]

Though Jesus proclaimed the Kingdom of God that is near, it was after the Easter episode that Jesus the proclaimer of the Kingdom became the proclaimed, the only means of attaining the Kingdom. The Church should be seen as a means to salvation. Pope Pius XI, once said that;

> men were not made for the Church, but the church was made for men:**Propter nos Homines et Propter nostram Salutem.**[51]

H. de Lubac also made an important assertion when he says;

---

48 Cf. E. Schweizer, **Church Order in the New Testament,** (SCM Press, London, 1961), pp. 13f.; H. Küng, **The Church**, (Doubleday & Company, Inc. New York, 1967), pp. 15f.; R. Schnackenburg, **The Church in the New Testament,** (Burns and Oates, London, 1965), pp. 9f.

49 Küng, H., **The Church**; p. 19.

50 Nkwoka, A.O., **New Testament Concept of Diakonia...** (1990), p.44.

51 Pius XI, **Allocution to the Lenten Preachers of Rome,** 1927.

Of course, just as Christianity is not the Church, so the Church, in so far as it is visible, is not the kingdom, nor yet the mystical Body, though the holiness of this Body shines through its visible manifestation.[52]

Every social or religious group has a rule by which they live. The description of the early Christian community will be based much more closely to the source of all Christian living – i.e., the teachings of our Lord, as contained in the scriptures. Jesus' office as a prophet gave him the authority to speak to the whole nation of Israel. In response to the approaching Kingdom of God, the whole of Israel was to be called to repent. Jesus tried to let Israel realize the importance of community-brotherly love and care:

So then, if you are bringing your offering to the altar and there remember that your brother has something against you, leave your offering there before the altar, go and be reconciled with your brother first, and then come back and present your offering (Matt 5:23).

This cautioned against the distortion of the community. One may also see some resemblance of the above sermon with the antithesis in the sermon on the Mount: "But I say to you: anyone who is angry with his brother will answer for it before the court" (Matt 5:22). Commenting on the above quotation Kahlefeld says;

Here, however, the words receive a new function; they warn the small band of disciples to remember that when they come before the face of God in sacrificial prayer as in the breaking of bread, only peace and brotherly love can purify their lips.[53]

What was recorded in the Gospels originally as a prophetic sermon to Israel, in effect, turned out to be a never-ceasing directive of our Lord for the community life of his followers. Matthew in his own narration suggests a family atmosphere as he says: "He sat down, and His disciples came around Him" (5:1).

There is another type of sermon directed specifically to the disciples. Jesus tries to distinguish His community from the rest of Israel. "If anyone gives you a cup of water to drink just because you belong to Christ, then I tell you solemnly, he will most certainly not lose his reward" (Mk 9:41); "For everyone will be salted with fire"(Mk 9:49). All these are to protect the community from dissensions. It is also in Mark, 9:31-50, that Jesus spelt out the rule of life for the community. And the early Christian communities knew how to

52 de Lubac, H., **CATHOLICISM: Christ and the Common Destiny of Man,** (Burns and Oates, London, 1962), p. 24.

53 Kahlefeld, H., "**Community Life in the New Testament**", in Hugo Rahner, (1958), p. 40.

apply the Master's sermons. They knew that Jesus addressed the whole of Israel, but they were also aware that these words would ultimately attain their full effectiveness only within the community of the redeemed.

The question whether Jesus founded a church can only be answered by how his followers saw themselves. Jesus started his public ministry by calling people and forming a community and from such a community he had the need of selecting a smaller group, who were called the Apostles. So to understand Christ's ministry is to see it in the line of the formation of a community of believers; as Schnackenburg states, anyone who denies Jesus' intention of gathering a community :

> misunderstands the messianic – eschatological thought of Israel, in which eschatological salvation cannot be separated from the people of God and in which the community of God necessarily belongs to his reign.[54]

Evidences abound in the New Testament that they saw themselves as a people called together for a new life. The Christian assembly is not just any type of gathering; it is God who gathers them. It is a community of faith in Jesus who is Christ. Pol Vonck puts it thus:

> The christian community are men and women anchored in Jesus the Messiah. Indeed the naval of the world is neither Zion nor the Torah; it is the story of Jesus, the Risen one. Accordingly the community is gripped by an overpowering task ('Go therefore'), yet this task can barely be fulfilled unless the community is truly community (process), notably a family of faith which manages to handle its own tensions in a spirit of reconciliation and compassion (Matt.18).[55]

A lot of people confuse the Church with its structure, hence the questioning of the foundation of the Church. Some get upset with the machinery of the Church, but fail to realize that since the Church is part of this world of tears, she needs some structures that will make her meaningful for the people. Hence Grabowski writes that;

> The Christian churches founded by the Apostle of the Gentiles developed themselves as enclaves within the existing civil society. The civil and political societies find the religious

---

54 Schnackenburg, R., **God's Rule and Kingdom.** (Herder and Herder, New York, 1963), p. 150; cf. G. Lohfink **Jesus and Community**, (1984), p. 26.

55 Vonck, P., "**Small is more than Beautiful**", in: **AFER**, vol. 20, 6(1988), p. 362.

communities forming and growing within their midst to be basically different from themselves and civil powers opposed them with all their might.[56]

The opposition and suppression of Christians, instead of destroying them, made them become more committed to their course, and new families are formed within them, the family of the new people of God. We see in the Apostolic community a new family, larger than a nuclear household. In the new family, anyone who has left brothers or sisters or mother or father, will have mothers or fathers. The plural fathers and mothers are an evidence that the early SCCs were larger than nuclear households.[57] The formation of community was necessary since the apostles understood their position as staying in the midst of the 'last things'. No wonder that the disciples left Galilee and headed to Jerusalem, where it was believed that the final revelation would appear. Lohfink saw their leaving Galilee thusly;

> The reason for this striking action of the disciples was their eschatology. They were convinced that they stood in the midst of the last things. As a result, they awaited the definitive revelation of the reign of God in Jerusalem, the place where, according to Jewish belief, the Last events would run their course.[58]

Since the end was eminent, it was imperative to summon all people to repentance and acceptance of baptism in the name of the Risen Lord. The baptism of repentance of John was replaced by the new baptism in the name of Jesus the Christ.

The early Christians understood themselves to be a new people of God and not a sect of the Jewish religion. They addressed themselves as the *ekklesia* of God (cf. 1 cor.15:9; Gal. 1:13). It is important to note that the Septuagint used *ekklesia* to translate *qahal*, so it is not the popular assembly of the political community, but the assembly before Yahweh of the Old Testament people of the covenant. To this effect Lohfink remarks:

> Here ekklesia is understood as the true people of God, separated from all unholiness and impurity. If the earliest Christian community called itself the 'ekklesia of God' against this background, it must have seen itself as the chosen people of God, the true Israel.[59]

---

56 Grabowski, J.S., **The Church: An Introduction to the Theology of St. Augustine,** (B. Herder Book Co., St. Louis, 1957), p. 166; cf. W. Ziegenfuss, **Augustinus: Christliche Transzendenz in Gesellschaft und Geschichte,** (Berlin, 1948), p. 116.

57 Cf. P. Vonck, **Small is more than Beautiful;** art. cit., p.361.

58 Lohfink, G., **Jesus and Community**. (1984), p. 75.

59 Ibid., p. 77.

Whatever happened, the early church knew itself to be the community of Jesus, the Messiah whom God raised to his right hand – a traditional position of authority (Acts 2:32 – 36; 3:13 – 15, 20f.; 5:30f.).

Does this mean that the community was formed after the Easter episode? Schnackenburg remarks that Luke creates the impression of a band of disciples which persisted without interruption from the days of Jesus' early life into the time after Easter, which was not dispersed by the passion of Christ nor completely cast down by his death, and which re-formed after Easter and became firmer, consolidated and expanded (Cf.Acts I:14, 15).[60] It is also striking to note how the Apostles insisted on maintaining the circle of twelve as Jesus had originally intended. The Lord's supper was shown as an integral part of the life of the community. From the point of view of fellowship, Pentecost cannot be the birth of the Church, as some authorities hold, but instead was its endowment with the power of the Holy Spirit, (Lk.24:49; Acts.1:8), that energized the Church for its missionary work.

Scarcely any thought intensified the church's eschatological awareness and feeling of solidarity so much as this conviction of having received from God the gift of the Holy Spirit through the medium of Christ. It is the Spirit who, according to the Acts of the Apostles, guides the early church and its missionaries (cf.5:3, 9; 8:29, 39; 9:31) and according to the Apocalypse speaks to the Churches (2:7,11,...)[61]

Boff affirmed that the church arose from a historical decision by the apostles, enlightened by the Holy Spirit.[62] He is of the opinion that the messianic eschatological community of the twelve as established by Jesus was convoked by the Spirit to become the Church. In his view, it was the disciples who, convoked by the Spirit, made the decision to concretely found the Church. It seems here that Boff is confusing the expression of the Church with the Church's institution. Christ advised the Apostles to remain in Jerusalem until they receive the Holy Spirit. This is a Spirit of courage, knowledge and strength to go out and proclaim the Kingdom of God, which is present in the person of Jesus the Christ.

The institution of the Church cannot be a decision of the Apostles, for they had no alternative but to express what they are, i.e., the Church, the people of God called by the Spirit of the Risen Lord. The community existed before the Pentecost episode, for they were meeting in secret places. The convocation of the community of the twelve was not to become Church as such but for the **mission** of the Church. To this effect Schnackenburg says:

---

60 Cf. R. Schnackenburg, **The Church in the New Testament**, op. cit., (1974), p. 12.

61 Ibid., p. 16.

62 Boff, L., **Church Charism and Power,** op. cit., p. 147.

The descent of the Holy Spirit at Whitsun (Acts.2) is for Luke a fundamental event for the whole epoch and efficacy of the church. It is not indeed the hour of the church's birth, at least not in the sense that from then onwards Jesus Christ's community existed (it was already there in Acts 1:15); but it is the moment of its endowment with the 'power from on high' (Lk.24:49; Acts 1:8), which alone qualifies it for its earthly task, its work of salvation in the world, and confers on it the mystery of its supernatural mode of existence.[63]

The Church, or Christianity, is something God initiated and communicated to men and can never be something men thought out or decided and proposed to God. "And it is in him that we were claimed as God's own, chosen from the beginning, under the predetermined plan of the one who guides all things as he **decides by his own will**" (Eph.1:11-12).

The distinguishing factor in the early christian community from other existing communities like the **Apocalypses, Qumran** communities, is the reception of the Holy Spirit. The original life of the Jerusalem community was somehow given in the Acts of the Apostles, which can be summed up as: (i) the activities of the Apostles, which were supported by works of wonders; (ii) the harmony and community sharing of "goods" – **Koinonia**; (iii) the liturgical life and worship which ended with the breaking of Bread.

Christ was born within a culture that valued small communities. Apart from the Qumran communities, there existed in the Jewish nation what one may call Jewish ancient communities, small societies of friends who met on the Sabbath eve for supper and prayer. They were called the **Chaburah.** It is not surprising that Jesus and his disciples formed such a company, although theirs was a more sincere bond and commitment. No wonder that the evangelist Mark records: "... and he appointed twelve, to be with him,..". It seems that Jesus more often chose to reveal himself in a smaller group (Cf. Transfiguration; the institution of the Eucharist – Last Supper; the Gethsemane episode; even after the resurrection in the breaking of bread etc.). The Church for a long time concentrated in the formation of small groups, who gathered to share with one another the intimate things, blessings and charisms as the spirit allowed them, such as in the house of Aquilla. Shead expressed what it meant to be a Christian in those days as;

In New Testament times to be christian was to belong to a fellowship of believers who had big things to accomplish and needed one another's support to get them done. But more than this they needed the common life centered in Christ. They banded together to talk about him, to listen to his Spirit speak to them, to read from the Scripture, to ponder the

---

63 Schnackenburg, R., **The Church in the New Testament**. (1974), p. 15. And for Lohfink, the existence of eschatological Israel began with the constitution of the twelve and their preaching of the reign of God. Cf. G. Lohfink, **Jesus and Community**. (1984) p. 10.

letters of their leaders, and to eat together the bread of communion at his table. He said he would come when two or three of them gathered together in his name. They believed his promise and felt his presence.[64]

The community of the Apostles after Pentecost was a real and intimate community. Before Pentecost, one may say that they were mere followers of Jesus. Community in the Gospels is somehow selective, with criteria of choice best known to God. Unlike those in OT or *umunna* communities, it is exclusive. Belonging entails faith in the Risen Lord and baptism, which are expressed in love.

Jesus summed up the Commandments as the love of God and neighbour. Every believer in Jesus should have the experience of a closer community love, just as Marcel Lequat wrote that every disciple of Jesus has to share the community experience of those first disciples, an experience of call, learning, joy, success, doubt, failure, betrayal, and forgiveness which always go with a smaller group.[65] We shall now look at the term "church" in different books of the New Testament, how the early Christians saw themselves or how they expressed their common belief. That will go a long way to help us in the understanding of what community means in the New Testament.

2.2.3. Community in Acts

Community in the Gospels is selective. The criterion is best known to God, and unlike that in the OT, it is exclusive the disciples had no sense of true community until Pentecost and were simply following Christ. This may be expressed in the Gospels to highlight the importance of the Pentecost event. The doctrine of the Church – community in the Book of Acts- presents a vital bridge between the Gospels and the other writings of the NT. For us to see the evidence of the community called Church in Acts, we shall consider its emergence, its mission and its administration. Considering its emergence, we must look for the dominating principles which guided the first group of believers to regard themselves as a Church.

There is no doubt in the Synoptics that the first disciples were conscious that the community they formed was foreseen and to some extent prepared for by Jesus. The Resurrection of Jesus was the key event that preceded the estab-

---

64 Shead, C.W., **How to Develop a Praying Church,** (Abingdon Press, Nashville/New York, 1964), pp. 12 - 13.

65 Cf. M. Leqaut, **A Glimpse of Tomorrow's Church,** Lumen Vitae, 1972, 2, pp. 185 - 216.

lishment of the Church. Through his resurrection, Jesus overcame death and showed that all he did was acceptable to God.

> The resurrection of Christ is viewed as the supreme display of divine power. It is the act by which the ceaseless round of death and corruption in human life has been checked. God has provided a way out of death into life, by raising his Son from death to life.[66]

Resurrection was the event that bound the disciples together and marked them out from the rest of men. They believed that Jesus was risen, and this faith meant that they were at once conscious of a continuity with the historical Jews. The Book of Acts portrayed the unanimity with which the disciples believed and proclaimed the resurrection as an objective fact.

The understanding of the emergence of the Church is only possible when one grasps the significance of the resurrection as an historical event. The Jesus of history, who died and rose to life, and his teaching, should be seen as the basis of the community. No wonder they demanded that the successor of Judas had to be a man who had been a companion of Jesus and had witnessed the resurrection. This, in effect, stresses the continuity between the historical Jesus and the resurrection faith. The community was the community of the risen Lord.

The promise made by Jesus of the gift of the Holy Spirit becomes another reason for the community. The believers gathered in Jerusalem to experience the descent of the Holy Spirit: both apostles, the disciples and some women. The inclusion of women in this gathering shows a new community that respects everybody, unlike the Jewish and other ancient world societies, who could not assign a value to women. The coming of the Holy Spirit was the critical event in the launching of the Christian community.[67] The community was activated by the descent of the Holy Spirit (Acts 2:1f). The Acts really showed that the Church was essentially a community of the Spirit that is transcendent. It was controlled, guided and directed by the Spirit.

Although these people saw themselves as new community, they did not discontinue their Jewish connections. As Jews, they worshipped in the temple (3:1ff), but gave their worship a new understanding, since they regarded them-

---

66 Guthrie, D., **New Testament Theology**, Inter-Varsity Press, England, (1981), p. 390; cf. M.C. Tenney, **The reality of Resurrection**, Harper, New York, (1963), pp. 146ff.

67 Cf. S.M. Gilmour, **"Easter and Pentecost"**, **JBL** 81, 1962, pp. 62ff. For Gilmour, it is Luke who has interpreted the event of the Pentecost as the beginning of the Church's world-wide mission. Some authors did disagree with his view, see J.D.G. Dunn, **Jesus and the Spirit**, SCM Press, London, (1975), pp.144ff.

selves as the true Israel.[68] The community in Jerusalem was made up mainly of Jews, but the rapid shift from an exclusively Jewish community to a mixed Jewish-Gentile community led to difficulties.[69] Aside from the issue of circumcision, it took a vision to convince Peter that Gentiles had as much right in the fellowship of Jesus as Jews. Gentiles are the foreign elements. But there is no doubt that the early Christian Church was in marked contrast to the Qumran community which found no place for strangers. Soon the Christian community realized the command of Jesus for the development of a universal *ekklesia*.

The life of the early Christians was of great importance in building a respected community. This is specifically mentioned twice (2:44; 4:32), with an emphasis on **they had all things in common**. There was a strong social concern which Christians felt towards each other. The needy were cared for (6:1). The community based their life on service and a sense of responsibility towards those who were socially deprived. Along with the common ownership of property, common worship in the temple and common meals in the Christians' homes were practiced.

The expression of fellowship was not only based on the sharing of material things, but on the combination of common worship with a common concern for the physical needs of each. These helped the believers to bind themselves into a fellowship and made them recognize their essential oneness in Jesus Christ. On the mission of the Community, Acts 1:8 clearly states that the task of the new community is to witness. This witness, which consisted of proclamation, has made some authors use the Greek word **kerygma** to denote the content of what is proclaimed.[70] Despite the dispute concerning **kerygma**, no one is left in doubt that the task of the Church was to proclaim the deeds of the Risen Lord (2:16; 3:13,24). Peter's speeches here were no specific appeals for the hearers to join the community; rather, he exhorted them to be baptized,

---

68 Cf. F. Hahn, **The Worship of the Early Church**, Eng. trans., Fortress, Philadelphia, (1973), pp.42f. Hahn critically looking at Acts argued that it was only when James took sole charge of Jerusalem Church that a Jewish Christian community developed. One may argue that office does not create community but for working of the community offices may be created.

69 Cf. L. Goppelt, **Apostolic and Post-apostolic Times**, Eng. trans., Black Press, London, (1970), pp. 68ff.

70 Cf. C.H. Dodd, **The Apostolic preaching and its developments**, Hodder, London, 1936, 2(1963); see also R. Bultmann's idea of using it to emphasize the act of proclaiming rather than the content of what is preached, **TNT** 1, pp.33f; cf. J.P.M. Sweer's discussion of the difference between these writers' use of the term **kerygma**, in: **"The Kerygma"**, **ExT** 76, 1965, pp.143ff; also see C.F. Evans, **"The Kerygma"**, **JTS** 7, 1956, pp.25-41.

which undoubtedly implied incorporation into the Christian 'body' and possession of this transcendent spirit.

So baptism became important in the mission of the Church.[71] Those who believed were baptized (2:38,41; 8:12,36; 16:15,33; 19:5; 22:16), and for them, this was the rite of initiation into the new community. It was an act that demonstrated the unity of all believers. The administration of the community in Acts can be likened to that of a family, since the organization was very loose. Acts presents us with a group of house communities scattered about in various cities, rather than with a unified Church. Each local group was an *ekklesia* of the area, but all stood for the same basic beliefs and all the ingredients existed for the concept of the one community of the Risen Lord. One can say that each local community was a microcosm of the whole Church.

The importance was placed on unity in Christ, which had a strong affinity with other natural groups who were similarly united. The Church organization at this period was a dynamic one. It was a living organism as opposed to an organization. The community relied more on the prompting of the Holy Spirit than ecclesiastical edicts or episcopal pronouncements. Decision-making was the prerogative of the whole company of believers (15:22). This does not show that the Church was run on democratic lines. There were leaders and office holders who saw their authority as service. Peter was a spokesman and leader. It was he, prompted by the Holy Spirit, who requested the replacement of Judas and the appointment of the seven **diakonein** (6:2). We can see that the Book of Acts of the Apostles constitutes the primary source, and also the safest and most conclusive one, on the Church's growth and multiplication.

The author of Acts saw the community from the point of view of eschatology and this is expressed in its preaching of repentance and baptism (Acts 2:38 – 42). Baptism was seen as a preparation for the things to come. Lohfink clearly states that;

> This baptism was considered an eschatological sacrament for Israel. The people of God was to be sealed in preparation for the coming end, in order to enable it to endure the judgement of the Son of man. The situation of John's baptism was picked up under new conditions. Early christian baptism also served the eschatological gathering and preparing of Israel.[72]

---

71 For more on baptism in Acts cf., W.F. Flemington, **The NT Doctrine of Baptism**, SPCK Press, London, 1948, pp. 37-51; G.R. Beasley-Murray, **Baptism in the NT**, Macmillan, London, (1962), pp. 93-125; H.G. Marsh, **The Origin and Significance of the NT Baptism**, MUP, Manchester, (1941), pp.153-166; S.I. Buse, in: **Christian Baptism**, ed. A. Gilmour, 1959, pp.115ff.

72 Lohfink, G., **Jesus and the Community** (1984), p. 76.

Luke also recorded the self-understanding of the early church as the circle of the twelve, which was reconstituted after the departure of Judas Iscariot by the election of Matthias (Acts 1:15 – 26).

Luke sees and stresses the fact that the outpouring of the Spirit is responsible for the growth of the community. The community life of the Apostles and the early Christians, as mirrored in Acts 2:41 – 47, hinges on four outstanding aspects of community life:

(i) The teaching office of the Apostles, who handed down the **didache ton apostolon**.

(ii) The brotherly and sisterly care they had for this community in the spirit of **Koinonia**.

(iii) There did somehow occur a break with the Jewish tradition, for they attended the Temple worship, but later retired to house churches for the breaking of bread.

(iv) They manifested the glorification and thanksgiving to God. These factors provide us insight into the religious and social life of the Jerusalem community and what made them a united and believing community, as Chris Manus says;

> Luke's community is a community of concord, a community sustained by its adherence to faith in Jesus Christ, and a community nurtured by the collegiate leadership of the Apostles' teaching and their **terata kai semeia** (miracles).[73]

This actually did mark the community as a separate community from the main Jewish community. Many people do not see Luke's idea of the church as sectarian, but Manus points out some traces of this sectarianism:

> In the whole of Luke – Acts, Lucan tradition shares with the synoptic gospels the fact that Jesus' movement stood out as a vehement protest, most probably unconsciously, against the legalism and externalism of Pharisaic religion of his time. The Mother church in Jerusalem, though represented by Luke as the ideal community, is without doubt, shown as an ekklesia in protest to the heathenism of contemporary Hellenistic associations (ekklesia) and social Clubs (collegia).[74]

The Christian community of Luke rejects the Greco-Roman socio-cultural settings upon which the larger society built its *Weltanschauung* and values. They had to fashion their own setting around the teachings of the Apostles in the life of Christ. They became knowingly or unknowingly members of an in-

---

73 Manus, C.U., "**The Community of Love in Luke's Acts: A Sociological Exegesis of Acts 2:41-47 in African Context**"; in: West African Journal of Ecclesial Studies; Vol.2, 1(1990), p. 22.

74 . Ibid., p. 23.

group, separate from the others. The walls that separated different ethnic groups were broken through their life of *koinonia*. Luke speaks loudly of the egalitarian nature of the *ekklesia* community in Jerusalem. Manus affirms that:

> The Jerusalem community is strengthened by the spirit of koinonia. Koinonia constitutes to my mind, the basis for their ethic of love – relationship. It helped for some time to hold conflict in check. The ethos of love was rooted, expressed and fully realized in their communal ritual. The 'breaking of bread' from house to house; that is, the Eucharistic ritual as the anamnesis of the Lord enhanced the internal coherence, unanimity, and equality of members.[75]

Luke tries to show how important ritual and sharing meals enhance the solidarity of the community. He saw the church as a cohesive community. For him all that is expected of the community is expressed in Acts 1:8. "...but you will receive the power..." From this verse, which is the leitmotif text, five basic truths are uncovered as dominant in the whole Book of Acts. Firstly, they have to realize that the Holy Spirit is the divine agent that initiates, supervises, energizes and accomplishes the purpose of God in the building program of the Church.

Secondly, the Apostles are presented as the representatives of the Church of Jesus Christ and the initial agents of the Holy Spirit, through whom the divine purpose is to be initiated and directed. Thirdly, the major means of accomplishing this purpose is through witnessing and oral communication. Fourthly, the content of the Christian message is Jesus Christ himself. Finally, the whole world is to become the sphere of God's gracious operations and gospel proclamation. Peters sees the change in old Jewish life thus;

> There is to be a directional change from the centripetal universality of the Old Testament to a centrifugal universality of the New Testament.[76]

One may be tempted to argue against the ecclesiological conception in this mission, but a closer look makes one realize that it was the response of Jesus to the previous question asked by the disciples, if he were 'to restore the kingdom for Israel' (v6): thus the ecclesiology that is implied can better be understood. Luke was an insider of the Church and he writes according to the living picture of the Church that he bears within him. There are other insiders of the Church in Acts, and one of the important figures was Paul.

---

75 . Ibid., p. 24.
76 Peters, G.W., **A Theology of Church Growth:** (1981), pp. 18 - 19.

2.2.4. Paul and Community

It is wonderful to see that he who once persecuted the Church of God and tried to destroy it has turned to be the chief advocate of the ideals of the Church (Gal.2:13; Phil.3:6). Luke even confirmed this when he wrote that Saul 'laid waste the church' (Acts 8:3), but after his conversion which was miraculous, "it is Paul in particular who shaped this concept of church."[77] Paul did establish that the members of the Church are true sons of Abraham, through faith in Christ, and are the new people of God. Procksch saw Paul's position thus;

> In the powerful historical sweep of Paul, the concept of the people of God has burst its national limits and come to be equated with the church of Christ. On the holy stump of the Old Testament people of God, the new branches from the Gentile world have been engrafted (Rom.11:17) and they are sanctified by the stump. The stump is obviously Christ as **he rhiza tou Iessai** (Rom.15:12) ordained to rule over the Gentiles [78]

Paul saw a new people of God emerging and taking over the old concept. He saw the community as being formed on the faith of the Risen Lord. On this new understanding of the people of God in Paul, Schnackenburg says:

> So it is clear that for Paul a new people of God has taken the place of the old, and one which, it is true, is formed on the basis of the old and more precisely on the promises of blessings made to it but for the rest stands on an entirely new foundation that of belief in the one heir to the blessings and sole mediator of salvation, Jesus Christ.[79]

For Paul the real ***communio sanctorum***, the Church, is the true people of God, the eschatological Israel, who have been chosen through the salvation wrought through Christ. In this way, the Church becomes the hope of Israel, through faith in the Risen Lord and in no way replaces the historical Israel. Schnackenburg says:

---

77 Coenen, L., **The CHURCH:** (1975), p. 291. Klauck says; "Andere Stellen ergänzen das bisher gewonnen Bild. Saulus verfolgt die Gemeinde und dringt dabei in die einzelnen Häuser, ihren Versammlungsort ein (Apg 8,3). Wenn man die Verben wegläßt, ergibt sich an dieser Stelle fast die paulinische Formel.... Nach seiner Bekehrung hält Paulus sich in Damaskus im Haus des Judas auf (9,11.17), später in Thessalonich im Hause Jasons (17,5). H.J. Klauck, **Hausgemeinde und Hauskirche im frühen Christentum**, (SBS 103, 1981), p. 51.

78 Procksch, O., "**Hagios**": **TDNT**, Vol. 1, pp. 92 - 93. Paul did come out with the idea that it is the church and not the synagogue which is now Abrahams's posterity as chosen by God (Gal.6:16; 1 Cor.10:18; Phil. 3:3; Gal.4:28f.). Cf. E. Schweizer, **Church Order in the New Testament** op. cit., p. 102.

79 Schnackenburg, R., **The Church in the New Testament**, (1974), pp. 79 - 80.

He also laid full claim to its actual privileges, and presents the church as the legitimate heir of the old people of God. Furthermore, he attempted to provide a theological basis for this inheritance by seeking to recognize the liniments of the new people of God of believers in Jesus Christ, in the text of the Old Testament itself newly interpreted. By that he certainly heightened and developed the primitive church's consciousness of being an independent society and even more prepared the way for the conception of the christian believers as the 'third race'.[80]

R. Grant pointed out how obvious but important this fact is, in that almost all the epistles of Paul are addressed to the Churches, even though the word 'church' occurs only in the letters to Galatians and Thessalonians.[81]

It is believed that these are the earliest of Paul's letters. Some scholars argue that the later use of the word *hagioi* instead of the earlier *ekklesia* portrays a development in Paul's theology. Paul really saw the Church in two extensive dimensions. At one end, the church is a sociological entity, whose standing in history is determined by time and space. And at the other end, it is an eschatological entity which looks beyond time and space to a reunion with the Risen Lord, and lives in the presence of God's saving graces.[82] The sociological entity is likened to that of a family and sees the members as one family in the Lord.

Paul, the builder of house Churches, always sent his greetings to the householders and the community that met in these houses.

My greetings to Prisca and Aquila, my fellow workers in Christ Jesus,.... My greetings also to the Church that meets at their house (Rm 16:3,5; Phil 1:2). Greetings to Asyncritus, Phlegon, Hermes, Patrobas, Hermas, and all the brothers who are with them (Rm 16:14-15).

Gaius' house as a meeting place really qualified as a eucharistic center, as the record shows. It may be that he had a larger meeting place or that he lived in a central place, so that many people had to meet at his place. "Greeting from Gaius, who is entertaining me and from the whole Church that meets in his house"(Rm 16:23). That bigger places existed for the gathering of many house Churches can be seen in Paul's admonition to the Churches in Corinth;

80 Schnackenburg, R., **The Church in the New Testament**, (1974), p. 81.

81 Grant, R.A., **A Historical Introduction to the New Testament,** (Collins, London, 1974), p. 397.

82 Cf. E. Schweizer, **Church Order in the New Testament**, (1961), p. 104. "..., as a society centered in heaven and striving towards eschatological fulfillment and the real nature of which is not grasped in its earthly, historical shape and form..." cf. R. Schnackenburg, **The Church in the New Testament** (1974), p. 84.

So that any uninitiated people or unbelievers, coming into a meeting of the whole Church where everybody was speaking in tongues, would say you were all mad (1 Cor 14:23).[83]

One has to understand that it was not every house that qualified for the house Church. Different families came to a house for the breaking of bread.

Since when the time comes to eat, everyone is in such a hurry to start his own supper that one person goes hungry while another is getting drunk. Surely you have homes for eating and drinking in? (1 Cor 11:21-22).

For the eucharistic celebration, many houses came together in a given place. Not every house really served this purpose.[84] It must be clearly stated that it is not the sum of the different house or local Churches that make up the universal Church. Every local Church is a realization of the universal Church. Even in Paul's letter to Colosia, the word *ecclesia* is used with three different meanings, standing for the universal Church, the local Church and the house Church.[85] Paul has some models or metaphors for the Church, be it universal, local or house Churches and method of membership.

2.2.4.1. Process of Membership

Whether Church universal, local Church or even the house Church, what is important is that the people gather in the name of Christ and are able to actualize the three basic foundations of the Church as were explained above. Paul sees the Church as a group composed of those who have encountered certain things and have done certain things.[86] It is the experience of the Risen Lord and the willingness to proclaim the Jesus' event that consists the starting point.

---

83 Cf. H.J. Klauck, **GEMEINDE. AMT SAKRAMENT...** (1989), pp. 15-16. "Nach einer anderen, alter Auslegungstradition war das Haus des Gaius der Treffpunkt der Ortsgemeinde von Korinth, vielleicht, weil es als einziges genügend Platz verfügbar hatte."

84 Klauck, H.J., says; Hier scheint es fast, als sei für Paulus nicht jedes Haus **eo ipso** Ort des Herrenmahls.... Für das Zusammenkommen der Hausgemeinden sind die gleichen Inhalte anzusetzen wie für die Vollversammlung: Gebet und Herrenmahl. Denn die Vollversammlung der Ortsgemeinde, die selbst nirgends anders Platz findet als in einem Haus, führt nur fort, was in der kleinen Hausgemeinde begann. **GEMEINDE. AMT SAKRAMENT...**, (1989), p. 16. This in a way is to forstall the Ghetto Church and enhance the universality of the Church. The mention of Onesimus shows that the house Church does not necessarily mean a blood related family Church.

85 Cf. ibid., "Festzuhalten ist ferner, daß im Kolosserbrief Ekklesia in dreifacher Bedeutung verwendet wird; fur die universale Kirche (1,18,24) für die Ortsgemeinde (4,16) und für die Hausgemeinde (4,15)"; p. 17.

86 Grant, R.A., **A Historical Introduction to the New Testament** (1974), p. 398.

The acceptance of Christ in faith makes Christ become real and present in their experience.[87]

This involves a change of heart and attitude in life which involves turning away from idols to serve the true God and waiting for the return of Christ (Thess. 1:9 – 10) The sinner must die to sin and rise to a new life of righteousness in Christ (Rom. 6:1ff; 2 Cor.5:17). Community of the elect for Paul appears as an event in which God fulfills his election through his personal call of those willing (Rom. 8:29f.). No wonder Paul uses such qualifications for members as "the elects"-***hoi eklectoi,*** "the beloved"-***hoi agapemenoi,*** and "the called"- ***hoi kletoi***. The action of calling is made by God and he insisted that circumcision should not be used as a criterion for membership (cf. Gal. 12:3 – 5; Acts 15). Schnackenburg expresses it thus:

> the blessing that was promised to Abraham for his physical offspring is transferred to Christ and through him to all who are bound to him by faith and baptism (Gal.3:14, 16,29), and in the Epistle to the Romans the spiritual descent from Abraham is directly ascribed to all who, like Abraham, allow themselves to be justified by faith, the uncircumcised equally with the circumcised (Rom. 4:11 – 17).[88]

Paul had the idea of the two covenants in mind which he wished to explore regarding the covenant community. He used the story of the two women. This can be regarded as an allegory. The women stand for the two covenants. The first who comes from Mount Sinai, and whose children are slaves. "... so, my brothers, we are not of the slave girl, but of the free-born wife" (Gal.4:24-31). This famous allegory on freedom deals on the two covenants, actually meaning, of course, the one made with Israel and that which was made with the new people of God.

Paul sees himself as one of the 'qualified' ministers of this new covenant community called church (cf. 2Cor.3:5, no wonder then, he makes use of an Old Testament passage (Ex.24:12) to describe the nearness of God to his people in the new covenant community. This covenant community is so important to him that he advocated that people should not be absent during the gathering or when the community meets. On this issue Schnackenburg has this to say;

> Like all the early Church, Paul knows no 'individual' Christianity but always has the Church community in mind in which the individual accomplishes his Christian life. Consequently the eschatological conception of the Christian life which is so powerfully worked

87 Coenen, L., **<u>CHURCH</u>** (1975), art. cit., p. 298.

88 Schnackenburg, R., **<u>The Church in the New Testament</u>**, (1974), p. 80.

out by him also benefits the concept of the Church: the Church itself becomes an ultimately no -cosmic reality, one already removed from this **aeon** in Christ.[89]

In addition, the author of the Letter to the Hebrews, who has Paul's style of expression, treats the whole Letter within the context of a comparison of the two covenants. For this author, Christ is the supreme and unique mediator of the new covenant community who constantly intercedes before the Father's throne for his people.

2.2.4.2. The Church as the People of God

Theological reflection on this extraordinary phenomenon was primarily the work of Paul. He reflected on the question of Gentile Christians belonging to the people of God, chiefly under the rubric of descent from Abraham.[90] Paul was of the opinion that, in order to qualify for participation in salvation, one ought to belong to the people of God and must be of the 'seed of Abraham'. The question raised was, how? Should one be circumcised or would a mere observance of the law of Sinai suffice?

For Paul, it is neither a question of believing as Abraham did, nor of circumcision, nor even of observing the law of Sinai, but instead, all who believe in Christ are the true descendants of Abraham, the true people of God.[91] It is really interesting to note how the idea of the people of God ran through all Paul's theology. In the use of certain terms, one without doubt can recognize that he is referring to the same concept of Christians being the people of God, without distinction between Jews and Gentiles. Such terms include:- Abraham is their father (Rom.4:12); they are his heirs (Gal.3:29); they are the children of the promise (Gal.4:28); they are the elect (Rom.8:33); they are the beloved (Rom.1:7); they are the children, the sons of God (Rm.8:16; Gal.3:26).[92] All these terms demonstrate a relationship which according to Jewish beliefs belongs only to the people of God and its members. All that the people of God

---

89 Ibid., p. 85; R. Banks, wrote concerning Paul and community that: "One can only be an individual in a community and a community can only function properly when each individual is playing his own distinctive role properly in the community; **Paul's Idea of Community,** (W.E. Erdmanns Publication Co., Grand Rapids, 1980), p. 70.

90 Lohfink, G., **Jesus and Community**, (1984), p. 78; cf. Rom. 4; Gal.3); cf. P.S. Minear, **Images of the Church in the NT**, pp. 66-104, he groups his evidence on the people of God theme under three headings: political and national analogies, metaphors drawn from the pastoral economy, and metaphors drawn from cultic traditions..

91 Ibid.

92 Ibid.

hope for is realized in the new people of God – the believers in the Risen Christ.

> For the Apostolic community the baptism of repentance and faith bestowed in this New covenant does more than restore that which was lost: by the spirit believers enter Christ's own communion with the Father. In the Eucharist, the memorial of the new covenant, believers participate in the Body and blood of Christ (1 Cor.11: 23f.), and are made one Body in him (1 Cor. 10: 16 – 17). It is communion with the Father, through the Son, in the Holy Spirit which constitutes the people of the new Covenant as the church, 'a people still linked by spiritual ties to the stock of Abraham'.[93]

This image of the Church in Paul was used by the Fathers of the Second Vatican Council to stress the ecclesiology of the Church. There has been a misunderstanding of this term 'people of God'. Some have taken it to mean a political association of people, and hence to call for what they call a democratic Church. On this misinterpretation of the term Kasper says;

> Then the word 'people' was interpreted to mean the 'ordinary, simple people', as distinct from the establishment. But as the Council uses the phrase, the people of God does not mean the laity, for example, or the rank and file, as distinct from 'the official Church', let alone in contrast to it. It means the organic and structured whole of the Church, the people gathered round their bishop, and attached to their shepherd, as Cyprian put it.[94]

For Paul, the people of God are a community of those who have been redeemed and for whom there is no further obstacle in their relationship to God. This is a reconciled community which becomes the true Israel.

2.2.4.3. The Church as the Body of Christ

The idea of the Church as the Body of Christ is expressed in various ways by Paul such as "in Christ", "in Christ Jesus" and "in the Lord." Barclay in his research, found out that "in Christ Jesus" occurred forty-eight times; "in Christ", thirty-four times; and "in the Lord" fifty times.[95] Due to human frailty, the

---

93 O'Conor, C.M., and M. Santer, **Church as Communion. An agreed statement by the Anglican - Roman Catholic International Commission 1,** (CTS, London, 1991), pp. 11 - 12.

94 Kasper, W., **Theology and Church,** (SCM Press, London, 1989), p. 162.

95 Barclay, W., **The Letters to the Philippians, Colossians and Thessalonians,** (The St.Andrew's Press, Edinburgh, 1979), p. 11; cf. E. Best, **One Body in Christ**, SPCK, London, 1965, pp.83ff; for detailed discussion of this theme see P.S. Minear, **Images of the Church in the NT**, Lutterworth, London, 1961, pp. 173ff; E. Kasemann, **Leib und die Leib Christi,** Mohr, Turbingen, 1933; F.W. Dillistone, **"How is the Church Christ's Body?" Theology today** 2, 1945, pp. 56-68; M. Barth, **A Chapter on the**

conception of the Church as, "the Body of Christ", which is often talked about, is rarely practiced in the Christian community. Since a body is a whole, there should be complementary parts and not discriminating and fighting parts.[96]

For M.R. Vincent, the Christian, being 'in Christ', is like a bird in the air, a fish in the water, or tree roots in the soil.[97] Just as these mentioned cannot have life without their environment, so will a Christian lose his life as a Christian without being in Christ, says Jesus, and Paul emphasized this. The use of this phraseology by Paul is seen by Schmidt thus;

> Since God acts **en Christo**, Christ is always mentioned in some places. The richest and all comprehensive example is 1 Thess.2:14. The words **tou Theou**, are implied even when they are not significantly added just as **Basileia** in the New Testament means **Basileia Theou**.[98]

This idea of the Church as the Body of Christ is somehow sacramental, since it is related to the Church's sharing in the Lord's Supper, (1 Cor.10:16f.). No wonder Cerfaux rightly concluded that the formula 'Body of Christ' received the seal that made it such a distinctive Christian expression.[99]

It is in this context that the inequality that exists in the Church nowadays could be levelled out (Gal.3:27 – 28), and a community of brothers and sisters built. The inequalities and discrimination that exist in the Church today are a contradiction to Paul's expression of the Church as the Body of Christ. It is Whiteley who rightly observes that when we say that the church is the Body of Christ, we are stating a fact by means of a metaphor.[100] Regarding this metaphorical expression, Nkwoka remarks that we should realize that each member of the Church functions as a limb, a part of an organism in which every part has its special function. No part is dispensable, not even the seemingly feeble

---

Church - the Body of Christ, Int 12, 1958, pp. 131-156; A. Wikenhauser, **Die Kirche als der mystiche Leib Christi nach dem Apostel Paulus**, Aschendorffsche Verlagsbuchhandlung, Munster, 1937.

96 See D.O. Via, **"The Church in the Gospel of Matthew"**, **SJT** 11, 1958, pp. 271-286; he takes the view that the background to the Body metaphor is the idea of corporate personality - the concept of unity in diversity. R.H. Gundry **Soma in Biblical Theology** - argues for a solidarity concept, CUP, Cambridge, 1976, pp.223ff.

97 Vincent, M.R., **A Critical and Exegetical Commentary on the Epistles to the Philippians and Philemon,** (I.C .C., T and T Clarke, Edinburgh, 1955), p. 11.

98 Schmidt, K.L., in: **ThW 111,** article **"Ekklesia"**, p. 84.

99 Cerfaux, L., **The Church in the Theology of St. Paul,** eds., G. Webb, and A. Walker, (New York, 1959), p. 146.

100 Whiteley, D.E.H., **The Theology of St. Paul,** (B.Blackwell, Oxford, 1974), p. 192; see G. Howard, **"The Head/Body metaphor of Ephesians"**, **NTS** 20, 1974, pp.350ff, he emphasizes the limb or feet as the primary connection.

and less honourable parts. The suffering of a part means the suffering of the whole body.[101]

After a close look has been given to this picture of the church as the Body of Christ, one is inclined to assert that Schnackenburg may be stating the obvious regarding the Pauline concept of the Church as the Body of Christ, as constituting the most mature result of New Testament thinking about the Church.[102] Thus the new Church's ecclesiology, echoed in Vatican II, got its spirit and power from this idea of the Church as the Body of Christ. And this will serve us well to fashion an ***umunna*** **– church** ecclesiology, where every one counts and complements the other. This image of the Church as the Body of Christ brings to light the unity of the Church.

Paul developed this image as his theological development progressed. In 1 Cor., and Romans, the concept of "body" expressed the unity in diversity of the community. Individuals have different functions, but their activities are directed to the same purpose or end;(cf.Rom.12:4 – 5; 1 Cor.12:12 – 31, 6:12 – 20). It is the gift of the spirit which unites the members of the body. "There are varieties of gifts but the same spirit..." (1 Cor. 12:4ff.). In Ephesians and Colossians, Paul builds on these images and takes them a step further.

Christ now becomes the head of the Body the Church, he is the beginning, the first born from the dead that in every thing he might be pre-eminent (cf. Col. 1:17; Eph. 1:22f.). The image stresses the Lordship of Christ, the total subjection of the Church to Christ, the need for living union through faith, hope and charity with Christ which is the basic foundation of the Church and the goal of the Small Christian Communities.

2.2.5. The House-Church of the Early Christians

The management by households in ancient societies constituted their basic operational units. In ancient Rome, households not only served as the foundation of the ***polis*** or city, but also of the ***basileia*** – the empire. The city or the empire mirrored the ordering of the household. This, in effect, was a natural order on a human level, which revealed the divine order.

---

101 Cf. A.O. Nkwoka, **New Testament Concept of Diakonia...**, (1990) p. 63; cf. M. Barth's extensive note in Ephesians, AB, Doubleday, New York, 1974, pp. 282ff.

102 Schnackenburg, R., **The Church in the New Testament** (1974), p. 165. It remains of course distinctively Pauline in the particular form it takes but has unmistakable kinship with other images and statements in the rest of the New Testament, as for example with the Johannine allegory of the vine and the branches. "The Church is the people of God as the body of Christ, in a sense which is determined by, or at least grounded on, the idea of the people of God." (pp. 165-166).

Households at this period in question organized themselves according to families and into villages, not only for protection and proximity to some natural resources, but also to better ensure basic reciprocal relations.[103] The principle of organization was kinship, like that of ***umunna***. It is this interaction of traditional reciprocity and redistribution within and among households and their relationship that gave rise to the village or community.

The house community later developed into social units larger than the household. Some of these units were due to the intention of Rome to solidify the empire and caused the household mentality to be transformed into urbanization. For administrative purposes, the villages were attached or attributed to cities. At the wake of the second and third centuries (A.D.), the policy of urbanization gradually transformed most non-urban territories into areas administered by cities.

The Roman empire provided the forum for the documentation of at least the first Gospel. The house was also at this point in time taken as a religious community. Every part of man's life and activity was seen within the household. Malina says;

> There was no freestanding social institution recognized as 'religious', no discernible separation of Church and State or Church and family, even if one wished to make such a separation.[104]

Having seen the role of household in the social order, we shall now examine its role in the New Testament, since the Church took almost the same structure as civic life.

> The basic structure of the earliest communities of Christian believers was the same as what was then the basic unit of civic life in the cities, namely the household. The *kata* in *he kat'oikon ekklesia* was used of groups which were based on a particular household, to be distinguished from (a) the whole church, which also sometimes gathered (1 Cor.14.23; Rom.16.23; see 1 Cor.11.20) and (b) the whole of the Christ movement, which is called *ekklesia*.[105]

---

103 For a description of the movement from household to lineage to village, to sub-tribe, to tribe, see M.D. Sahlims, "**TRIBESMEN**", **Foundation of Modern Anthropology Series**, (Prentice-Hall, N.J., 1968), pp. 14 - 20.

104 Malina, B., "**Religion in the World of Paul**", in: **Biblical Theology Bulletin**, 16(1986), p. 95. For the relationship between the make-up of the household and the gods and the differences that follow, see **Tacitus**, "**The Annals**", 14:44, in Moses Hades ed., **Complete Works of Tacitus**, trans., Alfred John Church and William Jackson Broadribb, (The Modern Library, New York, 1942), p. 344.

105 Schillebeeckx, E., **The Church with a Human Face: A new and expanded theology of ministry**, 2(SCM Press, London, 1989), p. 46.

Bayith is the Hebrew word that was translated in the Septuagint as ***oikos*** and ***oikia***. The meaning of the two words has given rise to a great many controversies. While Klauck claims that **oikos** represents lodging, room, and property, and ***oikia*** signify relatives, clients and servants,[106] Elliott took an opposite position, as he says:

> **Oikia** in the literal sense of "house" or "building" denotes the place where the ministry of Jesus and the Christian mission originated and developed. **Oikos** denotes a group of persons, a household as well as the domicile in which they lived; that is the basic social community to which the message of salvation was addressed.[107]

While the two authorities disagree on the actual meaning of the words, they have one thing in common: the household played an important role in the formation of the early Christian community.[108] The two words at times are used interchangeably in Matthew, as Crosby reports;

> while there are some uses of **oikos** in Matthew that have very specific and limited meanings, no clear-cut distinctions between the words can be found in Matthew; this lack of clarity generally supports interchangeability between the words.[109]

The difference between the two terms should only be seen from their use, rather than the etymological or lexigraphical distinctions. The constant use of

---

106 Klauck, H.J., "**Die Hausgemeinde als Lebensform im Urchristentum**", **Münchener Theologische Zeitschrift**, 32(1981), p. 2

107 Elliott, J.H., "**A Home for the Homeless: A Sociological Exegesis of 1 Peter: Its situation and strategy**", (Fortress, Philadelphia, 1981), p. 188.

108 Schillebeeckx says; "The early church made the *oikos*, that is, the Graeco-Roman city family house, the pastoral basis of the whole of the Christian movement: 'the *ekklesia* which meets in the house of Aquila and Priscilla' in Ephesus (1 Cor.16.19); 'the *ekklesia* which meets in the Prisca and Aquila' in Rome (Rom.16.5); 'the *ekklesia* which meets in the house of Philemon' in Colossae (Philemon 2); 'the *ekklesia* which meets in the house of Nympha' in Laodicea (Col.4.15); **The Church with a Human Face**, (1989), p. 46.

109 Crosby, M.H., "**House of Disciples...**, (1988), p. 33. G.D. Kilpatrick also argues that Mark is believed to be the foundation of Matthew, against interchanging **oikia** and **oikos**. "**Jesus, His Family and His Disciples**" in: **Journal for the Study of the New Testament**, 15(1982), p. 2. The references Matthew makes of **oikos** is not exclusive to the sphere of relations with cult: house of God (12:4; 21:13; 23:38), the house of Israel (10:6; 15:24), or the house of the demons (12:44). Matthew uses **oikos**, to refer to peoples' place of residence (9:6). So one can't easily distinguish the terms in Matthew. Cf. W. Bauer **A Greek-English Lexcon of the New Testament and other Christian Literature**, trans. W.F. Arndt and F.W. Gingrich, 2nd., ed., (University of Chicago Press, Chicago, 1979), pp. 556-561; Otto Michael, in: Gerhard Kittel and Gerhard Friedrich, eds., **Theological Dictionary of the New Testament**, vol.5, trans. G.W. Bromiley, (Eerdmans, Grand Rapids, 1981), pp.119-159.

the two terms in the New Testament, indicates the Gospels' and Epistles' contextualization within their environment.

The spread of Christianity owed much of its growth to the conversion of entire households. Naturally, the household provided a practical basis and theoretical model for Christian organization, as well as its preaching. Hence, our call for the use of the *umunna* community, an ensemble of households in Igboland, as the base for the formation of Christian community.

What is actually the relationship between *oikia* and *ekklesia*, one may ask? The relationship is seen thus: whereas the *oikia/oikos* referred to the basic unit of the empire, the *ekklesia* was a more political entity. The *ekklesia* referred to the regularly-assembled political body of free citizens gathered for deliberation.[110] During this time in question, not only all households were *ekklesia*.

The original meaning of *ekklesia* as we explained above (Section **2.2.2.**), did not involve inherent religious or cultic meanings; though all formal gatherings of people had some religious overtones.[111] Even at this period, the Roman Hellenistic empire had a wealth of associations and clubs, guilds, and fellowships. It is also striking that even in the second century (A.D.), Roman imperial officials, including anti-Christian writers, saw the many Christian ecclesae or assemblies in terms of a 'free association': ***Collegium quod est in domo Sergiae Paulinae***,[112]- the model of a free association which 'gathers at the house of somebody'.[113]

Meek gave four different descriptions of *ekklesia* as being: the Synagogue, the philosophical or rhetorical school, patriarchal households and voluntary associations.[114] Since the Jews wanted to extend the holiness of the temple to bed and board, the house-based congregation came into being, known as *ekklesia* in Greek. This was the practice at the time of Jesus. And for the first decades, for the Jews, the *gahal* (congregation) assembled in house-based synagogues. The Pharisees made their power-base at the village synagogues.

---

110 Cf. W. Bauer, **A Greek-English Lexicon of the New Testament and other Christian literature**, trans. W.F. Arndt and F.W. Gingrich, 2nd. ed., (University of Chicago Press, Chicago, 1979), p.240.

111 Cf. K.L. Schmidt, "**Ekklesia**", in: Gerhard Kittel, ed., **Theological Dictionary of the New Testament**, vol. 3, trans. G.W. Bromiley, (Eerdmans, Grand Rapids, 1982), pp. 513-516. For Robert Banks, it simply means "an assembly or gathering of people in a quite ordinary sense so that, as in Greek usage, it can refer to meetings that are quite secular in Character"; **Paul's idea of Community: The Early House Churches in their Historical Setting**; (Eerdmans, Grand Rapids, 1980), p. 35.

112 **Corpus Scriptorum Latinorum ,6. 9148**, cited by W. Meeks, "**The first urban Christians 222n. 17.**

113 Cf. E. Schillebeeckx, **The Church with a Human Face**, (1989), p. 48.

114 Cf. W.A. Meek, **The First Urban Christians: The social World of the Apostle Paul**; (Yale University Press, London, 1983), pp. 75 - 84.

The house-based Church in Christianity was short-lived at its first stage. Luke reports: "They preached everyday both in the Temple and in private houses..." (Acts 5:42). In their practice, the synagogue served as the primary setting for missionary preaching (Acts 9:20; 17:1-4; 18:4), while eucharistic worship continued to be ordered around individual homes. This was the second stage of the missionary growth. These stages progressed, as Walter Lowrie recorded. According to him, the third stage came at the end of the first century, and extended well into the third century, with private homes given over completely to ecclesial functions. The fourth stage arose before the middle of the third century, that found the building of larger edifices, especially in larger cities.[115]

It will not be quite proper to equate, as in Judaism, the house and Church, *oikia/oikos* and *ekklesia*. Paul made great use of the term *ekklesia* in various ways. In Romans alone, there were five different usage of *He kat' oikon*, using possessive pronoun, (Rm 16:5 the house of Prisca and Aquila). The Church was also linked to groups, not only being localized in the *oikia/oikos* (Rm16:4), to the *polis* (Rm 16:1), and eventually to the whole body as well (Rm 16:16). Elliott, in contributing to the relationship between *oikia/oikos* and *ekklesia*, points to some of the local and universal dimensions of the terms:

> Both terms, **oikos** and **ekklesia**, originally were employed by Christian missionaries to depict local individual households or public assemblies of believers, respectively. In the eventual expansion and consolidation of the Christian movement both terms also were used subsequently in a comprehensive manner to designate the sum total of Christian **oikoi** and **ekklesia** as constituting the one universal household or assembly of God.[116]

Although the *ekklesia* in the New Testament may not be considered synonymous with *oikia/oikos*, due to other political *ekklesiai* of the Greco-Romans and the synagogues of the Jews; the elements of *oikia* remained. These are seen in the notion of an actual gathering of people which met regularly: in connection to God (Acts 20:28; 1 Cor 1:2; 10:32; 11:22; 15:9; 2 Cor 1:1; Gal 1:13; 1 Tim 3:15) and to Jesus Christ (Rm 16:16; Eph 5:23-32; Col 1:18-24). These distinguished the Christian *ekklesia*. Crosby says;

---

115 Cf. W. Lowrie, **Art in the Early Church**; rev. ed. (Pantheon, New York, 1947), pp. 91f.

116 Elliott, J.H., **A Home for the Homeless: A Sociological Exegesis of 1 Peter: Its Situation and Strategy**, (Fortress, Philadelphia, 1981), p. 223.

The people who met as an ekklesia were those called by God and baptized in Christ Jesus; they gathered because of their faith in him and their baptismal bonds with each other.[117]

That Jesus knew the importance of household, in the sense of family, coming together, and caring for each other, is obvious in his teachings. In the Synoptics, Jesus sent his disciples to go from house to house and be prepared to win those living in them. "As you enter his house, salute it, and if the house deserves it, let your peace descend upon it" (Mtt 10:12-13) or "Whatever house you go into, let your first word be peace to this house" (Lk 10:5f.).

The disciples were sent first to win a household, and from there, they could continue their apostolic work (Lk 10:7; 9:4; Mk.6:10). The use of the house Church in the Synoptics has great advantages for the young Church. As the Good News is presented, the disciples also found new homes and new communities. The house community helped the converts to practice the Christian virtues of love, care and worshipping together.[118] Jesus knew the importance of the house Church. As he talked about the loss of one's family in order to gain others, he means the house Church and not the large parish structure.[119] Jesus used the house community as a place for catechesis. It was in the house that the disciples sought explanations on Jesus' teachings. The house was indeed a catechetical center for Jesus and his disciples. It provided the initial Church gathering; and from there, the mission to evangelize the world was launched, as Elizabeth Schüssler recalls;

The house Church was the beginning of the Church in a certain city or district. It provided space for the preaching of the word, for worship, as well as for social and eucharistic table-sharing. The existence of house Churches presupposes that some rather well-to-do

---

117 Crosby, M.H., **HOUSE of DISCIPLES: Church, Economics, and Justice in Matthew**; (Orbis Books, Maryknoll, New York, 1988), p. 35. **Kalein** or "call" is the root word for **ekklesia**; cf., K.L. Schmidt, "**Ekklesia**", in: Gerhard Kittel, ed., **Theological Dictionary of the New Testament**, vol. 3, (1982), pp. 487-491.

118 Klauck, H.J., points out; Damit ist eine weitere Funktion der Hausgemeinde erkannt, nämlich Stützpunkt für die Mission zu sein. Gastfreundschaft wird deshalb zu einer besonderen christlichen Tugend. **GEMEINDE. AMT SAKRAMENT: Neuetestamentliche Perspektiven**; (Echter, Würzburg, 1989), p. 19.

119 Ibid., Klauck also says; Die gegenläufige Bewegung: Verlust der eigenen Familie - Gewinn der Gemeinde.... Die neuen Häusern und die neuen Verwandten, das sind die Hausgemeinden, die dem Missionar Heimat bieten. p. 20; cf. H. Fürst, "**Verlust der Familie - Gewinn einer neuen Familie**" in: **Studia Historico - Ecclesiastica**, (Rome, 1977), pp. 17 - 47.

citizens – who could provide space and economic resources for the community – joined the Christian community.[120]

2.3. Conclusion

In this chapter, we showed Christianity as a community religion with the aim of providing a solid background for our thesis. In our exposition, we showed how the covenant takes place on both a vertical plane – a relationship between the Israelites and God – and a horizontal plane – a relationship among Israelites themselves. In both types, we witness a communion which is vindicated in their sacrifices and in their sacred rituals. The presence of the decalogue was meant to sustain and harness such relationship with the sole aim of maintaining order and unity. Hence one sees that the covenant inaugurates a community sealed with the blood of the lamb and as such, shows Israel as bound together to God and to one another. "I will be your God and you shall be my people".

Thus, the choice of Israel and her uniqueness in the covenant fact at Sinai does not exclude other nations, but rather presents Israel as the unique and immediate beneficiaries of the promise of God meant for all peoples. No wonder Christ came to break down the barriers that separated the Jew and Gentiles. Jesus, a community founder, was born into the Palestinian world. He grew up there and was part and parcel of their religion and culture and was even a victim of Jewish socio-political bondage to Rome. It was not strange for him to make use of the OT ideas of community. He completely identified with his own culture. His task was a gospel of social action, of service, compassion and generosity, of deeds as well as words. In order to bring these about, he gathered disciples, and from them he selected the Apostles. The community of the Apostles was a real and intimate one: a small Community, indeed. God chose members in a way best known to him, whether by faith, birth, settlement etc. In the case of *umunna*, membership is by birth and not by choice.

Christ gave an example of how to live in this community. He was a man for others, who became the focal point of a new way of being together. The Church thus becomes in the Gospels a body of people summoned by God to serve His purpose; a body that is universal; a means of salvation, a real and intimate community bound up in the new commandment of love, which are the characteristics of the Kingdom of God in Jesus. In the Acts and Pauline

120 Schüssler-Fiorenza, E., **In Memory of Her: A Feminist Theological Reconstruction of Christian Origins**, (Crossroad, New York, 1983), p. 175.

letters, the Church is seen to be guided by *Kerygma, Koinonia and Liturgia* (Acts 2:42), guided by the Spirit without distinction between Jews and Gentiles, since this salvation from Christ is for all (Acts 28:28), with shared responsibilities and a mission to witness to the Risen Lord.

The concept of the "people of God" and the "Body of Christ" expressed concretely in Pauline letters brings into sharp focus the meaning of Christianity as a community religion and as such is a help to our understanding of the community dimension of *umunn*a in Igbo society. The Church as the 'Body of Christ', where there is consanguinity based on the blood of Christ, based on sociology – a family gathering based on eschatology – looking towards the second coming of Christ – sincerely carries and sustains the idea of *umunn*a in Igboland and as such exalts *umunn*a to be the ground for inculturation process leading to the small Christian communities. Christianity as a community religion has been expressed in various ways at different periods of Church history. Sometimes the institutional aspect of the life of the Church is emphasized. One can say that there has been a quest for a relevant structure for the Church. We shall in the next chapter look at various models of the Church.

Chapter Three: The quest for a relevant structure for the church in Igboland

3.0. Introduction

Belonging to the Church for many means enrolling in a colossal organization rather than a small community of believers, where members become one another's keeper to restore what Cain lost by insisting that he should not be his brothers's keeper (Gen 4:9). Cain in the biblical narrative lost the care and importance of the community life, when he decided to kill his brother. It is a mark of selfishness and a life of non-sharing that distorts the backbone of the community life.

As the Church progressed in her organizational aspect, the Church that started as a "house Church" and later grew to become small community Churches, seemed for about sixteen centuries to have relegated the small community aspect to the background. The institutional aspect took the upper hand. There emerged a crowd or state Church, that saw the decline of the community life. This was followed by the gradual separation between the clergy and the laity. The Church also experienced the struggle for power both within and without. An individualistic and private spirituality emerged that provided sacraments and the spirit of saving individual souls rather than the community.

The Church then went in search of lost souls and the community aspect became obscured or a thing of the past. The structure of the Church took on the state structure and the living-community spirit of the house Church was sacrificed on the altar of a huge, organizational modern society. It will be our intention in this chapter to re-awaken the primordial community-oriented Church, by an analysis of the Church's understanding of community and how this community-oriented Church has fared through the years.

3.1. The Community Called Church

To look for a strict logical definition of church, as is seen in the Aristotelian sense of genus and specific difference, is like chasing a mirage. This type of definition works well with phenomenological objects, but the Church goes beyond mere phenomenology. The Church consists of both observable and unobservable elements. It is both temporal and spiritual, divine and human.

The Church can be paradoxically described. The Church is both an object of faith and also an object of sociological enquiry. There is always that tension between what the Church is and what it ought to be. The two faces of the Church, which are divine and human, can easily be misunderstood, when one aspect is over-stressed.

This divine-human institution cannot be exhausted. To be one-sided in the explanation of the Church is catastrophic; since the Church, being in this world, is a visible institution, one should not fail to recognize that the Church is also a pilgrim Church. The Church is the Kingdom of God here and now and is yet to be realized in the eschatology. Hence, John's summation of the Christian life is applicable to the Church:

> Beloved, we are God's children now, it does not yet appear what we shall be, but we know that when he appears we shall be like him, for we shall see him as he is (1 Jn.3:2).

The Church here and now is a sign or foretaste of the Kingdom to come. This is expressed in the doctrine of "realized eschatology". The future which we await, has already begun within the Church. The Church is a mystery. Cormac M.O'Connor says:

> The church is a mystery and we can never fully express the reality which it signifies, that is the love of God incarnate in Jesus Christ.[1]

This goes to express the fact that in Christ, God has broken into human history, in a manner that is both unexpected, disconcerting, illuminating and liberating. This led Rahner to say;

> Is not Christian doctrine rather a mysteriously simple thing of definite fullness, which can be propounded in an immense variety of statement while its mysterious and simple unity remains unchanged.[2]

These only boil down to the use of images or models in describing the Church. That the adoption of models is the best methodological approach is implicated in the mysterious character of the Church. Despite the mystery of the Church, it is also open to external examination, as Congar remarks;

> The church is a mystery. It is a reality imbued with the hidden presence of God. It lies therefore, within the very nature of the church to be always open to new and ever greater exploration.[3]

---

1 **O'Connor, M.C., <u>The Family of the Church</u>** (1984), p. 7.

2 **Rahner, K., "The Concept of mystery in Catholic Theology;" in: <u>Theological Investigation</u>**, Vol. iv, (Darton Longman and Todd, London, 1966), p. 37.

It is clear that models are necessary to give an adequate description of the Church. This means that the temptation of choosing ecclesiologies which tried to put the Church into a strait-jacket, as if the Church is purely human organization, and thereby remained closed to new ideas and models, have missed the essential nature of the Church. On the contrary, we run the danger of historically disincarnating the Church. Gustane Weigel during the debate on the scheme "De Ecclesia" at the first session of Vatican II, made this important observation:

> The most significant result of the debate was the profound realization that the church has been described in its two thousand years, not so much by verbal definitions as in the light of images. Most of the images are, of course, strictly biblical. The theological values of the images has been stoutly affirmed by the council. The notion that you must begin with an Aristotelian definition was simply by-passed. In its place, a biblical analysis of the significance of the images was proposed.[4]

Such a comment shows how the Council was going. The debate in the Church many times boils down to two extremities, and sometimes people forget that in the 'middle stands the virtue'. The Church is both Human and Divine. John D. Zizioulas has this advice to give concerning the two wings of the Church:

> Ecclesial being must never separate itself from the absolute demands of the being of God- that is, its eschatological nature, nor from history. The institutional dimension of the church must always incarnate its eschatological nature without annulling the dialectic of this age and the age to come, the uncreated and the created, the being of God and that of man and the world.[5]

In the opening address of Pope Paul VI, at the beginning of the second session of the Second Vatican Council, he declared that the Church has continually sought to further her self-understanding by meditation on the revealing images of Scripture.[6]

These are images that go with the life of the Church. Avery Dulles, in his book **Models of the Church**, provides an overview of the Church's ecclesiology. His principal contribution lies in the use of the notion of model as means of shading light on some aspects of Church life. A model is not an equation; rather, it is an heuristic 'angle of vision' which organizes our perception of

---

3 **Congar, Y. and D. O'Hanlon, eds., <u>Council Speeches of Vatican II</u>**, (Paulist Press, New York, 1964), p. 26.

4 **Weigel, G., "How is the Council Going"**, in: **<u>America</u>**, Nr. 109, (1963), p. 730.

5 **Zizioulas, J.D., <u>Being as Communion,Studies in Personhood and the Church</u>**, (St. Vladimir's Seminary Press, New York, 1985), p.20.

6 **Cf. H. Küng, <u>Council Speeches of Vatican II</u>**, op. cit., p.25.

Church in a particular way and sheds light on one dimension of the mystery which is the Church.

A model is a point of view, which serves to integrate the various components of our understanding of the Church. Each, though distinct, is linked to the whole. This use of the symbolic models serves to project, integrate, and organize one's varied insight into the Church. In the description of symbols as help to man, Dulles says:

> Symbols transform the horizons of man's life, integrate his perception of reality, alter his scale of values, re-orient his loyalties, attachments and aspirations in a manner far exceeding the powers of abstract conceptual thought. Religious images as used in the Bible and Christian preaching, focus our experience in a new way. They have an aesthetic appeal, and are apprehended not simply by the mind but by the imagination, the heart, or, more properly, the whole man.[7]

At this juncture we shall dwell on some well-thought-out models which theologians have articulated.

3.1.1. Church as an Institution

The institutional ecclesiology defines the Church in terms of its structures and highlights the structure of the government as the formal element of society. "Institution" literally means something set up, an establishment, a community or a society furnished with hierarchical agencies with the authority to guide and direct and preside over worship and represent the community in all matters affecting it. Hierarchy and institution are linked with each other. Institution is implied the moment hierarchy is mentioned.

In **the Teaching of the Church Fathers**, God and Jesus Christ were the absorbing interest that dominated the world of Ignatius, bishop of Antioch in Syria. Ignatius, being one of the out-spoken Fathers of the Church in the Second Century A.D., says that the constitution of the Church is strictly hierarchical. In the same book, he spoke of bishops, presbyters and deacons as men to whom obedience was due, and of the laity who were bound to obey. In his Letter to the Magnesians, Chapter 6, he remarked:

> I exhort you to be careful to do all things in the harmony of God, the bishop having the primacy after the model of God and priests after the model of the council of the Apostles,

7 Dulles, A., **Models of the Church**, (Doubleday, New York, 1987), p. 20.

and the deacons who are so dear to me having entrusted to them the ministry of Jesus Christ who from eternity was with the Father and at last appeared to us.[8]

It is St. Clement who advises the Church community to keep the peace and affirms that the task of the presbyterial college is to provide oversight – *episkope* – and leadership or service *leitourgia*[9]. Although Clement accepts the appointment of the presbyters as *episkopoi* and deacons in the Christian community[10], one has to observe that *episkopoi* is put in the plural and therefore does not mean 'bishop'; as presbyters, they are leaders – *hegoumenoi*. These presbyters seem to have a double function – episcopal and diaconal.

As understood in Clement's statement, this means that they exercise authority, but at the same time, in so doing, they are the servants – *diakonoi* in service of the community. There is thus no master-servant relation, but authority in service. But Ignatius' ecclesiology is that of an institutional Church of the clerics, with a tradition and liturgical prescriptions powerfully controlled and centered on one body – the clergy. No wonder that he remarked in his letter to the Philadelphians: nothing without the bishop, everything with the bishop.[11]

St. Cyprian's writings were directly linked to his works as bishop of Carthage. The administrative functions of his office preoccupied and influenced his writings. He expressed his views on the subject of the unity of the Church in his letter Nr. 43, and also in his treatise on the subject. His conviction on the unity of the Church revolves around the bishop.

The unity of the whole Church is maintained by the close union of the bishops who are glued to one another. Thus whoever is not united with his bishop is cut off from the unity of the Church, and cannot be united with Christ.[12]

The Vatican I Council did not shift from the apologetic counter-reformation ecclesiology. She presented the Church basically as a visible perfect society, and insisted on authority, the institutional and hierarchical structures, and, of

8 Willis, J.R., ed., **The Teaching of the Church Fathers**, New York, Herder and Herder, (1966), p.77. Similarly he continued in his letter to the Trallians, Chapter 2, that: "In the same way all should respect the deacons as they would Jesus Christ, just as they respect the bishop as representing the Father and the priests as the council of God and the college of the Apostles. Apart from these there is nothing that can be called a Church", p.77.

9 Clement, Ad. Cor. 44. 1-3, ed., J.A. Fischer, **Die Apostolischen Vater: Schriften des Urchristentums**, Darmstadt, 1970.

10 Ad Cor., 42, 4, p.78.

11 Ignatius, **Letter to the Philadelphians**, 7:1, p.8.

12 St. Cyprian, **The Fathers of the Church: "St Cyprian Treatise"**, vol.36; Roy J. Differrar, trans and ed., New York, Fathers of the Church Inc., (1958), p.92. Unity is understood in Cyprian's treaty as conformity and uniformity.

course, on the monarchical role of the Pope. R. Bellarmine saw the Church as a type of human community (*coetus hominum*). He clearly says;

> The one and true church, is the community of men brought together by the profession of the same christian faith and conjoined in the communion of the same sacraments, under the government of the legitimate pastors and especially the one vicar of Christ on earth, the Roman Pontiff.[13]

All these explanations take their root in seeing the Church as a society in comparison with the earthly society. The Church was seen as a perfect institution with all organs. Boff saw this institutional model as *Mater et Magistra*. According to this model, the Church is present in the world by virtue of a pact or treaty with the state that provides for all of the Churchs needs and guarantees its existence. There is, therefore, a relationship between two hierarchies, one civil and one religious. Church, in this sense, is synonymous with hierarchy.[14] One has to understand that missionaries were victims of their era. This was the period when Modernism became one of the major targets of the Church's teaching authority. It was thought that the Church ought to have a central government and that there should be a uniformity in her life.

To check the excess and intrusion of modernism, it is natural that the Church should have physical organs. There was some exaggeration on the part of authority and structure in the Church. In order for the Church to have control of what was going on, the Code of Canon law was published in 1919. For Luzbetak, the institutional model is a sort of a perfect society, with all the governmental offices one can imagine, as he says:

---

13 Bellarmine, R., **De Controversiis**, tom. 2, liber 3, De ecclesia militante, cap. 2, "*De definitione Ecclesia*" (Naples: Giuliano, 1857), vol. 2, p. 75; quoted by A. Dulles, (1987), p.16. J.Hamer deduced from Bellarmine's definition three elements: profession of faith (which corresponds with the magisterum; communion in the sacraments (which corresponds to the power of orders); submission to recognized pastors (which sum up the power of jurisdiction); cf. J. Harmer, **The Church is a Communion**, (1964), p.84.

14 Boff, L., **Church Charism and Power**, op. cit., p. 4. M. Kehl sees this thus; " In dieser Kirchenerfahrung rückt die hierarchisch-sakramentale Strutur der Kirche in den Vordergrund: Die Kirche wird geschätzt und verehrt als die vollkommene "Heilsanstalt" (societas perfecta), die von Gott mit allen notwendigen "Heilsmitteln" (also besonders ihren Ämtern und Sakramenten) ausgestattet worden ist". **Die KIRCHE: Eine katholische Ekklesiologie**, (Echter, Würzburg, 1992), p. 30.

The institutional model views the church as being primarily an identifiable society, an organization with offices, structures, order, discipline and obedience. The church is intended by God as his visible instrument of salvation.[15]

When one views the Church from the institutional model, the powers and functions of the Church are summed up as teaching, sanctifying and governing. Such a view leads to further distinctions between the Church teaching and the Church taught, the Church sanctifying and the Church sanctified, the governing Church and the Church governed. Azevedo sees such division thus;

Its underlying Christology is that of Christ as prophet, priest and king, with the threefold function of teaching, sanctifying and ruling.... Thus the Church is considered mainly from the juridical standpoint, in terms of the organization and dispensation of power. This shows up in three functions dealing with doctrine, sacrament and administration, which are explicitly linked up with their divine origin. The main consequence of this perspective is the hypertrophy of clerical power in the Church and the atrophy of the Holy Spirit's charismatic dimension as well as the importance and operative play of other segments of the People of God, especially the laity.[16]

This model has dominated Roman Catholicism from the Counter Reformation until the Second Vatican Council. Its chief exponent was Robert Bellarmine (1542 – 1621). The powers of government are stressed. Many people mistook institution for institutionalism, as Dulles explains;

Institutionalism... is not same as the acceptance of the institutional element of the church... the church of Christ could not perform its mission without some stable organizational features. It could not unite men of many nations into a well-knit community of conviction, commitment, and hope, and could not minister effectively to the needs of mankind, unless it had responsible officers and properly approved procedures.[17]

The Church needs the institutional aspect of her life to function as an organization. It is unreasonable to reject everything about the Church as an Institution. And there is the tendency of the modern man to fear authority, to reject

---

15 Luzbetak, J.L., **The Church and Culture;New Perspective in Missiological Anthropology**. (Orbis Books, Maryknoll, New York, 1989), p. 395. P.A. Kalilombe, says that the institutional model was characterized by clericalism,juridicism and triumphalism; op. cit., (1984), p. 25.

16 Azevedo, M. deC., **Basic Ecclesial Communities in Brazil**, (1987), p. 213.

17 Ibid., pp. 34 - 35. The argument against seeing the Church from the point of view of institution has made many to have a position that seems to have nothing to do with institution. Some went so far as to scrap hierarchy and institution from their vocabulary of what the Church means; or even see the Church as nothing more or less than a mere secular institution. Boff failed in his view to make the distinction between institution and institutionalism; cf. **"Church Charism and Power..."** (1985), p. 2.

the institutional model of the Church. The experience of Protestantism and its consequences in stripping all mystical attributes of the Church should be a warning to all, as H. de Lubac points out that;

> We do not 'attribute to the church what belongs to God alone....' All the more then do we reject monophysittism in ecclesiology just as we do in Christology, but none the less strongly do we believe that dissociation of the divine and the human is in either case fatal. If necessary, the experience of Protestantism should serve us as sufficient warning. Having stripped it of all its mystical attributes, it acknowledged in the visible church a mere secular institution; as a matter of course it abandoned it to the patronage of the state and sought a refuge for the spiritual life in an invisible church, its concept of which had evaporated into an abstract ideal.[18]

Dulles showed that institution does not imply necessarily institutionalism, any more than papacy implies papalism, or law implies legalism, or dogma implies dogmatism.[19] He sees institutionalism as where the institutional element is treated as primary, which is a deformation of the true nature of the Church. The opposition of institutionalism by a Christian does not mean opposing the institution; in actual fact one may oppose the former and be committed to the Church as an institution. The Church as an institution, viewed from the point of view of institutionalism, makes the Church rigid in all aspects, doctrinal and legalistic. It inhibits a creative and fruitful theological development. Boff's attack on the institutional model is precisely an attack on institutionalism, even though he never made this distinction when he said;

> Behind these practices lies an ecclesiology of the Church as a perfect society, parallel to that other society, the State. This is nothing more than a theological expedient for the affirmation of the Church's power, though it is seen as religious power. Religious power, here, is not understood by the Church as a way of understanding reality or as a "spirit" in which to embrace all things; rather, religious power is concerned with a narrow aspect of reality controlled by the hierarchy.[20]

Lumen Gentium, the dogmatic constitution on the Church, which is the basic guide for missiological anthropology, clearly does not endorse institutionalism but whole-heartedly supports the institutional character of the Church. Luzbetak, commenting on the stand of Vatican II concerning this issue, says:

---

18 de Lubac, H., **CATHOLICISM; Christ and the Common Destiny of Man**; (A.C. Books, London, 1961), pp. 27 - 28.

19 Dulles, A., **Models of the Church** (1987), p. 34f.

20 Boff, L., **CHURCH CHARISM and POWER: Liberation Theology and the Institutional Church**; (SCM Press, London, 1985), p. 3.

> The Council strongly emphasizes the fact that the church is far more than a visible society – that it is a mystery, the body of Christ, a sacrament, and Herald,... Vatican II views the juridical organizational aspect of the church in a much broader and deeper context than did the institutionists of the late Middle Ages and especially the defenders of the papacy during the Counter Reformation and particularly in the last few centuries up to 1950.[21]

There are many militant arguments against this model, since some criticize it of having meager basis in Scripture and in early Christian tradition. It is not as wide-spread as other models.

The institutional system tends to create a division between the governed and the governor; law and its observance takes the place of charity, and much clericalism tends to reduce the laity to a condition of passivity. But it also contains much to the benefit of the Catholics who practice it, not only in maintaining the right relationship with the hierarchy, but also in protecting and guiding the interior unity of a living entity. Lubac summed it up thus;

> The highly developed exterior organization that wins our admiration is but an expression, in accordance with the needs of the present life, of the interior unity of a living entity, so that the Catholic is not only subject to a power but is a member of a body as well, and his legal dependence on his power is to the end that he may have part in the life of that body. His submission in consequence is not an abdication, his orthodoxy is not mere conformity, but fidelity.[22]

For Lubac, destruction of unity is a corruption of truth, and the poison of dissension is as baneful as that of false doctrine.[23]

Therefore an institution is necessary to guide against disorder. But authorities in the Church must justify their position by seeing the office as service

---

21 Luzbetak, L.J., **The Church and Cultures** (1989), pp. 395 - 396. Bishop De Smedt spoke of the pyramidal pattern in which all powers is conceived as descending from the pope through the bishops and priests, while at the base the faithful people play a passive role and seem to have a lower position in the church. This is as a result of having the church as an institution. Cf. A. Dulles op. cit., p. 39. But thanks to the Encyclical **Mystici Corporis** of Pope Pius XII, who undertook to intervene and re-orient the thinking of the time and prepared a way for new ways of seeing the church.

22 de Lubac, H., **CATHOLICISM**..., op. cit., p. 28. In every generation the church has to face anew the problem of how to maintain its institutional strength and societal stability, so institution is necessary for this stability but care should be taken that it does not boil down to exaggerated institutionalism. Cf. A. Dulles, **Models of the Church;** op. cit., pp. 43 - 46.

23 Cf. H. de Lubac, **CATHOLICISM: Christ and the Common Destiny of Man**, (Burns and Oates, London, 1961), p. 46.

and be able to express the Church as a community of life and witness; a community that reconciles and unites humanity in the grace of Christ.[24]

3.1.2. Church as Mystical Communion

A real Christian community is expected to be as perfect as possible. In the model of the Church as a mystical communion, there is a realization that the Church is not only seen from its outer core society (*Gesellschaft*), but also in its inner core community (*Gemeinschaft*). While the society is the outward manifestation of the community, it exists in order to promote the realization of the community. For Dulles, the concept of the Church as Communion harmonizes with several biblical images: "those of the Body of Christ and the People of God".[25] The Church is united to God by grace as Dulles clearly states;

> The church is seen on the analogy of a human body equipped with various organs. It has an in-built vital principle, thanks to which it can grow, repair itself, and adapt itself to changing needs. The body of Christ as distinct from any natural organism, has a divine life-principle. On most explanations this is said to be the Holy Spirit.[26]

By the strength of the grace of the Holy Spirit, its members must lovingly be united to one another. The Church, being both divine and human, has its weaknesses. Sometimes it is obscure and says little about the raison d'etre of the community which is the Church.

The approach of the Church as a mystical communion is reflected in the writings of so many theologians, such as Johann Adam Mohler,[27] Yves Congar,[28] Jerome Hamer[29] and Heribert Muhler[30]. It is also echoed in the Vatican

---

24 Cf. A. Dulles, **Models of the Church:** op. cit., p. 45. "In spite of the over-emphasis on the institutional in the official Roman Catholic theology especially since the Reformation, the institutional model of the church has rarely been advocated in its purity... They tempered the institutional with more spiritual and organic conceptions, such as those of the communion of grace or the body of Christ. For a fuller understanding of moderate institutionalism, therefore one must draw upon the communitarian and mystical views of the Church..."

25 Dulles, A., **Models of the Church**, (1987), p. 50.

26 Dulles, A., **Models of the Church**, op. cit., p. 50.

27 Dulles commenting on Möhler says: "The ground work for this revival was laid in the nineteenth century by Johann Adam Möhler and his associates in the Tübingen school. Reacting against the aridity of the institutional models, they popularized the notion of the Church as a supernatural organism vivified by the Holy Spirit, a fellowship sustained by the outpouring of divine grace"; **Models of the Church**, p. 50.

28 Congar, Y., **The Mystery of the Church**, (Helicon, Baltimore, 1960), pp. 97 - 117.

II document, especially in **Lumen Gentium**. This model uses the biblical images of the people of God and the Body of Christ in order to elucidate the mystery of the Church.

This method had an endorsement of the Vatican II Council, and was emphasized by the Extraordinary Synod of Bishops of 1985.[31] Despite wide acceptance of this model, one should not lose sight of its pitfalls. Such an image of the Church may lead people to become too introspective and have nothing to do with the world outside the Church community. The mission of the Church will be lost when it concerns itself only with the joy and blessing of Christian fellowship. When the people are so introspective, they will naturally forget the Kingdom for which the Church exists. Another danger that lurks in this understanding of the Church lies in speaking of the Church as "the people of God" and as the "Body of Christ", we become too mystical and possibly get lost in cliches and platitudes. It may also result that we concentrate so much on the communal character and loose the importance of the institutional dimension of the Church.[32]

Boff, in criticizing this model, saw no connection between the Church and the Kingdom or the world. He sees this model as that of the City of God. And as he raised the question regarding its future, he went on to answer it thusly:

> Theologically, it has been widely eclipsed by Vatican II.... As new ecclesial practices gain ground, the model of the church as Civitas Dei is left behind and becomes more openly reactionary rather than traditional. The future is linked to those bishops who allow history to assert its rightful place in the church. As such, this model of the church appears to have not much hope for survival.[33]

Boff wants to equate this model with the physical structure of the Church, which unfortunately does no good. The Church as mystical communion should go beyond the structures, as Kasper rightly suggests;

---

29 Hamer, J., **The Church is a Communion**, (Sheed and Ward, New York, 1964), pp. 93ff.

30 Muhler, H., **Una Persona Mystica**, 3rd. ed., (Schöningh, Paderborn, 1968), p. 50; cf. S.J. Kilian, "**The Holy Spirit in Christ and Christians**", in: **American Benedictine Review**, 20(1969), pp. 99 - 121.

31 Cf. **SYNOD REPORT:** The Final Report and Message to the People of God of the Extraordinary General Assembly of the Synod of Bishops Rome, 24 November - 8 December 1985, on the theme: "**The Second Vatican Council; A celebration, reaffirmation and a carrying forward of its work**"; (CTS, London, 1986).

32 Cf. A. Dulles, **Models of the Church**, (1987), pp. 55 - 61; R.I. McBrien, **CATHOLICISM**; 2 vols., (Winston Press, Mineapolis, 1980), p. 713; L.J. Luzbetak, **The Church and Cultures**, (1989), p.377.

33 Boff, L., **Church Charism and Power**, op. cit., p. 3

The term communion does not initially have anything to do with questions about the church's structure. The word points rather to 'the real thing' (res) from which the church comes and for which it lives. Communio is not a description of church's structure. It describes its nature or, as the Council puts it, its 'mystery'[34]

The Church is seen as a communion of men and women. This communion is primarily an interior reality, but it is also expressed by external bonds of creed, worship and ecclesiastical fellowship.[35]

Hamer rejected Bellarmine's definition that would characterize the church only in terms of its external, institutional features. He also disputed the ideas of Sohm, who taught that the essential nature of the Church stands in antithesis to all law.[36] He also opposed Brunner's idea, that would see the institutional Church as illegitimate. Brunner argues that the Church in the biblical sense (the *ecclesia*) is not an institution but a brotherhood (*Bruderschaft*); it is "a pure communion of persons (*Personengemeinschaft*)".

It is this position that he held which made him reject all laws, sacrament and priestly office as incompatible with the true being of the Church.[37] The Church has been, as history tells us, battling with the school of extremities. Hamer, maintaining with Congar that both aspects are essential, went on to combine the aspects under the notion of communion. He asserts that;

the mystical body of Christ, is a communion which is at once inward and external, an inner communion of spiritual life (of faith, hope and charity) signified and engendered by an external communion in profession of the faith, discipline and the sacramental life.[38]

3.1.3. Church as Sacrament

In speaking of the Church as a sacrament,[39] we want to illustrate or show how the Church is viewed as a sign of Christ's continued action in the world

---

34 Kasper, W., **Church and Theology**, (1989), p. 151.

35 Dulles, A., **Models of the Church**, (1987), p. 55.

36 This is the view of Sohm as expressed by Emil Brunner in his work: **The Misunderstanding of the Church**, (Lutterworth, London, 1952), p. 107.

37 Brunner, E., **The Misunderstanding of the Church**, (Lutterworth, London, 1952), p. 17.

38 Hamer, J., **The Church is a Communion** (Sheed and Ward, New York, 1964), p. 93; cf. L.J. Luzbetak, op. cit., "there is the danger that the communal character can become so dominant that the institutional dimensions of the church can be made to appear unimportant". p. 377.

39 **The new standard Encyclopaedia** loosely describes" sacrament" thusly: In Christianity, a religious rite or practice that is believed to have been instituted or commended by Jesus Christ and is held especially sacred for this reason. This description misunderstood

through the Holy Spirit, to bring about God's promises. This sign is made visible through the liturgical life of the Church. Dulles, looking at the Church as sacrament, brings out the mediating role of Christ. The good and merciful God, despite man's sinfulness, wants to communicate with man. God's redemptive will is powerful and efficacious and effects history. Dulles says;

> Our belief in the superabundant power of grace when confronted by evil is founded upon the historical tangibility of God's redemptive love in Christ. Jesus Christ is the sacrament of God as turned toward man. He represents for us God's loving acceptance of man and his rehabilitation of man notwithstanding man's unworthiness.[40]

Such a sacramental view of Christ is seen in the light of his Godliness, but he is also God made man. Thus in Christology there is the tendency of man toward communion with God; Christ, through his grace, enables man to achieve this. Christ is simultaneously the sacrament of God's self-gift and of man's fully obedient acceptance[41].

The mutual acceptance of God and man, initially signified by the history of Israel, reaches its consummation in Christ's cross and resurrection. Christ, as the sacrament of God, contains the grace that he signifies. Conversely, he signifies and confers the grace he contains. In him, the visible grace of God takes on visible form. But the sacrament of redemption is not complete in Jesus as a single individual.

In order to become the kind of sign he must be, he must appear as sign of God's redemptive love extended toward all mankind, and of the response of all mankind to that redemptive love.[42] The Church seen as sacrament has both

---

sacrament as a sign and had little or nothing to offer the reader spiritually. (Standard Educational Corporation, Chicago, 1988). **The Webster comprehensive Dictionary** (encyclopedic edition: J.G. Ferguson Publishing Company, Chicago, 1988); had more to offer than the New Standard Encyclopedia as it expresses it as; A rite ordained by Christ or by the church as an outward and visible sign of an inward and spiritual grace. From the above descriptions one can look at the church as sacrament from the point of view of visible and invisible, material and spiritual.

40 Dulles, A., **Models of the Church**, (1987), p. 67.

41 Since the Church, in Christ, is in the nature of sacrament - a sign and instrument, that is, of communion with God and of unity among all men - she here purposes, for benefit of the faithful and of the whole world, to set forth, as clearly as possible, and in the tradition laid down by earlier Councils, her own nature and universal mission (**Lumen Gentium, Nr. 1**).

42 Dulles, A., **Models of the Church**, (1987), p. 68. Azevedo says; "The sacraments, then, contain the grace they signify, and confer the grace they contain. Tradition has always associated the sacraments with the social dimension of the Church, not with the isolated individual, even though they are administered and received by individuals. For the human being, then, the sacraments bring together and link the visible and invisible orders,

outer and inner aspects. The outer aspect is expressed by the institutional model, without which the Church will not be visible. Visibility is essential, for it is in it, that the sign or communion of the Church is seen. The institution also helps to connect the Church of today with that of the past. Otherwise the Church could not appear as the sign of our redemption in and through the historical Jesus. Sacrament is eventful and dynamic.

> The Church becomes Church insofar as the grace of Christ, operative within it, achieves historical tangibility through the actions of the Church as such.[43]

The Church is not only a 'sign' but a sacrament. Where the Church is present as sacrament, there, the grace of Christ will not be absent.[44] The Church thus becomes an event of grace. Boff saw the Church as the focus and the celebration of the universal salvation; this salvation is not only on the eschatological domain but on the here and now – *hinc et nunc*. He puts it thus:

> The church, in turn, becomes universal in the measure that it points out the salvific love of the Father for all people through His Son and in the power of the Holy Spirit. Because this is the case, so-called worldly realities are also possible means of salvation and grace.... This theological perspective colours the commitment of Christians in their struggle for the building of a more just and fraternal world.[45]

This image relates the visible aspect of the Church to the continuing vitality, of the grace of Christ and of the redemption which he has promised.

The Church, then, is seen as a sacrament, the sign and instrument through which Christ and his spirit act for the realization of the Kingdom within the world in an explicit and concrete way within the Church, as Boff likes to express it. Luzbetak sees this model thusly:

> By a sacramental model, we mean that the church is viewed as a sign of Christ's continued action..., the church as being the 'universal sacrament', we mean that Christ the sacrament now works through his Body the church. 'Where two or more are gathered in my name, there am I in their midst also'(Mtt.18:20), and where Christ is, there is also his Church.[46]

---

the individual and social planes. We can sum it up by saying that Christ is a sacrament and so is the Church. **Basic Ecclesiastical Communities**, (1987), p. 216.

43 Dulles, A., **Models of the Church**, (1987), p. 69.

44 Collins, R., **Models of Theological Reflections**, (London, 1984), p. 133.

45 Boff, L., **Church charism and Power**, op. cit., p. 6.

46 Luzbetak, L.J., **The Church and Cultures** op. cit., p. 381.

The Church's life makes itself into a sign and instrument of God's loving presence and grace. The Vatican II expresses the Church as a universal sacrament;

> The church, to which we are all called in Christ Jesus, and in which by the grace of God we acquire holiness, will receive its perfection only in the glory of heaven... Rising from the dead (cf. Rom.6:9) he sent his life giving Spirit upon his disciples and through him set up his Body which is the church as the universal sacrament of salvation...[47]

For the ministry of the Church to be meaningful to man, it has to be actualized in a concrete situation. It should be visible and expressive. Dulles affirms that;

> Man comes to himself by going out of himself. He becomes active only in reception, and receives only through encounter with the world about him. The body mediates that encounter. Without contact with the world through the body, the spirit simply would not actuate itself.... Whatever takes place in the recesses of the human spirit somehow comes to visible or tangible expression through the body.[48]

This statement tends to reconcile the extremities of institutional and sacramental models of the Church. Although man shares in the divine life, this sharing is done in a human way, due to his nature as man.

The visible and social expression of the life of grace in the Church does not merely signify some spiritual reality that exists prior to its expression, but it sustains the reality of the spiritual activity that it expresses.[49] The understanding of a sacrament from the point of view of a socially constituted or communal symbol helps us to comprehend it as the presence of grace coming to fulfillment. Dulles beautifully expresses how the church as sacrament can be seen and understood in every culture.

> The church therefore is in the first instance a sign. It must signify in a historically tangible form the redeeming grace of Christ. It signifies that grace as relevantly given to men

---

47 Flannery, A., **Vatican II, "Lumen Gentium" 48**, p. 407f.; cf. **GS. 45; AG. 2 - 5.** There were different views within the council that no one fixed ecclesiology can be said to have emerged. "This is because in reality most of the documents were the outcome of a juxtaposition of or an uneasy compromise among divergent views which kept clashing against one another during the whole Council 'without finally reconciling themselves in **osculo pacis**;" cf. P.A. Kalilombe, "**From Outstations to Small Christian Communities**," **SPEARHEAD**, (1984), p. 26; G. Dejaifve, **L' ecclesiologia del Concilio II**, in: G. Thils, and A. Angel, et alia, **L'ecclesiologia dal Vaticano I. al Vaticano II** (Facolta Teologica Interregionale, Milano, Brescia: Editrice La Scuola, 1973), p. 94.

48 Dulles, A., **Models of the Church**, p. 65.

49 Cf. Ibid., pp. 65 - 66.

of every age, race, kind, and condition. Hence the church must incarnate itself in every human culture.[50]

O'Connor, in his own analysis of the ecumenical implications of the church as sacrament, says:

> A sacrament is never just a sign of grace, it is rather a sign which brings about or effects what it signifies. The church as sign has ecumenical implications, for it enables each body of christians, without denying any aspect of its self-understanding to look out at fellow christians and work for a reconciliation and unity that will enable the sign or sacrament to be a more visible and effective expression of Christ's presence among his people.[51]

Both Dulles and O'Connor understand the implication of human situations. These situations should be taken into consideration both for the understanding of the Church in a given area and for the Church's call to "go and make disciples of all Nations".

3.1.4. Church as a Herald

Seening the Church as sacrament, an ecclesiology that deals with the outward sign of the inward grace, emphasizes the present reality of the grace of Christ in the world. As such, the Church is always seen as the sign of this reality. In the "Church as herald", the "Word" takes a more prominent position than the sacrament.

This model can rightly be called the kerygmatic model. It sees the Church as gathered and formed by the Word of the Lord. The mission or task of the Church is to proclaim that which it has heard, and received, believed and commissioned to proclaim.[52] Dulles sees this model thus:

---

50 Ibid., p. 68.

51 O'Connor, C.M., **The Family of the Church**, (1984), p. 8.

52 Dulles, A., **Models of the Church**, (1987), p. 76; for Azevedo in this model, "the Church is seen primarily as the bearer of the *word of God.* Receiving that word, it is to pass it on to human beings. Its *proclaiming* is also a *convoking*, bringing together those who hear and accept the word in faith and who are maintained in faith and union by the strength of that divine word. Thus the word of God is constitutive of the Church. But the Church is its herald, not its ultimate addressee. Thus the word of God emerges as the crucial axis of an ecclesiological perspective that is kerygmatic, prophetic, and missionary"; **Basic Ecclesial Communities**, (1987), p. 221; Klostermann looks at the duty of the christian community thus: "Die erste Aufgabe der Christlichen Gemeinde als Kirche am ort liegt zweifellos im ungekürzten und unverfälschten Weitersagen, im Ausrufen der Botschaft Jesu, die auf die missionarische Gründung neuer christlicher Gemeinde zielende Evangelisation (Apg. 13:3f.), und die so-gennat inner gemeindliche

> This model is kerygmatic, for it looks upon the church as a herald – one who receives an official message with the commission to pass it on. The basic image is that of the herald of a king who comes to proclaim a royal decree in a public square.[53]

This ecclesiology is summarized by the words of Richard McBrien:

> This mission of the church is one of proclamation of the Word of God to the whole world. The church cannot hold itself responsible for the failure of men to accept it as God's word; it has only to proclaim it with integrity and persistence. All else is secondary. The church is essentially a kerygmatic community which holds aloft, through the preached word, the wonderful deeds of God in past history, particularly his mighty act in Jesus Christ. The community itself happens wherever the spirit breaths, wherever the word is proclaimed and accepted in faith. The church is event, a point of encounter with God.[54]

The model has a good biblical base, seen in the prophetic tradition of the Old Testament, and the letters of St. Paul. It provides a clear sense of mission and identity for the Church, especially the local Church, which can be seen as an evangelizing community. The fruit of its spirituality is a firm hope in God's sovereignty and the knowledge of man's infinite distance from him. The Church as a herald leads to obedience, humility, and readiness for repentance and reform. It is an eventful ecclesiology.

This model leads to a rich theology of the word.[55] We should be very careful in over-stressing this model, for it runs the risk of not stressing the incarnational aspect of God's Revelation. It runs also the risk of falling into the exaggerations of the biblicists and fundamentalistic sects, who may have an exclusive focus on witness to the neglect of action.

The over-emphasis on witnessing makes it too pessimistic or quietistic, with regard to the function of the Church for a better human society, and the duty of Christians to participate in this common effort.[56] The Church cannot com-

---

Verkündigung" F. Klostermann, Vgl., **Kirche: Ereignis und Institution:** (Wien, 1976), p. 34f.

53 .Dulles, A., **Models of the church**, op. cit., p. 76.

54 McBrien, R.P., **Church: The Continuing Quest**, quoted by A. Dulles, ibid., p. 76 - 77. McBrien unfortunately plays down on community aspect of the church. For him even preaching in the TV, or Radio qualifies as his own imaginary community. Cf. Paul VI's **Evangelii Nuntiandi; San Paolo Conference, (Rome, 1980).**

55 Cf. L.J. Luzbetak, **The Church and Cultures: New Perspectives in Missiological Anthropology**, This model according to him has, "the distinct advantage of giving the Church members a deep sense of mission and identity. It generates a deep love for and commitment to the Scriptures, and it produces zeal for the kingdom: "(1989), pp. 385-386.

56 Luzbetak went on to give some of the problems inherent in this model of ecclesiology as; "make Christians so absorbed in the word that they neglect other dimensions of the

municate without the human medium of communication. Culture, being the underlying code for social behaviour, cannot be sidetracked.

The more the Church understands the underlying cultural codes for behaviour and the symbolic systems of peoples, the more concretely she understands its mission. The gospel needs a fertile soil, and the concept of *umunna* community offers this opportunity. This kerygmatic model uses communication as the best tool available. Paul had this in mind when he says;

> But they will not ask of his help unless they believed in him, and they will not believe in him unless they have heard of him, and they will not hear of him unless they get a preacher, and they will never have a preacher unless one is sent, but as the Scripture says: The footsteps of those who bring good news is a welcome sound (Rom.10:14 – 15).

Here Paul not only stresses the duty and action of the Christian community in the spread of the gospel, he also acknowledges the authority that one has to be sent. He sees an organized community of believers. Luzbetak, in a way, sees all the models of the Church as having their root in this kerygmatic model. For him it is the base of all that the Church is and does.

> To speak of teaching and prophesying..., is to speak of communicating. No matter how we look at the mission of the church no matter what model we choose, we see the church communicating. Thus the communal character of the church is maintained largely through communication; the church as a sign of God's active presence produce in itself a form of communication; the church as servant must serve in word and action, communicating the church's human and divine knowledge and providing the validity of its message by living in accord with what the church believes and teaches. It is also through communication that the church progresses along its arduous pilgrim part towards the fulfillment of the kingdom and through which the church organizes itself into a visible body.[57]

From Luzbetak's assertions, one can easily conclude that the Church is the creation of the word. We know quite well that not only verbal communication

---

Church including the institutional, the sacramental, and the social...", **The Church and Cultures**, (1989), pp. 385-386.

57 .Luzbetak, L.J. **The Church and Cultures** op. cit., p. 385. K. Barth; see **Dogmatics in Outline**, (Harper Torch Books, N.Y., 1959), pp. 142 - 143, and R. Bulmann; see also his work: **Theology of the New Testament**, vol. 1 (Scribner's, N.Y., 1961), pp. 306 - 314; can be called pillars of this model, for they laid emphasis on the church as Herald, announcing definitively the word of God in Christ for our time. J.V. Taylor, in his work: **The Go Between God**, says:"The church exists by mission as fire exists by burning" (1987), p. 133. For K. Barth's ecclesiology, see Colm O'Grady, **The Church in the theology of Karl Barth**, (1968); and **The Church in Catholic Theology: Dialogue with Karl Barth**, (1969)

is required by the kerygmatic nature and mission of the Church, but also non-verbal communication.

Just as the saying goes, 'action speaks louder than words' so do actions make the Church's words understandable and credible. The function of the Church among other things is that of service, which takes us to the next model. But we should not loose sight of the importance of faith, which is the principal bond of communion.

3.1.5. Church as a Servant

In our on-going ecclesiological inquiries, one easily deduce two characteristic features on the ones we have so far seen. Firstly, they are centripetal, i.e., they place attention on the internal reality of the Church. The Church is presented as an organized and self-sufficient institution, as a sacrament, realizing and dispensing the sacraments; as kerygmatic, to proclaim the word of God it has received, believed and commissioned to proclaim.

Secondly, these models stress the inner vitality of the Church and its self-sufficiency in relation to the world. The Church is seen existing, as it may seem, outside the known world, but with the duty of controlling the activities of the world, with a view of making the world free from sin, by issuing moral codes to be followed. There emerged a kind of world which was colonized by the Church.

But the world, with the advent of modernity, became independent from the Church. The world could no longer look on the Church for ethical norms. Azevedo expressed it thus;

> The advent of modernity and the world's growing awareness of autonomy drew it further and further away from dependence on the Church. The world took up stance involving criticism of the Church and even confrontation. For centuries the Church tried to reinforce its own sacred identity. It took a defensive, indeed often aggressive, position vis-a-vis the modern world.[58]

The effort of the Church to discipline the world by force of authority was met by the world going its own way, neglecting the ecclesiastical influence and power. Such a parallel movement was halted by the Second Vatican Council, which recognized the modern world as an interlocutor, with its own proper identity and autonomy.

---

58 .Azevedo, M. deC., **Basic Ecclesial Communities in Brazil**, (1987), p. 226; for the process, see also his book: "**Inculturation and the Challenges of Modernity**, (Gregorian University Press, Rome, 1982).

The Church had a new look on the world. This new orientation on the part of the Church can be seen in John XXIII's opening address to the Council, in **Gaudium et spes**, and various papal, episcopal, and ecclesiastical documents, after the Second Vatican Council. This role of the Church in the world did generate some sort of secularization, which is evident in some Protestant circles.[59]

This helped to dispose the Church to see herself as one of universal service to all humanity, in all the concrete realities, where human-beings may be found. Then the diaconic ecclesiology was born. This ecclesiology of service has a lot to do with the spirit common in an *umunna* ensemble. And it offers the Church the opportunity to see humanity as one big family. By so doing, it transcends the boundaries of an ecclesiology of communion,

> centered solely around unity in the faith or membership in the institution. Communion widens out to take in humanity as a whole. The doors of the Church are open, and now this Church also wants to serve the world even though it is more realistically aware of its own frailty and inconsistency.[60]

In today's world, serving is not a pleasant duty, but this is the duty, of all who profess Christ as Lord, are called to undertake. "For the son of man himself did not come to be served but to serve, and to give his life as a ransom for many." Christ the head of the Church or the Church par excellence had this guideline for himself. What is then expected of the Church? The Church is actually called to serve.

The Church as servant of the world was dramatically developed in the Second Vatican Council document on the Church in the modern world. This 'diaconal' model of ecclesiology underscores the special competency of the

---

59 Some of the big names include Dietrich Bonhoeffer, who in his posthumously published *Letters and Papers from Prison*, calling on a humble and servant Church says; "The Church is the Church only when it exists for others.... The Church must share in the secular problems of ordinary human life, not dominating, but helping and serving"; rev.ed., (Macmillan, New York, 1967), pp. 203-204; cf. G. Winter, **The New Creation as Metropolis**, (Macmillan, New York, 1963); H. Cox, **The Secular City**, (Macmillan, New York, 1965); J.A.T. Robinson, **The New Reformation?** (Westminister Press, Philadelphia, 191965).

60 Azevedo, M. deC., **Basic Ecclesial Communities in Brazil**, (1987), pp. 227-228; cf. Y. Congar, **Pour une eglise Servante et Pauvre**, (Paris, 1963); G. Gutierrez, " **L'Irruption du Pauvre dans la theologie de l'Amerique Latine**", in: **CONVERGENCE**, 1-2(1981), pp. 22f.; idem, "**The Irruption of the Poor in Latin America and the Christian Communities of the common people**", in: Sergio Torres and John Eagleson eds., **The Challenge of Basic Christian Communities**, pp. 107-123.

Church to keep alive the hopes and aspirations of men and women leading towards the Kingdom of God and its values. Luzbetak writes:

> By viewing the church as a servant, we emphasize a very basic characteristic of the mission of Jesus Himself. His mission was a total self-giving and an unreserved commitment to the kingdom of God, a kingdom of love, justice, peace, and freedom in a world of oppression and sin.[61]

For the Church to be true to her calling, true to her name and represent her founder, she has to be the servant of humanity. The Church should offer guidance and prophetic criticism to the changing world.

The Church would do this by promoting the mutual reconciliation of human beings, and by initiating them in various ways into the Kingdom of God. The model points to the urgency of making the Church contribute to the transformation of the secular life, and of impregnating human life as a whole with the values of the Kingdom of God.

For McBrien, the Church is a universal sacrament of salvation and the Body of Christ and because the Church is both a universal sacrament of salvation and the Body of Christ, it has the duty and mandate to serve. He writes:

> The church must offer itself as one of the principal agents whereby the human community is made to stand under the judgment of the enduring values of the Gospel of Jesus Christ: Freedom, justice, peace, charity, compassion, reconciliation.[62]

This diaconal model tries to build a mutual brother/ sisterhood among those who join in Christian service towards the world. Dulles is of the opinion that the Church's mission in this regard is not primarily to gain converts for itself, but rather to be able to place herself at the service of all, wherever they are. "The special competence of the church is to keep alive the hope and aspiration of men for the kingdom of God and its values.[63]

The history of the Church has always shown the effort by the Church to preserve and enhance the community of the 'People of God'. The models we have already seen show that each and every model represents this communio, but each does so to a different degree. We have so far seen how different models, though pointing at the same thing, have stressed one side of the Church's life.

The Church is the copy of the *Communio* whose original lies in the Holy Trinity and is expressed in the Vatican II document;

---

61 Luzbetak, L.J., **The Church and Cultures** op. cit., p. 386.

62 McBrien, R.P., **Church: The Continuing Quest:** op. cit., p. 85.

63 Cf. A. Dulles, **Models of the Church** op. cit., p. 97.

> Hence the universal church is seen to be 'a people brought into unity from the unity of the Father, the Son and the Holy Spirit' (LG.4).[64]

3.1.6. Vatican II and the Church Structure

The establishment of the Sacred Congregation for the propagation of the Faith in 1622 saw the task and aim of the mission as "plant the Church" (*plantatio ecclesiae*). This meant trying to set up in non-Christian territories more or less the same Church structures and life as were common in Europe and North America. They saw Christianity as a civilization, and the result of this way of presenting Christianity still lives with us in Nigeria today. Burrows says;

> The nineteenth century missionary movement, which today is coming to a conclusion of sorts, was a success in bringing many people and nations to embrace faith in Jesus Christ. But it had presuppositions which need un-earthing if we are to grasp the issue which today makes the passage of the young Churches from dependence to independence so precarious. The most basic of those presuppositions... is the policy that the Church in the third World must adopt the structures of the Church in Europe and North America.[65]

For a long time, the Church has relied on the pyramidical structure which mapped out territories for specific ordained pastors to take charge of. The method of *plantatio ecclesiae* produced Euro-churches in mission lands. There was a misplacement of unity for uniformity. The missionaries created parishes, so large that they became like service stations dishing out sacraments to those who came around. Even though there came a time when outstations emerged, they only served the priest's administrative purposes. The emphasis of the outstation strategy was on the universality of the Church rather than on the people. Commenting on this, Kalilombe says;

> it is evident that the pastoral set-up based on parish-mission and its outstation puts heavy emphasis on the Church rather than the grassroots structures. It is geared toward promoting the sense of the oneness and Catholicity of the Church, and values uniformity. In

---

64 John Paul 11, Christifideles Laici: "The communion of Christians with Jesus has the communion of God as Trinity, namely, the unity of the Son to the Father in the gift of the Holy Spirit, as its model and source, and is itself the means to achieve this communion: united to the Son in the Spirit's bond of love, Christians are united to the Father." (CTS., London, 1988), p.18. Cf. Pope's addresses and Homilies at the Extraordinary General Assembly of the Synod of Bishops, 1985: "Without that divine, Trinitarian communion there would not exist here on earth that created, human communion that is the Church." (CTS., London, 1985), p. 338.

65 Burrows, W.R., **New Ministries: The Global Context;** (Maryknoll, New York, 1980), p. ix.

this case, religion is not really the product of communities at the base but of the body of 'special spiritualists' at the service of the client majority.[66]

Steps were taken for the unity of the Church, but they did not stop people from looking for a more personal and community or grassroots-oriented pastoral set-up. The Second Vatican Council gave impetus to this search for alternative Church structure.

Vatican II introduced a new way of looking at the Church and its structure. There was stress on the organization of the parish as a community of the baptized and confirmed Christians. The priest now sees himself as a co-worker and leader of a community, and together with some specialized cooperators and with the parish council organizes and coordinates a big spectrum of activities of the community. This model of parish structure can be equated to concentric circles[67], as shown in the diagram on the next page.

Fig: A

Concentric circles

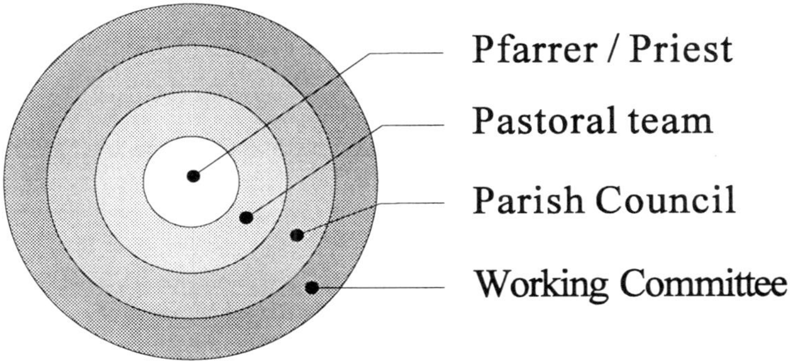

Inasmuch as this structure offers the pastoral work a team atmosphare, we cannot fail to comment upon the friction between the priests and the team of

---

66 Kalilombe, P.A., "**From Outstations to Small Christian Communities**", in: **SPEARHEAD;** Nr. 82-83 (Gaba Publications, Eldoret, 1984), pp. 59-60; cf. the reflections of Kuno Fussel, in "**The Socio-economic Conditioning of the Church**", in Virgil Elizondo and Norbert Greinacher, eds., **Concilium**: "**Tensions between the Churches of the First World and the Third World**" (Edinburgh, 1981), pp. 15-16.

67 Cf. L. Karrer, "**Erfahrungen von Gemeinde ohne Pfarrer am Ort**", in: **Gemeinde Ohne Pfarrer am Ort; Ergebnisse einer Untersuchung in Schweizer Pfarreien**, (1987), p. 222.

helpers. Some of the specialist workers are neither priests nor lay people; at least they do not know where to place themselves. There has been a struggle to determine who does what. These hosts of spiritual or theological specialists tend to build a position or cast, where they act as specialists, taking care of the community, instead of being identified with the community.

With the influence of Vatican II ecclesiology, coupled with the inspiration of BCCs/SCCs of Third World countries,one can today talk of 'Basic ecclesiastical communities'. That is seeing a parish as a community comprised of many communities. Here the emphasis is on the community as a whole and can be called a network of communities of a parish (see the next page for the figure describing the network of communities).

Fig. for Net-work of communities

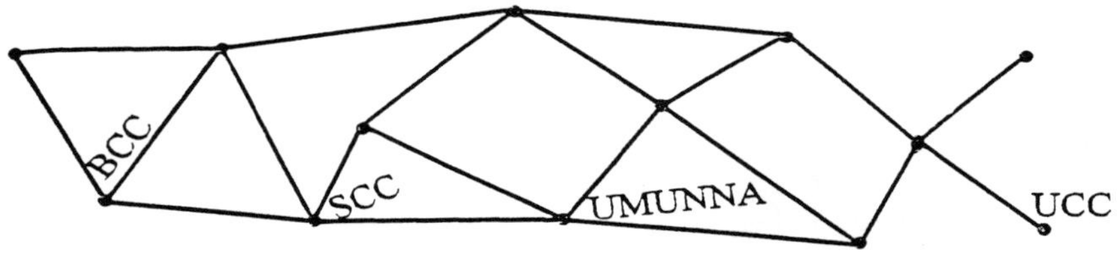

It is in this network of communities that the prayer taught by Christ to his disciples is realized. He taught us to call God our Father, so we are all God's children (*umunna*). This is the greatest expression of the community; with God, we all share the communio of the faithful. Pope John Paul II expresses it thus:

> From the communion that Christians experience in Christ there immediately flows the communion which they experience with one another: all are branches of a single vine, namely Christ.... For this communion Jesus prays:'that they may all be one;...' (Jn.17:21).[68]

The seriousness with which the Vatican II expressed the Church as the 'People of God' has called for a new understanding.[69] The People of God from

---

68 John Paul 11, **Christifideles Laici:** op. cit., p. 18. Cf. **Synod Report: The Final Report and Message to People of God of the Extraordinary General Assembly of the Synod of Bishops, 1985;** "Through the Church which is his body, Christ is ever present in the midst of humanity. We are all called, through faith and the sacraments, to live, fully, communion with God. Inasmuch as she is communion with the living God, Son and Holy Spirit, the church is, in Christ, the `mystery' of the love of God present in the history of mankind. (CTS., London, 1986), p. 2.

the community of the faithful with one another and for one another, in the life of the Triune God, expressed in the Church. It is Christ who summons and sustains this community.[70]

The base of every communio is Christ for all humanity. Vatican II, on the subject of the dogmatic Constitution on the Church, states;

> Hence that messianic people, although it does not actually include all men, and at times may appear as a small flock, is, however, a most sure seed of unity, hope and salvation for the whole human race. Established by Christ as a communio of life, love and truth, it is taken up by him also as the instrument for the salvation of all; as the light of the world and salt of the earth (Cf. Mtt. 5:13 – 16) it is sent forth into the whole world (LG:9).

Communion is achieved by the grace of God given through the sacramental life of the Church, which is summed up in the Eucharist. Man cannot separate Church and the Eucharist, for the Eucharist is the starting point for the deep consciousness of community life between God and man, man and man, chosen as Christians.

The Vatican II Council gave the understanding of the Church a new awareness by the expression of the Church as being the people of God united together in word and action of Christ. With this ecclesiology, the Church no longer sees herself as a one-sided fixed structure, but as a place of living interchange, through which exist mutual interest, love and care for one another.[71]

There is a relationship of communio and the three persons in one God which is the origin and source of the Church. For Kasper, the communion of the Church is prefigured, made possible and sustained by the communion of

---

69 A. Wagner puts thus: Im 2. vatikanischen Konzil wird die Darstellung der Kirche als 'Volk Gottes' besonders betont und damit die urchristliche Aussage neu ins Leben gerufen: Eine Zentralidee für das rechte Verständnis jedes Christen und jedes in die Gemeinschaft der Kirche Berufenen, fur die Kirche Bestellten und Geweihten."**Kirche als Communio"**, in: **Anzeiger für die Seelsorge**, Heft 5 (Mai, 1990), p. 171.

70 Cf. J. Ratzinger says; Immer ist Jesus Christus der Urgrund und Quell, das Vorbild und die Wegweisung; er selbst führt in Eucharistie die Kommunion mit ihm ein und dadurch die Verpflichtung zur Communio unter-einander; er führt den Christen zur gemeinsamen Sendung hin. **"Kommunion - Kommunität - Sendung",** in: **Schauen auf den Durchbohrten**, (Einsiedeln, 1984); cf. A. Wagner, "**Kirche als Communio**", 5(1990), p. 171

71 Kasper formulated the rudiments of the ecclesiology thus: "Die Kirche ist ja communio als Teilhabe der Trinitarischen Communio, und das heißt, sie ist Vielfalt in der Einheit". **Zukuft aus der Kraft des Konzils: Die außerordentliche Beschofssynode 1985,** (Herder, Freiburg - Basel - Wien, 1986), p. **88;** cf. P.L. Byeng-Hun, **Leben aus der Communio mit Gott und Untereinander: Zur ekklesiologischen und praktischen Bedeutung des Communio - Prinzips für eine evangelisierende Pastoral.** (Seelsorge/Echter Verlag, Würzburg, 1991), p. 49.

the Trinity. Ultimately, as the Council says, echoing Cyprain the martyr bishop, it is participation in the trinitarian communion itself (LG.4; Unitatis redintegratio 2).[72] The Council Fathers said that since the Church, in Christ, is in the nature of sacrament – a sign and instrument, that is, of communion with God and of unity among all men (LG.1) – the trinitarian communion can be seen as the source and basic principle of the Christian life and its structure. The proposal we will like to make in this work is to see how this communio can be more understood and lived in the set up of the Igbo people, hence a call for *umunna* ecclesiology. The final Report of the Bishop's Synod says:

> Because the church is a communion, the new so-called 'Basic Communities', if they genuinely live in the unity of the Church, are a true expression of communion and an instrument for fashioning a more profound communion. They thus offer great hope for the life of the Church.[73]

The Council Fathers explained the complex word "communion" as meaning fundamentally a matter of our "communing" with God through Jesus Christ in the Holy Spirit. This trinitarian communion comes to us through the Word of God and the sacraments. The passport, visa and foundation of this, is baptism, while the Eucharist is the source of the whole Christian life and its summit.[74] Thus the Council expressed the basic foundations or functions of the Church for a better understanding of the Church community.

No one model, nor the old parish structure, can effectively bring about this *communio ecclesia*, hence the call for a more effective way, which is being seen in the formation of basic or small ecclesial communities. In our own situation, it is *umunna* that is the primary and proper locale for the concrete embodiment of this communion. *Umunna* sociologically allows for a change and improvement in interpersonal relationships in the Church and is also open for all the models raised by Dulles. *Umunna*, as we explained in Chapter I, in its elasticity in usage can be applied here as *ekklesia*. The concept of its universality (Church Universal) should not be taken to be a philosophical universality that has no concrete context. It is different from a generality. It is similar

---

72 Kasper, W., **Theology and Church**, op. cit., p. 152. Lim Byeng - Hun says: Sie ist das Grundprinzip der Kirche, das aus dem trinitarischen Wesen der Kirche hervorkommt. Sie ist orientiert am kirchlichen Leben und führt die Kirche zu ihrem ziel, op. cit., p. 49.

73 **Synod Report, (1985),** op. cit., p. 19; cf. **Evangelii Nuntiandi, Nr. 58.**

74 Cf. **Synod Report:** "Communion with the Body of Christ in the Eucharist signifies and brings about, or builds up, the intimate union of all the faithful in the Body of Christ, which is the Church, op. cit., p. 15; cf. LG. 11; 1 Cor. 10:16. John Paul 11, **Christifideles Laici**: "The Body of Christ in the Holy Eucharist sacramentalizes this communion, that is, it is a sign and actually brings about the intimate bonds of communion among all the faithful in the Body of Christ which is the Church..." op. cit., pp. 18-19.

to the *universum concretum* as realized Christologically in the Person of Christ – the Risen Christ, who is the 'exalted master' over every community. In this case, ecclesiological universality can only be universal if it is also concretely realized in the local Church and in a given community – *umunna*. Every Christian Community has relevance for the universality of the Church.[75]

Ecclesiologically, *umunna* offers a base for reading and interpreting life and is a catechetical center both, for the assimilation of the word of God and the spreading of it. The *umunna* communal life leaves no one out in sorrow, need and happiness. Where eventually an *umunna* Christian community consciousness is formed, it will amalgamate and integrate the conscious, subsidiary co-responsibility of all, under the action of one and the same spirit, into the overall body of one and same Church. The development of the Church has given rise to the parish structure.The required Christian community under the present parish structure will not be attainable. Let us see how the Church communities evolved to be parish establishments.

3.2. Church Development and Emergence of the Parish

A look at the old parish structure will show how difficult it will be to realize *communio ecclesia*. Even the old Code of Canon Law, in 'Book II' deals with *De Personis*,[76] individuals, and mostly about the officials and their roles; however, the new revised Code talks, in the same 'Book II', of "the People of God".

> A parish is a certain community of Christ's faithful stably established within a particular Church, whose pastoral care, under the authority of the diocesan Bishop, is entrusted to a parish priest as its proper pastor (Can.515, art.1).[77]

When one looks at the old Code, there is no doubt that it considers the parish as a determined, geographical part of a diocese, whose pastoral duties are

---

75 Cf. W. Kasper, "**Kirche als Universal Sakrament**", in: **Glaube in Proceß für K.Rahner**, Hrsg., von Elmar Klinger und Klaus Wittstadt (1992).

76 **C.I.C.**, Lib., 11: **De Personis:** (Canon 216) "Territorum cuiusliebet dioecesis dividatur in distinctas partes territoriales; Unicuque autem parti sua peculiaris ecclesia cum Populo determinato est assignanda, Suusque peculiaris rector, tanquam proprius eiusdem pastor, est praeficiendus pro necessaria animarum Cura; cf. G. Alberigo, "**The People of God(le Popolo Dio) in the Experience of Faith**" in: **Concilium**, 176, (6/1984), p. 34.

77 **The Code of Canon Law**, in English translation, the Canon law Society Trust, (Collins Liturgical Publications, London, 1983), p. 92.

assigned to a priest by the bishop (Can.216, arts. 1,3; 451,1). Such a concept suggests that the diocese must be created prior to the parish.[78]

The history of the parish holds that at first it did not exist as we have it today, where a priest has a parish of his own. Christian communities did exist, and were looked after by *Episcopoi* (bishops), as seen at Ephesus with Timothy as the overseer; Titus, for example, looked after Crete. Even where a college of priests existed to act as helpers (Acts 20:17), they were just that – mere helpers for the bishop, received their assignments from him.[79] As the number of Christians increased, the house church started giving way for a more elaborate gathering places. In the old Canon, we had the territorial parish, which is entrusted to the priest as the Father, as it were, and every other person in the area becomes automatically his sons or daughters.

Since culture unfortunately is not static but dynamic, and as man molds culture so does culture mold man, one can say that we are in a situation of constant changes. Looking at the history of the origin of the parish and today's parish situation, one notices actually that nothing has drastically changed, especially in Nigeria, or even Igboland.

The same problems that existed centuries ago still rear their ugly heads, such as problems of pastoral structure, parish-priest, deacon, money, property, Church and state relationship, distribution etc. These are human problems that are expressed within the human side of the Church. The parish as we have it today started in the 4th century; before then, there was no such structure, where each parish had a pastor.

In the post-Apostolic period, pastors were met only in titular churches, like that of Rome.[80] These titular churches comprised about 30 or 40 people, who gathered for prayers, a typical Small Christian Community. There was nothing like territorial jurisdiction; no wonder that St. Justin wrote: "We gather not all at the same place but each one where he can join the celebration in christ's name." Here, we experience an early Christian practice of decentralization in favour of pastoral care. Such communities were scattered all over the Christian world. It was reported that in North Africa alone, with their sense of community, there existed at least 500 residing Bishops; each bishop had a

---

78 Cf. W. Croce, "**The History of the Parish**", in: **The Parish from Theology to Practice**, ed. Hugo Rahner, (The Newman Press, Maryland, 1958), p. 9.

79 Cf. Bihlmeyer-Tuechle, "**Christian Antiquity**",**Church History**, vol. 1, trans., V.E.Mills, (The Newman Press, Maryland, 1958), pp. 103ff.

80 Croce, W., records that one of the oldest house-Churches in Rome belonged to one Pamachius. This house was named Titulus Pamachi, after the owner of the house. Such houses were small, and can take in 20, 30 or 40 people. See His article on "**The History of the Parish**" in: Hugo Rahner (1958), pp. 9-14.

community.[81] These bishops were simply what we today have as parish priests.

The early Church gained a lot from the African sense of community life; which was first made manifest by St. Anthony of Egypt in his anachoretic community. After him came Pachomius, with his Senobitism. Senobitism derives itself from *coenobium*, the latin translation of the Greek *Koinonia* – meaning community. Pachomius brought the African community into the Christian world.[82]

The turn of the 4th century saw the introduction of assigning priests permanently to a particular locality. This gave birth to what we have today as parish. W.Croce says;

> At the turn of the 4th century, the practice of permanently stationing priests in the most distant villages was introduced. Thus arose the first parishes in the modern sense of the term. In the fifth century, there were already many such parishes.[83]

The spread of these parishes had their own coordination problems with the sending bishop. The problem was somehow solved by the creation of "the Choir Bishopric". Such bishops had the task of maintaining unity between the diocesan bishop and the rural clergy.[84]

---

81 Karrer, L., **Abhebung der Pfarrei von der Bischofskirche:** "Allerdings gab es auch im lateinischen Westen für die Leiter einer sozusagen örtlichen bzw. Städtischen Gemeinde noch verschiedene Bezeichnungen: Pastor, Episcopus, Dominus, ja selbst Papa. Noch Grego von Tours (+ 594) gebraucht `sacerdos' und episcopus' als Synomnyme (**De gloria Confessorum**, C.79). Und wenn es in einem Bericht aus dem 4. Jahrhundert. (M. Pfligler, a. a. o., 70) heißt, dass in Nordafrika 500 Bishöfe residierten, dann kann man wohl mit Fug und recht annehmen, dass diese der Weihe nach Bischöfe, also ordinarien mit eigener Vollmacht, waren, dem pastoralen Wirken und Umfang nach wohl aber `Pfarrer' im heutigen Sinn." (Kirchl. Altertum, unpublished monograph, University of Freiburg, Schweiz, n.d.), p. 111.

82 Cf. K. Baus, and E. Ewig, "**Die Reichskirche nach Konstantin dem Großen; von Nikaia bis Chalkedon;** in: **Band die Kirchengeschichte**, Band 11/1, (Herder, Freiburg, 1985), pp. 348-369).

83 Croce, W., "**The History of the Parish**" in: **The Parish from Theology to practice**, ed. Hugo Rahner, trans. Robert Kress, (The Newman Press, Maryland, 1958), p. 12. In a letter to **Leo the Great** (440-461), Theodoret of Cyrus reports that, in his province, 800 parishes had been established. St. Zorell, "**Die Entwicklung des Parochialsystems bis zur Ende der Karolingerzeit**", **Archiev für kath. Kirchenrecht, Lxxxii**, (1902), p. 90.

84 Croce says; "It is interesting to note that, with the rise of these rural parishes, the choir bishopric came into existence. These bishops had as their task the maintenance of unity between the diocesan bishop and the rural clergy. These bishops had the right to appoint minor clerics, but they could not ordain deacons or priests. This was reserved to the diocesan bishop. "**The History of the Parish**" (1958), p. 12.

During the time of Constantine, the Church became a state and almost city religion, and the Church was influenced by the state structure. The Roman Empire brought a great influence on the church life; then there came a shift in the role of the bishop from being a pastor to a leader, organizer, *episcopoi* – overseer of a well organized diocese.

At the end of the Roman empire, the Germans exerted their own influence, which also affected the structure of the parish, mostly regarding property ownership. They stressed private ownership, which gave kings and wealthy citizens, the right to rebuild destroyed churches and own them. These Kings took these churches as personal property and that could decide which priest worked in them. These Churches were the so-called proper or private Churches *(Eigenkirchen)*.[85]

The priest had to become one of the king's workers. The clerical duties of such priests consisted in keeping the candles at certain times, saying Mass and above all, performing all kinds of blessings: blessing the fields, the animals, the house, the barns, against sickness and storms and the like.[86] The Bishops struggled to save such priests from the enslavement which they suffered from these kings, by building new Churches and naming them parishes and depriving the private Churches of the right to be parish churches.

> The only step that could be taken against it was to build as many churches as possible on the land belonging to the bishop. These churches were endowed with the right to perform baptisms and were thus raised to the status of parish churches. Further, the obligation to belong to one determined parish was introduced. It was forbidden, at least on the greater feast days, to hold services in the small private oratories.... As a rule, the right to baptize and bury remained with the mother parish, which was also entitled to a determined part of the income of the auxiliary church.[87]

The struggle lasted quite a while; since the private Church was helped by the policy of secularization in vogue at this period. The first secularization episode was the work of Charles Martel. He needed money to prosecute the war, so he appropriated the Church's property. It was at this time that was

---

85 "In the fifth century, the barbarian migrations began. The Germanic hordes overran the Roman Empire. In the resulting confusion, many of the old parishes were destroyed. After the baptism of Chlodwig (496) and the conversion of the Germanic tribes, the labor of building churches was again undertaken.... But it was no longer the bishop alone, but also the king, the nobility, and the rich landowners who established churches, chapels, and oratories on their property"; W. Croce, "**The history of the Parish**", (1958), p. 13.

86 Cf. W. Croce, "**The History of the Parish**", in: Hugo Rahner (1958), pp. 14-15; G. Schnuerer, **Kirche und Kultur im Mittelalter**, (Paderborn, 1929) 11, 65.

87 Croce, W., "**The History of the Parish**" in: Hugo Rahner, **The Parish from Theology to Practice**, (1958); p. 15.

called the compulsory loan, the *precario verbo regis*. The laymen who bought the Church property considered them to be their private possession, including the Church that stood on it.

The bishops had to struggle to remedy the situation. Such struggles continued until 746, when Pope Zachary demanded from Pepin the right of the bishops to appoint the pastors of the private Churches. Even earlier, in 743 at the Council Germanicum convoked by St. Boniface, in order to have control over the priests and their appointment, it was stipulated that during Lent, every priest had to render an account of his ministry to the bishop. The priest had to procure the holy chrism from the episcopal see and had to be prepared to receive the bishop on his visitation.

These stipulations were officially recognized during the Synod of Frankfurt (794). The situation of the private churches remained basically unchanged well into the Middle Ages. It was Alexander III (1159-81), who tried another approach to the problem, by transforming the right of the private church into the right of patronage. With such approach, the landowner did not have dominion over church property, but only the right of administration. This did not help matters, for since one could now acquire just as many patronage as one desired. They, in effect, ruled the Church and administered its property at will.

Monasteries, with financial difficulties under the old order, took advantage of the new situation and acquired numerous patronages as means to increase income. What actually emerged from this right of patronage was known as "incorporation". Because of this, the parishes became too large, and no one was willing to split his parish into smaller units, since to do so would be to entail financial loss. The parish priest became attached to his parish for the sake of finance to the point that no other clergy was allowed to minister to his parishioners, even at the point of death.[88]

The Church witnessed a decline in pastoral care, but hope was raised at the emergence of the Franciscans and Dominicans in the thirteenth century. These groups took to the spirit of their founders and went out in search of souls. Their popularity attracted the wrath of the parish priests, who in turn forbade

---

88 For such extremely unpleasant scandals, see the case of Honau and Wanzennau, as narrated from the history of the Alsatian Church. L. Pfleger, "**Untersuchungen zur Geschichte des Pfarrinstitutes im Elass**", in: **Archiv für elsaessische Kirchengeschichte**, (1933), pp. 100ff. Here two towns: that stood on the both sides of the Rhine River. On the right stood the parish of Honau, incorporated by the monastery of St.Peter in strassburg. On the left bank was Wanzenau, which belonged to the parish Honau. For Church services they have to cross the Rhine, and the crossing was often dangerous. They pleaded for their own parish, but because of loosing the finance due to Honau, their request was not granted. It was not uncommon that people were drowned while trying to cross the river.

their parishioners to attend the sermons of the Friars Minor and to give them alms. Whoever did not heed these regulations was subject to excommunication and denial of the last sacrament.[89]

After this period came the influence of the Council of Trent.[90] This Council emphasized the territorial importance of the parish – this, in a way, diminished both the influence of the itinerant preachers and private churches of the rich. Each diocese finally had organized, clearly geographically defined parishes, and each parish had its own pastor.

The Council defined the duties and rights of the parish priest. The Council also put sactions on the laity who had such great influence on the economic life of the parish and abused it. The concept of rights for the Council had great a deficiency, since they built the church too much on the clergy and forced the laity into passivity. The Council carved out these territorial parishes, where the priest was the parish and the parish the priest. The main duty of the priest was to save the souls of the dying.[91] For the council, the bishop was the proper pastor of his diocese and must reside there, and this was also the position of the priest within the parish. The parish priest had the odious task of caring for the souls. At this time, the care of souls was seen not as the fulfillment of a duty on a contractual quid pro quo basis, with financial interest as the main purpose, but as a supernatural labor of love.

The parishes now received definite boundaries and were not supposed to be too large. This Council of Trent made the parish priests conscious of their mission, and the territorial parish was created. This type of structure centralized the powers in the person of the parish priest.

---

89 Ibid., p. 132; cf. W. Croce, "**The History of Parish**" (1958), p. 19.

90 Cf. A. Schrott, **Seelsorge im Wandel der Zeiten**, (Graz, 1949), pp. 79ff.

91 Leo Karrer expressed it thus:" Die herkömmliche Territorialpfarrei war das Leitbild bis zum Zweiten Vatikanischen Konzil. Unsere Elterngeneration ist davon geprägt. Die Katholiken einer gebietsmässig klar umschriebenen Pfarrei wurden vom Pfarrer und 'seinen' Vikaren und Kaplänen seelsorglich betreut. Das grundlegende Motto aller pastoralen Bemühungen und die Sorge für alle Seelsorger lautete: 'Seelen retten'. Das Gewicht lag dabei auf dem einzelnen Christen und weniger auf der Gemeinschaftsbildung. Die Pfarrei war sozusagen eine Verwaltungseinheit der Grosskirche, einer Art `Agentur'. Alles, was kirchlich von Belang war, ging durch die Hände des Klerus". **Erfahrungen von Gemeinden Ohne Pfarrer am Ort. "Einige Überlegungen und Anfragen aus praktisch - theologischer sicht".** in: **Gemeinde ohne Pfarrer am Ort**, Hrsg. Schweizerisches Pastoral - soziologisches Institut, (NZN Buchverlag, Zurich, 1987), pp. 220 - 221. A. Dulles says:"Since the Reformation the Catholic church has tended to regard its mission as an exclusively regious one, aimed at preparing individuals through faith, worship, and right behavior to attain eternal life." **The Reshaping of Catholicism:** op. cit., (1988), p. 31.

Fig. for territorial parish

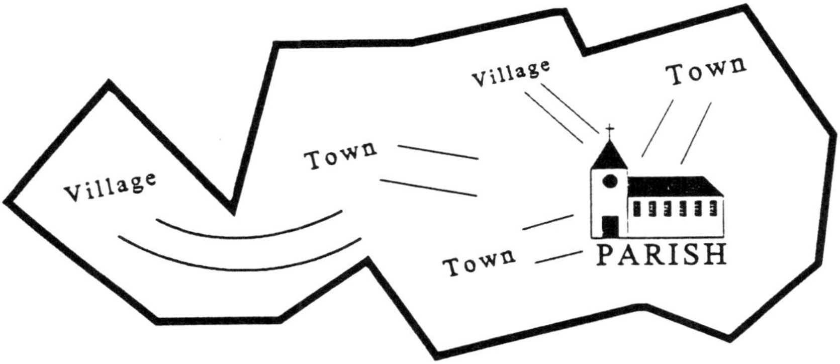

However, a change came about during the era of Enlightenment.

The period of Enlightenment brought a great deal of influence onto the life of the Church. There was a change of attitude in the faithful as to the meaning of life, and there was a loss of close religious unity which went with traditional feastdays. The Church lost a great deal of her influence on the people. Since the territorial parish structure encouraged a collection of individuals, rather than forming a community, people saw the church as belonging to the priest and his close associates and no longer felt a need for it, especially in the West.

Pyramid Fig.

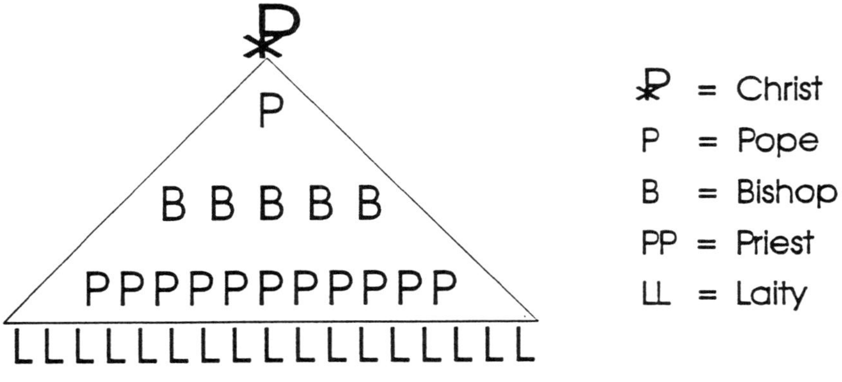

The Church at this time was pyramidically structured.

It is almost a platitude to assert that the Catholic church from the Middle Ages until Vatican II was pyramidal in structure. Truth and holiness were conceived as emanating from the pope as commander – in – chief at the top, and the bishops were as subordinate officers carrying out the orders of the pope.[92]

This parish structure continued until Vatican II as a kind of administrative district of the Church, a kind of church agency. The activity of the parish was concerned with sacraments. Vatican II brought about a lot of changes and people started to question the structure and see the Parish as a Community (*Gemeinde*) as we shall see later in Section **4.1**. of Chapter **4**.

3.3. The History of Today's Structure in the Igbo Church

Nothing can possibly prevent this Section from being a delicate one which easily inflames passion and prejudice. Any account that endeavours to consider only the experience of the African peoples themselves is certain to be written off by some apologists as failing to give due credit to the good intentions of many Europeans who paved the way during this particular part of history. When one lauds the potentially good gifts of Europe to Africa, such as new food crops, elaborate technology, writing and Christianity, one is seen as having a colonial mentality. However, the story of change in the African cultural community cannot be fully told without a look at the missionary activities there.

In Africa, south of the Sahara, Christian missionary activities either preceded or accompanied colonialism. If the African polity and social structures were disorganized by the colonial power, it was the effect of missionary activity, which was not only supportive of the colonial administration but also discredited the African way of life. Charles Agu argues that;

Colonial rule, aiming at economic exploitation of the land and its people accordingly affected the matter of the Igbo, the missionary, by introducing and propagating his religion, attacked their spirit. The former alienated the body, the later the soul of the Igbo. And when it is borne in mind that colonialism and missionary work did not operate one after the

92 Dulles, A., **The Reshaping of Catholicism**, (1988), pp. 24 - 25. And presenting the position of the priest in the same line of pyramidic structure, L.Karrer says; "Der Pfarrer war der Hirte der Pfarrei, der die Schafe weidete, für die unverfälschte Weitergabe und Einhaltung der kirchlichen Lehre und Gebote verantwortlich war und der als Vater der Pfarr-Familie die Gläubigen betreute. Zu Beginn der Predigt konnte der Pfarrer noch ungeniert zu seinen 'geliebten Pfarr-Kindern' sprechen. Dieses Leitbild hat ohne Zweifel über lange Zeit die Probe bestanden". "**Erfahrungen von Gemeinden Ohne Pfarrer am Ort...**" **Gemeinde Ohne Pfarrer am Ort**, p. 221.

other, separated in time and with objectives clearly distinct in the natives's view, but rather simultaneously, interrelatedly, and in a mutually complementary manner, then the socio-political stress and the cultural strain on the Igbo by the two combined forces can best be imagined.[93]

The problem of the Europeans at the time of colonization and missionary activity was due to a preconceived idea that the African has no history, no intelligence, that the African "is a child of nature". He has no historical background "outside the fact that he had been a slave in history".[94] Such thoughts are made manifest by what Margery Perham wrote in her report concerning tropical Africa. According to her,

> Until the very recent penetration by Europe the greater part of the continent was without the wheel, the plough or the transport-animal; almost without stone house or clothes, except for skins; without writing and so without history.[95]

Perham's argument showed that the colonizer and the missionary came to Africa expecting to see the same way of life and structure in Europe, but found a different structure and way of life; surprisingly, they failed to realize that man's physical environment influences his economic and cultural activity. Referring to this, Ayandele argues that,

> Without the help of objective anthropology, therefore, nineteenth-century missionaries in Africa could not conceive that what they met on the spot was civilization of some kind; the idea of civilization as taking diverse forms was beyond their ken. Therefore missionaries could not think that Nigerians had their religions, laws, social and moral sanctions, aesthetic appreciation, insight into the meaning of life and its philosophy, types of human relationship and loyalties and reverence which were different from those of Europe and America but were evolved in and best for the Nigerian environment. Hence they did not make any conscious effort to study Nigerian customs and institutions, understand their in-

---

93 Agu, C.C., **Secularization in Igboland:Socio-religious Change and its Challenges to the Church Among the Igbo**; (Peter Lang, Frankfurt, Bern, New York, (1989), p. 257; cf. F.I. Nzimiro, **Family and Kinship in Iboland; A Study in Acculturation Process:** Inaugural-Dissertation for Promotion to the Doctorate Grade in the Faculty of Philosophy, the University of Cologne (1962), p.32. "In fact, it is difficult to disentangle the church from the company (Royal Niger Company) since it was evident that the Church had interests in the financial profit of the Niger trade.

94 Azikiwe, N., **Renascent Africa:** (London, 1968; reproduction of 1944), p. 179; cf. I.K. Okonjo, **The Role of Women in Social Change Among the Igbo of Southern Nigeria Living West of the River Niger:** Submitted in partial fulfillment of the requirement for the degree of Doctor in Philosophy, (Boston University, Boston, 1976), p. 33; "The early missionaries believed that the Igboman had no religion or that whatever religion he had was primitive and destined to perish and disappear".

95 Perham, M., "**The British Problem in Africa**;" in: **F.A.** 29(1951), 638.

ner meaning, the reasons for their existence and the purposes they were expected to fulfill.[96]

Perham's insistence that because the Africans can not write, then they have no history, tends to suggest that history is interchangeable with writing and for her any history that is not documented is no history. It suggests that writing itself has no history. These arguments seem to suggest that there was no history until writing was invented in Africa.

This was the European idea of "history" as a documented happening. But for the African, history is transmitted through stories or orally. No wonder then that the missionaries were imbued with the desire to impart the Gospel of salvation to these "abandoned souls" to the "unlettered barbarians, the downtrodden people of the dark continent, who were sunk in heathenism and were animalistic to the core".[97]

The atrocities the Royal Niger Company perpetrated in Southern Nigeria notwithstanding, Goldie, a colonial administrator, in a letter to Fox Bourne, expressed their task as:

> Sacrificing time, money and health in the arduous work of introducing civilization into one of the wildest and most barbarous regions on earth.[98]

The preconceived idea regarding the traditional Africans can be summed up from Perham's report on the Igbo thusly:

> These people struck the Europeans from the first as being not only unorganized but particularly barbarous and intractable. Reports are almost uniformly unfavourable, not only from traders but also from administrators and missionaries. In the sixteenth century one of our sea captains reported them as "a people of beastly living, without a god, law, religion or

---

96 Ayandele, E.A., **"The Missionary Impact on Modern Nigeria 1842-1914: A political and Social Analysis"; in: Dr. K.O. Dike, Ibadan History Series**, (London, 1966), p. 245; cf. F.B. Welbourn, "**Missionary Stimulus and African Response", in: Colonialism in Africa: 1870-1960; Profiles of Change, African Society and Colonial Rule,** Victor Turner ed., vol. 3, (Chicago, 1971), pp. 330f.

97 Agu, C.C., **Secularization in Igboland..:** (1989), p. 258.

98 Goldie's letter to Fox Bourne, 7/11/1889, quoted by C.C. Agu, op. cit., p. 258; cf. E.A. Ayandele, "**The Relationship between the Church Missionary Society and the Royal Niger Company, 1886-1900**", in: **JHSN**, iv, (1968), 401. For more of such remarks about Africa, see J.P. Jordan, **Bishop Shanahan of Southern Nigeria**, (Dublin, 1949); A.G. Leonard, **The lower Niger and its Tribes**, (London, 1968)2, p. 75; F.K. Ekechi, **Missionary Enterprise and Rivalry in Igboland 1857-1914**, (London, 1971), p. 49.

commonwealth", while in the following century, another declared them "Born and bred villains. A man of integrity is as rare among them as a white falcon".[99]

It will be difficult for such a preconceived idea of a people to change overnight. The missionaries never gave many Africans the chance to explain themselves or do things their own way. They were as one of the prayers formulated for the Africans said: "People wandering in the desert of sin with the devil as the lion looking for them to devour" (in a prayer for the conversion of Africa – *Ekpere maka ntogha nke Africa*).

One will quickly mention here that there were two types of missionaries working in Africa at this period: a large number who collaborated with the colonial administrator; and a small number, who were burning with the zeal of their Father's house, trying to bring as many Africans as possible into heaven. Luke Mbaefo says:

> there were the missionaries whose interest was primarily evangelical, to bring the light of the Christian Gospel to a heathen people. Their mandate comes from the Gospel; "Go, teach all nations". These missionaries belonged to various religious faiths, Catholics, Anglicans and Protestants. It has become clear that missionary work is not only to be understood solely in the religious sense. There is the secular missionaries whose main interest was to convert the natives from savage culture to civilization. In many cases they used the Christian religious missionaries to accomplish their motives... Generally, the religious missionaries preached against superstition, against slave trade and started off the natives on the way to self-reliance and their dignity as persons.[100]

On the Igbo/missionary relationship, Agu reports that "... for the missionary the Igbo were not only sunk in heathenism like their brothers elsewhere throughout black Africa, but they were literally in the firm shackles of the devil".[101]

With such preconceived ideas that there was nothing good in the people and their way of life, the missionaries set out to work among the savages. They were prepared to bulldoze everything they encountered, everything that existed in the form of rituals, customs, tradition, even the communities, and of course the traditional religion. Ekechi, looking at the activity of the missionaries, said:

> The truth is that European missionaries were imbued with the idea that indigenous religion must be destroyed before Christianity could be expected to effect changes in the society. Under no circumstances, therefore, should the new religion be grafted onto the old. And since idol-worship was considered one of the greatest"fortress which impede the es-

---

99 Perham, M., **The British Problem in Africa.** op. cit., p. 21.
100 Mbaefo, L.N., **The Reshaping of African Traditions**: (Enugu, Nigeria, 1988), p. 45.
101 Agu, C.C. **Secularization in Igboland...**,(1989), op.cit., p. 259.

tablishment of the true faith and true morals in this numerous (Igbo) nation", it was therefore felt that the faithful should reject idolatry from the start.[102]

The devastating blow on the Igbo traditional religion and culture by missionary strategies helped in destroying her community structure. The Missionaries' idea of conversion meant removing people from their respective homes, communities and forming a new community of the people of God.

In reality they created a division between brothers, sisters and parents. The idea of believers and non-believers was a construction of the missionaries. Agu, commenting on this division, says;

> Since the adherents of the new religion regarded themselves as the only people who knew God and, naturally, who had a religion, there arose again for the first time in Igbo society believers and non-believers.... But as soon as a few people were converted to Christianity there came into existence a group which considered itself the sole possessor of the true God vis-a-vis all others whose gods were declared false.[103]

The converts to Christianity were taught to underrate the so-called unbelievers and there came to be a big division among a people that had lived happily for centuries. The believers were isolated from their kin and kept in "Christian villages".

> With the 20,000 Francs granted annually to the society of the Holy Ghost Fathers by Rome, specifically for the purchase of slaves, the society encouraged the institution by buying slaves from eager Ibo sellers. These slaves were settled in Christian villages and they constituted the nucleus of the Catholic community in Eastern Nigeria.[104]

The new converts became segregated from others and were forbidden to take part in village activities. They had been washed clean with the water of baptism and were to communicate no more with the unbelievers, who were regarded as the devil's agents.

One of the earliest Christian villages in Nigeria was founded with Chief Idigo of Aguleri around 1892, and contained 202 out of the 15,000 inhabitants of the town. The missionaries gave such immunity to the new converts that they had no respect for the local traditions. This really created a social disintegration, and forced Jordan, one of the earliest missionaries, to admit that;

---

102 Ekechi, F.K., **Missionary Enterprise and Rivalry in Igboland 1857-1914**, (1972), op. cit., p. 148.

103 Agu, C.C., **Secularization in Igboland...**, (1989), op. cit., p. 262.

104 Ayandele, E.A., **The Missionary Impact on Modern Nigeria 1842-1914...**, (1966), op. cit., P. 332; cf. J.P. Jordan, **Bishop Shanahan of Southern Nigeria**, (1949), op. cit., pp. 86-93.

every exclusiveness (of the converts in them) was arousing suspicion and opposition from the rest of the natives... their immunity from native law and custom attracted law-breakers seeking refuge from retribution.[105]

Since the majority of the early converts were mainly slaves bought over by the missionaries and criminals seeking refuge, one thus understands why they dealt rather ruthlessly with the people's institutions, with the backing of the missionaries. Ekechi recorded once how Christians in Onitsha were expressly instructed and encouraged to "do whatever Onitsha forbids to be done in the town".[106] Such encouragements given to converts to break with their pagan environments and relations whom they were taught to regard as non-believers and, as such, their inferiors, ruptured the socio-cultural life of the people.

No wonder a certain chief in Igboland preferred to go to hell where his kin were, according to the missionary, because they were not baptized, instead of going to heaven where his community, with his kin and ancestors, was non-existent. On this division of the people's community, Charles Agu wrote;

Children were trained to look upon their parents as living a life of sin, thus introducing a subversive element into the household. Native authority was therefore seriously menaced, for, asks Morel, "how can the convert entertain his former respect for rulers whom he has been taught to regard as morally and spiritually his inferior?".[107]

Orishatuke Faduma, a Sierra Leonian Yoruba, while addressing the congress on Africa at the 'Gammon Theological Seminary', in Atlanta, and commenting on the destructive role of some missionaries ventures, sarcastically defined a Christian in that era thus;

That which distinguished a heathen from a Christian is not moral character or allegiance to Christ, but outward dress. The stove-pipe hat, the feathered bonnet, the high-heeled

---

105 Jordan, J.P., **Bishop Shanahan of Southern Nigeria**; (1949), op. cit., p. 30.

106 Ekechi, F.K., **Missionary Enterprise and Rivalry in Igboland...**,(1972), p. 36.

107 Agu, C.C., **Secularization in Igboland...**, (1989) p. 267; cf. E.D. Morel, **Nigeria: Its Peoples and Its Problems,** (London, 1968), p. 215, quoted by C.C. Agu, ibid. Ayndele writes: "And although the missionaries might not intend it, the children were being taught to be disrespectful to their parents in regarding them as indulging in vile and inhuman practices. The effect was to sever the children from the home, the fountain-head of their lives, and from all the instincts, moral teachings, ideas and inspirations connected with it. Consequently they became deluded with the idea that the less African they were the more Christian they became"; cf. **The Missionary Impact on Modern Nigeria 1842-1914**, (1966), op. cit., p.243

shoes, the gloved hands, and all these under the burning tropical heat, make a man a Christian gentleman.[108]

There was total disrespect of what the people stood for. The people's shrines, which had acted as gathering points and a cord for community life, were destroyed.

Defiantly and imprudently, they killed and ate animals offered to and reserved for the gods, an act which in many communities were taboo. Agu correctly wrote that masks, which were regarded, revered and dreaded by some communities as embodiment of the spirit of their ancestors, were unmasked and defiled with impunity.[109]

The dwindling and final abolition of the slave trade forced the missionaries to seek a new strategy for evangelization, which they found in education. Although education helped greatly in improving the people's life, it was through it that the missionaries completed the program of destabilization, disintegration and revolutionization of the traditional African society and culture. The programs in the schools were often geared at biasing and turning the minds of the children against the custom and tradition of their fathers.[110] Education also brought about class distinctions among Africans. Those who were educated by the missionaries saw themselves as being between the Africans and the Europeans – and naturally looked down on their kin who were not equally privileged. Such class distinctions helped in breaking the community.

It seems that the missionaries were so preoccupied with preparing the Africans for heaven that little attention was paid to their earthly harmony as expressed in the traditional African community life. The Christian community was composed of men drawn from different lineages, and their attitude towards each other was that of fraternity existing among members of one faith. The community became a new social group in a pagan community, and the Church did not attract, during her early period, the traditional leaders of the

---

108 Cf. J.W.E. Bowen, quoted by E.A. Ayandele, **The Missionary Impact on Modern Nigeria 1842- 1914...,** (1966), p. 246.

109 Agu, C.C., op. cit., pp. 267-268; cf. E. Isichei, **Entirely for God: The Life of Michael Iwenesi Tansi,** (Macmillan Press, London, 1980), pp. 42f. For further information concerning the missionaries and the early converts see Chinua Achebe's **Things Fall Apart,** pp. 161ff., Idem, **No Longer at Ease**, p. 151; Idem **Arrow of God**, p. 47; J. Munoye, **The only Son**, (AWS Nr. 21, London, 1966), p. 57; Oliver Onwubiko, **Principal Elements of Igbo Traditional Religion**, (unpubl. BD Dissertation, Bigard Memorial Seminary, Enugu, 1980), p. 267; F.K. Ekechi, **Missionary Enterprise and Rivalry...**, (1972),op. cit., pp. 9, 36, 161f.; C.K. Meek, **Law and Authority in a Nigerian Tribe: A Study in Indirect Rule**; (1950), p.48.

110 Cf. F.B. Welbourn, "**Missionary Stimulus and African Response**, in: **Colonialism in Africa 1970-1960,** vol. 3, V. Turner ed., (Chicago, 1971), pp. 321-330

community.[111] It is thus evident that there was some resistance to whatever was going on at this period. The Church can only be better incarnated in Africa, by first of all studying African social institutions and culture, and secondly, by allowing the Gospel of Jesus Christ to manifest itself or shine through African Culture.

One other obstacle that faced the missionaries was the question of polygamy. Although the non-conformity of polygamy with Christian doctrine is understandable, one may question the destruction of family or community life by asking already polygamous men to renounce all their wives but one in order to be Christians. Our concern is on community life and the effects it had on its members.

> the preposterous regulation that polygamists who wanted full membership and privileges of the Church must first disown all wives but one.[112]

This regulation upset the traditional African community and what it stood for, and unfortunately, at this period, every one that was somebody in Africa was a polygamist. No wonder conversion was more effective on the children than adults.

This disruption of the traditional African community created enmity among families and villages. The missionaries never saw this as a problem, since their concern was with the individual, rather than with the community. They failed to realize that the indigenous African society was community oriented. Ayandele notes that;

When a missionary converted individuals in a community he removed units from organic whole and thereby undermined the monolithic structure of the community. The converts not only imbibed a new set of religious beliefs but began to nurse alien ideas, economic ambitions and political aspirations of their own, detrimental to the welfare and solidarity of the community.[113]

The renunciation of traditional religion in Africa without a grounded Christian doctrine left the traditional African hanging in the air, since he could neither hold on to the traditional religion which was the source of his morals, civil and political obligation to his community, which were now played down upon, nor could he hold to the new religion, in which he looked up to the Europeans of the Royal Niger Company and some of the missionaries around him in his search for good examples, but found them wanting.

---

111 Nzimiro, F.I., **Family and Kinship in Iboland: A study in Acculturation Process**, (1962), p. 65.

112 Ayandele, E.A., **The Missionary Impact on Modern Nigeria 1842-1914...**, (1966), p. 330.

113 ibid., pp. 330-331.

As we earlier mentioned, our task here is not to assess the marvelous works of the missionaries, but to look at the failures of the Church at this period and to recommend a more effective pastoral strategies. One should note that it was the mission schools and their policies that contributed to the nationalist movement all over Africa. The missionaries contributed immensely, though indirectly, to the achievement of independence in Africa.

They taught and encouraged people to fight for their rights through schools and the establishment of journals and magazines, which made observations on political events in the African situation. Education made Africans think back and question their existence and hope in life. These questions opened the way to the recovery of their past values.

3.3.1. Welfarism as a Method of Evangelisation

When we talk about moving towards an *umunna* ecclesiology, it means another way of being Church that is meaningful to the Igboman. This presupposes that the old way needs a modification or a reappraisal. When the missionaries arrived, they did not find things easy, being faced with hydra-headed problems ranging from the language barrier, harsh climatic condition, or tropical diseases, to how to bring the Good News to the people.

The Catholic Church, being a latecomer when compared with the "Church missionary society", (C.M.S.), sought ways and means to attract the natives. It is a pity that in this period of evangelization, much emphasis was laid on number than on the quality of converts.[114] Being victims of the period, the welfare system of evangelisation was opted for. Ozigboh described this initial evangelization thus:

> The missionary policy of the Prefecture during the first fifteen years (1886-1900), may be characterized as the use of charity as an instrument of evangelization. Charitable programs were embarked upon as a means to one desired end: to gain the good will and the conversion of the people to the catholic religion... They rendered their services 'free of charge', asking in return no more than that the people should be appreciative of and receptive to their religious message. Their charity was not disinterested. It was indeed, a *Quid Pro Quo*, an investment for which the expected dividends would be spiritual and psychological.[115]

---

114 Probable reason being that these missionaries get subvention from their mother countries according to the number of converts they have. Since the greater the number, the more work expected.

115 Ozigboh, I.R.A., **Roman Catholicism in South Eastern Nigeria (1885-1931): A Study in Colonial Evangelism;** (Etukokwu Publishers, Nigeria, 1988), p. 58. The missionaries

This strategy was in use until the end of the civil war. These welfare methods took different strategies. The missionary activity in Igboland took place during the period of slave trade and the missionaries used this opportunity and other methods they deemed fit.

3.3.1.1. The Christian Village

The initial policies and method of evangelisation had far-reaching effects, and the missionaries led by Father Lutz opted first of all for the salvation of the slaves who were either meant for human sacrifice or exportation. They opened up Christian villages where these ransomed slaves could stay and be taken care of and be taught the Christian message. This was also an institutionalized charity or welfare system.[116]This method of buying back slaves was considered the most favourable method under those circumstances. There the Catholic faith was taught and this led to the formation of Christian villages.[117] For P.B.Clarke, the philanthropic missionaries of the 1890s saw the Christian village as the most powerful weapon for the attack on *la traite* and the best method of civilizing and Catholicizing. I use the word "Catholicize" because the missionaries never intended merely to Christianize. They were of the Roman Catholic Church – the one, true Church.[118]

There was a disruption of community life, families were divided into pagans and Christians. They saw themselves as warring factions. Father Relling's report of 1894 gives a survey of the situation as he expressed:

> The converts are not admitted indiscriminately into the Christian village. They have certain conditions to subscribe to; (a) The man must have one wife or promise to have only one. This must be done before he comes into the village.[119] (b) He must have nothing to do

---

had no time to study the culture of the people and psychologically they defeated the people by inculcating in them that everything of theirs was pagan and as such must be avoided. European way of life became synonymous with christianity and to be a christian was to behave like an European.

116 Ozigboh says: "The cluster of houses in which these persons were quartered in and close to the mission station, gradually developed into a village, distinct from the indigenous villages. This village was under the direction of the missionaries". ibid., pp. 66-67.

117 Cf. C.A. Obi, **A hundred Years of the Catholic Church in Eastern Nigeria**; (FEP Publishers, Onitsha, Nigeria, 1985),p. 35.

118 Clarke, P.B., "**The method and Ideology of the Holy Ghost Fathers in Eastern Nigeria", in: Journal of Religion in Africa**, Vol. vi, 2(1974), p. 107.

119 This is an action which is still persistent today that needs to be looked into. There is no rationale in asking a happy family of more than one wife to destroy such a community in accepting Christianity. The promise of having only one wife can be applied to those not yet married or have only one wife before embracing christianity, but to separate the al-

with idols.[120] (c) He must be willing to be instructed in the christian faith and to follow other christians in the exercise of piety and to live unreproachable life. If any of these is broken later, the person is immediately expelled. The christians in the village are happy and they know we love them and are devoted to them. We try to repress the ancient habits by limiting the contacts of our christians with their pagan countrymen and even with their friends and relations (meme avec leurs amis et parents)...[121]

The above report is self contradictory. How on earth can love, care and happiness be expressed when the people's freedom is limited at the point of refusing them to communicate with their kin and friends? It was a sort of forced monastic life.[122] It seemed this method worked for some early missionaries in Africa. For P.B.Clarke, it was a prototype *village de liberte*, a system employed by the French in the Western Sudan to include the flotsam and jetsam uprooted by the Jihads waged by the Islamic leaders such as Al Haji Omar and warriors like Samovi. The *village de liberte* and the Christian village were in effect a temporary compromise between the social institutions of Europe and Africa.[123]

3.3.1.2. The School Apostolate

Education was part of the overall strategy of the welfare evangelization and an important one, since it was difficult to communicate without breaking the language barrier. Father Lutz indeed laid the foundation for literary education. Obi documented that:

---

ready happy family, which in most cases brought enmity in the community, must be addressed as a pastoral issue.

120 There was more to this, since every Igbo culture for the missionaries, was superstitious and fetishst, converts are not to live their own life rather the imported life. Jordan reports that the influences (pagan) were certainly considerable because everything in native life from the cradle to the grave bore the stamp of false worship... So there was quite a strong case for removing neophytes from such a host of evil influences and placing them in surroundings that would foster instead of choking their newly acquired Supernatural life of Grace. Cf. J. Jordan, **Shanahan of Southern Nigeria,** (Dublin, 1971), p.28.

121 "**Bubendorf to superior General**", **APS**, **B. 191/v/xii**, Onitsha, 10th March, 1897, quoted by I.R.A. Ozigboh, op. cit., p. 74.

122 Cf. E. Isichei, **A History of the Igbo people**; (London, 1976), p. 162.

123 Clarke, P.B., **The Methods and Ideology of the Holy Ghost Fathers in Eastern Nigeria**; op. cit., p. 1.

children were put into nursery schools, boys and girls in primary schools, the young men and women learnt different trades according to each one's aptitude.[124]

After the educational foundation of Lutz and his band of three, came the man whose educational strategy worn him a lot of admiration. This was Shanahan, who later became the Bishop in 1920. He employed the pragmatic policy of using school education as a principal instrument of missionary evangalisation. This method is sometimes referred to as "the magic school wonder of Bishop Shanahan". Jordan described Shanahan thus:

> The school was for him all things else, an instrument of the apostolate. It might give Counsel about hygienic living quarters, pure water, treatment of fever and dysentery, prevention of leprosy and a host of other things... And no school would be completely successful in his eyes, as long as a single pagan child remained outside its portals and its influence.[125]

The school system apart from helping to educate the pupils was to a large extent the bedrock for the consciousness of African identity in both world politics and culture. The system also concentrated more on children leaving their parents out. These schools produced the first Church hierarchies like John Cross Anyogu, who later became bishop, Michael Iwene Tansi,[126] Wil-

---

124 Obi, C.A., **The French Pioneers, 1885-1905**, in: C.A. Obi, ed. "**A hundred Years of the Catholic Church in Eastern Nigeria 1885-1985**", op. cit., p. 36. Cf. I.R.A. Ozigboh, op. cit., p. 78. The first mention of school in the carefully kept journal of the mission was on 18th. Oct., 1887, 22 months after the arrival of the Catholic missionaries at Onitsha... It would seem that the school was stared when the children of school age were ransomed in reasonable numbers... Education remained just an aspect of the general apostolate for children (**Oeuvres des enfants**). Cf. C.A. Obi, **Igbo Response to the Holy Ghost Missionary presence at Onitsha and its Environs 1885-1930**, (London, 1980), p. 23. "The pioneer Holy Ghost Fathers - Father Lutz and his band of three, Father Joseph Horne and two lay brothers, Hermas and John Gotto...", brought the early educational experience to bear on the Igbos.

125 Jordan, J.P., **Bishop Shanahan of Eastern Nigeria**; op. cit., p. 98. D.B. Abernethy, wrote: "All the mission-groups in Southern Nigeria were interested in educating the common people, but none served this cause more energetically than the Roman Catholics of the Eastern Region"; **The Political Dilema of Popular Education**, (Stanford University Press, California, 1969), p. 39.

126 Cf. C.I. Eke, **Priestly and Religious Vocations,** in: C.A. Obi, ed., op. cit., p. 306. The beatification Course of Michael Iwene Tansi has already started. The Diocesan Tribunal for the Course of his beatification was formally inaugurated in the Archdiocese of Onitsha, on the 20th of January, 1986. Although he died and was buried as a Cistercian Monk in England, January 1964, his remains were brought back to lay among his people at Onitsha in Sept. 1986. For further information see S.N. Ezeanya, **Lord, Increase our**

liam Obeleagu – these were pioneer seminarians. Great politicians and businessmen and women are products of the mission schools.

3.3.1.3. The Hospital Apostolate

The missionaries were burdened with the hopelessness of the system of medical care in Igboland on their arrival. There existed the traditional herbalists and medicine men and women, whose art and methods were not only crude, but beyond the comprehension of the missionaries. The traditional medical care took the whole person into consideration – physical, spiritual and psychological, and as such the practices of the herbalists were easily mixed with occultism. Because of this, the indigenous medical practice was branded magical and superstitious.

> The use of psychology and emotional appeals laid traditional medicine open to accusation of magic and superstition. Traditional medicine is also suspect and despised for several reasons: Its practitioners are generally illiterate, unduly secretive and shady in their medical practice.[127]

The missionaries had to battle with both their health and those of their would-be associates. This was not an easy task. The mission houses became 'sick-bays' because of the white man's medicine, and Lutz, who had a little experience in medicine and an overwhelming interest in the practice, utilized the opportunity. He once wrote:

> A form of ministry very consoling to us and which gains us the good-will of all, is the care which we daily give to the sick.[128]

In order to have a healthy mind in a healthy body they went out of their way in helping the sick. The caring of the sick later became the tool for evangelisation and conversion, as observed by Lutz, that "morning and evening, a long file of their unfortunate sick arrive at the mission so that we might soothe their

---

Faith: Lenten Pastoral of Onitsha Archdiocese, 12th. Feb., Onitsha, 1986, pp. 16-18; E. Isichei, op. cit.

127 Ozigboh, I.R.A., **Roman Catholicism...** op.cit., pp. 59-60; **The Image of Africa: British Ideas and Action 1780-1850**; (University of Wisconsin Press, Madison, 1964), chapter 14. The death of many Europeans merited West Africa as being the most dangerous climate in the world. At this time no one including the Europeans knew that the fevers were due to mosquitos which carry plasmodial parasites.

128 APS, B. 191/B/1; The Propaganda Fide concession runs in part, "...**privilegium exercendi per se vel per missionaros sibi subjectos aetes medicinate at Chirurgiae extra tamen sanguinis effusionem**". The general permission to all catholic missionaries was given later in 1936.

ills. They are of all ages but, the number of them are children... In caring for their bodies we have the sweetest consolation of saving their souls too".[129]

Once in 1890, when a dysentery epidemic ravaged Onitsha, Lutz utilized the opportunity to get more money for the health care projects. And one of his strategy to get this money from his sponsors in France was to insist that the hospital would make it possible for patients to receive more religious instructions or baptism when death became imminent.[130] This does not play down on the importance and seriousness with which they cared for the sick.

Most of the inmates of the Christian villages were ex-slaves and the village n'er-do-wells, so the community never took them seriously. The Christian village method of evangelisation was later abolished by Father Shanahan in 1904, using, instead, the school as a means of evangelisation.[131] The school system produced the first agitators for independence and since they saw the Church as collaborating with the colonial masters, they alienated themselves from the Church.

But the fruits of the mission schools are many. After the Nigerian Biafra war, not only were the missionaries asked to leave, the schools were taken over by the Government. Thus the Church lost her weapon of evangelisation. The hospitals could not help matters, since it was no longer on a welfare or charitable basis, and rather had to compete with the Government and other private institutions in health care services. Even the mission hospitals are now more expensive than the Government ones.

This means that they can never be used as an effective method of evangelisation. The question now is, since these three major methods are no more operational, what other alternatives can be suggested for the propagation of faith? What is the position of the Church in Igboland today regarding community and people's participation in life of the Church?

---

129 APS, Bulletin General, vol. xv, p. 546. Lutz was correct in describing them as unfortunate, because without the sickness they would have never dared to come.

130 Cf. APS, Bulletin General, vol. xvi, p. 334. This method is coupled with the Europeans paying for the baptism of any mission child by getting the benefit of the child bearing his or her name. A practice that is still used by some missionaries in Africa today. For them the African names are pagan names, even when the African's name is **Chibuikem** (God is my strength), the European name Stanley or Kennedy is preferred.

131 Cf. C.A. Obi, **The Missionary Contributions of Bishop Shanahan, C.S.Sp., 1902-1932**, in: C.A. Obi ed., op. cit., p. 108. At this time slave trade had also dropped.

3.4. A Relevant Structure for the Church in Igboland

Having investigated the method, history, nature and function of the Church as was expressed by the missionaries, one may ask: how is the Church structured and how does it function two decades after the missionaries' exit from Igboland? It is surprising to note that in Igboland, the mission or parish is considered for pastoral purposes as consisting of a certain number of outstations, i.e. territorial subsections of the mission. Despite the fact that so many towns are now parishes (as one-town parishes), the old missionary system remains the official policy. The consideration is primarily geographical, organizational (C.W.O., C.F.O., Youths etc.), and administrative.

The priest is the dominant person in the parish. It is his job to organize everything and so he arranges the Mass attendance schedule. He visits the sick, hears confessions and buries the dead. People approach him with their problems and to seek advice. Many a time, the priests are exhausted trying to be providers for needs which are far too many for them to handle. The whole Church activities revolve around the priest. He has to perform his priestly office publicly for men in the name of Christ and the primary ministry with the power of the holy Orders is to offer sacrifice and to remit sin.

Whatever happens in the Church, be it 'the Church in action' or 'action in the Church', it was or is around this function of the priest 'to offer sacrifice and to remit sin'. The point is that the priest is the principal pastoral agent and so pastoral action is determined by his activities. This function of the priest as the principal actor, centered around the Eucharist and Confessions, is further amplified in conferences and pastoral letters of bishops, in order to highlight the role of the priest. An example of such pronouncements can be seen in Archbishop now (Cardinal) Francis Arinze's pastoral letter of 1977, where he says:

> The work assigned to clerics in the Church is to Sanctify the people of God (by Holy Eucharist, other sacraments, prayer, blessing), to give the Word of God (by preaching, catechetics, religious books) and to gather the people of God together (to rule them). Clerics are called to give leadership to all in the Church in the proper discharge of this threefold function. No other activity of theirs can supply for the absence of this.[132]

The people are passive regarding the Church's life. Their duty is to come to Mass as families, couples or by themselves. They have a common faith, stand together in Church and pray together. They also share a common loyalty to the Catholic Church and to their parish. The only identification to the parish is the

132 Arinze, F., "The Christian as Leader", **Lenten Pastoral 1977**, Trinity Press Onitsha, (1977), Nrs. 22, 23. The words in italics are mine.

reception of all their needs for salvation. They are receivers as described in the Canon Law, which was published in 1917 stating that they have the right "to receive from the clerics spiritual goods and strong help for salvation" (Canon 682). In 1983 the New Code of Canon Law described the role of the laity in much more positive tones. Yet the attitude of the laity in the Church remains passive. They wait for the parish priest to give commands.

There are many Catholics who want to be more involved in the life of the Church. They get involved in so many parish activities, but they still see themselves as priest's helpers. One can see that the apostolate of the laity as seen as subordination to the priestly ministry did not, however, restore their role, which is contrary to **Lumen Gentium** Art.33. The activities of the laity are not those of participation, but that of assistance rendered to the priest, which is also contrary to **Ad Gentes** Art.23. The lay person in Igboland do not see their role as a member of the Church in actively sharing in building up the Church – conveying grace to individual human beings.[133] Some years ago, Pope Pius XII described such active Catholics and their work with the term "Catholic Action". In the Congress of the members of Catholic Action who gathered in Assisi on October 14, 1951, the Pope said: "Catholic Action... is a tool in the hand of the hierarchy and should, as it were, be its prolonged arm".[134]

Even though the Pope modified his position six years later in his address to the Second World Congress of members of Catholic Action, the situation in Igbo Church has not changed much. The Pope at this time said that: "This apostolate always remains an apostolate of the laity and does not become a 'Hierarchical apostolate', even if it is exercised with ecclesiastical mandate".[135] This new view of the Pope was emphasized further by the Fathers of the Second Vatican Council six years later.

The introduction of the parish Council did not help much, for the priest is still dominant. Sometimes it is the priest who invites people to be members of the parish Council instead of using the Igbo method of representation. The Councilors do not represent any particular group of parishioners. Their task is often reserved to certain maintenance jobs around the Church buildings, taxing and collecting dues from the people, and preparing for the harvest thanksgiving and launching of parish projects.

The Church is still referred to as *Uka-fada* (Rev. Father's Church), not "our Church". A lot of people have evaluated missionary success or failure according to the degree of Western modernization which the missionaries induced among the evangelized people. Since the ideal for christian missionary work

---

133 Rahner, K., **Theology of Pastoral Action**, Herder and Herder, New York, (1968), p. 68.

134 Pius XII, AAS 43, (1951), 789.

135 Pius XII, AAS 49, (1957), 928.

was to help the backward cultures to move up the ladder and join the more developed Western civilization[136], they neglected the people's way of life. The exit of the foreign missionaries did not result in a change in method. Community life is still relegated to the background.

The sacraments are yet to be community celebrations. One notices how enthusiastic the people are during the traditional initiation rites within *umunna* and how unconcerned they are during a Church baptism. For the Christian initiation rites, it is a common practice to see a woman presenting her child to the priest without the presence of her husband or relations, and sometimes even the Godparents are missing. Initiation sacraments are being reduced to private ritual acts between the priest, the speechless child and the ignorant mother. The priest goes through the rites alone, while the community spirit is exhibited during traditional initiations or naming ceremonies with pomp and with every member of *umunna* in attendance.

The sacramental system focusses more on the rites, stresses Church attendance and the reception of the sacraments. To be a good Catholic is measured by the regular attendance to confessions, Mass, reception of holy Communion, membership in pious societies and payment of dues and levies. The pattern that centers activities of the Church around sacramental life has been the main blueprint for evangelisation. It makes the parish center, and sometimes station Churches, loci of intense religious activities, which unfortunately do not influence Christian life in the villages, *umunna* and families. These local places are where the life of the people are expressed.

Having seen the life of the Igbo and their community spirit, it would do the Church a disfavour to place a great accent on the reception of the sacraments and introduction of pious societies in a way capable of causing a split between faith and people's everyday life, especially the community life. When a split occurs, an integrated grasping of and experiencing the sacraments cannot be achieved. The communal life of the Igbo is called for, to make these celebrations more meaningful. Instead of relying on the ecclesiology of Vatican I, which was basically apologetic Counter-Reformation, insisting on authority, the institutional and hierarchical structures, we have to turn to Vatican II ecclesiology, that is, *communio*.

Dulles describes Vatican I ecclesiology as being an institutional one, characterized by clericalism, juridicism and triumphalism.[137] Although there are

---

136 Ranger, T.O., **Themes in the Christian History of central Africa**, edited by T.O. Ranger and J. Weller, London, Ibadan, Heinemann, 1975, p. 93; P.A. Kalilombe, "*From Outstations to small Christian communities*", in: **SPEARHEAD**, Nr.80-83, Gaba Publications, Kenya, 1984, pp.8-9.

137 Dulles, A., **Models of the Church : A critical Assessment of the Church in all its aspects;** Garden City, New York, Doubleday and company, (1974), pp. 13,31,36.

some traces of the spirit of Vatican II in the Igbo Church, the principal policy is still that of Vatican I. There is an intensification of centralization and uniformity within the Church. It is nice to remark that some bishops are realizing that their vocation is that of service and some have already started to allow or encourage participation, partnership and have given responsibilities to all levels of the church structure.

We must also admit that changes are not easy. There is a tendency of holding to the old order which the Irish missionaries bequeathed to the Igbo Church that makes changes very difficult. People prefer to take to the old ways than opt for a change. Any positive move towards inculturation is barred by the fear of some Church leaders about Rome's reaction. Even a rector of a major seminary thought it was an achievement to tell a papal nuncio that the seminarians as of 1976 were still saying their prayers in Latin. The Church leaders want to maintain a good names of holding fast to what the missionaries handed over to them.

There is marginal involvement of the laity in ecclesiastical issues, and this does not help in the formation of a really caring community. Because the Church was involved in the building of schools, hospitals and giving of arms, the majority of the lay people think that the Church is very rich. This brings them to seek personal and material gain for every service they render to the Church. This is alien to the spirit of *umunna*. The Church as such is not seen as "our" Church. Thus the *umunna* spirit is lacking since the Igbo cannot identify himself with the Church. The *umunna* spirit works where one is accepted as what one is and be able to identify oneself with the group. The Church in Igboland today is still far from giving this option or opportunity: hence a call goes out for *Umunna* Christian Communities.

3.5. Conclusion

In concluding, we venture to say that though the Church operates on many models, there is yet the need to find one that appeals to all peoples at all times. Even to find one that appeals to a particular people to bring them into full realization of the Gospel of Christ remains a challenge to the Church. Hence the charge of the Second Vatican Council that an alternative model be found for the Church.

The realization of the *Communio Ecclesia*, cannot even be achieved by the existing parish structure in Igboland without modifications, since the problems that existed centuries ago are very much prevalent today in their modern intensity. There as the attachment to the parish churches to so many considerations other than the love for the children of God. Also a community spirit was missing in the parishes.

It does appear that the entire effort of the missionaries boils down to welfarism. This is exemplified and summarized by the missionary modes in Christian village, school and Hospital apostolate. The idea behind these methods appears to lie in the distresses and uncomfortable dispositions with which the missionaries were confronted. A jewel was contained in the earthenware that was the uncivilized nature of the way of the life of the traditional Igboman. This jewel is the *umunna* community.

It is painful to realize that even after the white missionaries had gone, the native work force that inherited the evangelisation could not effect any change in method: foreign unworkable models continued and the Church remained *uka fada*, a cultic affair. It is at this point that we wish to unveil the *umunna* Community as the veritable alternative that will bring the traditional Igboman to be involved in the spread of the Gospel, both to himself and to others. Thus there is the need for a more relevant structure of the Church in Igboland – a small basic community, namely, the *Umunna* Christian Community.

In our next Chapter, we shall attempt to explore some other, similar models to the *umunna* that have worked and are working extraordinarily well in other Third World countries to substantiate our claim for the *umunna* ecclesiology. This will review the BCCs as an effective means of evangelisation: the BECs in Latin America and those of African countries. These considerations will launch us into the full ramifications of the *umunna* community as the basic Community.

Chapter Four: Basic christian communities and evangelisation

4.0. Introduction

Christ did not come to abolish the laws and the prophets, thus his Mystical Body is also not here to abolish the people's way of life, but to sanctify them. We give thanks to the Fathers of the Second Vatican Council, who did not treat the Church abstractly as an ahistorical or metahistorical monument sheltered from the concrete course of history, but as an existence in history made more relevant in its nearness and usefulness to culture as a people's way of life.

Just as the Sabbath is made for man, so also is the Church made for human beings.[1] The Church's structure and functioning should take cognisance of the people's culture. It ought to make use of the past to project the future and not be tied to the past, as if it is a fixed historical reality set in some ideal time or past that is to be taken as the sole reference-point or criterion in trying to understand and evaluate it. Azevedo puts it more clearly:

> The whole past will live on in the consciousness of Church members today, but ecclesiology need not confine itself to that past... be constructed on the present of a Church that lives in the midst of human beings and a complex world, finding its reason for being in service to both... Operating in the present, then, ecclesiology is always asking questions about the future of our past.[2]

This is exactly what the Fathers of the Second Vatican Council did. In this Chapter, we shall examine the Second Vatican Council's understanding of the basic foundations of the Church. The deliberation of the Council Fathers has already produced some fruits, and we shall look at these fruits by glancing at the BEC of Latin America; and the AMECEA Countries and Zaire, both in Africa. The council Fathers explained the word "communion" as fundamentally meaning our "communing" with God through Jesus Christ in the Holy Spirit. This trinitarian communion comes to us through Word of God and the

---

1 Cf. R. Alves, **Theology of Human Hope**, Corpus Books, Washington D.C., (1969), especially chapter iv, p.13; J.M. Bonino, "Historical Praxis and Christian Identity", in: R. Gibellini, ed., **Frontiers of Theology in Latin America**, Maryknoll, New York, Orbis Books, 1978.

2 Azevedo, M.deC., **BEC in Brazil...op.cit.,** (1987), p. 188.

sacraments. The foundation of this is faith that leads to baptism. The Council expressed the basic foundations or functions of the Church for a better understanding of the Church community. Eucharist is the nourishment and building up the Christian life of the members of the mystical Body of Christ to be like the real Body of Christ.[3]

4.1. The Basic Foundation of the Church Community

The elementary aspect of Christian way of life and the understanding of the New Testament concept of Christian community as a place where Christian living is made manifest, a place where the word of God is made present, make the basic function of the Church clearer to us. They lead to the basic, center and heart of the life of the Church.

There is a three-fold definition of the basic foundations of the Church, which is based on faith, hope and love. These make up the basic life of the Church and nourish the Christian life. The Church as mission is seen as a basic natural movement, with the responsibility to receive, to praise and to distribute.

The New Testament reports these three basic characters of the community are to give witness to the faith and hope, to hear the Good News; to celebrate the Eucharist, to pray, sing and to share, give and receive in solidarity – *agape – diakonia*. The Fathers of the Second Vatican Council mentioned these three basic concepts of Christian community life and threw more light onto the issue by their reference to the teaching of the church Fathers, who saw the three-fold functions of Jesus as that of a teacher, priest and king. These became the basic elements of the teaching of the Church. In the Constitution on the Church, the Fathers related these functions to those of the Bishop and priests as teacher, priest and king. They affirmed and described the Church as having the task to hear the word of God, to practice Christian fraternity and to celebrate the Eucharist.

A Christian community experiences in itself the presence of the Risen Lord as Jesus says: "Where two or three are gathered in my name..." He is the head of the Church; the faithful are members of his Body. The most important characteristic of the community is to be in union with Christ and open to the

---

3 Cf. **Synod Report:** "Communion with the Body of Christ in the Eucharist signifies and brings about, or builds up, the intimate union of all the faithful in the Body of Christ, which is the Church, op. cit., p. 15; cf. LG. 11; 1 Cor. 10:16. John Paul 11, **Christifideles Laici**: "The Body of Christ in the Holy Eucharist sacramentalizes this communion, that is, it is a sign and actually brings about the intimate bonds of communion among all the faithful in the Body of Christ which is the Church..." op. cit., pp. 18-19.

Holy Spirit and to bear witness to Christ in three ways, as we will soon see in the forthcoming paragraphs.

4.1.1. Martyria

This is giving witness to the faith and announcing the Good News. This term *martyria* is a basic term which includes the complete action of the community to spread and deepen the faith in the Risen Lord. Pope Paul VI's statement that the Church "exists in order to evangelize" (EN 14), has inspired many authors.

Taking Paul VI's position, David Bohr defines evangelization so broadly as to include proclamation by word and by deed and in fact practically the whole life of the Church. And for him, the primary goal of evangelization is conversion.[4] For Jon Sobrino, the Church achieves its goal when it effectively proclaims the gospel to the poor by Word and by deed.[5]

Roger Haight, expressing his own view, says that the Church exists in order to turn outwardly to the world by participating in the mission of God, especially through evangelization and human development.[6] The basic action of giving witness to the Resurrection or rather the paschal mystery is always the life of the Christian.[7] And in the end it is the relationship of each Christian with Jesus who calls God his Father. And it is the life that comes from God through Jesus to each man, and the opening up of God to each person, as the

---

4 Bohr, D., "**Evangelization: The Essential and Primary Mission of the Church**", in: **Jurist**, 39(1979): 40-87.

5 Sobrino, J., **The True Church and the Poor**, (Maryknoll, Orbis Books, New York, 1974), especially see chapter 9, "**Evangelization as Mission of the Church**", pp. 253-301.

6 Haight, R. "**The 'Established' Church as Mission: The Relation of the Church to the Modern world**", in: **Jurist** (1979): 4-39; cf. R.D. Haight, **An Alternative Vision: An Interpretation of Liberation Theology**, (Paulist, New York, 1984), pp. 178-185.

7 Concerning catechesis and evangelization with reference to the encyclical **Catechesi tradendae;** R. Bleistein wrote:"Ein Katechese steht weder im Gegensatz noch in Trennung zur Evangelisierung. Es besteht aber auch keine einfache Identität. Beide sind vielmehr eng miteinander verbunden, indem sie sich gegenseitig ergänzen und vollenden". R. Bleistein, **Kirche Jungendarbeit**, p. 97, quoted by Lim Byeng-Hun, op. cit., p. 87; Cf.Acts 13:3f; F. Klostermann, **Kirche. Ereignis und Institution**, (Wien, 1976), p. 34f; cf. **Synod Report:** "The mystery of divine life which the church shares must be proclaimed to all peoples... Evangelization is the first duty, not only for bishops, but also for priests and deacons, and indeed for all the faithful", p.13; **Ad Gentes, nr. 2; Lumen Gentium, nr. 25**. And the 1985 Synod of Bishops declared that: "Evangelization is the first duty, not only for bishops, but also for priests and deacons, and indeed for all faithful." **The final report and message to the people of God of the Extraordinary General Assembly of the Synod of Bishops;**" (1985), p.13.

action of God, as his promise, that we experience and try to live up to.[8] The giving witness and the content of this message comes from the hearing and the life of those who give this witness.[9]

The first task of the Christian community at each place usually is to give on the message of the good news, to start new communities. It is always an evangelisation within the community itself and beyond. The Good News is never kept in a bookshelf, it is lived and made visible in the society.[10] The missionary aspect of the church and the announcing of the Good News are one and the same thing. Mission is therefore not just a side aspect but essential for the spreading of the Good News. Through example, preaching, sacraments and other means of grace, the Church leads its members to participate actively in the salvation mystery, according to the Second Vatican Council:

> The mission of the Church is carried out by means of that activity through which, in obedience to Christ's command and moved by the grace and love of the Holy Spirit, the Church makes itself fully present to all men and peoples in order to lead them to the faith, freedom and peace of Christ by the example of its life and teaching, by the sacraments and other means of grace. Its aim is to open up for all men a free and sure path to full participation in the mystery of Christ (**Ad Gentes**, Nr.5).

To evangelize means therefore to bring the Good News to all mankind, to all levels of the society; to change man from inside.[11] In this basic function,

---

8 Cf. Paul VI, **Evangelii Nuntiandi**, nrs. 17f. "Evangelization is made by means of witnesses; but a witness testifies, not just by words but by his own life too." **Synod Report**, p. 13

9 Byeng-Hun, puts it thus: "Das Zeugnis durch das Leben als Verbindung des Inhaltes der frohen Botschaft mit dem konkreten Leben ist die zentrale Aufgabe der Martyria". op. cit., p. 86; Cf. L. Karrer, op. cit., "**Erfahrungen von Gemeinden ohne Pfarrer am Ort...**", (1987), p. 229

10 Karrer says: "Unsere Zeit bedarf nicht weniger als frühere Zeiten der religiösen Sinnfindung und der sprachlichen Ausdrucksformen des Religiösen. Der einzelne Christ gewinnt somit nur über andere Menschen und über die Erfahrung mit christlicher Gemeinschaft Zugang zu Leben und Wort Jesu. Versagt sich der einzelne diesem Dienst oder versagt dieser Dienst der Gemeinde, dann wird der Glaube unversehens totgeschwiegen: er wird sprach-los und blind". op.cit., "**Erfarungen von Gemeinden ohne Pfarrer am Ort**", (1987), p. 230.

11 A. Reise says: "Evangelisierung bedeutet, den wahren Gott ansagen, der in Christus sich manifestiert hat, und ihre Sache verteidigt, der sein Volk aus Ungerechtigkeit, Unterdrückung und Sünde befreit". **Basisgemeinden und Befreiung in Lateinamerika**, (Mainz, 1980), p. 367. L. Karrer, wrote: "Mit der Glaubensverkündigung (Kerygma) ist die gesamte glaubenerweckende und - vertiefende Grundfunktion angesprochen... Eine unübertragbare Aufgabe der Gemeinde als Kirche am Ort liegt darin, dass sie die Botschaft Jesu unverkürzt und unverfälscht weitersagt und dass sie die Kunde von Jesus und

each community must remain faithful to the unity with its apostolic origin and with the universal Catholic Church. Each local church is carried by the universal and taken to task by other communities. For a deeper understanding of the revelation, great faith is needed; it is the basis for a Christian life.

Because the Christian community is a community of faith, it is of little wonder that Luther once said that the Church and the individual community is a creation of the Word. A community is a Christian community as far as it evangelizes. It is its task, its origin, its reason for existence, it is its life to evangelize. Evangelizing means to announce the true God, who manifested Himself in Christ and through whom salvation and liberation from sin and oppression reached us.

The Good News should be accepted like a treasure which in turn had to be handed on, considered as a living process that needs a constant flow of give and take.[12] A community has a multiplicity of tasks of activities:- religious instructions, courses in faith and theology, pastoral dialogue which help to pass on the gospel through liturgical celebrations.

4.1.2. Liturgia

The second task is the celebration of the memorial of Christ; which is not a past event but a re-enactment. It not only induces conversion but also reconciles and unites the individuals with the Risen Lord. Such is the nature of the celebration of other sacraments. Liturgy is the most visible and profound way in which the community gives physical expression to its fellowship, which normally ends in the breaking of bread in the case of early Christians. Coming together for the breaking of bread indicated a great sign of unity among Christ's followers.

---

seinem Lebensenwurf in die unmittelbaren gesellschaftlichen und politischen Verhältnisse hinein ausruft. **Gemeinde Ohne Pfarrer**, op. cit., pp. 229 - 230.

12 Ibid., Lim rightly says: "Der Glaube ist erst durch die Verkündigung der Glaubensmeinschaft möglich. Der Glaube des einzelnen verdankt sich der unaufhörlichen Verkündigung des anderen und kann nur in Verbindung mit der Communio der Glaubenden ursprungstreu bewahrt bleiben". p. 88; cf. P. Wehrle, "**Der Katechismus in seiner theologischen und kirchlichen Bedeutung**", in: **Informationen**, Hrsg.: (Erzb. Freiburg Jg.1986), p. 81.

They went as a body to the Temple every day but met in their houses for the breaking of bread; they shared their food gladly and generously; they praised God and were looked up to by everyone(Acts 2:46-47).[13]

It is in the Liturgy or the liturgical life of the church that the lordship of Jesus is manifested; from him we live, believe, hope and love. When we accept Jesus as the Lord of all in a given community, we are then more conscious of our brotherhood and sisterhood.[14] This Good News must reach people, hence the importance of the celebrations relating to this Good News. In the liturgical rites, the communication of the word, sermons and actual celebration should be always a sign, a new hope given in the paschal mystery.[15]

Liturgy should take into consideration the life situation of the people. It is a fact that the Jewish people lived the paschal feast, the mystery of the redemption and the liberation from slavery in their paschal celebration. The paschal celebration of Christians is seen as liberation from sin. It is really a great gift from God that we have a new life in Christ. Liturgy as a service of God is radically different from the service of the world, but there is also certain relationship between them. It seems that worldly interests, power and position tend to pull down the spiritual aspect of the liturgy, but the spirit that always guides the Church is ever at work.[16] Meditation and recollection strengthens our spirit and make our judgments more objective. The anthropological idea of liturgy is clear: man in our secularized world will find or rediscover himself again as a person in the liturgy. There he rediscovers his own conscience his freedom and basic values which is more than just performing and functioning.

---

13 L. Karrer describing one of the functions of the Christian community says; "Eine weitere wichtige Aufgabe der christlichen Gemeinde ist die Feier ihrer 'Gabe', nämlich die erinnernde, zur Umkehr einladende, versöhnende und befreiende, mit Christus verbindende und danksagende Feier seiner Gegenwart: also Gottesdienst, einschliesslich der Vielfalt der sakramentalen Praxis, mit dem Zentrum in der Eucharistiefeier. **Gemeinde Ohne Pfarrer am Ort**, (1987), p. 230.

14 Cf. L. Karrer, **University monograph**, op. cit., p. 146a.

15 Ibid. "In der sakramentalen und gottesdienstlichen Praxis bringt die Gemeinde durch Wort und Zeichen zum Ausdrück, wie sie in der glaübigen Erinnerung an den Tod und die Auferweckung Jesu Christi und im hoffenden Vertrauen auf den Geist Jesu angesichts von Lebenssituationen, die für den einzelnen Christen wie für die Kirche entscheidend sind, Grenzen des Menschseins überwindet". , p. 147a. Dulles says: "The sacraments are signs intended to remind Christians of what God is doing and wills to have done throughout the world. Worship, therefore, is both a celebration of what is happening everywhere and a summons to the members of the Church to measure up to their responsibilities in the building of the kingdom of God". **The Reshaping of Catholicism: Current challenges in the theology of the Church**, (1988), p. 141.

16 "Gottesdienst unterscheidet sich radikal von Weltdienst, dennoch stehen beide nicht bezeihungslos nebeneinander.. L. Karrer, ibid., p.148a.

Liturgy has a very important anthropological function, in so far as man learns that in our lives there exist other values, such as being generous, simply living for God and our fellowmen. Liturgy gives meaning to life. The fruit of such liturgical actions and opening up makes us truly human, shows us that it is a virtue to praise God, the liberty to thank God and man, and to experience our life in a way that is not otherwise known, because we allow ourselves to be nearer God, be united with Him. Such a personal and community spirit formalizes itself in a community prayer, in praying for oneself and the need of others, formulating their hope and love and giving them a new basis for life and functions.

The community strengthens its members insofar as no one is deserted, neither in time of difficulty and misfortune, nor in time of fortune. No human situation should be excluded from the liturgy of the community.[17] Sacraments are the concentrated experience of our nearness to God. In these related experience, we deepen our faith in Jesus, we gain a new hope to risk ourselves in Christ.[18] The extraordinary General Assembly of the Synod of Bishops (1985) confirms, that the liturgy must nourish and illumine the sense of the sacred. It should be filled with the spirit of reverence, and of giving worship and glory to God.[19]

4.1.3. Diakonia

Diakonia is simply expressed as solidarity, brotherly and sisterly love and is the third basic aspect of the Christian community, intrinsically united with the other two. Faith, hope and love belong together and are one. Solidarity is perhaps a drier expression of what love means. We are told that the first Christians shared every thing in common and there was no one who was in need (cf. Acts 4:32 – 35).

Even the celebration of the Eucharist was originally carried out together with the evening meal in which the rich shared with the poor. Such a descrip-

---

17 Cf. K. Koch **Streifzüge durch Gottes Gegenwart**, (Zürich, 1984), p. 83.

18 Boff comments that: "Möglicherweise empfindet der moderne, säkularisierte Mensch.. die Anwandlung, sich des religiösen Symbols gänzlich zu entledigen. Wer aber solches tut, schiebt nicht nur einen bedeutenden Reichtum innerhalb der Religion beseite, sondern schliesst zugleich auch Fenster seiner eigenen Seele, denn das Symbolische und Sakramentale bilden tiegreifend Dimensionen der menschlichen Wirklichkeit". **Kleine Sakramentenlehre**, (Düsseldorf, 1978, 2.), p. 11.

19 **Synod Report.** op. cit., p. 15. They advised that Bishops should explain the theological foundation of sacramental practice and of the liturgy to the people for a better appreciation of the liturgy.

tion can be said to be idealistic, expressing more of what the Church ought to be, rather than what the Church at any given point in time is; it is a sort of Christian imperative rather than the ecclesiastical indicative.[20] However, Paul in his first Letter to the Corinthians, already criticized this solidarity, which hit the rocks and even became a scandal.

In spite of this initial human problem, the task of bearing witness to this solidarity remained an important aspect of the Christian community. The two terms *Diakonia* and *Koinonia* indicate the two aspects of this service. *Koinonia* brings together and builds the community; *diakonia* serves the poor, needy and also renders help to those outside the community. It is therefore the task of the community to care for the various needs and to stand up for peace, justice and freedom.

A community cannot live outside society, neither can it live as if the societal problems do not exist. The community has to be present in the mist of society and must feel itself responsible for the marginalized, the oppressed and the poor. That notwithstanding, the Second Vatican Council had the intention to go right into great social problems of the contemporary period. The council supports its position by quoting Pius XI: "It is necessary never to lose sight of the fact that the objective of the Church is to evangelize, not to civilize. If it civilizes, it is by means of evangelization" (GS 58). The Council in the pastoral constitution expressly declares: "The specific mission (*missio propria*) that Christ entrusted to his Church is not political, economic, or social order. The purpose which he set before her is a religious one" (GS 42).

The Church, of course, knows that its religious mission has ramifications in the temporal sphere (GS 40). It has at various points commented on the relationship between evangelization and humanization. The Council Fathers also insisted on the social responsibility of the faithful.

How can one reconcile the Council's insistence on the social responsibility of the faithful with its doctrine that the Church has no proper mission in the social, political and economic orders? One can rightly argue that on the side of the Church, there is no inconsistency; while by "proper" mission, the Council "presumably means, that which is specific to the Church, and would remain undone unless the Church existed. To preach faith in Christ and to administer the sacraments are in this sense proper to the Church."[21] The social obligation

---

20 Cf. B. Hearne, "**Small Christian Communities: Let's go Ahead**", in: **AFER**, vol. 26, 5(1984), p. 246.

21 Dulles, A., **The Reshaping of Catholicism: Current Challenges in the Theology of Church**, (1988), p. 148. Ricardo Ramirez says this of the Church in Latin America; "The Church in Latin America, through its Bishops' statements, has raised moral and justice issues of universal scope. Principles of our teaching tradition on morality and social justice are applied to concrete and specific situations in these statements. They are a

within a society, for one another are made aware of in the *Diakonia*.[22] The *Diakonia* liturgy should make people more open to the needs of others, because to know about other people's needs, makes it possible for one to help. Therefore the spirit of *Diakonia* should be able to open people's hearts, not just to know the needs but to do something about it, because love and solidarity are one and the same thing.

> Take the case, my brothers, of someone who has never done a single good act but claims that he has faith... Faith is like that: if good works do not go with it, it is quite dead (James 2:14 and 17).

One can give either material or spiritual things. In giving, one gives oneself and gains others. For one to understand the life and hope aspect of the Christian life, one has to face especially the problems of the dying, the sick, the aged etc. The two lives of man, the one here and the one to come, are important; neither should be treated at the expense of the other. The life of Christians who contemplate the life received from the altar of our Lord without being concerned with the hungry and homeless will be a tragic one. If our life hope is not put into action in love, the liturgy remains an empty ritual or an ideology. If we do not practice our love, the liturgy loses its force.[23] The three basic functions of the Church, *martyria*, *liturgia* and *diakonia*, are linked together and are complementary. To stress one at the expense of the other, is unchristian. With all these explanations, the second Vatican Council gave the

---

reminder that the teachings of the Church's principles on such matters are not irrelevant to the late twentieth century but, on the contrary, are very much on target and at the cutting edge of contemporary issues. The Church does have something of paramount importance to say on issues of justice, peace, human dignity, and political and social reform"; R. Ramirez, Chairman bishops committee for the Church in Latin America, 1985-88; "**Medellin and Puebla from a U.S. Perspective**", in: **Path from Puebla**, (U.S. Cath. Conference Inc., Washington, D.C., 1989), pp. 10 - 11.

22 Byeng-Hun, P.L., writes: "Die Communio mit dem Herrn bewirkt auch Communio der Menschen untereinander: Die Communio mit dem Herrn wird in der Communio untereinander in Liebe konkretisiert und sichbar gemacht. Erst mit dieser Verwirklichung der Diakonia durch die Communio mit allen in Liebe, als Vollzug der Sendung der Glaubenden zu den jeweiligen Lebenswelten, erreicht die Feier der Liturgie ihren eigentlichen und vollen Sinn". **Leben aus der communio mit Gott und untereinander:** (1991), p. 102; cf. D. Zimmermann, **Diakonie**, 10; K. Lehmann, **Christliche Gemeinde**, 496; H. Wieh, **Konzil**, 217. See also P.L. Byeng-Hun, op. cit., pp. 102 - 109.

23 Karrer, L., **Gemeinde ohne Pfarrer am Ort**, "Die Glaubwürdigkeit einer Pfarrei steht und fällt somit mit ihrer Dienstarbeitschaft und Offenheit zu solidarischen Handeln. Kriche und christliche Gemeinde sind nicht Selbstzweck, sondern sie sind für die Menschen da. Jesus verband mit dem Abendmahl die Fusswaschung; und in der Urkirche gehöhrten Eucharistie und Mahlgemeinschaft zusammen; op. cit., p. 231.

Church a new understanding. The green light was given for the resurgence of the basic Christian community that had been historically swept into oblivion. As a response to this teaching, a lot of Basic Christian Communities started springing up all over the world, especially in the Third World countries, as an on-going process of the implementation of the principle of the Second Vatican Council. It is the combination of these three basic functions of the Church that mark the life of the authentic Basic Christian Communities.

4.2. Basic Ecclesial Communities (BECs)

With the teaching of the Second Vatican Council, the neglected concept of basic Christian Communities, that is as old as Christianity itself, that for some time now was relegated to the background, regained its rightful position among people and cultures.

(i) BCCs: Terminology and origin: There are a lot of terms used in reference to Basic Christian Communities (BCCs): we shall come to some of them in the course of our study. The reality and concept of this term Basic Christian Community (BCC) or Small Christian Community (SCC) may seem recent, but it is as old as Christianity itself. Kalilombe commenting on this says;

> The origin of the SCCs pastoral system is more recent, even if what it is attempting to implement is as old as the church itself.[24]

This term as a new phenomenon came to light in South American countries, with the name "Ecclesial Communutes de Base" (E.C.B), some call it Basic Christian Community (B.C.C.). It is worth noting that the BECs are not mentioned in the documents of the Vatican II. They came to light in an official Church document in Pope Paul VI's Apostolic Exhortation **Evangelii Nuntiandi** (Nr.58). Some have equated different groups in the Church with Small Christian Communities. It is due to such multiplicity of conceptions that necessitated Pope Paul VI's comment in his **Encyclical Evangelii Nuntiandi**, a report on the discussion of the 1974 Roman synod of bishops. Here the Pope deplored the fact that many different groups with different orientations claim the name of Basic communities.[25]

---

24 .Kalilombe, P.A., "**From Outstations to SCCs, SPEARHEAD**, Nr. 82-83 (Eldoret, Kenya,1984), p. 60.

25 Cf. Paul VI, "**On Evangelisation in the Modern World**", Encyclical: **Evangelii Nuntiandi**:- "Die letze Synode hat sich sehr mit den Kleinen Gemeinschaften oder 'Basisgemeinschaften' befaßt, denn in der Kirche von heute ist häufig von ihnen die Rede..." **EN,** par. 58, in: **Ordensnachrichten, Nr. 91** (Mayer & Comp., Wien, 1976).

But recently attention has been given to it in official Church documents, especially in Pope John Paul II's Apostolic Exhortation **Christi fideles Laici** (e.g. Nrs. 19, 26, 61). This was actually a follow-up to the 1987 Synod of Bishops on the Laity. No matter whatever terminology this concept uses, there are three key words that indicate that they are saying the same thing, namely, "Basic or Small", "Christian or ecclesial" and "Community". Despite these, there are a lot of groups within the church today that claim also the same status as the BCCs or SCCs, such groups include small prayer groups, charismatic groups, Bible class groups, family and liturgical groups, factional circles opposed to traditional church order, the new '*offene Kirche*' and so on.

The development of this modern concept 'BCC' started in ernest after the Second World War. Due to the devastating nature of events during that time, there was a search for an alternative society; groups did emerge but never qualified as Basic Christian communities.[26] These varieties of communities interested D.Clark and he made a study of them and eventually came out with three categories which he named as follows:

(a) Intentional community: This involves those who have not only contracted to share a common interest but also a common way of life, which involves living together in one place.

(b) Group: These are people who gather around a common concern or cause, they may meet frequently, but do not live together in one building nor share so fully in a common way of life.

(c) Network: "a web of communities/or groups with similar concern, linked together often over the country as a whole."[27] From D.Clark's study, we can see that none of them can actually qualify as BCC/SCC, but the nearest to it may be the 'group'. It is Frank Ponce who tried to sketch the origin of BCC when he wrote:

> Historically, the BCC began in Latin America, in Brazil and especially the experiment of San Miquelito in Panama.(They now exist in all over the world, and are active especially in Africa, Asia and Italy). Originally they began in the 1950s as movement for educating masses of poor people, by bringing them into small groups where they knew each other and had more courage to speak out. But they didn't stay there. Gradually, church leaders and organizers realized that here were really the seeds for building genuine community rooted in Christ.[28]

---

26 Cf. D. Clark, **Basic Communities: Towards an Alternative Society:** (SPCK, London, 1977); S.B. Clark, **Building Christian Communities,** (Ave Maria Press, Notre Dame, Indiana, 1972).

27 Clark, D., op. cit., p. 19.

28 Ponce, F., "**Building Basic Communities: Communidades ecclesiales de base in the U.S. Experience**", in: **Developing Basic Christian Communities; A HandBook**

Antonia M.Pernia writing on the origin of BECs says:

BECs first originated in Brazil in 1956(Barra do Pirai Diocese) and in Panama in 1963(San Miguelito Parish), as a creative pastoral effort supported by the Bishops but emerging from the local lay people as a church from below.[29]

Many people are in agreement with Frank Ponce's position, but there are those who have other views regarding the origin of BCCs. Boff wrote that it all began with the lament of one humble old woman who could not enjoy Christmas for lack of a priest:

Christmas Eve, all three Protestant Churches were lit up and full of people. We could hear them singing... And the Catholic Church, closed and dark.... Because we can't get a priest.[30]

The story of the woman gave Dom Angelo food for thought. He began questioning himself of what will become of Christians when there are no more priests. He decided to train community coordinators,

to do everything a lay person can do in God's Church in current ecclesiastical discipline. At the least, these catechists will gather the people once a week for religious instruction. Normally they will also celebrate daily prayer with the people. On Sundays and Holy Days they will gather the people from all over the district for a Massless Sunday, or 'priestless Mass', or 'Catholic worship', and lead them spiritually and collectively in the same Mass as is being celebrated by the pastor in the distant mother Church. They will recite morning and evening prayers with the people, as well as novenas, litanies, May and June celebrations, and so on.[31]

The above explanations are born out of necessity and each is explaining a particular incident, that is peculiar to the place of description. We cannot in principle accept Boff's legendary story, that all began with the Christmas episode, no matter how captivating the story may seem.

The Church has for centuries had services without priests. Uriel Molina Oliu narrated the origin of BCC in Manaqua, which at first was a movement in the Church,a renewal along the line suggested by the Second Vatican Council

---

(National Federation of Priests' council, Chicago, 1979), p. 25; cf. A. Shorter, **The Church in the African City.** (1991), p. 102.

29 Pernia, A.M., "**The Ecclesiology of the Base Ecclesial Communities**", in: **Studies in Philosophy and Theology**, Vol. xv, Nr.2; (Graduate School Divine Word - Seminary. Tacaytay City, Philippines, 1990), p. 56.

30 Boff, **L., Ecclesiogenesis: The Base Communities Reinvent the Church.** (London, 1987), p. 3 These are legends used to illustrate the origin of the BECs.

31 Agnelo, D., **Revista Eclesiastica Brasileira,** 17(1957), 731-737; quoted by L. Boff, ibid.

for people in areas where priests are lacking. At the same time, another movement outside the Church was also going on, i.e., the *Frente Sandinista de Liberacion Nacional.*

These two parallel renewal movements in Nicaragua, developed independently, were brought together at Medellin. Christians began to find renewal as they organized themselves into basic communities.[32] This type of movement spread all over Nicaragua and also among students and they combined the claims of Christianity with the revolutionary struggle. As these movements were going on, similar movements were taking place in other countries in South America, and as Gustavo Gutierrez rightly says;

> The self-awareness of the Christian community is conditioned historically by the world of which it is a part, and by its way of viewing this world.[33]

Each country or place which was confronted with the problem of life and faith set out in search of a solution. But it is certain that BCCs started in Brazil and Panama (San Miguelito parish) in the 1950s as what one may call a creative pastoral effort which was endorsed by the Bishops. Azevedo, confronted with the problem of the origin of BECs, turned to Alvaro Barreiro who says;

To my Knowledge, there does not yet exist a meticulous historical study of the origins of BECs in Brazil.[34]

Just as in the Christianity it represents, the BCCs had humble beginnings composed of small groups of neighbours in impoverished rural villages and urban slums. It was really a kind of sub-divided outstation of the missionaries (as we have in Nigeria) with the goal of easing priests' work, and many sprang up in parishes which lacked priests. The people, in coming together and sharing the life of the Church, began to participate in their neighbours concern, such as water-projects, schools, roads etc.

There was a growth in the understanding of the Bible as a story of liberation. In the sharing of the Word of God, they were able to relate it to their life situation. And through cooperatives and other associations they tried to change their poor and oppressed situation and were able to have a voice in the things

---

32 Oliu, U.M., "**How a People's Christian Community (Comunidad Cristiana Popular) is structured and how it functions** in: **Concilium**, L. Boff, and V. Elizondo, eds. **La Iglesia Popular**: 176 (UK., 1984), p. 4.

33 Gutierrez, G., **The Power of the Poor in History.** (Orbis Books, Maryknoll, New York, 1983), p. 27.

34 Barreiro, A., "**Raizes da consciencia eclesial das CEBs,**" in: **CONV.**, 17/158 (1982): pp. 602-609; quoted by M.deC. Azevedo, **Basic Ecclesial Communities in Brazil. The Challenge of a New Way of Being Church,** Transl. by J. Drury, (Georgetown University Press, Washington, D.C., (1987), p. 23.

that concern them. Christianity was seen as a life to be lived, instead of a pack of Codes; and solidarity was the watchword. Later, during the 1960s and 1970s, a wide variety of BCCs sprang up in other countries of Latin America such as Chile, Peru, Paraguay, El Salvador and Nicaragua. These groups were people of convictions rather than convention; it was a grassroots movement. A new way of being Church was born where the poor people became subjects of their own history. Healey quotes Jose Marins as summarizing the BCCs in Latin America thus:

> the dynamic reality of an evangelical,liberating and prophetic community opting preferentially for the poor and therefore constituting a new model of Church and the seed of a new model of society.[35]

For Azevedo there are two, complementary outlooks at the origin. There was the stress on the context of ideas, the currents of thought, that were the order of the day as the BECs emerged. The second approach focussed on certain facts of events that really anticipated the BECs.[36]

From Azevedo's exposition one can conclude that the first approach focusses on the search for community, the rise of small groups, the struggles and aspiration of parishes to become communities, in which the Vatican II was instrumental; while the second approach tries to identify concrete facts and events in the Church that acted as forerunner of BECs.

BCCs can only be described and not really defined, as Pernia says;

> It is not only difficult to give a clear-cut definition of the BECs, but to do so would also deprive them of one of their fundamental characteristics, that is, flexibility, openness to change and the tendency to reverse patterns.[37]

Definition we shall not dare, but some description will suffice by looking at the important operational words involved which are: Basic, Christian/ecclesial and community. The word Basic has four expressions or connotations: sociological, theological, descriptive and strategic.[38]

From the sociological point of view, it denotes the grassroots, the rural and those of the lowest level in society. This is what Pernia described as 'of the base' with emphasis on the social origin of the membership of the BECs.

---

35 Healey, J., "**BCCs in Africa and Latin America**"; in: **AFER**; vol. 26, 4(1984), p. 224.

36 Cf. M.deC. Azevedo, **Basic Ecclesial Communities in Brazil:**, (1987), p. 23.

37 Pernia, A.M., **The Ecclesiology of the Base Ecclesial Communities.** op. cit., p. 57.

38 Cf. G. Gutierrez, **The Irruption of the Poor in Latin America and the Christian Communities of the Common People, in the Challenge of BCCs**, S. Torres and J. Eagleson, eds., (Orbis book, New York, 1981), pp. 116, 135, 236.

> BECs are communities of faith at the base both of the Church and society. At the base of Church are the laity, while at the base of the society are the poor.And very often in Third World countries, those at the base of society and of the Church are the same people.... Thus, BECs are communities of faith made up of the poor and the lay faithful.[39]

Theologically speaking, it pertains to the *Anawim Yahweh*, the poor, the marginalized and simple people.[40] The level of growth is from the bottom or the base, from below to the top, a movement which is not forced down on people, but rather grows up naturally from the people. Strategically, it entails the pillars, the roots, the foundation-stones.The movement we are talking about has a common and primary denominator which is Christ. The word 'Christian' points to the primary root of the phenomenon. It is not just any group or community, but one that has a common faith in the Risen Lord Jesus Christ.

They got their name from whom they are following, the anointed One, the Christ (Acts,11:26). The last word 'Community' can be broken down to give us:-*Com* (from "come") and "Unity"; the two words will give us com-unity, which is coming to unite. It implies a strong sense of belonging, communitarianism, solidarity, sharing, caring and all that show a mutual living. Boff says:

> Community must be understood as a spirit to be created, as an inspiration to bend one's constant efforts to overcome barriers between persons and to generate a relationship of solidarity and reciprocity.[41]

Pernia is not left out, he sees the word "community" in BCCs as an attempt to set a pattern of Christian life, which is deliberately in contrast to two realities.

---

39 Pernia, A.M., **The Ecclesiology of the Base Ecclesial Communities**, p. 58.

40 Healey adds that: "The very term communion *(the underlying principle of BCC)* connotes people, all people, each one with aspirations, needs and gifts. The great majority are the powerless and voiceless, the so-called silent majority". J.Healey, "**Comment on the 1987 Synod of Bishops Topic on the Laity**", in: **Tablet**, Sept. 12, (1987), p. 962.

41 Boff, L., **Ecclesiogenesis**, op. cit., p. 5. An eyewitness to what is happening in the small group reports that; "We are witnessing a phenomenon of a group of people who are discovering themselves through the realization of their own worth. The people are changing, they feel they are in contact with reality, that they are discovering the real causes for that reality. They are taking on more responsibility for each other in a process of greater self confidence and confidence in each other which becomes evident in the unity they feel themselves. Thus they are enabled to confront their problems". J.B. Libanio, "**A Community with a New Image**", in: **International Review of Mission**, vol. LXVIII, 27(1979), p. 245.

(1) Contemporary Western culture, which is generally regarded as individualistic, competitive and centered on the self. Against this, BCCs want to live the faith not as a privatized but as a shared experience which is nurtured and supported by the community, and at the same time, which nurtures and supports the community...

(2) Traditional Church life, with its vertical structure in the exercise of power and authority, whereby the lay faithful are simply passive recipients of decisions made on top. Against this, BCCs emphasize the idea of 'participation', whereby the lay faithful have their role in the decision-making process in the Church.[42]

Pernia is suggesting that the BCCs are the architects of this ecclesiology of participation. One may rather say that it is the ecclesiology of the Second Vatican Council; that BCCs are trying to put into practice. According to Latin American bishops in 1968, during their conference at Medellin, BCC is described as: "the core group, the most reduced expression of the Church".[43]

The operational words are 'core' and 'reduced' expression of the Church. It is not just any gathering of people, but instead, is made up of those who are called and gathered in Christ whose Body is the Church. The conference stressed the smallness of the number – 'core' 'nucleus', 'reduced'. This is a group where intimacy and solidarity is at its utmost level. Naab puts it beautifully:

This emphasis underlines the intimate or close relationship that can exist within such a small group of people. The factor of closeness as a result of fewness would appear to be the force behind the cohesiveness of the community while largeness in numbers would tend to foster looseness, easy disintegration, and anonymity. This element further points to the fact that, the Church as a universal body is essentially alive in the concrete grassroots communities.[44]

In the same line of thought as at Medellin comes the description of BCC by Cardinal Silver Henriquez of Santiago, Chile:

---

42 Pernia, A.M., **The Ecclesiology of the Base ecclesial Community**, pp. 57-58. Hetson calls BCCs; "the place where the poor people can speak, exchange their experience and find hope. They do not provide intellectual discourse or cold, impersonal sermons. They use living gestures, symbols, drama, posters, songs, stories and speeches full of grammatical mistakes, but even fuller with passion and life. They do not know what 'ideology' means, but they understand perfectly well what it means to feel hunger for justice and thirst for God"; J. Hetson, "**An Assembly of Brazilian Communities,"** in: **AFER**, vol. 23, 4(1981), p. 277. Hetson is describing a church life, where praxis comes before theory.

43 Cf. J. O'Halloran , **Living Cells: Building BCC:** (Dominican Publication, Dublin, 1980), p. 14.

44 Naab, J.T., "**The Basic Christian Community in Biblical Perspective**", in: **Incarnation Monograph Series;** Nr. 1. (Assumpta Press, Owerri, n.d.), p. 12.

as a living cell within the church, a reduced group with human warmth; a group in which the Gospel can be lived totally and where people help one another.[45]

The Cardinals definition is more biblical; though he stressed the smallness of the number, he put more emphasis up on love – human warmth and care for one another, which is actually the characteristic of the Christian community – " see how they love themselves " (Acts.) It is also of importance to comment that the definition said, a living cell within the Church, and not outside the Church, for the cell will then be dead if it is outside the body. Joinet, in his own contribution, describes BCC as;

a small group of people who feel related through an awareness of brotherhood in Christ and wherever possible, rooted in a human or natural community. [46]

The feeling of being related here goes with knowledge and conviction of one fatherhood of God and brotherhood in Christ. And the definition adds something more when it expressed 'wherever possible, rooted in a human or natural community'. This supports the idea of making use of the natural existing communities as base, instead of destroying them, as is the case in Africa.

Joinet will actually accept the role *umunna* will play in the theology of the small Christian community in Igboland. Stephen Clark, in his own contribution, states that,

a Basic Christian Community is an environment of Christians, which can provide for the basic needs of its members to live the Christian life.[47]

Any environment that allows the practice of Christian life is for Clark a basic community. Although his description somehow corresponds to the ones already mentioned, he is silent on the size of the community. The environment in which the faith can grow may be large or small, so his holistic view or approach did no justice to the smallness of the group. Shorter gives his understanding of what 'basic' in Latin America is;

In Latin America, however, a community is described as 'basic' when it identifies with the lowest social strata, the poor and the oppressed.[48]

---

45 Cf. J. O'Halloran, **Living Cells: Building BCC**; (1980), p.5.

46 Joinet, B., " **Practical Steps Towards building Christian Communities"**, in: **AFER**, 19, 2(1977), pp. 77 - 78.

47 Clark, B.S., **Building Christian Communities**. (Ave Maria Press, Notre Dame, Indiana, 1972), p. 70.

48 Shorter, A., **The Church in the African City.** (Geoffrey Chapman, London, 1991), p. 100.

Such a concept is not only misleading, but also creates a division in God's house and may fuel a class struggle which Christ never preached. What happens when the poor are not included within a given group?

Enrique Dussel gives three interpretations of the term 'base' which can be summarized as: (1) Sociological – where he brings out the context between a macro-scale society, which is anonymous and impersonal, and a micro-scale 'base' community that is "local or environmental, which allows for personal, fraternal contact between its members.[49] (2) Societal duality – where he traces the bipolarity in the Church, boiling down to hierarchy and laity. (3) Political commitment – here he sees the role of the base in a strictly prophetic sense as a sign of eschatological liberation.[50] Dussel never confined himself exclusively to any of these three meanings, but did stress the ecclesiological aspect of the term. One may not accept that material poverty is *ex opere operato* an evangelical sacrament. There is no guarantee that there is an automatic, reliable linkup between the proletariat (the poor) and liberation. Numerous initiatives in history, particularly in the last century and a half, does not suggest such a notion. Dussel and C. Boff many a time seem to link the poor and BECs to the project of liberation without doubt or question. Often they also overlook the poor who do not embody that project or participate in it. There is no doubt that in their thinking they automatically exclude from that project those who are not economically impoverished, thereby creating an unchristian situation.

After going through some of these definitions or descriptions of BCC, we can rightly say that they revolve around these key words: 'Basic', 'Christian' and 'community'. All agree that the community should be such that it's size can be managed. Small is beautiful, as one author puts it, and the smaller the group, the more effective the operational mechanism.

Another, very important word in their definitions is 'faith' in the Risen Lord. Without this common faith, the group could be anything but Christian. Thus faith in Jesus should be the motivating force and center of all members. It is a shared faith. Last, but not least, is the stress on community, as opposed to what Leonardo Boff calls a modern society, "that has produced a wild atomization of existence and a general anonymity of persons lost in the cogs of the mechanisms of the macro-organization and bureaucracies".[51] This stress on

---

49 Cf. Medellin Final Document on, **Joint Pastoral Planning**, Nr.10.

50 Cf. E. Dussel, "**A base na teologia da libertacao**", in: **Concilium**; 104, 4(1975); C.M. Olseu, **The Base Church: Creating Community through Multiple Forms.** (Forum House, Atlanta, Ga., 1973 see also M.deC. Azevedo, **BECs in Brazil...** (1987), pp. 75f.

51 Boff, L., **Ecclesiogenesis**, (1987), p. 1.

community shows a fundamental reality and a fundamental human longing. Walter Kasper says;

> Only in Polis – in community with other people – can a man or woman find fulfilled humanity.[52]

Generally speaking, and this concurs with our research, BEC is a group of persons or a combination of groups, in which there is a primary, fraternal and personal relationship as expressed within a given community. For it to be ecclesial, it has to live the totality of the life of the Church, expressed in service, celebration and evangelization.[53] There can be no doubt about the importance of the term 'ecclesial' in the definition. This is a term that differentiates the group from all other diversified groupings in the broad, pluralistic context of today's world. The Church's understanding of the Second Vatican Council is bearing fruit everywhere in the formation of Basic Christian Communities.

4.2.1. Basic Ecclesial Communities in Latin America

Azevedo sees the official launching of BECs in Brazil, after the fruits of their labours began to be evident and concrete experiences picked up, as taking place a few years after the issue of the "emergency plan" in 1962 of the National Conference of Brazilian Bishops.[54] The pastoral Plan that followed activated the laity, and set in motion an integral evangelization. Following these, is the 'nature of social relations within the community'. The decentralization of the parish became a necessary event, not in the sense of creating new juridical parishes, but in the sense of awakening and activating basic communities. Commenting on these set-ups, Azevedo writes;

> In them Christians would not be anonymous persons seeking merely the performance of a service or the fulfillment of obligation. They would be faithful members feeling accepted

---

52 Kasper, W., **Theology and Church.** (SCM Press, London,1989), p. 148.

53 Cf. A. Gregory, "**Comunidades eclesiais de base: Utopia ou realidade"**; in: **Maringa Seminar**. Appendix 2, p. 83; see also M.deC. Azevedo, **"BEC in Brazil;"** (1987), p. 74.

54 Cf. M.deC. Azevedo, **BECs in Brazil:** (1987), pp. 27-28. This plan was limited in scope and duration. It was at the request of the Holy See but the formulation was that of the National Conference of Brazilian Bishops (CNBB), as one will expect there were some misgivings. The first joint Pastoral plan (PPC) took place between 1965 and 1970.

and responsible as an integral component, living in communion with Christ and all their brothers and sisters.[55]

The BEC in Latin America received an official Church recognition at Medellin in 1968.

4.2.1.1. Medellin

All the different community movements in Latin America had their first official ecclesiastical attention at the conference of Latin American Bishops at Medellin in 1968. This was a period of turmoil in the whole of South America, as the chairman of Bishops committee for the Church in Latin America put it:

> Medellin was held in 1968, a year of confrontation that was approaching the culmination of a decade of strife and turmoil in many parts of the world... Medellin confronted head-on the historical situation in which Latin America found itself in 1968. The conference fathers observed the happenings around them as signs of the times that must be interpreted in the light of revelation and Church teaching, particularly that of Vatican 11, (Gaudium et Spes)... The title of the Medellin documents reveals its intent: The Church in the Present-Day Transformation of Latin America in the light of the Council.[56]

This conference gave a turning point in the life of the Church in Latin America, in that the option was for the poor. Bishop Ricardo Ramirez went on to numerate the themes that run throughout the documents as:

> Social sin and the poor (2.1.7), unjust structures that are responsible for oppressed people (1.2), 'institutionalized violence' as description of the situation of injustice that violates fundamental rights (2.16), promotion of the human dimension of life; fidelity to God and fidelity to the human person, need for a profound conversation and for authentic liberation (1.2.3), and conscientization (1.3.17).[57]

The word 'Liberation Theology' was at this conference not mentioned as such, but the influence is obvious in the document. A new theology was born,

---

55 ibid.; The BECs in Brazil as well as else where had its humble beginnings and long history. They showed up in different areas and in different shapes - like rural chapels, the work of small groups in neighbourhoods and blocks acts sometimes as modalities of this orientation.

56 Ricardo, R., "**Medellin and Pueblo from a U.S. Perspective**", in: **Path from Pueblo, Significant Document of the Latin America Bishops since 1979. Bishops Committee for the Church in Latin America National Conference of Catholic Bishops.** (Washington, D.C., 1989), pp. 11-12. We must also comment that it was at this period (1968) that Nigeria was involved in a bloody civil war.

57 Ibid., p. 12.

and the movement *Comunidades eclesiales de base* (Base Christian Communities) became the instrument that popularized these themes and approaches to pastoral life and the means whereby Medellin reached the masses. At this conference the Bishops were able to define what they meant by basic Christian community as:

> The primary and fundamental ecclesial nucleus, responsible at that level for maintaining and expanding faith, and for the cult which expresses faith. It is the initial cell of ecclesial structuring, a place of evangelisation, and already a foremost factor in human promotion and development.[58]

In the same line of thought Karl Rahner wrote in his book *The Shape of the Church to Come*, the future Church will be a "Church from roots", built up from below by basic communities, or Small Christian Communities.[59]

It was in Medellin that the Latin American Bishops took note of the incipient reality of base-level groups and communities, seeing them as a fundamental factor in living the faith as community and effectively expressing it in social commitment. Azevedo saw the focus of the Medellin on the communities as more sociological and religious, than ecclesiological, a point that has not been sufficiently noted in analyses of its documents.

But there can be no doubt that Medellin was fundamental in the launching of BECs by the Church. The controversies arising from Medellin and the misunderstanding of its spirit which followed called for another conference in Puebla in Mexico.

4.2.1.2. Puebla

The conference at Puebla was first convoked by Pope John Paul I, but due to his sudden death it could not take place till Pope John Paul II had given the green light. The Medellin conference had produced a lot of heated arguments all over the world regarding Liberation theology. There were hopes in certain quarters that Puebla will be answering the questions arising from what some may call excesses of the Medellin.

But from the beginning the Puebla conference clearly declared its intention of following in the footsteps of Medellin, especially expressed in the docu-

---

58 Hearne, B., ed., "**The Community called Church: Vol. 5 of an Experimental Sourcebook for religious education"; SPEARHEAD:** Nr. 60 (Eldoret, 1979), pp. 16-24; cf. "**Medellin Documents"**, Ch. 15, Section 10, in: J. Gremillan, ed. **The Gospel of Peace and Justice**, (Orbis Books, New York, 1976).

59 Cf. K. Rahner, **The Shape of the Church to Come:** (SPCK, London, 1975), pp. 120-125.

ment on the "preferential option". The first Chapter of the document opens thus:

> With renewed hope in the vivifying power of the spirit, we are going to take up once again the position of the second General Conference of the Latin American episcopate in Medellin, which adopted a clear and prophetic option expressing preference for, and solidarity with, the poor. We do this despite the distortions and interpretations of some, who vitiate the spirit of Medellin, and despite the disregard and even hostility of others.[60]

The word that featured much in this conference was "solidarity". Pope John Paul II, in his opening address at the Puebla conference, admonished the participants (Bishops) to exercise their principal duty of pastors and to be :

> teachers of truth – not a human or rational truth, but Gods truth, which is the principle of authentic liberation.[61]

This admonition is necessitated by the use of marxist ideology by some people in the Theology of Liberation. To put the record straight, the sacred Congregation for the Doctrine of the Faith gave instruction on certain aspects of the Theology of Liberation, where it states:

> The 'theology of liberation' makes wide use of readings from the book of Exodus. The exodus, in fact, is the fundamental event in the formation of the chosen people. It represents freedom from foreign domination and from slavery. One will note that the specific significance of the event comes from its purpose, for this liberation is ordered to the foun-

---

60 **Pueblo Documents**: Nr. 1134; quoted by G. Gutierez, **The Power of the Poor in History**, (1983), p. 127.

61 John Paul 11, "**Opening address at the Puebla Conference**", in: **Puebla and Beyond**, p. 58. The Pope's message can be seen as double barrelled:- comprising both a warning and encouragement. Warning against using Christ as a political activist involved in class struggle and he encouraged them to stand up for the poor. Moises Sandoval gave a summary of the Pope's talk thus; "... the needy and marginalized (i.e., all those whose lives reflect the suffering countenance of the Lord). He spoke about proclaiming the complete truth about human beings: 'human beings are not pawns of economic or political processes,... instead these processes are geared towards human beings and subject to them' (I.9). He called for the advancement of human liberation, asking that the Church's voice 'when the growing affluence of a few people parallels the growing poverty of the masses' (III.4). He emphasized that 'there is a social mortgage on all private property' (III.4). He spoke of the 'sometimes massive increase in violations of human rights in many parts of the world...the right to be born; the right to life; and the right to responsible procreation; the right to work; the right to peace, freedom, and social justice; and the right to participate in making decisions that affect people and nations" (III.5). in: J. Eagleson, and P. Scharper, eds. ***Puebla and Beyond.*** **Documentation and Commentary**, (Maryknoll, N.Y., 1979), p. 34.

dation of the people of God and the Covenant cult celebrated on Mt.Sinai (Exd.24). That is why the liberation of the Exodus cannot be reduced to a liberation which is principally or exclusively political in nature.[62]

In their document, the Fathers of Puebla expressed their satisfaction in the role played by Basic Ecclesial Communities, how they created more personal inter-relations and a wider acceptance of God's Word, and led people to re-examine their lives and reflect on reality in the light of the Gospel. They supported the multiplication of small communities as an important ecclesial event, which stand as the hope of the Church, as centers of evangelisation and as the moving forces for liberation and development.[63]

But it was not all easy going, as Moises Sandoval observed; he described the meeting in Puebla as being held in a spirit of tension and fear. There were two camps present at this conference, the so-called progressives and the conservatives; the ambiguity of the document was meant to please both camps. The most significant contribution of the Puebla conference was its pastoral-theological themes, which can be applied wherever the Church exercises her mission.

The themes from this conference had a universal Christian acceptance, some of which include:

(i) The Church and Kingdom vis a vis the World.
(ii) The dignity of the human person.
(iii) Social justice as Liberation.
(iv) Charity (*agape*) as a wellspring of justice.
(v) Poverty as a theological concept.
(vi) The Church as servant.
(vii) Young people as a preferential option.
(viii) Prophetic role of Bishops.
(ix) The spirituality of popular Catholicism, especially devotion to Mary.

One can argue that Puebla moved a step further than Medellin by devoting time to the people's religiosity. The uniqueness of BCCs is summed up by William Cook by the following:

(a) They represent a new understanding of the social reality, looking at the Church as the people of God, where inequality is levelled up and only brotherly love reigns.

(b) The BCCs are a new way of being the Church, seen in the life of solidarity, communitarian, holistic and inclusiveness.

(c) The BCCs are a new way of 'doing theology'. That is an option for the poor but not at the exclusion of the rich but seen from the perspective of the

62 **Libertatis Nuntius: <u>SGDF</u>** (C.T.S., London, 1984,), p. 9.
63 Cf. **<u>Pueblo Documents</u>**.

oppressed and marginalized. Christ never preached class struggle or class distinction.

(d) The BCCs are a new way of carrying out a mission: emphasizing the 'denunciation' part of the 'denouncing- announcing' dyad of the Gospel.[64]

The ecclesial structure that found expression in Puebla "preferential option for the poor", is seen from the point of view of the Church. To truly be a Church, she should not disassociate herself from the base. It is only through the base that the Church which be transformed and be transformative. No wonder Africans, who are known for their community life, are opting for the establishment of Small Christian Communities.

4.2.2. Small Christian Communities (SCCs) in Africa

The Second Vatican Council, having provided us with a new understanding of Church, made a lot of changes in ecclesiology. The fruits of this great Ecumenical Council are being felt all over the Christian world. We have seen the impressive job being done in Latin American Countries. Here we shall look at the African response. The AMECEA Countries are in the forefront in localizing the Church with the option for Small Christian Communities.

4.2.2.1. Association of member episcopal conferences in eastern africa (amecea)

Its origin and scope: The ASSOCIATION OF MEMBER EPISCOPAL CONFERENCES IN EASTERN AFRICA (AMECEA) came into being by the efforts of 50 bishops and prefect-apostolics from Kenya, Tanganyika (Tanzania), Uganda, Nyasaland (Malawi), and Northern Rhodesia (Zambia). The architect of this noble association was His Lordship, Bishop J.M.Blomjour, then Bishop of Nwanza, Tanzania. It was in June 1960 that the ordinaries of Tanzania (Tanganyika) at their General Meeting discussed,

> the possibilities of joint meetings with the Hierarchies of the neighbouring territories for purpose of encouraging common policy on problems that several of the territories shared equally.[65]

64 Cf. W. Cook, quoted by J.Healey, **BCCs in Africa and Latin America**, art. cit., p. 225.

65 **Cf. Record,** p. 3; P. Lwaminda, **The Theological Analysis of AMECEA-Documents in the Local Church with Special Emphasis on the Pastoral Option.** unpublished article, n. d. p. 5.

Such an idea sailed through in the assembly, and all the Bishops decided to communicate 'their belief' to the Episcopal Conferences of Kenya, Uganda, Malawi and Zambia. Then on July 17 – 26, 1961, 51 Bishops from Kenya, Tanzania, Malawi and Zambia met in Daressaalam in a study conference. One of the things that emerged from this Conference was the decision to set up, subject to the approval of the Holy See, an Inter-territorial Episcopal Board, representative of the five territories.

> The first meeting of the AMECEA countries (then called ITEBEA) took place in July 1961 at Dar es Saalam. It was inspired by a desire to coordinate the pastoral approach of the Church in Eastern Africa as much as possible.[66]

After obtaining the approval of the Holy See, in their meeting at Nairobi Sept.5, 1962, the Board decided on the official name as: the Inter-territorial Episcopal Board of Eastern Africa. Finally, during the second session of the Second Vatican Council, on November 4, 1964, 37 Bishops of ITEBEA met in Rome to renew a draft consultation for their organization; it was here that the association took the name of Association of Member Episcopal Conferences in Eastern Africa (AMECEA). It is interesting to note that, in 1979, the Episcopal Conference of Sudan joined AMECEA as a full Member, while the Episcopal Conference of Ethiopia became an associate member and later became a full member. Now, AMECEA is comprised of seven Episcopal Conferences: Ethiopia, Kenya, Malawi, Sudan, Tanzania, Uganda and Zambia.

4.2.2.1.1. The Birth of Small Christian Communities (SCCs)

The Church in Africa, just as in every other place, has emphasized the importance of grassroots communities in different ways. There has been a one-way-traffic sort of evangelization, following a service station model or pipe-line theory model, where the sacraments and other pastoral services were delivered to the Churches or groups. The people have been always on the receiving end. As the priest dispenses the sacraments, the laity are made passive, so much so, that the Church is seen as the priest and the priest the Church. In line with the teaching of the Second Vatican Council, and in order to put an end to this model of the Church, the AMECEA Bishops sought to establish Small Christian Communities (SCCs).

In 1967, the Assembly that followed the Second Vatican Council had the theme:"Pastoral Perspectives in Eastern Africa after Vatican II." They tried to evaluate the task ahead of them pastorally and sought new methods of evan-

---

66 .Mwana`A Nzeki, R.S.N., "**Implementing AMECEA's Pastoral Priority.**" (Plenary Presentation paper), in: **AFER**, Vol.21 5(1979), p. 286.

gelisation. Other topics that surfaced during this Assembly included priestly formation, ecumenism and marriage customs.

In their August 1970 Assembly, which took place at the Dominican Convent school, in Lusaka, Zambia, they decided to discuss the topic: "The Priest in Africa today." Being confronted with the problem of shortage of priests, the Bishops decided to educate and encourage their communities to minister to themselves as much as they could.[67]

The 1973 Assembly, the "MAGNA CHARTA" for SCCs, was held in Nairobi (Kenya) under the theme: "Planning for the Church in Eastern Africa in the 1980s". During their deliberation, the Bishops studied among other things, the search for identity, relative and local autonomy, and self-reliance in the institutional, economic and ideological life of the Church. The Assembly bore great fruit. The Bishops committed themselves not only to establishing a local Church, but also to a new way of being Church, a Church with a human face, made manifest in Small Christian Communities. They declared;

> We are convinced that in these countries of Eastern Africa it is time for the Church to become really 'local', that is: self-ministering, self-propagating and self-supporting. Our planning is aimed at building such Local Churches for the coming years. We believe that in order to achieve this we have to insist on building Church life and work on basic Christian Communities, in both rural and urban areas. Church life must be based on communities in which every day life and work takes place; those basic manageable social groupings whose members can experience real interpersonal relationships and feel a sense of communal.[68]

The 1973 Assembly was really the "magna charta" for SCCs. Joseph Kelly says;

> Although SCCs were to spread at a later date, the year that marked the early beginnings of the notion of SCCs was 1973. It was in this year that several things happened that were to contribute greatly to the evolution of the notion of SCCs.[69]

For the AMECEA bishops, the old method of parish/out-station should give way to SCCs.[70] They understood the Church to be a sign of all that Christ

---

67 ibid., p. 14.

68 "**AMECEA:Guidelines**", in: **AFER**, 16, 1-2(1974), pp. 9-10; see the study by M-F.P. Jassy, **Basic Community in the African Church**, (Maryknoll, Orbis Books, 1973), conducted among the Independent Churches of the Luo people of North-eastern Tanzania, indicates some of the essential elements of what are authentic African (Christian) communities. See also her "**Forming Christian Communities. An Evaluation of Experiments in North Mara**", Tanzania,(Eldoret, Gaba Publications, n.d.).

69 Kelly, J., "**The Evolution of SCCs**", in: **AFER** Vol. 33, 3(1991), p. 110.

70 "**AMECEA Guidelines: For the Catholic Church in Eastern Africa in the 1980s**", in: **AFER**, Vol. 18, 1 & 2(1974), pp. 8-9.

stood for and as the dynamic leaven for wholesome transformation of the sick egoistic World. It is their task to find the means of man's total development, as they declared:

> In our sincere efforts to achieve true human development we seek to respond to Christ, and through this response we hope for the fulfillment of the Kingdom and our own final and eternal life in union with God in his Kingdom of love and brotherhood.[71]

The question of brotherhood, which Christ taught and died for, was a cause for concern in some of these countries, where discrimination and racism were a stumbling block for the propagation of Christian faith. The Church, in order to fulfill her mission of universal brotherhood, must live and work in the world, not in isolation, but with everyone, irrespective of race, colour, social condition, sex or creed. The Church, to be true to her vocation, should have respect for all men and women, be ready to collaborate for the common good, and must continue to be a dominant factor in the society.

> We believe that the Church in our countries, called to continue the prophetic mission of Christ, must defend those authentic human values which have been the basis of the life of our people. The Church must stand up against all that would tend to degrade the human person or lead to injustice, violence, oppression, racism, wars and evil of all sorts.[72]

The Church of Christ is universal, but its universality is seen and lived in a communion of small local Christian churches. The option for SCCs was seen by Kalilombe as:

> A decisive landmark in our pastoral policy in Eastern Africa. For the Bishops, the resolve to base Christian life and witness on SCCs is not just one way among many possible ones; it is not just following a passing fad in the Church today.It is a basic commitment: a serious shift in pastoral emphasis. It is deliberately intended to modify deeply our pastoral system, policy and practice. Until now the avowed common system was to base the life of the Church on the parish level, rather than on the sub-parish level... in these circumstances of Eastern Africa, what we call missions or parishes cannot be taken as the basic units of the local Church. If so, the Church is doomed to failure. We need to adopt a new system, whereby the basic units of the Church are those smaller communities where the ordinary life of the people takes place.[73]

The outcome of this Assembly was so important that it occupied the next two Assemblies that occurred in 1976 and 1979.

---

71 ibid.

72 ibid.

73 Kalilombe, P.A., "**An Overall view on Building Christian Communities**", in: **AFER**, Vol. 18 5(1976), pp. 266-267.

(i) The 1976 Assembly. The 1973 Assembly provided the raw material for this Assembly, which focussed on the theme: "Building SCCs in Eastern Africa." Their deliberations provided the key pastoral priority for the years to come; they concluded:

> The Christian communities we are trying to build are simply the most local incarnation of the one, holy catholic and Apostolic Church... The task of building Christian communities is more of creating and developing awareness of what our renewal vision of the Church means in practical terms and relationships, than one of building new structures.[74]

This explanation is important, lest the whole thing boil down to the same old structure with a new name. Building SCCs became a pastoral priority; communities that are self-ministering, self-propagating and self-supporting. There is a new understanding of the Church as the "people of God". There is a shift in emphasis, from the hierarchy to the laity, with both elements seeing themselves as one apostolic team.

(ii) The 1979 Assembly. An unexamined life, says Aristotle, is not worth living. No wonder the Bishops in this Assembly preferred to have as the Theme:

> "The implementation of the AMECEA Bishops' Pastoral Priority of Building Small Christian Communities an Evaluation".

For a better understanding of this pastoral priority, the small Christian communities need much attention and nurturing hence:

> We the Bishops of AMECEA, have spent several days together, reflecting on the progress made since 1976 in the task of building SCCs in Eastern Africa, a task which we then accepted as the pastoral priority for our times in our countries. Living together as a fraternal community, united in the one Holy Spirit, listening together to God's word, and celebrating together the sacrament of unity, the Eucharist.... This policy represents the most appropriate way of expressing the mystery of the Church as a communion of faith, hope and love, as well as being an excellent means of involving all the members of the people of God in the common task of continuing the reconciling mission of Christ in the world.[75]

This session was an evaluation indeed. They saw the SCCs as the means by which the Church could be brought down to the daily life and concerns of people in their locality. It is within these groups that the Church can take on flesh and blood in the everyday situation of the people. It is here that the people are able to experience the Church as a new way of being together in Christ.

---

74 **"AMECEA,"** in: **AFER**, 18 5(1976), p. 250.
75 **AMECEA**, in: **AFER**, Vol. 21, 5(1979), p. 265.

4.2.2.1.2. The Concept of the Small Christian Community

Although Jesus addressed individuals and insisted that each individual decide freely to follow him, he was not concerned with a collection of individuals. As A. von Harnack once taught, the reign of God does not come to a community, but comes to an individual. He was quoted as saying:

> The individual is to hear the good news of mercy and adoption, and to decide if he wishes to stand on the side of God and eternity or on the side of the world and time.[76]

Jesus was indeed concerned with Israel – the New Israel, the people of God, who could neither be founded nor established, but only gathered and restored. So the concept of SCC is, as it suggests, a small group of the people of God, a community where no one is left out.

> It is in this community that Christian commitment is fully lived, deepened and becomes the leaven and light of its members. It is also in this small group that the Church of Christ is as it were, given a 'human face' in its fellowship, service and witness, for here authentic Christian life and work emerge.[77]

This type of Christian community is the most local incarnation of the One, Holy Catholic and Apostolic Church. The size of such small groups breaks the needs and problems of the Church into a smaller dimension, and the involvement of the community leading to the solution of problems is more readily achieved.

In such a group, there is bound to be seen a true sense of co-responsibility and the principle of subsidiarity permeating every member of the group. There is little or no bureaucracy or "redtape" in implementing agreed policies. It is really in the small Christian community that the universality of the Church shines out and is localized. Care must be taken that such a group does not boil down to a ghetto community. There should be an ongoing contact with the parish, the deanery and the diocese.

> They (SCCs) remain firmly attached to the local Church in which they are inserted, and to the universal church, thus avoiding the very real danger of becoming isolated within themselves, then of believing themselves to be only authentic Church of Christ, and hence of condemning the other ecclesial communities.[78]

---

76 von Harnack, A., **Das Wesen des Christentums**; quoted by G. Lohfink, **Jesus and Community**. (Paulist Press, New York, 1984), p. 2.

77 Mwana A'Nzeki, R.S.N., "**Implementing AMECEA's Pastoral Priority**"; in: **AFER**, 21, 5(1979), p. 288.

78 **Evangelii Nuntiandi**, section V. Nr. 58.

The concept of SCCs is based on the understanding of Vatican II of the Church as the people of God, which carry out a mission, are actively self-reliant, self- propagating and self-ministering. The idea is based on a renewed vision of the Church, with a new spirit.

> This church of Christ is really present in all legitimately organized local groups of the faithful, which, in so far as they are united to their pastors, are also quite appropriately called churches in the New Testament. For these are in fact, in their own localities, the new people called by God, in the power of the Holy Spirit and as the result of full conviction.[79]

During the AMECEA Plenary Conference of 1976, it was declared that;

> The Christian community at every level is authentically the fullness of the Church because in it the Mystical Body of Christ is fully present and He, Himself, unites it and gives it life through His ordained minister, and through all the gifts which the spirit of Christ pours on the whole community.[80]

The SCC should be seen as essentially Eucharistic, which is both oriented to the Eucharist and finds its fullest meaning in it. The truth and importance of the Eucharist in the life of the church is obvious. It is the center of the life of the community, the manifestation of Christ's presence and the expression of the unity and the catholicity of the community.

(ii) *The structure of SCCs*. Since the SCC is suggested to be comprised of a group who feels related and lives in a localized situation, they should also deepen their commitment to the Risen Lord and the Christian way of life in order to qualify as a Christian community. For such a SCC, the structure must be based and dependent on the charisms of the community, its various ministries and services to its members. No matter what structure the SCC may take, it should be borne in mind that the exact words of Jesus, which are the base for every church structure are:

> I give you a new commandment; Love one another; just as I have Loved you, you also must love one another. By this love you have for one another, everyone will know that you are my disciples (Jn. 13:34-35).

The structure must always try to reflect the Church as an institution of brotherhood, of communication and of dialogue. The structure should allow communication among all different levels and among groups and individuals within the Church, to be able to fulfill its true role as the Church of Christ.

---

79 **Vatican 11, <u>Lumen Gentium</u>,** 26. A. Flamery, p. 381.

80 "**AMECEA Plenary Conference 1976,** in: **<u>AFER</u>** Vol. 21, 5(1979), p. 310; cf. **<u>Vatican 11</u>,** Documents on priests, Nr. 2, 6.

The structure should be in such a way that there exists great cohesion and at the same time a steady decentralization. In such a structure, there should be a flow of ideas and dialogue from top to bottom ,and vice-versa.

> If the pastoral option of building SCCs is to be really effective, a serious effort has to be made to re-educate clergy, religious and laity according to the authentic principles of Vatican II, especially in ecclesiology... Bishops and priests are apostles and teachers, but also disciples and learners.[81]

Following the ecclesiology of the Vatican II, the structure should take into consideration that the Church is the people of God. For all those who seek salvation in God, He wishes to deal with them as a community, as his children joined together into one family of brothers and sisters in His household. Inasmuch as He does not ignore the individual, God makes His Children conscious of the great brotherhood that ought to exist in the community, in the extended family of His Church. Pope Pius XII summed up this in his **Mystici Corporis** thus:

> It is clear enough that Christians stand in absolute need of Divine Redeemer's help. But it is also certain, surprising though it may seem, that Christ needs his members.... Dying on the Cross, he bestowed upon His Church the boundless treasures of the redemption without any cooperation on her part. But in the distribution of those treasures, He not only shares the work of sanctification with her, but wills it to arise in a certain manner out of her labour. This is truly a tremendous mystery; that the salvation of many souls depends on the prayers and sacrifices of the members of the Mystical Body, and on the cooperation which pastors and faithful, especially parents must give to our Divine Saviour.[82]

The structure calls for every member of the Body of Christ to participate fully in the life of the Church. The office should be seen from the evangelical concept of authority and leadership, which is expressed in service to and by the community, that is, the Church as the people of God.

The structure should encourage a community of faith, where every member of the community helps to strengthen one another's faith and make it relevant to daily life. Though the AMECEA Pastoral Priority of SCCs came from what may be termed the top, that is, from the official statement of the Church, it really expressed the needs of a time when African Christians were looking for the expression of their own values of community, harmony and solidarity in the context of their Christian faith.

---

81 **"AMECEA Guideline,"** op. cit., p. 270.

82 Pope Pius XII, **Mystici Corporis**, Nr. 42; cf. AMECEA Guidelines, op. cit., p. 270.

4.2.2.1.3. The Churches in East Africa and SCCs

After tracing the birth of SCC and the road to it, we shall now see how far SCCs have spread in the countries belonging to AMECEA. As was usual everywhere else, the Church in these countries were structured hierarchically. The Vatican II ecclesiology broke the old hierarchical pyramidal structure of the Church and gave a new explanation of what hierarchy means in the life of the Church – service. The Church is seen from the point of view of the Vatican II as being the "people of God".

In the old order, the Dioceses were sub-divided into territorial parishes for administrative purposes. The term "parish" refers to territorial, and not personal, parishes. By territorial parish is meant a stable community of the faithful within a particular area whose pastoral care is committed to a priest as the pastor under the authority of the diocesan Bishop.[83]

The parish embraces all the Christians in a given territory belonging to this pastor, who acts like a manager (cf. C.I.C.518). It may be more specific to say here that the difference between a territorial parish and personal parish is that the latter is established based upon rites, language, nationality or other determining factors. Some of these parishes are comprised of many towns, so many that they celebrate the Eucharistic only periodically. The priest acts as a father, even though he may be twenty years old, and members of the parish are his children and must be fed with spiritual milk.

It was not easy for a priest to cover the vast area, so the missionaries created sub-parishes which became outstations, or as they address them, "bush" stations. In these areas, catechists were appointed without formal education; they were Father's errand boys, money collectors and interpreters. Some of the catechists were used as a means of distributing old clothes to the poor and sometimes they would conduct services without a priest. Some of these outstations had masses once every two or three months. The missionaries were really care-takers of the Christians in their area. Gatamu expressed it thusly:

> The missionaries catered for the people who were working for the settlers, people who had very little to do with one another except meeting when picking or weeding coffee or pyrethrum shambas, maize or sisal plantations; people who met when the priest came for mass or religious instructions on sacraments, the ten commandments and on church. People

---

83 Provost, J.H., "**Code, Community, Ministry**"; **Canon Law Society of America.** (Washington, D.C. 1983), p. 61.

who met when they gathered around the catechist to receive old clothes or christmas gifts from the parish house.[84]

For the Catholics at this period, what mattered most was the priest and the Eucharist. The attendance of the mass was the only Christian activity and many were never able to follow what was going on at mass because the priest spoke only Latin. It was a common occurrence to see people busy reciting their Rosary while the mass was going on.

There was no dialogue, the clergy had to give their pastoral care to the best of their ability, and the faithful passively received the care, with their local leaders acting merely as intermediaries.[85] The priest was everything. Christianity followed colonization and to be a Christian means to be civilized in the western thinking, so any music or song that had no "musical so-fa notations", were regarded as uncivilized and hence pagan. To prepare people for the sacraments, especially baptism and confirmation, emphasis was laid on memorizing the questions and answers of the Dutch Catechism, with little or no emphasis on the life itself. Christianity was not then presented as a life to be lived everywhere, to be experienced and manifested to others.[86]

Pious societies took over the religiosity of the people. They visualized the Church as a service organization. People paid their annual mission collections (A.M.C.), not because they were Catholics, but because they want to go to confession and receive Holy Communion and other sacraments. This practice persists in many mission lands today. Those who pay their A.M.C. are permitted to receive the sacraments. The receipt obtained at the payment of these dues acts as a pass permitting access to some of these sacraments. Laws and regulation became too important. In this way, Christianity was seen as a list of arbitrary rules which one had to carry out completely.[87] There was a great effort to save individual souls; the sense of community was destroyed, and nothing was done to salvage it. The ecclesiology of the Second Vatican Council has opened the new way of expressing the Church and the new way of being Church. People are realizing that the Church belongs to every Christian, or rather that we are the Church -clergy and laity. The period before the Vatican II belonged to a Church that overstressed the juridical aspect of the life of

---

84 Gatamu, J.P.W., **SCCs in the Catholic Diocese of Nakuru:** A Thesis in fulfillment of the requirement for the degree of M.A./ Specialized Licentiate in Theology. (Catholic Higher Institute of Eastern Africa, Nairobi, 1986), pp. 22-23.

85 Cf. P.A. Kalilombe, "**An Overall View On Building Christian Communities**", in: **AFER**, Vol. 18, 5(1976), p. 268.

86 Cf. D. Kyeyune, **The Role of Liturgy in Pastoral Life of the Church**, ad usum auditorum, (CHIEA, 1985), p. 1.

87 Cf. K. Rahner, **Theology for Renewal**, (Sheed and Ward, New York, 1964), p. 71.

the church, a Church that was so individualistic and indifferent that it was, as some prefer to call it, "a church in the sacristy".[88]

This situation led the AMECEA bishops to opt for a change. This is not a new Church as some have said and written but a new style of "dancing to the old music or old song". The stress is on the Jesus of yesterday, today and tomorrow; therefore the ecclesiology of the Second Vatican Council is a new way of being Church. Because the Latin American BCCs offer Christians a new understanding of social reality, a new way of being Church, a new way of doing theology and a prophetical way of carrying out the Church's mission in our time, this has affected the Church in Africa.[89] The introduction of SCCs took place at a time when almost the Member Countries of AMECEA were achieving their independence. The AMECEA Bishops had other reasons for embarking on SCCs. Some of those reasons included the lack of priests and the fears that missionaries would be shown a red card as soon as independence was won since the nationalists regarded them as cooperators of the colonial masters. A Gikuyu proverb summarizes this fact:

> there is no catholic priest and a European both are the same.[90]

The thought of losing the missionaries who mark the bulk of priests in this area really occupied their mind. At the time when missionaries were still there, there was: "a shortage and maldistribution of priests".[91] What the fate of Christianity would be when the missionaries left was a legitimate question that needed an urgent answer. Gatamu wrote:

> Hence the precaution was to conscientize the people that they are the church and christianity is here to stay and that it is a way of life. The best too was starting SCCs which would help the church be self-supporting, self-propagating and self-ministering.[92]

The ecclesiology of the Second Vatican Council gave impetus to this line of thought. Looking at the Church as the People of God and the expression of the life of the Church in people's culture, the council fathers admonish priests, saying;

---

88 Cf. D. Kyeyune, **Eucharistic celebration as the basis and foundation of Christian Life and activities, ad usum auditorum**, (CHIEA, Nairobi, 1985), p. 12. Cf. P.W. Gatamu, **SCCs in the Catholic Diocese of Nakuru**, (1986), pp. 24-29.

89 Cf. A. Shorter, **The Impact of BCCs**, unpubl. article, quoted by P.M. Gatamu, **SCCs in the Catholic Diocese of Nakuru** (1986), p. 39.

90 Mbiti, J., **African Religions and Philosophy**, (Heineman, Nairobi, 1983), p. 12.

91 O'Halloran, J., **Living Cells**, (Dominican Publications, Orbis Books, New York, 1984), p. 12.

92 Gatamu, P.W., **SCCs in the Catholic Diocese of Nakuru** (1986), p. 39.

as they sanctify and govern, under the Bishops authority, that flock entrusted to their care, make the universal church visible in their locality. (L.G.28)

The SCC was introduced in order to realize the local Church, where people will be able to know one another, and live in daily contact with one another. This is "where the action is" and it is there that the Church can be found. Functions are shared according to the gifts of the spirit and ability. Now people can take decisions on their own. There is on-going awareness within the villages, discussion about the meaning of the SCCs and necessary actions taken.

It is interesting to see how far this has gone to help the local Church. The apostolic spirit of the laity is reviving in different ways and people are beginning to realize that they have a common task and mission in the Church and the community to share.

4.2.2.1.4. Evaluation of SCCs in AMECEA Regions

In my interview with Bishop P.A.Kalilombe (one of the architects of SCCs in East Africa), he once said that people cannot be forced or just be told to form communities; they should know and realize the need and challenges it entails. But is it not exactly that which the Bishops are telling the people?

Let us from the point of view of intellectual honesty and openness to reality before us have a critical look at the way SCCs have gone within the AMECEA regions since its inauguration. The Church in a way is an institution, and will rot away if she does not re-examine herself and make changes where they are necessary.

The effort of renewal in the Church is not new. It has been an on-going activity which is often carried on silently. Renewal sometimes needs a more open degree of consciousness and a more articulated and clear sense of direction. Pope Paul VI, in his first encyclical letter, **Ecclesiam Suam** of 1964, counselled that the church has reached the hour in which it, "should deepen its consciousness of itself, in which it ought to mediate on that mystery which is peculiar to it, in which it ought to examine, for its own enlightenment and for its own development, a particular doctrine that it already knows and that it has formulated and made known during this past century. That doctrine concerns the origin of the church, its nature, its mission, its ultimate destiny, a doctrine never sufficiently investigated and understood.."(Nr. 9).

It is this desire of renewal and examination that motivated the AMECEA Bishops to establish SCCs. The Bishops took this bold step and proposed that SCCs be made into an integral dimension of the vision and structure of the Church in the region.

> The main reason among others was to make 'Christianity African' that is to help christianity to influence the African to an appreciatable degree. In other words to influence the African, the way the traditional religion did, Africanizing the church. Making the church local in such a way that it will be concerned with politics, social life and economic struggle of the African people. Making christianity a way of life and not a fashion by making it truly African.[93]

How far has these been realized? For the past 21 years, the formation of SCCs has been the pastoral priority of the church in AMECEA countries. The ideals of the SCCs are clearly documented in the reports of the Plenary Conferences of the AMECEA, which took place in 1973, 1976 and 1979 respectively.

The primary preoccupation of these conferences was the planning, choice and execution of pastoral priorities. The plan was to help to bring people into psychological, sociological and ecclesiological communion with one another, and with the larger Christian communities. There are problems associated with the implementation of such pastoral planning and execution.

First of all, we have to admit that, since the creation of SCCs took place within the hierarchy, i.e. from above, it will not be surprising to encounter some implicit contradiction in its methodology. The question of forming communities, without first acknowledging the felt need of the people, and the lack of prior formation of pastors and leaders, for the real implementation of the guidelines based upon SCCs, has been a great stumbling block for the progress in the growth of the SCCs in Eastern Africa.

It has been difficult to achieve the aim and aspirations of the Founding Fathers, due to poor education and enlightenment programs. This does not in any way suggest that no progress has been achieved. Guiney saw the effort thusly:

> However, the effort to establish communities in which genuine interaction might take place, and where the church could be really localized and incarnated has been a slow and challenging process. On one hand, SCCs have either been confused with prayer groups, or with parish out-stations, and turned into administrative tools under the control of some authoritarian parish priests, and with little sharing of responsibilities.[94]

---

93 Gatamu, P.W., "**SCCs in the Catholic Diocese of Nakuru** (1986), "... those basic and manageable social groups whose members can experience real inter-personal and feel a sense of communal belonging both in living and working. We believe that Christian communities at this level will be best suited to develop real intense vitality and to become effective witnesses in their natural environment". Cf. "**Planning for the Church in Eastern Africa in 1980s**", **AFER**: Vol. 16, Nr. 142, (Gaba publications, Eldoret, 1974), pp. 9 - 10.

94 Guiney, J., "**Comparing BCCs in South America and Africa**", in: **AFER**, Vol. 30, 3(1988), p. 169.

It is noteworthy that the SCCs do not only arise in an ascetically religious soil; they can and often do arise from a need felt in everyday life. Particular social, cultural, and economic circumstances and situations have a notable bearing upon the rise of such communities. Thus, to concentrate on catechesis will not only be difficult, but will create more division, instead of cementing the community.

Experience has shown that people have more feelings towards life's concrete necessities, such as water projects, schools and other similar needs. The preoccupation of the hierarchy was still the salvation of the soul with little or nothing for the body. They were building or shaping the people for the life to come and little emphasis to the existent life.

In the program there was not much to incite the people to stand up for the rights that had been trampled upon for a long time. They seemed to fall back to the routine pedagogy of separating the religious life from the political/social life. Though the church may have no particular political mission as some say, but the Church must evangelize. And this evangelization includes awakening the people's consciousness to things that concern them.[95]

Inasmuch as the SCCs is the decision of all AMECEA Bishops, the growth and interest of some dioceses seem to suggest that some voted for it without actually understanding their full implications and far-reaching effects, as Healey puts it:

> Implementation of AMECEA guidelines reveals a mixed experience. In the seven AMECEA Countries relatively few dioceses have really established SCCs as a new model of church with its vast implications for grassroots decision-making, varieties of lay ministries and simple, community-oriented lifestyle. Other dioceses are caught between the traditional clerical, centralized parish structures and the revolutionary plan of modeling the local church from the bottom, with lay people truly responsible for their church. Other dioceses for political or pastoral reasons have hardly begun to implement the AMECEA Pastoral Priority.[96]

Robert M.Gay tries to show that despite the many meetings and resolutions, the progress in terms of establishing SCCs in these lands is yet to be seen:

> Pastoral vision and policy are often to be found well defined in the various documents of official church documents. It is well known for instance that the S.C.C pastoral option has been stated and adopted by all the Bishops of Eastern Africa since their Plenary Meeting of AMECEA of 1973... an option of priority concerning the launching of S.C.C. as the basis

95 Romero, O., **Voice of the Voiceless**, (Orbis Books, N. Y. 1985), pp. 50f.

96 Healey, J., "**BCCs in Africa and Latin America**", in: **AFER**, VOL, 26, 4(1984), p. 227.

of their pastoral planning. However, when one seeks to identify concrete realization of S.C.C., the list is rather short.[97]

It is true that recent research into the situation of SCCs in East Africa has shown that the objective has not been universally implemented.

It would be demanding so much to see that all be achieved within this period in time. There are a number of dioceses which have taken this pastoral priority seriously with the encouragement of their ordinaries. O'Halloran in his report said that by 1983 there were about 10,000 SCCs in East Africa.[98] In some dioceses there are examples of some level of success in implementing the AMECEA vision.

From my interviews, I realized that the most prominent Bishops who are interested in the implementation of this are Bishops C.Mwoleka of Rulenge,Tanzania and P.A.Kalilombe, then of Lilongwe, Malawi. From my interview with Bishop Kalilombe, I also realized that not very much has been achieved in translating the ideal of SCCs as the primary and fundamental local churches into reality. The actual obstacles militating against this include the authoritarian attitudes of some pastoral agents and the reactionary policies of others, which are expressed in excessive clericalism and episcopal apathy. Gatamu puts this problem in this way:

> The major one is that many priests have not taken this issue seriously... And this cry goes a step further to prove that the priests are still very isolated from the real center of activities, 'homes' where one can detect the climate of christian living,through observation, and actually helping where necessary are not visited as needed.[99]

Despite the number of SCCs and the talks and seminars about SCCs, nothing seems to have changed from the concept of the parish as the center of administration and only source of the sacramental ministry of the Church. The outstation is still the outreach of the parish. More is said and written about

---

97 Gay, R.M., **The Role of Expatriate Missionaries in the Local Church of Eastern Africa.**, p. 17.

98 Cf. J. O'Halloran, **Living Cells: Developing Small Christian Communities**, (Dublin, Dominican Publications, 1984), p. 21; **Signs of Hope: Developing SCCs**, (Maryknoll, Orbis Books, 1991); Cf. L.J. Goodwin, "**Ecclesiological Dimensions of Eucharistic centers in the Diocese of Mbarara**", (Uganda, An Inquiry into Christian community structure and Ministry, Ph.D. dissertation, mimeo, Washington, D.C., Catholic University of America, 1984

99 Gatamu, P.W., **SCCs in the Catholic Diocese of Nakuru** (1986), p. 137; and in another place, he also says, that where priests are not interested in SCCs, or not make a fellow-up, the original objective of SCCs are not met. Some priest allow inexperienced catechists to run such organizations; p. 132.

SCCs in East Africa but one can say that less action is observed. Practical action or praxis is what establishes the church in a locality.

Initially, there seems to have been confusion in distinguishing the SCC from outstations and village churches. It is difficult to look at the SCC as a new way of being the Church, or as Leonardo Boff calls it, 're-invent the church'. Some took the SCC on its face value, not realizing the enormous work and energy that had to be put into it, in order for it to work. No wonder so many SCCs ended up in becoming mere prayer groups within the Church structure. It may be of interest here to recall how Aloisio Lorscheider (Bishop of Fortaleza and president of the Latin American Episcopal Conference) looks at the BCCs/SCCs:

> To speak of basic ecclesiastical communities is the same for us to speak of church renewal, of an enormous hope; it's like speaking of the living church, of its vitality, of its dynamic quality; it's speaking of the church as Vatican Council 11 really wanted it. In fact, basic ecclesiastical communities offer us a new image of the church, or, rather a new image of ecclesiastical life.[100]

The AMECEA Bishops admitted the inadequacy of the existing structures, though there is no call for new ones; what that means is that inadequate structures need to be renewed. Timira looked at these structures critically and says;

> It is painfully obvious that many of the structures related to the community to ministry are now inadequate to meet the demands and thinking of the African Church, especially in dioceses where there are too many catholics and too few priests; too many marginal Christians and too few committed catholics; too many nominal catholics and too few involved lay people; too many parishes and too few ministers.[101]

Because of these inadequacies and lack of priests to preside over the Eucharist at regular times of worship, many Christians are discouraged and even abandon their religious duties. Such problems were not adequately looked into and no provision were made, such as creating new ministries to take charge of such problems.

The Church is still capsuled in her old ways, but efforts are being made to allow in some changes. Theses changes are necessary for the SCCs to survive and to be able to be an authentic Church in a given locality, otherwise they will boil down to a mere glorified prayer groups. The methodology of the SCCs constitutes another problem, since there is no blue print or prototype,

---

100 Lorscheider, A., "**BECs in Latin America**", in: **AFER**, Vol. 19 3(1979), p. 142.

101 Timira, A., "**BCCs and the Participatory Church Theology**"; in: **AFER**, Vol. 27, 6(1985), p. 379.

but efforts have to be placed on the education of the clergy and laity. Timira, in trying to suggest ways of improvement, says;

> Yet, one of the necessary elements, besides a change of mentality, is spontaneity and commitment that goes hand in hand with education or conscientization of both the clergy and the laity about Small Christian Communities.[102]

After so many years, one wonders that the same old mentality still raises its ugly head; reliance on the Western Church, Christians' dogmatic dependency on the priests, and of course, the priests clinging to authoritarian administration, legalism, clericalism and the like are still present.

Some of the priests are afraid of losing their parish-kingdom to splinter groups or sects. Some are not interested in the formation of these SCCs, and some who are interested over police these communities to the extent of stifling local leadership and spontaneity. It is good to remark that the best place to re-educate the future priests about SCCs for the good of the Church is in the seminary. Timira, continuing his remarks, says;

> One could again ask, how much preparation is given to future priests in seminaries in view of equipping them with right knowledge, vision and even skill to deal with SCCs later on in the ministry? Moreover, it has been evident that some church leaders merely give the pastoral priority no more than lip-service when it comes to diocesan pastoral strategy. That indifference leaves the SCCs formation on individual priest's initiative or lay people without any defined directions on the diocesan level.[103]

At this time, some people in these areas still see the SCCs as one of the ways the priests are using to organize their parishes, and not as a way of being Church. Jose Marins puts the point more bluntly when he says:

> the parish is seen as a sort of spiritual service station, where christians go to receive sacraments, practice their devotion, fulfil their obligations but have no deep experience of life-sharing or even a backing of their mission.[104]

This way of thinking can be attributed to the fact that the idea of the SCCs came from above and not from below.

The SCCs as we have mentioned, should not be seen from the point of view of catechesis but instead, and most importantly, the conscientization approach start from the people themselves by helping them to become more aware of

---

102 Ibid.

103 Ibid., pp. 379 - 380.

104 Marins, J. and T. Trevisan, **Basic Ecclesial Community: "Church from the Roots"**, Bangare National Biblical Catechetical and liturgical Center, 1981, quoted by P.W. Gatamu, **SCCs in the Catholic Diocese of Nakuru** (1986), p. 138.

their problems and needs in their life situations. There should be programs to help people stand up for their rights and face their problems squarely.

Often, priests and religious in a given area see themselves as teachers and masters instead of brothers and sisters in the family of God's people. The degree of involvement of priests and members of religious orders in SCCs is still not encouraging; it may be due to their formation. Since they are referred as *segrigatus apopulo*, wrongly translated as separated from the community, rather than taken among the people, to serve and share within the community in cultic duties. So many members of religious orders still find it difficult to be identified with the community in which they live and work; looking at such a life, E. van Huet remarked:

> They have great difficulty when they are asked to function in small groups. Many of them have developed such a teaching approach that it is very hard for them to share personal feelings and faith experiences, to listen to others without attempting to judge and evaluate what others share.[105]

Many priests and members of religious orders suffer a from 'teacher complex', and they feel that they have answers to every problem. Does our line of thought suggest that nothing good has come form the introduction of the SCCs? On the contrary, SCCs in East Africa are the best thing that ever happened in the history of evangelization in Africa.

Inasmuch as the option for SCCs as a pastoral priority came from the top, it has become the expression of a need which has been felt to change the church structure to make it be in harmony with African cultures and structures. Gatamu sees the new development within SCCs as:

> Today decisions are no longer taken in mission houses but in SCCs. The whole of SCC is based on the fact, that everything comes from the grassroots level, though the priest has the last word in every major problems or in matters pertaining to morals or sacraments that need the stress of the universal church.[106]

---

105 van Huet, E., "**Religious and AMECEA Key Pastoral Priority**" in: **AFER**, Vol. 23, 5(1981), p. 266; cf. P.W. Gatamu, **SCCs in the Catholic Diocese of Nakuru** (1986), where he says; "However, what surprises one is the fact that some of the priests do not really fulfil their roles in SCCs. That is the roles of co-ordering, facilitating and animating them in God's name. Also serving, teaching and guiding them, and governing them in the context of service as in Mtt.20:25 - 28; approving them and again relating not only to SCCs but also to other organizations;" p. 133.

106 Gatamu, P.W., **SCCs in the Catholic Diocese of Nakuru** (1986), p. 130. We have to remark that Gatamu's conclusion here is with regards Nakuru Diocese where it applies it is an exception rather than the rule. For the old mentality of the church and decisions belonging to the priest still holds.

Our goal is to make the Church to be our Church in the communal spirit of the African, instead of calling it the "priests' church". Healey described this thought thus:

> The AMECEA Bishops opted for the SCC pastoral priority as the best way to build up local churches that are truly self-ministering, self-propagating and self-supporting. The AMECEA Pastoral Priority of SCC has effectively questioned the whole system by which pastoral ministry is carried out. Also, the AMECEA study conference in 1979 stressed that SCCs are the best means of developing African christianity stating that small communities also seem to be the most effective means of making the gospel message truly relevant to African culture and tradition.[107]

As SCCs advance these objectives, there is no doubt that they are also committed to serve as the most important source of human advancement and development.

Many groups such as prayer groups, charismatic, close neighbours (like the Ujamaa villages) have gone on to become SCCs. No doubt this goes to prove that SCCs in no small measure are contributing to christianizing the ordinary African neighbourhood. The smallness of the group acts as a help to the individual, and brotherly correction is readily available. The formation of a Christian consciousness can be attributed to the effort of the SCCs in the AMECEA countries, through a series of seminars and work-shops. There is a greater awareness among many Christians now than before as to what it means to be Church and what a Christian life entails. From the research in some of these countries, it has been recognized that the exodus of some Catholics to other churches has been minimal since the introduction of the SCCs. A lot of cooperation between priests and their co-workers is being experienced, though in a low key. But sometimes such progress is blocked by the struggle for power. Gatamu says this of the Londiani SCCs:

> About 20 SCCs were started, within a few weeks, three of them dropped out and again within three to four months some more collapsed due to strife, ambition for leadership.[108]

There is much work still to be done in these places make the idea of the founding fathers of AMECEA into reality. The future lies on more education so that people will be more appreciative of this noble pastoral strategy. And

---

107 Healey, J.G., "**Basic and Small Christian Communities**", **ADS**, 48, Nr. 284, (Nairobi, 1984).

108 Gatamu, P.W., **SCCs in the Catholic Diocese of Nakuru** (1986), p. 140. This is normal for formation of such groups when the initiative comes from outside the group as the case in AMECEA Regions.

emphasis should be laid on what unites the tradition of the people with Christianity, especially shared care.

4.2.2.2. The Zairian Experience

The implementation of the teaching of the Vatican II is also felt in Zaire. The Basic Christian Community (*Communautes ecclesiales de base*) in Zaire has come a long way in helping to incarnate the Christian faith in Africa in general and Zaire in particular. Just as it did in the AMECEA countries, the Episcopal Synode of Zairian Bishops, held in Kinshasa, opted for the introduction of BEC as a pastoral priority.

4.2.2.2.1. The Process of Mokambi wa Paroise

Mokambi wa Paroise is a system of running a parish in Zaire, where a lay person takes charge of a parish administratively and runs it like the parish priest, as Bertsch puts it:

> *Der Mokambi ist vom Bischof beauftragt, am Dienst der Wortverkündigung teilzuhaben. Bei seiner Einsetzungszeremonie überträgt ihm der Bischof diesen Auftrage: Lehren Sie die Christen das Wort Gottes so wie ich es Sie gelehrt habe. Der Dienst der Wortverkündigung wird in der Katechese, in der Predigt bei Gottesdiensten sowie in anderen Formen der Glaubensunterweisung ausgeübt. Der Mokambi übt diesen Dienst vor allem im Bereich der Katechese.., der Vorbereitung auf ein christliches Leben und der Glaubensvertiefung aus. In diesen Bereichen hat er weitreichende Verantwortungen zu übernehmen.*[109]

Since the 1970s, the *Mokambi wa Paroise* position has been promoted in Zaire, particularly in the Archdiocese of Kinshasa. The architect of this new way of being church, following the ecclesiology of the Vatican II and due to lack of priests was Cardinal Malula as Bertsch rightly observed;

> *Kardinal Malula hielt seine Entscheidung für gerechtfertigt durch die besonderen Umstände der Erzdiözese Kinshasa: den Priestermangel, die dringende Notwendigkeit der Afrikanisierung und die Sorge um die verantwortliche Beteiligung der Laien an der Einpflanzung der Ortskirche.*[110]

---

109 Bertsch, L., "Laien Als Gemeindeleiter: Ein afrikanisches Modell; Texte der Erzdiözese Kinshasa" in: **Theologie der Dritten Welt**; Band 14, Freiburg, Herder, 1990, p.196.

110 Bertsch, L., **Theologie der Dritten Welt**, p.202; cf. *Les bakambi de paroisse - les bakambi du quartier,* **in: Documentation et informations africaines**, 4, S. 121f. Kinshasa, 1975.

Zaire must also be included in the list of countries accusing early missionaries of being collaborators with colonizers, and at independence, there was a quick struggle for an authentic African Church. Salvatore Coppo says:

> The events and the struggle towards African authenticity in Zaire, marked a turning point in the church as well. The cultural alienation of which the church appeared as the retrograde agent in an independent country, led it to recognize already in 1961, some mistaken collaboration with colonialism.[111]

The problem the bishops faced was that of putting it into practice. How could their resolutions and talks be brought to reality? How could the Church be Africanized? They realized that the Church can never be African as long as it is dependent on foreign aid in personnel, money, thought and lifestyle.

It will be difficult, if not impossible, for a non-African to Africanize the Church in Africa. It became imperative to animate the Christian communities, using pastors chosen from among themselves in order to help them in living their Christian faith, according to their African way of life.[112] The Church should be, just like every other thing in Africa, "our" Church.

Although much is talked about and written about inculturation, at the same time, almost all the parishes in Zaire were run by foreign missionaries. How can the Christian communities survive in the hands of those who know little or nothing of African community mentality? Then there was a call for Zairians to minister to themselves if the SCC were to succeed. Malula had to take the bull by the horns, by introducing the first parish to be manned by a lay, unordained, married pastor who is called *Mokambi wa paroise*, according to the stipulation of the new code of Canon Law.[113] During this epoch making event the cardinal declared:

> To day you are inaugurating a new style of dancing. Be it clear to you: If you dance well, we shall follow you; but if your dance is not good, we shall not join... We have to

---

111 Coppo, S., "**A Truly African Church**", **SPEARHEAD**; Nr. 99, (Gaba Publication, AMECEA, Eldoret, 1987), p. 4.

112 Ibid.

113 Canon 517, section 2, "If, because of a shortage of priests, the diocesan Bishop has judged that a deacon, or some other person who is not a priest, or a community of persons, should be entrusted with a share in the exercise of the pastoral care of a parish, he is to appoint some priest who, with the powers and faculties of a parish priest, will direct the pastoral care". **The Code of Canon Law** (Collins, London, 1983), p. 93. Bertsch also writes: "*Bei der rechtlichen und theologischen Begründung des Laiendienstamtes des Mokambi greifen sowohl Kardinal Malula wie auch andere Gruppen, z.B. die Verfasser der Schrift "Die Laiendienstämter in der Ortskirche von Kinshasa" (Dokument 5), immer wieder auf can. 517 § 2 des Kirchlichen Gesetzbuches zurück*"; **Theologie der Dritten Welt**, p.184.

recognize – witness Mongu Ekongo and his wife – that at Saint Adrien they did not dance so badly.[114]

One may call this an experimental stage that opened the door for a new way of being Church.

4.2.2.2.2. A Novelty in the Tradition of the Church

After the period of incubation, when much research and hard work had been done regarding the lay ministries and church Africanization, the cardinal made the private dance of Mongu Ekongo and his wife an archdiocesan dance. Observing this historic event Bertsch says;

> *Der Mokambi ist an der Ausübung des Hirtenamtes beteiligt. In der Einsetzungszeremonie als Pfarr-Mokambi überträgt ihm der Bischof diesen Sendungsauftrag: "Führe die Christen dieser Pfarrei auf den Wegen, die Jesus Christus den Menschen gewiesen hat." Er ist also berufen, die Gläubigen auf den Wegen des Evangeliums zu führen.*[115]

It was in September of 1973 that the project was made known to all the archdiocesan pastoral agents in Kinshasa. The cardinal gave his main guidelines as:

> We want to entrust entirely some parishes to lay animators who will have followed a three-year training cycle and will have already given a clear sign of their dedication to the service of the community.... This project must not lead us to forget the urgent need of promoting, or favouring other lay ministries in all the parishes. It is also necessary to initiate lay ministers committed to the pastoral care of the sick.[116]

It is interesting to note that the Cardinal stressed the willingness and dedication to the service of the community. The emphasis is on service and not on the rank of people or position (not of making a difference between those who will see themselves as married priests or between priests and lay people).

> *Er muß fähig sein, das Leben der Gemeinde zu erleuchten. Dies fordet von ihm das fortwährende Studium des Wortes Gottes wie auch der Lebensbedingungen und Bedürfnisse der Gemeinde. Er muß Erzieher im Glauben sein, den Christen helfen, zu be-*

---

114 **Telema**, 3(1982), p. 68. We notice here the use of the term "We" by the cardinal showing the African "we" mentality.

115 Bertsch, L., **Theologie der Dritten Welt**, p. 199.

116 Malula, J., **Notes Pastorales**, Kinshasa, Nr. 73, (Sept. 1973), pp. 484 - 485. Cf. S. Coppo, **A Truly African Church**, (1987), pp. 5 - 6.

ten und das Wort Gottes zu meditieren und das durch Vorbild seines Lebens in den Christen das Verlangen wecken, Christus mehr nachzueifern.[117]

After the training, there is a danger at first of the lay pastor seeing himself or herself as a "small" priest, and that results in his or her not being a either priest or a lay person. Although the ministry of the priest is needed, but there should be a line of demarcation regarding duties and cooperation between the priest and the parish *Mokambi.*[118]

Secondly, because of the constant availability of the priest, the *Mokambi* may be turned into a priests errand boy like the old catechists. Thirdly, it gives the priest the chance to devote much time to prayer and preaching, as Peter once told the community.

It would not be right for us to neglect the word of God so as to give out food; you brothers, must select from among yourselves seven men of good reputation, filled with the Spirit and wisdom, we will hand over this duty to them...(Acts 6:2 – 6).

This method of using the *Bakambi* (plural of *Mokambi*) in the parishes has given rise to many Christian communities. Although the priest is ordained for the sacraments and preaching the word, evangelisation is not and cannot be the task of the ordained alone, but must be a duty of the whole baptized Christian community. Commenting on everyone participating in the building of the Christian community, Bertsch says;

Wenn jede under jeder in der Gemeinde ihre Aufgaben zur Auferbauung der Gemeinde und zur Weitergabe des Glaubens wahrnehmen, wird die Kirche ihren Auftrag erfüllen können und wird sie als die von den Sakramenten der Taufe und Firmung aller ihrer Mitglieder getragene Communio von Priestern und Laien in der von soviel Zusammenhanglosigkeit bedrohten abendländischen Gesellschaft Zeichen der Hoffnung sein können.[119]

---

117 Bertsch, L., **Theologie der Dritten Welt**, p. 200.

118 Bertsch summarizes it thus: "*Es ist notwendig, daß es zwischen beiden einen häufigen und regelmäßigen Austausch gibt, bei dem alle das Pfarrleben betreffenden Probleme zur Sprache kommen, damit beide wirklich eins sind im Dienst der Pfarrei.., daß sie miteinander im Dienst der Kirche stehen und gemeinsam verantwortlich sind für die gleiche Aufgabe, die zu erfüllen beide - jeder auf seiner Ebene - von ihrem Bischof gesandt sind.*" **Theologie der Dritten Welt**, pp. 200-201.

119 Bertsch, L., **Theologie der Dritten Welt**, p. 188; cf. **Presbyterium ordnis**: "*Mit allen nämlich, die wiedergeboren sind im Quell der Taufe, sind die Priester Brüder unter Brüdern, da sie ja Glieder ein und desselben Leibes Christi sind, dessen Auferbauung allen anvertraut ist*"; (**PO 9**).

The spread of the Good News is a commission for every Christian through his words and deeds, under the supervision of the Apostles. A case at hand would be the Jerusalem council:

> We hear that some of our members have disturbed you with their demands and have unsettled your minds. They acted without any authority from us...(Acts 15:22 – 29).

These people were recognized as members of the church but they had no authority from the Apostles. That is to say, they were not sent. According to the *manuel du Mokambi wa paroise*, the *Mokambi* takes charge of the parish with the mandate from the Bishop as:

> He exercises his functions as a delegate of the bishop, who sends him to animate and guide the christian life in a portion of his diocese; the parish.[120]

One may quickly jump to the conclusion that the erection of parishes under lay people was simply due to lack of priests. This is a determinant factor, but it is coupled with a rapid growth of Christian communities. These communities need to be looked after and encouraged to realize the active Church at the local level as a follow-up of the Vatican II document. Pope Paul VI's encyclical, after specifying the specific vocation of the laity in world, adds:

> One cannot, however, neglect or forget the other dimension: the laity can also feel themselves called or being called to work with their pastors in the service of the ecclesial community, for its growth and life, by exercising a great variety of ministries according to the graces and charisms which the Lord is pleased to give them (Evangelii Nuntiandi, Nr.73; also see, Nr.70).

The Vatican Council and the Pope's encyclical had much impact on the Church in Zaire, who quickly recognized the importance of the Council's theological and pastoral renewal. Coppo analyzed the minutes of the Zairian Bishops' sixth and seventh Planers and came out with the conclusion that they were motivated with:

> First, the enlightenment of lay people seen as the means of bringing closer the church leadership and the mass of christians who, after the primary evangelisation mainly by foreign missionaries, hardly felt themselves full members in a church which remained foreign. Secondly, the new theology of the laity allowed them to rediscover their traditional cultural

---

120 **Manuel du Mokambi wa Paroisse**, (Kinshasa, 1975), p. 2. "*Der Mokambi ist vom Bischof beauftragt, 'an der Wahrnehmung der Seelsorgaufgaben teilzunehmen`. Im allgemeinen Rahmen dieser Beauftragung weist ihm der Bischof als besondere Aufgabe im einzelnen die Verwaltung der Pfarrei und die Organisation der Seelsorglichen Aktivitäten zu.*" Bertsch, L., **Theologie der Dritten Welt**, p. 193.

and social African patrimony, the importance of community life, co-responsibility and solidarity of all the members of the christian community. Thirdly, the bishops' invitation to the lay people to assume responsibilities in the church was the beginning of presenting Christ's message meaningfully through African thought expressions and local structure that 'incarnate' it concretely among the faithful.[121]

Lamenting the passivity of the laity in the Church the bishops declared:

> It is necessary that lay people be the very ones responsible in the church. In our church of Zaire, responsibility belongs too exclusively to the clergy. The christians are now so used to it that they adopt a passive attitude proper of a consumer and not of an active member. An immense effort must be done to change this situation. It is not a question of inviting lay people to assume their own responsibility in the fields of worldly activities. It is within the very church – institution and at all levels, that they have to behave as responsible members.[122]

The archdiocese of Kinshasa was in the forefront of the implementation of the decisions of the Assembly, due to the energetic and foresightedness of Cardinal Malula, who in 1968 declared that the task of the church in Kinshasa include:

> to put at the service of the country the dynamism which must introduce into our society the faith and hope of the believers .... To do so, the function of the a committed laity is put in a crucial and decisive manner for our diocese.[123]

For the Cardinal to realize this type of informed and active Christians is not an easy task. There should be re-orientation of both clergy and the laity, and he decided, that to come towards the needs of decentralization of action, and as an efficacious source, to connect the Church structures on the natural social structures, it is indispensable to develop where they already exist, and to start basic communities elsewhere, the running of which is to be entrusted to the lay people.[124] Seventeen years after the introduction of the BEC, came a document which stated, from experience, how these communities are to be formed and lived. The Document, dated January 21, 1987, was approved by the bishops' Council. This Document defined the Christian Basic Community, its formation, function and aim. Since the declaration of this 'pastoral option', the archdiocese of Kinshasa has placed the building of Christian Basic Com-

---

121 Coppo, S., **A Truly African Church**, (1987), p. 14.

122 **Actes de la VIIemme Assemblee Pleniere de l'Episcopat du Congo,** Leopoldville 1961; (Kinshasa, 1967), pp. 39 - 41.

123 Malula, J., **Lettre du 14 Avril 1968** ; cf. S. Coppo, op. cit., p. 14.

124 Malula, **Mission de L'Eglisa a Kinshasa: Options Pastorales**, (Kinshasa, 1970), p.18; cf. S. Coppo, **A Truly African Church** (1987), pp. 14 - 15.

munities as the most important aspect of her pastoral life. Bertsch summed this pastoral option of the Zairian thusly;

Im Falle des Priestermangels und auch, so glauben wir, um viele Laien für ihre Mitverantwortung in der Kirche wach zu machen, wird diese Pfarrstruktur in der Erzdiözese Kinshasa für eine Reihe von Pfarreien künftig eine rechtmäßige, nützliche und gültige Form darstellen, die auch weiterhin dem Volk Gottes wertvolle Dienste leisten wird.[125]

This pastoral option has its base and foundation in the Scriptures and should not be taken as one of the new movements. God willed it, as we mentioned earlier in this work (Cf. Ex. 19:5-6; Jer. 31:31-34; Mtt.1:21; Jn.11:51-52; 1 Pet.2:4-10). It is the experience of the first Christians who lived these community lives, together with a call from Vatican II to revive this important aspect of Christian life, that actually necessitated these movements.[126]

4.3. A Basic Community as a Community of Umunna

The *umunna* community is not only an abstract concept but a mystique. It is seen as the supreme phenomenal principle of cohesion, as well as the morally efficient cause of the sense of responsibility of the individual. The *umunna* community determines strength and guarantees safety. It is a principle that goes on satisfying the inner longing in man which God recognized in the dawn of creation and which led Him to create a helpmate for him (cf. Gen. 2:18). The *umunna* community phenomenon is, in fact, the Igboman's effort to fulfill that divine charge in Gen 1:28, to go out into the world and subdue it. The Igboman has become what he is by the dynamics of the *umunna* community phenomenon – *umunna bu ike* (*umunna* has the strength).

The philosophy of the Igbo must determine that the *umunna* phenomenon will continue to be a controlled one. It must remain an effective but handy, small community of relationship, where everyone knows everyone else, a place one runs to for protection. This mentality is apparent by the Igboman's aversion to mere number. Quantity is detestable and hence he does not literally

---

125 Bertsch, L., **Theologie der Dritten Welt**, p. 213.

126 L. Bertsch says; "Es ist also gerade der Wille zur Treue zu unseren biblische Quellen, der uns drängt, in Gemeinschaft mit allen und mit Beteiligung aller die Kirche als Volk aufzubauen. Daher wollen wir den Getauften die Möglichkeit geben, in der Gemeinschaft Gläubige zu sein, die sich ihrer Berufung bewußt sind und die in der Erfüllung ihres Sendungsauftrags engagiert Verantwortung übernehmen. Somit steht unsere option auch in Einklang mit den Richtlinien des Zweiten Vatikanischen Konzils". **Laien Als Gemeindeleiter: Ein afrikanisches Modell; Texte der Erzdiözese Kinshasa** :Theologie der Dritten Welt, Band 14, (Herder, Freiburg. Basel. Wien, 1990), p. 90.

count his issues as he would his flock. He values communality, but understands that this cannot be possible with an amorphous group.

The *umunna* community is a gauge that points towards itself as a paradigm in its two-way movement. It promotes and enhances a teachable community that can be predicted in their identity as one in body and soul. The family members which are its base thought of themselves as one, and all their language and behaviour emphasized their unity. The basic goods of life were 'our food', 'our land', 'our home'. The Igbo *umunna* is our inculturated form to describe and work in the purpose of *koinonia* of the early Church and the *Qahal* of the OT people of God. The *umunna* community phenomenon can be said to be an abstract existential. This means that it is a term that transcends the phenomenon and belongs in essence to an existence other than that of man, informing and forming the corporal existence of man. It is because of this nature that the Igboman, wherever he may be, whether far or near, is controlled and tends towards this *umunna* community. Even far from home, he forms the *umunna* (cf. Chapter 1).

4.4. Conclusion

The new way of looking at the Church has turned to be a revival of early Christian life. The Vatican II Council, being more biblical in her deliberations, re-awakened the understanding of the Church as the 'people of God'. A call was made for the Church's renewal; to see the Church as the faithful members of a community and office in the Church as that of service. The community of the faithful is summoned and sustained through the Holy Spirit by Christ Himself. Communion of the summoned is achieved by the grace of God given through the sacramental life of the Church, which has the Eucharist as the central point.

The understanding of the Church given by the Second Vatican Council gave a new awareness by the expression of the Church as the people of God united together in the words and actions of Christ. This notion has made the Church to see herself no more as a one-sided, fixed structure, but as community of living persons, where mutual interest, love and care for one another exist. The community is a sharing community which participates in the trinitarian communion. It is a community guided by the Holy Spirit to perform its works. The basic foundations of this community is expressed as giving witness to the faith and announcing the Good News, celebrating the memorial of the Risen Lord and fraternal solidarity. These led to the basis, center and heart of the life of the Church. These understandings of the nature and life of the Church bore fruits the world over. The results are seen in the formation of Basic or Small

Christian Communities. Examples are seen in Latin American countries, East African Countries and Zaire, testifying to the importance of looking at the Church as the people of God.

A frank study of the Second Vatican Council's ecclesiology should convince every Christian in Igboland that he is neglecting part of the NT witness and is also not being true to the Igbo culture. The ecclesiology of the Second Vatican Council is actually a new way of being Church. The Small Christian Communities are to be formed not simply for the reasons, sometimes alleged, that they are emphasizing 'community' as opposed to 'hierarchy' or 'institution' or because of their impressive sharing. These are the lives experienced in the early Church. Just as J.O'Halloran expresses it "the newness lies in the irruption of the poor and the powerless on to the world and Church scenes, clamoring for freedom and participation..."[127] It is a way by which every Christian matters, and finds the belongingness and solidarity for which the Church stands. The formation of Basic Christian Communities, which agrees with the fraternal spirit, is actually an effective means of evangelisation.

The Basic communities are where love, care and solidarity abound. In love of neighbour, the kingdom of God is present, and the *umunna* community qualifies for this; since it is a community where no one is left out in health or in sickness, poor or rich. Everybody in *umunna* counts. In the next Chapter, which is also the last Chapter of this work, we shall attempt to bring out those elements, structure and values of *umunn*a, which makes it a Christian community.

127 O'Halloran, J., **Signs of Hope: Developing Small Christian Communities**, Orbis Books, Maryknoll, New York, 1991, p. 141.

Chapter Five: En route to a umunna christian community (UCC)

5.0. Introduction

Grace builds on nature and does not destroy it. This dictum is exemplified in Christ's very mission on earth. Jesus came not to destroy, but to fulfill what is contained in the law and the prophets (Matt 5:17). Instead of inventing new structures, he made use of the existing ones in forming his new community. This is seen in his use of their synagogues and temples as places for prayer and worship. Like the great teachers of his time, he made use of riverside and mountainsides as the proper places to impart knowledge to his numerous followers. Inasmuch as he came to bring a new way of worshiping God in spirit and in truth, he used the Old Testament metaphors and proverbs to explain the Kingdom of God. His constant references to the OT, giving reason and justification for his actions, was to show that he had not come to destroy but to fulfill. His followers represented the new chosen people of God.

The Church in recent time has displayed an accommodating spirit towards other peoples' cultures. The spirit was reaffirmed in the Second Vatican Council, in the Fourth Synod of Bishops on Evangelisation (1974), and in Pope Paul VI's Apostolic Exhaltation, **Evangelii nuntiandi**.[1] This last document insisted that the correct attitude toward local ways of life would be nothing less than "a radical and profound understanding" of the ways and values of the people, an adjustment that would be more than "a thin veneer" or that would be "purely decorative" in nature (EN 52). Paul VI proposed that the proper attitude towards the ways and values of a local Christian community would have to affect the particular group "in a vital way", "in depth" and "right to the very roots" – that is, "in the wide and rich sense of the pastoral constitution on the Church in the Modern World" (EN 53).

In this final Chapter, we shall try to use this primary grouping in Igboland – the *umunna*, as a basic community in our search for an in-depth Church Evangelisation. The *umunna* grouping would then be made, as it were, the primary agent involved in incarnating the Gospel. It will do this with the help of the Holy Spirit, for the benefit of the local Christian community and the Church at large. *Umunna* could become an important agent for the Church in Igboland,

---

1 Issued Dec. 8, 1975; English translation, (Washington D.C., U.S. Catholic Conference); cf. L.J. Luzbetak, **The Church and Cultures** (1989), p. 69.

since faith is grasped and lived in a profoundly personal way, which readily generates originality and creativity in spirituality, liturgy, art and above all, in theology.[2] In a succinct appreciation of this, Cenkner had said:

> A theology which does not draw upon the legacy of those to whom it speaks usually exhibits little creativity and development, quickly loses relevancy, and gradually alienates the believer from the social and cultural context in which he lives.[3]

In this Chapter, we shall highlight those elements of *umunna* that are of positive significance for the deepening of the Christian faith. In this case, we shall look at the structural, theological, ecclesiological and pastoral significance of *Umunna* Christian Community. Such values as fraternal love, sharing, solidarity will be examined. This will elucidate the process for the realization of the *Umunna* Christian Community (UCC), as well as explain the basic functions of the Church within an *umunna* social structure.

5.1. *Umunna* as a Basic Structure for Christian Communities

The concept of *umunna*, as explained in the first Chapter, will be applied here as we look at the structure for *Umunna* Christian Communities. The use of the structure of *umunna* as a Basic Christian community is employing an informal method of community formation. In this case, all the Christians within the community are called to participate actively in the so-called secular institutions which strive to promote human good. As we have seen in Chapter One, *umunna* as Igbo basic community is known for promoting human good, be it social, political or religious.

People of the same *umunna* meet to discuss their problems, to share what they have and to bring about reconciliation. The Christians within this community should utilize this opportunity to establish a Small Christian Community. In such communities, the Christian should get involved, not as an outsider, but as an integral member of the community. He brings with him the Christian way of life, that could help to influence the lifestyle of the community. The activity of the Christian is very important within his or her own natural grouping for the renovation of pastoral commitment, as the Latin American bishops in Medellin affirmed:

---

2 J. Saldanha, "**Theological Inculturation as a Missiological Problem**", in: **Indian Theological Studies**, 14, 4(1977), p. 335.

3 W. Cenkner "**The Emergence of an Indian Christian theology**", in: **Indian Missionary Review**, 57, (1973), p. 81.

> The Christian ought to find the living of communion, to which he has been called, in his 'base community', that is to say, in a community, local or environmental, which corresponds to the reality of a homogeneous group and whose size allows for personal fraternal contact among its members. Consequently, the church's pastoral efforts must be oriented towards the transformation of these communities into a 'family of God', beginning by making itself present among them as leaven by means of a nucleus, although it be small, which creates a community of faith, hope and charity... This community becomes then the initial call of the ecclesiastical structures and the focus of evangelization, and it currently serves as the most important source of human advancement and development.[4]

The structure of *umunna*, being the Igbo basic community, could be adopted by the Church for the formation of Christian communities. It provides a fundamental base for the establishment of the Christian community, since in this community, there is a dominance of shared experience.

People know each other by name and get involved in each other's joys, sorrows, pleasures and difficulties. The *Umunna* community shapes and produces the individual so that he lives a communal life. The Church, as community, should carry out the work of Jesus by permeating its values into the cultural, religious and social reality of the people, becoming incarnate in and with the people, "in virtue of her mission and nature and is bound to no particular form of human culture, nor to any political economic, or social system" (GS 42). *Umunna*, with its sense of solidarity and communalism, is a prophetic presence which could check the tendency towards materialism and individualism in the community. Efforts should be made to integrate the Christian Community into the *umunna* structure. Integration is not to be confused with assimilation. Through the policy of assimilation, people are forced to give up their language, culture, values and traditions and to adopt a form of life and worship foreign to them in order to be accepted as Church members.

The majority of the Igbo feel distant or marginated from the parish establishment. The life of the Church has been limited in many cases to Sunday liturgies and a sacramental preparation which has often not stressed a profound conversion that integrates the dimensions of faith, spiritual growth, solidarity, and justice for the transformation of society. This, in our opinion, would be taken care of with the use of the *Umunna* Christian Community. The participation of Christians in these natural communities is to introduce into them or uphold whatever Christian values that may be appropriate. Their involvement would constitute an occasion of checking the aberrations that may be inherent in these communities and help them to keep to the path of Christian love. It

4 **Title of the Conference Report:** *The Church in the present-day Transformation of Latin America in the light of the Council,* 2 vols., 2nd. ed., (Washington: Division for Latin America - **USCC**, 1973), p.201.

will be a great disservice to the Christian cause for Christians to be aloof to such natural communities, or to pretend to make amends when they get into the Church. The Church should be seen where the people live, work and share their lives. The *umunna* communities are the vehicles that Christians should use to build the Kingdom of God; the involvement of Christians in these communities is a must.

No matter how laudable these communities are, they do not always exhaust the wealth of Christian values. In this case, it is necessary for Christians, to introduce new ways which involve formal transmission of Christian ideas, while supporting the objectives that are Christian, in the *umunna*. They do not have to bring in new structures, but use *umunna* as a platform, with the new understanding as the people of God. Using *umunna* as a starting base for the Christian community, some of the functions within *umunna* may have to be carried over to the *Umunna* Christian Community.

As the Christians of the same *umunna* meet, all the ideals of the group have to be followed with the addition of the Christian teaching. Different groups in *umunna* should be used by the Christian community as Catholic Action groups, such as *Umuokorobia* (the youth), *otu ndi Nne* (Christian mothers organization), *Ndi okenye uka* (elder of the Church). These do express certain aspects of Christian life. The elders in the Christian community should be respected as in the *umunna* community. The parish priest should realize their importance and consult them regularly for pastoral work in the area. This is imperative, for they are the means through which Christian communities can be established in the formal sense. It is really vital to base them on the *umunna* community in order to make Christian communities effective as bearers of Christian ideals.

The recognition of the existence of the *umunna* community is a prerequisite if we have to form effective Christian communities and if Christianity is to take root in Igboland. The spirit of community in its diverse forms is at the basis of Igbo social structure and therefore could serve as a springboard for the establishment of Christian communities. A Christian community cannot exist in the air, but is based first and foremost on some form of living or existing community. Since the *umunna* structure gives recognition to individuals, giving them rights and responsibilities, and thereby fostering inter-action and communication, it becomes a God-sent unit that allows such elements as are mentioned above which are vital to a basic Christian community.

Structurally speaking, *umunna* embraces political, economic, social, and religious functions and thereby takes care of the members with regard to their spiritual and material needs. Such a life marked the lives of the early Christians, for 'none of their members was ever in want' (Acts 4:34). *Umunna* gives a member a sense of belonging, makes him feel at home and wanted. These are also values similar to the Christian values of brotherhood which should be tapped by the *Umunna* Christian Community. This spirit of communion is essential in a truly Christian community. But experience has shown that in *umunna*, women and children are not given prominent positions or not even consulted. Christianity has a function of lifting *umunna* to the higher level of equality among the children of God.

It is pertinent to note that the assumption of an *umunna*-based structure by the Christian community in Igboland does not deprive it of reflecting the Church as an institution of brotherhood, of communication and of dialogue. In actual fact, it is a help in this regard. For this scheme to work there should be a change of mentality.

5.2. A Theological Interpretation of the Umunna Community

Through God's revelation of Himself, he invites men to participate in the life of the Trinity and to share this life among themselves. The Church in essence is made up of those who through faith and baptism commit themselves to this Trinitarian life. The Church members freely enter into covenantal vertical relationship with God and a horizontal one with all the believers. The profession of faith in Jesus through baptism forms a basis for and entrance to the Christian community. Belonging to the *umunna* is not by choice; instead, one is born into it. The *Umunna* community is for all who are of the same agnatic descent or who can trace their link to a common ancestor.

However, the actual initiation into *umunna* takes place at the naming ceremony. The Igbo say that a child without a name belongs to no community and no one can care for such a child. A basic Christian community is also a small group of people who feel related through an awareness of brotherhood in Christ. Such a relationship will be better if it is rooted in a human or natural community. *Umunna* offers the Christians such fertile ground for community building. People who do not feel related will not form a real community. The Igbo traditional naming ceremony, which is an official initiation rite into *umunna*, can be introduced into Christian initiation after due examinations.

Belonging to a Christian community entails faith in the Risen Lord and reception of the Holy Spirit, of which the Christian initiation (baptism) is an external sign. It is in baptism that all the faithful share and exercise in Christ's priesthood, share in his prophetic office and in a mission of justice and solidarity (LG 10, 12; GS 29-32). This is a mission that makes the Kingdom of God present. *Umunna* can be seen as a concrete reflection of the Kingdom of God, since in traditional *umunna* community justice, love, care and solidarity reign. The direct contact of the priest or the catechist is very important in bringing the message of Christ to the *umunna* community. This contact will not only bring or spread the word of God, but will gradually lead the traditional *umunna* meetings to a form of *umunna* Christian meeting. When the community has shown great interest in the Christian teaching and life, the priest has to make an official inauguration of the *umunna* Christian Community. At this point the eucharist can be celebrated. The word of God so immersed into the *umunna* community will not only purify the mundane life and some initiation rites, but also rid the people of the fear of witches and evil spirits which enslaves them.

The person of Jesus introduced or preached as the one who liberates or saves people from the power of evil spirits will actually help to remove the fears of evil spirits. Jesus Christ, having triumphed over Satan, shares this victory with his followers. The faith in the Risen Lord will help members of *Umunna* Christian Community realize that "no evil spirit, no wicked forces... can separate us from the love of God in Christ Jesus" (Rm.8).

There is a belief in a Supreme God among the Igbo. The Christians also have the same belief. This belief in the Supreme God (*Chukwu*), form a basis for Igbo solidarity. The concept of One God helps the Igbo to create and live the life of community and solidarity among themselves and with the spiritual world. It is obvious that both the Church and the Igbo (*umunna* community) have a common theocentric basis for community and solidarity which is based on the belief in a Supreme God. No matter how similar this may seem, the Church is called upon to purify the Igbo concept of God by introducing the Trinitarian God of the Christians, since the Igbo do not believe in the three Persons in One Supreme God. Contributing on this, Mozia writes;

> Since the Igbos already possess the "seed of the Word" through their faith in the One Supreme God, and since they also have a partial sense of personal and convenantal relationship with the one God, the first theological implication of the Church's trinitarian solidarity is to recognize and accept this "seed of the Word" in the Igbo Community (umunna) and to use it as a starting point for presenting a covenantal and trinitarian solidarity to the people.[5]

Idowu, realizing the importance of covenantal relationship within the African framework, talks of the use of the African belief in it, with one God as a basis for presenting the Christians' covenantal relationship with Christ. He went on to say;

---

5 M.I. Mozia, **Solidarity in the Church and Solidarity among the Igbos of Nigeria**, 2(Claverianum Press, Ibadan, 1987), p. 251.

> The basis of the African belief and practice is the covenant. It is the heart of all cults in Africa. Africans count it a serious sin to break the covenant... If efforts had been directed in making Christians, showing clearly to Africans that they are entering into personal-covenant-relationship with the living God and personal saviour, we should not have been facing our present embarrassment.[6]

The use of the authentic expression of faith shared by the Igbo in the Supreme God, especially their modes and terminologies of designating God, is of paramount importance. These modes and terminologies manifest and crystalize for them the different attributes of God. Such attributes will help to build a type of Igbo/*umunna* theology of community. Some of the attributes include; *Chukwu* (the great God), *Chineke* (God the creator), *Osebuluwa* (the Lord of the whole world).

These attributes of God show the relationship between the Igbo and God, man and the world. The traditional Igbo, as we have mentioned, lack the knowledge of the revelation of the mystery of the Blessed Trinity. Because of this, it is impossible to express the universal brotherhood which was taught and lived by Christ.[7] This lack of universal brotherhood in *umunna* set-up is what the Church has to supply, to make *umunna* a truly Christian community. It will not be difficult, since from the point of view of creation, the Igbo recognize a person as a child of God, hence such names as *Nwachukwu* (child of God), *Chinwe* (God owns), *Chukwukere* (the great God creates).

With such an understanding, it can serve as a theological basis for presenting Christ to them as the son of God, "who, through the mystery of Incarnation, has come to unite all men into one family."[8] If through God-made-man, all men participate in the sonhood of God, then through Christ, and in the unity of the Holy Spirit, all men are the sons of God. "Everyone moved by the Spirit is a son of God..."(Rom 8:14-17; cf. Gal 4:6f.; Eph 1:4-14).

This explanation will equip members of the *umunna* community to see how Christ transforms the natural and created relationship to a supernatural and universal one. It will help them to form a community in Christ. The community that finds its root in mankind's participation in the universal sonhood through Christ, as Paul puts it; "Before the world was made, he chose us in

---

6 B. Idowu, "**The Predicament of the African Church**", in: C.G. Beata ed. **Christianity in Tropical Africa**, (OUP, London, 1968), p. 434. Some of the embarrassment Idowu is talking about include living in two worlds, not relating to Christian God as having anything to do with them, and not really being committed since there is no breaking of a covenant. Covenant in Igbo is called **Igba ndu** (to unite life) it is belief that only death can break a covenant.

7 M.I. Mozia, **Solidarity in the Church and Solidarity among the Igbos of Nigeria**, (1987), p. 252; words in brackets are mine.

8 Ibid.

Christ, to be holy and spotless, and to live through love in his presence, determining that we should become his adopted sons, through Jesus Christ" (Eph 1:4-7). This new relationship of human beings with God the Father, through the Son, makes men and women sons and daughters of God. Christ has created a new freedom for all as the children of God, communing with one another and God. With such a method, the members of *umunna* are led through their knowledge of community in the natural setting of man to a higher community that comes about through the mystery of Incarnation. Then they will enjoy the freedom of the children of God. Kakuba-Kapia pointed out;

> The freedom of the children of God guarantees their rightful participation in divine Kingdom. They are bound together, as brothers and sisters through and beyond their biological, cultural and spiritual networks.[9]

Jesus is not only the Son of God but also the saviour of the world, who shed his blood to redeem mankind. It is through his death and resurrection that he removed every barrier that separated people, and liberates them from sin. The Church has the task of bringing the *umunna* community to the understanding that Christ is the saviour, who calls all men to enter into a saving community.

The Igbo see salvation in the context of solidarity in a community.[10] Some Igbo names affirm this, names such as *Chizoba* (God saves). Mozia commenting says;

> Although Igbo moral life is characterized by fear of punishment from God and the ancestors, it also has some element of grateful response. In response to the care and protection they enjoy from God and their ancestors, the people accept the obligation to maintain justice and see that no member of the community is neglected or unjustly treated... an interpersonal relationship between the dead and living members of the community helps to form a creative and liberating solidarity among the people... faith in their interpersonal union

---

9 Kakuba-Kapia, "**A Theology of fostering ecclesial communities**", in: **AFER**, vol. 33, 3(1991), p. 127.

10 For more information concerning the Igbo concept of salvation see C.C. Osuji, **The Concept of Salvation in Igbo Traditional Religion**, (Pontificia Universitas, Roma, 1977), pp. 68ff. An old man in Igboland as the missionaries recorded, refused baptism because he was told by the missionaries that he would be the only person saved from the hell fire. He would go to heaven after baptism when he dies but all his forefathers and ancestors would be in hell. The man decided to go where he can be in communion with his kin and ancestor rather than go to white man's heaven. Since there is no community with those he knows.

with the ancestors serve as a strong basis for solidarity among the members of the community.[11]

Tradition and religion are vital in Igbo life and may not be ignored in our *Umunna* Christian Community. The figure of the historical Jesus and the community of the Church have been the fundamentals of Christian faith. The first Christians, reflecting on the situation after the death of Jesus, who lived and spoke as no one had before, bestowed upon him titles which were borrowed from contemporary culture. It was not easy to change these titles.[12] Theologians are questioning the meaning of these titles today. Some of these titles, they claim, are puzzling for people and often serve to obscure rather than to illuminate the message of Jesus.

These theologians are now striving to recover the genuinely human dimension of Jesus, in order to make his message more meaningful to the modern man, instead of being wrapped in some ancient and often incomprehensible metaphysical idiom.[13] Since the Western theologians are calling for such reinterpretation, the Africans, especially the Igbo who have received Christianity in foreign wrapping, have a more urgent need. In Igbo society, which is characterized by strong ties with and respect for ancestors, to present Jesus Christ analogically as an ancestor (which Bujo refers as a Proto-Ancestor[14]) is an asset. The practice of honoring ancestors among the Igbo serves as basis for effective community. The cult of ancestors is the core of a lasting personal and intimate bond with all the members of a given *umunna* community. This type of bond is based on a natural association, as opposed to a voluntary one.[15]

---

11 M.I. Mozia, **Solidarity in the Church and Solidarity among the Igbos of Nigeria**, (1987), p. 184.

12 E. Schillebeeckx, **Interim report on the books *"Jesus" and "Christ"***, New York, 1982, pp. 25ff.

13 Cf. B. Bujo, **African Theology in Context**, J O'Donohue transl., Nairobi, St. Paul Publications; see H. Kung, **On Being a Christian**, New York, 1978. Also see E. Schillebeeckx, **Jesus, an experiment in Christology**, New York, 1979. Idem., **Christ, the experiment of Jesus as Lord**, New York, 1980.

14 According to B. Bujo "We can perceive the importance of Jesus for the Africans in regard to ancestor-theology. This importance does not come from looking at Jesus christ simply as an ancestor. The term *ancestor* can only be applied to Jesus in an analogical, or eminent, way, since to treat him otherwise would be to make of him only one founding ancestor among many. That is why the term **Proto-Ancestor** is reserved to Jesus". **African Theology in Context, Christian Leadership in Africa Series**, transl. by John O'Donohue, Nairobi, St Paul Publication, 1992, p.80.

15 Cf. P.J. North, **People in Society: An Introduction to Sociology**, 3(Longman, England, 1986), pp. 15-23, 120-126. Pope Paul VI, commenting on the African family says; "Another Characteristic element of African tradition is the sense of family... For the Africans the family thus comes to be the natural environment in which man is born and

From the point of view that *umunna* is a natural grouping, one can assert that it is willed by God, who makes the individual in the community a descendant of a particular ancestor. K. Rahner, writing about traditional African ancestor-worship and its importance, says that it is :

> perhaps conceivable that Christian theology in Africa, if it wishes to become truly African, will introduce a new, independent form of ancestor-worship, and that from there it might be imported into Christian theology in the rest of the world. It would be extremely regrettable and ominous for the future of Christian theology as a whole if this African contribution were to meet with nothing but indifference from the rest of the Christian world[16]

The words, actions and rituals which are associated with the ancestors, and also with the elders of the community in general, have a deep meaning in the life of the Igbo people. Giving the title ancestor analogically to Jesus fits in very well with the Igbo understanding. Jesus is then understood as an elder in the community, an intercessor or mediator between God and man, one who guards and protects the human community.

It is pertinent to note that most of those who qualify as ancestors normally give their farewell addresses before dying. These words are words of life, setting the seal on the experiences and example of one who, while withdrawing from the community, yet truly lives on within it, along with the other forefathers. These last words given to us by those good persons are normative for those of us who are left behind. Jesus really lived the Igbo ancestor-ideal in the highest degree and brought it to an altogether new fulfillment.

The new fulfillments are seen in his works of miracles, healing the sick, raising the dead to life. One of the last words of both Igbo ancestors and Jesus – our Proto Ancestor – is that of Love. Our ancestor advised his children to love each other and be in unity, since the welfare of the community was in his mind, especially his immediate family. The same advice preoccupied Jesus' farewell address to his apostles. He prayed that they be one and that they love one another as he loved them (Jn.13). As Bujo explained:

> The last supper which Jesus took with his disciples is like the final hour which a father of a family spends with his children. He gathers his children about him to give them his final blessing and to pronounce his last will. Jesus' last will was: serve one another, love one another. Only those who carry out the terms of this will have life, and only they can

---

acts, in which he finds the necessary protection and security..." ***Roman Document: Africae Terrarum,*** "**A message of Pope Paul VI, to the Countries of Africa**", in, **AFER**, vol.x, 1(1968).

16 K.Rahner and J.B. Metz, **The Courage to Pray**, (SPCK, London, 1980), p. 45.

transmit life to others. "If you know these things, blessed are you if you do them" (Jn. 13:17).[17]

Jesus as a "Proto Ancestor" has opened up a new relationship. The Igbo ancestorship, which is based on a biological relationship, assumes a new dimension in the blood of Christ. Jesus transcends the Igbo ideal of the ancestor and brings it to a new completion. Jesus is our ancestor in an eminent way. Through his death on the cross, a rejuvenating blood was shed on mankind, to bring about a new family of people of God and a new brotherhood, and in doing so, he became the means of salvation. Bujo clearly says:

> Through the resurrection of Jesus, God brought into being a new creation, a creation which infinitely transcended the first creation, including the world of the African ancestors. Jesus Christ is the ultimate embodiment of all the virtues of the ancestors, the realization of the salvation for which they yearned... Jesus Christ is the Proto-Ancestor, the Proto-Life-Force, bearer in a transcendent form of primitive "vital union" and "vital force".[18]

There is a natural constant communion between the ancestors and the members of the *umunna* community, and the ancestors are believed to be actively involved in the communitarian efforts to build up an authentic community among the people. This community, can be seen as relating to the ecclesial significance in the eschatological dimension of solidarity in the Church.[19] One may add that, through union with one's ancestors, the Igbo retains his community in death. Considering the help such an understanding could give, Shorter says;

> Ancestors are certainly comparable to the Christian cult of saints in as far as it is an expression of the moral ideals of the society, and Christian experiment in exploiting African's attachment to their ancestors has usually met with success.[20]

We should not fail to point out some dissimilarities in the cult of both Christian saints and Igbo ancestors. One of the most important dissimilarity is

---

17 B. Bujo, **African Theology in its social context**... op.cit., p. 80.

18 B. Bujo, **African Theology...**, op.cit., p. 81.

19 Cf. La Roche, "**African Theological Interpretation**", in, C.G. Baeta, ed., **Christianity in Tropical Africa**, (Oxford University Press, London, 1968), p. 146. See also M.I. Mozia, **Solidarity in the Church...**, (1987), p. 257; One of the possible aspects in the belief in ancestors that immediately comes to mind is found in some of the moral qualifications for becoming an ancestor. Some of these qualifications are comparably parallel to Christian qualifications for becoming saints, e.g., the need for fidelity to God's laws and the need for a good moral life; cf. C. Nyamiti, **Christ as our Ancestor**, (1984), pp. 103-120

20 A. Shorter, **African Christian Theology**, (Geoffrey Chapman, London, 1975), p. 126.

that the saints are not only in union with Christ, but also provided a universal model for all Christians to emulate. This universality is lacking in the *umunna* ancestors.

Another dissimilarity concerns the importance the Igbo attach to having offspring. Having children is one of the qualifications for becoming an ancestor. The Christians seem to extol celibate life as one of the evangelical virtues. Paul advises, "it is a good thing for a man not to touch a woman..."(1 Cor 7:1), and in (v 8) he adds, ... for the sake of widows and those who are not married: it is a good thing for them to stay as they are, like me."[21] It is this lack of universality in the person of the ancestor and the question of begetting children among the Igbo that bring problems. They trace their root to a common ancestor and make no effort to include all humanity. In Christianity, Christ the Son of the Father is adored, in the traditional Igbo religion, the ancestors are not adored but reverenced.

Umunna should be helped to extend its relationship to include people of the group and beyond. This will make the *umunna* community to go beyond its encapsuled self to reach out to the rest of humanity. While accepting the notion of fatherhood among the Igbo, it is necessary to give it a Christian orientation and wider dimension. It would be necessary to present to them the Christian notion of a spiritual and universal fatherhood of God.[22]

Also important in this line of thought is the spirit of hospitality. It is a value of African traditional life which has its origin in solidarity. Hospitality shows an attitude towards others which is in harmony with the Gospel. This may form the basis for the mutual aid among the members of an *Umunna* Christian community. It can also provide an incentive to a larger community which goes beyond *umunna*, the Church or the nation. The Igbo, as we pointed out in Chapter 1, are hospitable. They extend their love and care to strangers. Hospitality is a religious duty for the Igbo. Visitors and strangers are often astonished by the way the Igbos receive them. This way of life is inherited from their ancestors who held that God will only help the villagers if the villagers are kind and open-hearted to everyone, including strangers.[23] Mozia says;

---

21 Though one can argue that this Pauline position is only disciplinary.

22 M.I. Mozia, **Solidarity in the Church and Solidarity among the Igbos of Nigeria**, (1987), p. 260.

23 E.M. Umeasiegbu, **The way we lived**; (Heinemann, London, 1979), p. 39.

it is their religious zeal to enjoy the support and fellowship of God and their ancestors during their life, and to be reunited with them in the next world, that motivates all their actions of hospitality.[24]

The acceptance of visitors among the Igbo is demonstrated by the presentation of a kola-nut,[25] a mark of friendship and love. The presentation of a kola-nut is the most important sign of a whole-hearted welcome.

The sharing of food and liquor is not as important to the Igbos as the sharing of kola-nut.... It always comes first. It is the King. To be presented with a kola-nut is to be made welcome...[26]

People with such open hearts in receiving strangers will also be open to a wider bond and support for the universal community – the Church. The *Umunna* Christian Community may be the greatest service of the Church to the changing Igbo society today, since it would support and strengthen the existing Igbo values which are close to the Christian teachings. This will help make a changing Igbo society a better place to live in, where mutual care, support and bond are expressed. If the Church is to mirror the life of Christ to the world, she must recapture this basic concept of Christian community. Being conscious of living for others, Christians will commit themselves totally to the service of others.[27]

In Igboland, the immediate response to human needs (hunger, thirst, clothing and housing) is met generally by the kinsmen. The community is outstanding in providing such care, hence names like *Azu-atalam* (let there be more kin) or *Ikwuakolam* (I shall not lack *ikwu* [28]), which are also expressed in Igbo prayers. A typical African traditional community is thus expressed in Nyerere's *Ujamaa* philosophy;

---

24 M.I. Mozia, **Solidarity in the Church and Solidarity among the Igbos of Nigeria**, (1987), p. 194.

25 **Kola-nut** is symbol of friendship, reconciliation, and summoning of the living and the dead, during the eating of kola-nut. It is communion per se.

26 V.C. Uchendu, **The Igbo of Southeast Nigeria**, (Holt, Rinehart and Winston, New York, 1965), p. 74.

27 This does not show that the early Christians did not have their share of problems in, jealousies, selfishness, mistrust, anger, lies etc., (cf. 1 Cor 1: 10-11; 6: 7ff; 9: 12; Gal 5: 15; 6: 1; Eph 4: 31ff; Phil 2: 3, 4, 11; Jas 3: 16).

28 See **Ikwu and Ibe** in chapter I, **1.3.** M.H. Crosby speaking about the familial care says; "While basic, immediate needs were to be continually met through familial care,.. kinship ties expressed in care and redemption were to address individual needs within households. If households (**oikia/oikos**) would be reformed, it would lead to structural release..."; **House of Disciples: Church, Economics and Justice in Matthew**, (Orbis Books, Maryknoll, New York, 1988), p. 190.

The traditional African family lived to the basic principles of ujamaa.... They lived together and worked together because that was how they understood life, and how they reinforced each other. The results of their joint effort were divided unequally between them, but according to well-understood customs. And the division was always on the basis of the fact that every member of the family had to have enough to eat, some simple covering, and a place to sleep, before any of them had anything extra. The family members thought of themselves as one, and all their language and behaviour emphasized their unity. The basic goods of life were 'our food', 'our land', 'our cattle'.[29]

In an *umunn*a there is a dominance of shared experience. People know each other well and thus get involved in the joys, sorrows, pleasures and difficulties of their neighbours. This is an actualization of Paul's admonition to Christians to rejoice with those who rejoice and mourn with those who mourn.

The stress here, both in the Christian community of Paul and *umunna,* is on "man-in-the-community". This is a cooperative life which builds communities that upholds the spirit of love. John Mutiso-Mbinda, describing the community life in Africa, says;

The ordinary African community could be described as a neighbourhood. Everybody knows everybody else, because this is a primary group relationship in which the members are actually involved in the life of the group, constantly and fully. The whole life of the individual is affected by the group. The people who live in a typical African community like an ujamaa village (umunna),.. or a rural neighbourhood, cooperate with one another in meeting the basic necessities of life. Hence they will build houses together, weed gardens together, attend village meetings, funerals and weddings. They will participate in planning events together.[30]

This is close to what one expects of a Christian community. The feeling of being wanted and at home, makes it possible or easier, "for individuals to be integrated into the wider society, especially in a time of rapid change".[31] This is building a more humane society, where love, care and support reign. In such a community, the kingdom of God is made manifest, as C.S.Song says;

Human community and divine communion are interdependent. It is not a question of either – or, but of both – and. Nor is it a matter of which comes first – communion with God or community with other human beings. They both come first: they take place simultaneously. Communion with God without human community may be possible in the world of metaphysics but not in the real world of human persons. Human community without

29 J.K. Nyerere, "**Freedom and Socialism / Uhuru na Ujamaa**"; **A Selection from his writings and speeches 1965-1967**, (OUP, Nairobi, 1967), p. 337.

30 J. Mutiso-Mbinda, "**African Background for community Building**", in: **AFER**, vol. 19, 6(1977), p. 300. Word in bracket is mine.

31 Ibid.

communion with God inevitably yields broken humanity. It is no longer community. It is hell.[32]

There is no way of showing our love for God except within the human community. No wonder John, in his first letter, says that our love for God is not genuine unless it is manifested in love for our brothers and sisters (1 Jn 4:19-21). The bond and support one experiences in the *umunna* unit show the depth of love that is practiced by the members. It is from the structure of the community, as well as from respect for the ancestors, that the Igbo derive their moral precepts, including respect for elders and leaders. It is these that make the working of *umunna* ecclesial.

5.3. Umunna as a Visible Ecclesial Community

The African social context demands a definite relevant structure to enhance evangelisation, a structure that would not separate religion and God from the individual's ordinary, communal life, and at the same time ensure the salvation of body and soul. *Umunna* Christian Communities bring together faith and life. The Church is characterized by communion as a way of being in the Church. It is presented as a sign and sacrament of the communion of men and women with God and of the unity among people (LG 1). This allows all members of Christ's flock to participate in the mission of the Church. Every Christian participates in her or his own way in the priestly, prophetic and kingly office of Christ. They are called to exercise this mission of the Church in the world. The ecclesial basis of cooperative exercise of this mission is deeply rooted in the very nature of the Church as a communion, as well as in the very nature of Christ's faithful as members of the people of God.

We should give thanks to the Fathers of the Second Vatican Council for reiterating that in God's relations with those who seek salvation in Him, He deals with them as a community. He sees them as His children joined together into one family, united to each other as brothers and sisters in household. This does not mean that God ignores the individual. He loves all personally, but does not want His children to ignore each other. God wants His children to be conscious of the great brotherhood that should exist among them as one family of His Church. In **Mystici Corporis**, Pius XII wrote:

It is clear enough that Christians stand in absolute need of the Divine Redeemer's help. But it is also certain, surprising though it may seem, that Christ needs His members... Dy-

---

32 C.S. Song, **Theology from the Womb of Asia**, (Orbis Books, Maryknoll, New York, 1986), p. 154.

ing on the cross, he bestowed upon His Church the boundless treasures of the redemption without any cooperation on her part. But in the distribution of those treasures, He not only shares the work of sanctification with her, but wills it to arise in a certain manner out of her labour. This is truly a tremendous mystery; that the salvation of many souls depends on the prayers and sacrifices of the members of the Mystical Body, and on the cooperation which pastors and the faithful, especially parents must give to our Divine Saviour.[33]

This shows that the wholehearted cooperation of every member of the people of God (*umunna*) is called for in the service of the Church. Everyone's contribution is very important.

In the *Umunna* Christian Community, just as the traditional *umunna*, everyone must work, not merely for their own sake, but for that of others. This is in the spirit of 'togetherness'. Those in *umunna* work for the good of the community; such a spirit of self sacrifice will also be employed by members of UCC for the good of others. Christ said in this respect; "For their sake I consecrate myself, so that they too may be consecrated in truth" (Jn 17:19). The *Umunna* Christian Community should be seen or understood to be the people of God, born anew by baptism. It means that the first truth about members of a given *umunna* is that they are now members of a new *umunna* in Christ. This new family is brought about by baptism.

The Igbo view about *umunna* corresponds to the Vatican II vision of a people structured ministerially. This structuring of *umunna* allows all members to be active, and none to be a passive receiver. The Church, the people of God, as we know, is a two-way sharing in the life of God and among members of the community. The *Umunna* Christian Community is an attempt towards making this communion of God's people a living reality.

There should be a wider distribution of the services (ministries). The ministries in UCCs should not be seen as the prerogative of the priest or the catechist. The people should be led to realize that the whole community (as in the traditional *umunna*) is called to participate. It is not just a matter of lay people looking for something to do in order to feel useful. The community has all sorts of needs that ought to be fulfilled, so there is no lack of urgent work to be done. These tasks should be seen as ministries. Each person within the UCC should contribute his or her share, according to one's charisms and talents. Some of these ministries include instructing the catechumens and children for first communion and confirmation; visiting the sick and praying for them; organizing marriage courses; organizing social and recreational facilities; cultural revival groups; organizing meetings; leading singing; providing a treasurer for finances; someone to coordinate the community with other com-

---

33 Pius XII, **Mystici Corporis, Nr.42**. The parents' cooperation about which the Pope talks concerns also the *umunna* community where children are schooled in morals.

munities or with the parish. These are ways in which the people serve the community, and share in the mission of the Church. The work is imbued with dignity, because it is a part of Christ's mission to preach the gospel. In this way, we are building a Church that is self-ministering, self-propagating and self-supporting.

People in *umunna* like to be involved in things that concern the community. They perform, and most importantly, cherish leadership positions in community engagements. An ecclesiological significance of the UCCs is seen not only in the work the priest and the catechist do, but in the fact that all members, each in its own capacity, can fulfil ministerial obligations. The Church is now 'our Church' and no longer that of the bishops, priests and catechist. From the point of view of service, the Church practices an essential equality of all the members, insofar as all have to contribute to the well-being of the whole, the special tasks of various members notwithstanding. Therefore, no one should put himself above the other in this reciprocal service.[34] The future of Christianity in Igboland will be affected by the way bishops, priests and the entire church leadership handle the Church ministries.

There are many challenges facing the Church in Igboland today. Such challenges include the one being posed by the proliferation of African churches, the aggressive Islamization of Nigeria, the praise of traditional religion in the name of cultural revival, and an increasing spirit of secularization. It is obvious that, if it is to survive these onslaughts, the Igbo Church must think of a grassroots ecclesiology similar to that which the UCC can offer. This is done by recognizing and accepting these ministries in the whole community, so that the church will cease to be *uka fada* (the priest's Church) and become 'our Church'. The entire apostolate of the laity must receive our close attention and reassessment. Then, the role of the priest, apart from his ministerial office and that of his catechist, will be that of an animator, who coordinates activities in the Church.

The Trinitarian life of the community is participation at its best. God always wanted us to share in His divine life. In creating man, God says: "Let us make man in our image; in the likeness of ourselves..." (Gen 1:26). This likeness and image is seen in the Trinity. By revealing the Trinitarian life to man, God invites us to participate in his life and to share this life among ourselves, while he becomes the Father of mankind. The most Blessed Trinity is the principle and the *raison d'etre* of the Church, which is in its deepest and most specific reality, a 'people assembled in the unity of the Father, the Son and the Holy Spirit' (LG 4). Community is born from the gift of communion. In it the believer receives, lives and transmits the gift of communion. The community is

34 Cf. 1 Cor 12:4-11; also **De Ecclesia** 4, Nr.35.

constituted basically on the visible and stable relation which links the believers among themselves in the common profession of faith.[35] Participation is one of the great values one observes within *umunna.* We have also stressed that Christianity ought to be presented as a participation in the life of the Trinity. Participation in recent times has occupied a central position in the ethical discussions in many parts of the world, both in ecumenical movement of Western theology,[36] and in the Latin American theology of Liberation.[37]

But in the Igbo context, participation has a distinctive character due to the structure of the *umunna* community. It is one of the values responsible for running the *umunna* community smoothly. The *Oha* principle which allows every member the right to participate is central in the *umunna* community. The *oha* constitutes the assembly, in which every citizen can take part. In other words, the *oha* is the sovereign body in the State to decide national affairs, great and small. The citizens have a considerable amount of opportunity to take part in the executive and judicial administration.[38] This is why the Igbo approach to life is centered on people, not as individuals but on a living community, where life is shared not only with the living but also with the ancestors.

In Igboland, the commitment to God and humanism are interrelated. Participation is seen in sharing, just as in the Trinitarian life, as Nyamiti observes;

> In the Trinity, participation implies the communication of the One single divine life and power among the three Persons. This in no way implies having a part of the divine life or power, the Father shares his entire being with the Son and the Spirit. Hence the African sense of participation is closer to the truth than is the Western "pars capere," to have a part.... It is a question of having communion in the same divine life shared equally and to-

---

35 C. Rocceta, ***La Communione, dono dello Spirito alla chiesa,*** **Presenza Pastorale,** 57(1982), p.19.

36 **Cf. Anglican-Roman Catholic International Commission (ARCIC II) Salvation and the Church,** with commentary and study guide by M. Cecily and T. Bradshaw, **(CTS,** London, 1989)

37 Cf. M.de C. Azevedo, **Basic Ecclesial Communities**...(1987), p.36.

38 Cf., O. Mbachu, **Ohacracy as a system of Government in Igbo culture area of Nigeria**; A Paper presented at the first Annual Conference of the Center for Igbo Studies, Imo State University, Okigwe; (unpublished article, Okigwe, July 11 - 13, 1991), p.12. Frostin, commenting on the African life of participation, says; "The "African" conception of participation is characterized as both theocentric and anthropocentric. The theocentric concern is substantiated by the assertion that "participation is closely linked with the sacred - the supernatural;" the anthropocentric concern is explained with reference to the notion that the African "wants to share in cosmic and sacred forces" because community is the only way to life and power". Per Frostin, **Liberation Theology...,** (1988), p. 53.

tally among the divine Persons who are, as a consequence, one and identical in life, nature and power.[39]

God is the creator of the universe, and since God is perfect communion in the Trinity, and views His creatures as a people, then it follows that community life ought to be a vocation for all men. Participation in the Trinitarian life, as we have explained, should be a longing for a complete and authentic human community. This longing is experienced in the *umunna* spirit.

The spirit of communitarianism gives rise to ecclesial being. Zizioulas clearly says;

ecclesial being is bound to the very being of God. From the fact that a human being is a member of the Church, he becomes an "image of God", he exists as God Himself exists, he takes on God's "way of being." This way of being is not a moral attainment, something that man accomplishes. It is a way of relationship with the world, with other people and with God, an event of communion and that is why it cannot be realized as the achievement of an individual, but only as an ecclesial fact.[40]

The life in *umunna* is a life of communion. *Umunna* as a Christian community will help the Church to be incarnated and her participatory life assured. It is in *umunna* that the Church can take on flesh and blood in an everyday situation.

At the *umunna* level, the Christians will help the gradual and steady maturing of the Christian community. This will call for a sense of responsibility for all, and the Christians will in no time discover the meaning of a truly Igbo expression of Christian faith, and thus be able to respond to Pope Paul's call on Africans in Kampala that; "You may and you must, have an African Christianity".[41] Because in the *umunna* community, everyone is involved in the activities of the group, be it social or political, this will be one of the major ways through which laymen and laywomen will participate actively in the life of the Church. While proposing kinship as the basis for Small Christian Community, Lumbasi said;

---

39 C. Nyamiti, "**African tradition and the Christian God**," (1977), p. 73.

40 J.D. Zizioulas, **Being as Communion: Studies in Personhood and the Church**; (St. Vladimir's Seminary Press, New York, 1985), p.15.

41 Paul VI's address, quoted in the AMECEA Plenary assembly 1979 document, in: **AFER**, vol. 21, 5(1979), p. 270; cf. P. Lwaminda, **The Theological Analysis of AMECEA - Documents in the Local Church with special emphasis on the Pastoral Option: Emergence of a new conception of the Church in Eastern Africa;** (unpublished article, no date, Nairobi), pp. 17 - 18.

> Because of all this, (their relatedness and communion) Christians interacted happily together in feasts or in common projects for development. They were able to discuss their daily problems and settle them amicably, rather than going to accuse one another.[42]

It is a common practice for the members of a given *umunna* to assist in erecting a building for a member or work in his or her farm. Mwoleka, commenting on the task of the Church, says;

> The main occupation of Church members must therefore be the work of forming Christian small communities imbued with dynamism to undertake to meet genuine needs of man in collaboration with all men. They must be committed to the work of transforming human affairs and human relations. The field of this undertaking is the ujamaa village.[43]

The involvement in the life of *umunna* by Church leaders is a *conditio sine qua non*, if Christianity is to be incarnated in Igboland. What W. Schools, a missionary in Tanzania, says of Ujamaa, can readily be seen in the *umunna* unit;

> the experience of living with and close to the daily life of the people in the Ujamaa village has contributed to my being more concerned about persons than about structures or nice records in books.... Living the daily events of the village-life would help the Christians to understand more deeply the value of their every day-life.[44]

The primary motive of forming UCCs is to bring about an ecclesiological change, whereby new relationships could be formed, enabling the entire community to be called Church, a Church rooted in the local society. This is essentially the "mystical communion" ecclesiology, as promoted by Vatican II. From our study of *umunna*, one notices that not only communion is emphasized, but also mutual service. *Umunna* as a people of one large family is perceived as the new family of God's people, where there should be no distinction between Jews and Gentiles, but all share in the priesthood of Christ, through baptism. The ministerial priesthood, though essentially different, is in service of this common priesthood. UCCs, as small groups of people gathered together, live the fraternity of the common priesthood, in a special way. This

---

42 G.W. Lumbasi, "**Kinship and Small Christian Communities**," in: **AFER**, vol. 26, 6(1984), p. 374; words in brackets are mine.

43 C. Mwoleka, "**Ujamaa and Christian communities**," (1976), p. 12; the literal translation of **Ujamaa** as we have explained is "familyhood," though it is a deliberate policy of Tanzania Government to transform the lives of the people of Tanzania and knit them into one great family, it has the same philosophy with **umunna**.

44 W. Schools, "**Personal reflections on the new way of sharing in community**," in: **Ujamaa and Christian communities**, eds., C. Mwoleka, and J. Healey, **SPEARHEAD**, Nr. 45, (1976), p. 52.

means that they can effectively enjoy the rights and fulfill the duties deriving from the common priesthood.

Members of the UCC have some responsibilities in the building of the community, according to the talents given to them by the Spirit. Some will be called to fulfill special functions in the community. With time, they may be ordained to carry out these functions, which are essential to the very life of the Church. Just like the role of the leader or head of the traditional *umunna* unit, one of the chief roles of the ordained minister is to be pastor or shepherd of the UCC, and in so doing, to notice, encourage and channel the gifts of the members, so that these gifts can be recognized, appreciated and utilized for the good of all. Then the Church becomes a mystery of communion between God and the people, and amongst the people themselves.[45] The Church is at the service of the Kingdom of God, revealed by Jesus. The Church then proclaims and serve this Kingdom, by incarnating itself in the life of the people at the local level.

5.3.1. Leadership

Jesus came not to be served, but to serve. The leadership in the traditional Igbo community is more of service than authoritarianism. *Okwara* leads the community in the sense of offering inspiration and shape. The Church in Igboland needs a leadership that is articulate, dynamic, committed and at the same time, ecclesially conscious. A leader that takes the community as his life, casts off apathy and indifference. The way the *Okwara* and elders interact with their people must be explored by the church. Leadership has a strong religious aspect in Igbo traditional society. The leaders are supposed to be fair, just and truthful. It would offend the ancestors to disobey the *umunna* leader. God is seen as the ultimate ruler of all people, and it is He who provides His people with His own visible intermediaries to lead and guide them.[46]

The leadership in *umunn*a is comparable to that of the Zulu, who say; "The chief is our father and we are the members of his family". The *umunna* leader is also seen as a shepherd and head of the community. This image is biblical. In the *umunna* community, the purpose of leadership is not merely to make decisions, but also to help the community reach its own decision through consensus. It is not a one-man show, but a real exercise in participation. It is a

45 R. Munoz, S. Torres, and J. Eagleson, eds., **Ecclesiology in Latin America: *The challenge of Basic Christian Communities***, New York, Orbis, 1982, pp. 150-160.

46 J. Mutiso-Mbinda, **Ministry: *Service in the Church and the World***, **SPEARHEAD**, Nr. 61, Kenya, Gaba Publications, 1980, pp. 45-49.

leadership ready to serve the community. This is in response to Christ's advise: "Let the first be the servant of all". The leadership in Igbo traditional society is a shared one of collegiality, which is of great help to the leadership in UCCs.

Although there is a great respect for authority because of its religious overtones, it will be expected of a leader to be more of a facilitator for the life in the community than a solitary ruler, more of a listener than a speaker. This will actually help us to lay a better foundation for a perspective of service and will enable various ministries to arise, depending on the needs of the community.[47] In so doing, the Igbo traditional approach to leadership could form the basis for shared leadership and shared responsibilities in the UCCs. The position of a leader is such that he has many functions, including cultic, judiciary and mediatory.

The mediatory role of the leader/priest is fulfilled in sacrifices, offerings and prayers. One will notice that this role was also played by the pre-Christian priesthood of the OT. Our emphasis here is on the traditional value of integrity required of the priest, and not on reintroducing the OT concept of priesthood, where the priest sees his role as purely cultic. The priests should see their role not only that of 'saving souls', but as one that truly concerns the whole human person, being careful of the division between the things of the spirit and the things of the earth.[48] Theologically viewed, *umunna* breaks the dualism of secular and sacred, spiritual and material.

Another role played by the traditional priest is that of healing. In the *Umunna* Christian Community, emphasis should also be placed on Jesus Christ the healer. Jesus as healer is at the heart of the NT. Christ as the healer brings all ecclesial communities together. But this is not enough. Christ as our saviour must not be overlooked. Therefore the redemptive work of Christ as exemplified in his passion, death and resurrection must have a prominent place in presenting Christ as a healer. In *umunna*, the role of Jesus as a healer should become a reality through preaching and teaching, through sacraments and sacramentals. This is demonstrated by making the eucharist the center of the healing ministry. The old catechesis has neglected this aspect; that is the reason many people are seeking help of other forces, rather than Jesus. In Igboland, sickness is experienced in a religious context, which indicates the importance of this approach for the Christian communities. The idea of Jesus as a healer should be expressed in the people's prayers for the sick and in the practice of exorcism.

47 See J. Hetsen and J. Holmes-Siedle, ***Aspects of Christian Community building in Africa***, **SPEARHEAD**, Nr.75, (1983), pp.13-14.

48 J. Mutiso-Mbinda, in: **Ministry...** op. cit., p.48.

When the Igbo Church starts presenting Jesus in this manner, they would be taking more seriously the challenge issued by Pope John Paul II in 1980 on his visit to Kenya in East Africa. Here the Pope spoke of the need to move towards a deeper understanding of the mystery of Christ.

> There is no question of adulterating the word of God or emptying the cross of its power (cf.1 Cor.1:17) but rather of bringing Christ into the very center of African life and of lifting up all African life to Christ. Thus not only is Christianity relevant to Africa, but Christ, in the members of his body, is himself African.[49]

In this context, we can speak of a *umunna* Christology, since there are popular christological images. It is within the *Umunna* Christian Community that life tries to respond to this desire, to give expression to religious values and concrete life situations. The *Umunna* Christian Community portrays the meaning the community has given to Christ in their *sitz im Leben*.[50] This Christology is born out of the community's reflection on the word, and the mandate to evangelize. With this understanding, the *umunna* places Christ – the Proto-Ancestor – as the master of the community from whom all the ancestors within the community take their existence. After this position is established, every member looks up to Christ as the elevated Master and will be prepared to proclaim him. The veneration and sacrifices given to the ancestors has to be given to Christ as the supreme ancestor. The *umunna* ancestors become his collaborators.

Umunna cannot be a concurrence of parochial establishment since it does not plan to be a separate Church; instead, it will enhance the development of the parish into community of communities. *Umunna* is not a unit of the State authority, but is essentially cultural in character. One can rightly conclude that the *Umunna* Christian Community is a providential form of Small Christian Community and Basic Christian Community, just like the religiosity of man is providential to Revelation. Patricia Hafey, a nun who was overwhelmed by the life of sharing in the African community says;

> Just living and sharing in the lives of the people has been such a powerful experience that I wonder if this is what God is calling us to do. It seems to be an Evangelical virtue just to appreciate people in their culture, their standards of living, their values in life, ap-

---

49 John Paul 11, ***The African Bishops' challenge***, an address to the bishops of Kenya given on the 7th May 1980, in: **ORIGINS**, 28 May 1980, p. 29.

50 S.U. Njoku, **From Station to BCC: *with reference to Nguru Parish***, (unpublished MA thesis) CIWA., Port Harcourt, 1986, p. 55; Njoku calls it ***pietistic Christology***. For further readings on the images of Christ see J. Miguez Bonino, ed., **Faces of Jesus**, New York, Mary Knoll, 1977.

preciating them and their lives as they are. As missionaries I see this as our opportunity to give witness to the Incarnation, to give expression to God's presence with us.[51]

Such experiences of religious men and women, working in a typical African traditional rural group, show the importance of everyone working together, like brothers and sisters in the one Risen Lord. Participation is not only a matter of working and sharing material things, but also includes decision-making as it affects the *umunna* group.

Pope John Paul II reiterated the importance of people participating in decision-making in his message for the World Day of Peace. He warned that violence and injustice can hardly be avoided, when the basic human right to participate in decision-making and action taking is denied;

> A world of justice and peace cannot be created by words alone, and it cannot be imposed by outside forces: it must be desired and must come about through the contribution of all. It is essential for every human being to have a sense of participating, of being a part of the decisions and endeavours that shape the destiny of the world. Violence and injustice have often in the past found their root causes in people's sense of being deprived of the right to shape their own life. Future violence and injustice cannot be avoided when and where the basic right to participate in the choices of society is denied.[52]

It is a common practice now that no priest can work in a parish without the help of the parish council, the Christian Mothers Organization (C.W.O.), Mary League girls and the youth-groups. Although such organizations exist and are active, many of them are executors of the parish priest's ideas. They contribute little or nothing by the way of decision-making. This has to change with the use of UCCs.

The *Umunna* Christian Community model will actually decentralize authority and allow the people to participate actively in the affairs of the Church. This is what Uzukwu means when he said:

> An African Church must reflect in a fundamental way the communal aspects of traditional African society, only then can it belong to Africa and be liberated to bear witness to the Christian message interpreted in African concepts and symbols.[53]

---

51 P. Hafey, "**Personal reflections on new ways of sharing in community**," in: **Ujamaa and Christian communities...** (1976), p. 53.

52 John Paul II, "**World Day of Peace Message**" in: **L'Osservatore Romano**, vol. 17, Nrs. 52-53, (4th Dec. 1984), p. 11, parag. 9; cf. J.X. Labayen, "**Basic Christian communities**", in: **AFER**, vol. 30, 3(1988), p. 137.

53 E. Uzukwu, "**Christian Missions and An African Church**," in: **AFER**, vol. 20, 2(1978), p. 82.

It is such a Church that will give the Igboman the chance for active participation and solidarity.

In *umunna*, everyone's life is centered on community. The parish set-up is too large and indifferent for the Igbo. Igbo Christians have their daily lives centered on the small communities (*umunna*) to which they belong and not the parish. Only when the traditional parish takes on a new outlook as a community of communities (of different *umunna*), can the people eventually bring this community spirit with them when they gather in church on Sundays.

This structure begins not from the parish as we are traditionally accustomed but rather from the other end. That is why we call it the community of communities. This model begins with the 'home – *umunna*' – ecclesial community. It is an assembly of a neighbourhood whose gathering together forms a Christian community. It is the Church at the grass-roots, in the people's homes, where they actually live most of their lives. This is like the house-Church of the early Christians. The Church thus ceases to be *uka fada* (the priest's Church) but 'our Church'.

Umunna Christian Communities meet around the Word of God, nurturing and deepening their faith through sharing the gospel. Since there is already a sense of belonging in the *umunna*, members will take part in the mission of the Church in the world – caring for each other and the needy,celebrating weddings, facing and opposing injustice, burying the dead.

On the Lord's Day, these *umunna* communities gather around the Table of the Eucharist. The Eucharist is the center of the Church's celebration, in order to be meaningful to the Igbo, it should be a communitarian action. In this case, the whole old parish can then meet as a community, since they have experienced Christian community already in *umunna* through sharing the gospel and working together, both in the spirit of *umunna* and of Christ. Sunday gives them the opportunity to celebrate their unity. It is at the Eucharist, really, that they become the fullest sign of Christ's Body on Earth, the community of believers. This model of ours is in contradistinction to the traditional model of the Church, where the Sunday Eucharist is often the only time for believers to nourish their faith, to pray and listen to the Word of God. After an hour's Church service, it is difficult for such Christians to have received enough to carry them through the next week. In this case restructuring the parish as a community of *umunna* communities, will allow the people to come to the Sunday Eucharist with their faith already alive and nurtured.

5.4. The Umunna Christian Community: A More Effective Locus for Pastoral Work

Having established the theological and ecclesiological significance of UCCs, our task now is to reveal the pastoral significance, which entails the presentation of some concrete pastoral tools that are more *ad rem* with the use of *Umunna* Christian Communities. *Umunna*, as we have mentioned, is not a closed unit that is cut off from the rest of society, but strives to form a community which can act as the salt of the earth and light of the world (Matt. 5:13-16).

In our method of presenting the concrete pastoral tools, we shall fall back upon the basic foundations of the Church's life. These basic foundations or functions of a Christian community are the *kerygma* (message) which entails the proclamation of the word of God and conversion, the *koinonia* (communion) – fellowship in Christ with one another, and finally, the *diakonia* which is the aspect of service.

5.4.1. Kerygma

The Igbo Church is used only to catechesis programs for children, where adults are left out. This is contrary to Christ's system of teaching adults and blessing children. Even this is no longer effective, since the State's takeover of the schools. With the introduction of UCCs, we are recommending (a) an adult catechesis program in addition to a more effective children catechesis program; (b) a more communitarian catechumanate; (c) infant baptism as a community celebration.

The adult catechesis program should take the form of the '*umunna* council', where all eligible adults meet and participate actively. This forum should be used to conscientize the people about their life situation, to stimulate them to action, and should also be used as an ongoing formation which would aim at educating people to another vision of the Church, to another model of Church life. Here they will see the Church as 'our church' where responsibility is born by all. Those involved in the conscientization should avoid indoctrination or the old "question and answer method" of the penny catechism as the first step. The method proposed by Richard McGarr[54] should be preferred. This method gives room for discussions on life themes. After such discussions, a traditional

54 R. McGarr, "A village Catechesis", Pastoral Paper, in SPEARHEAD, Nr. 23, (Gaba Publication, Kenya, 1972).

approach should be used to discover the Christian attitude, according to a text of the Gospel. We have to re-enforce basic traditional values and aim;

> to arrive at a really indigenous Christian way of thinking and life-style, which will make people feel at home in their ordinary living situations, both as Africans and as Christians.[55]

Evangelization in *Umunna* Christian Communities should be essentially centrifugal and horizontal. With the *umunna* community, there should be a shift of most pastoral and religious activities from the parish center, to the *umunna* community. This is a catechesis that is self-propagating. It will help people to have a critical role regarding the local customs and culture, since it makes people think at the grassroots level about how the Gospel touches their lives. With the help of the priest, the people will be able to recognize the good values inherent in their culture that should be good for the propagation of the faith, and to see that the ones contrary to Christian teaching should not be allowed. *Umunna* then gives the Christian community in Igboland a basis for originality and incarnates it into the local situation.

A person's first allegiance is to the *umunna*. Names like *Umunnakwe* (if the *umunna* agrees, or permits), or *Umunnabuike* (*umunna* is my strength, or power) illustrate the position of an individual within the *umunna* unit. An individual in an *umunna* unit does not loose his autonomy or self-determination,[56] but that autonomy and self determination is exercised within the constraints imposed by the community.[57] The *umunna* guides and protects its members. No wonder that some great sacrifices such as that of the "scapegoat", *oriko* (sacrifice of communion) are practiced for the good of all by the entire *umunna*.

An example of a real-life situation would be a simple way of explaining the sacrificial death of Christ, with the analogy of the Igbo sacrifice of scapegoat.[58] The self-propagating, self supporting aspect of UCC allows a much greater localization of the Church than does the traditional parish structure.

---

55 Ibid., p. 1.

56 One pursues one's private goals and is not hindered by the **umunna**, rather the ***umunna*** structure helps one to achieve one's aim in life by communal encouragement. Cf. P.O. Iroegbu, **Communalism: A Theory of Justice for Contemporary African Political Communities**, (1989), pp. 143-144.

57 Included in these constraints are: moral conventions, cultural traditions and shared values and goals of the community. And it is in the ***umunna*** unit, that such values are cultivated.

58 For the Igbo traditional sacrifice of "**escape-goat**" see A.F. Arinze, **Sacrifice in Ibo religion**, (Ibadan University Press, Ibadan, 1970), pp. 36-90; P. Osuchukwu, **Home-sick for Paradise Lost. The place of sacrifice in Traditional Ibo Religion and the Bible with particular reference to Amauzari Town**, (1988), pp.33-35.

The ohacracy or traditional democracy of consensus and the recognition of the ability and gifts of members facilitate this localization. The adult catechesis will make people aware of their needs; these will be reflected in the light of the Gospel and of the possible solutions available.

Holmes-Siedle, speaking of the use of dialogue in adult catechesis in the rural groupings, says;

> In general it could reinforce basic African attitudes and values, as solidarity, sense of community, awareness of the gratuitousness of life, value of fecundity and sense of festivity; but it could also oppose any abuse of power, corruption, abuse of sexuality, etc.[59]

The catechetical center that has been in the Church premises, after being shifted to the *umunna* units, becomes a practical realization that the mandate "go and preach the Gospel" applies to all Christians.[60] Making the *Umunna* Christian community the catechetical center is making Christian homes into the catechetical base. When this is achieved, the cry for returning schools to the Church for the purpose of religious instruction will be taken care of.

Within the *umunna* catechetical center, different Igbo traditional values will be incorporated into the corpus of the Christian principles and inculcated in the children, e.g., the value of hospitality. The *Umunna* Christian community used as a catechetical center will of maximize the traditional involvement of all adults in the up-bringing of children. It will also help to prepare all adults according to their capacities in educating the children in the Christian principles. For a more practical method, the *obi*[61] *umunna*, village halls, or squares could be used for both catechetical and other Church activities.

In the urban areas, a group of residential houses has to be organized to function like the *umunna* community. The different streets, organized into zones, become an out-station frequently visited by the priest. The priest should also establish personal contact with these house (yard) groupings. These should be catechetical and prayer centers. Members gather on a more regular basis to pray and reflect together on the Scriptures. The use of the existing Block Rosary centers, common in most urban areas in Igboland, will be of great help here.

---

59 J. Holmes-Siedle and J. Hetsen, "**Aspects of Christian Community Building in Africa**", in: **SPEARHEAD, Nr. 75**, (1983), p.30.

60 Cf. **EN 13**, At baptism and confirmation the faithful receives such obligation and the special grace to carry it out. By baptism, he enjoys the priesthood of the people of God, and becomes a member of the Mystical Body of Christ, and receives the mandate to proclaim the Gospel according to his capacity. At confirmation he is guaranteed special help from the Holy Spirit to be active and zealous in this mission and in his Christian life.

61 **Obi** is the socio-political as well as religious meeting place for families, ***umunna*** meetings. It simply a reception small hall, visitors are normally entertained.

These societies are not only the 'militant' arm of the Church, they are also veritable carriers of the Word of God into all homes in the community. They actually enrich the apostolic life of the *Umunna* Christian communities. They act as catechetical agents and help in no small way in bringing about Christian community living and solidarity. The adult catechesis program or '*umunna* council' catechesis, with its conscientization aspect could make people aware of the community dimension of the church and of the fact that 'we are the Church'. The Church becomes 'our' Church, and then people will be prepared to propagate and support it.

We are also calling for a better organized and more communitarian catechumenate. Much is learned during the liturgical celebration. The whole *umunna* community should be encouraged to participate in the catechumenate ceremonies. The *okwara* leader of the *umunna* community should be allowed to declare publicly that they want to present and support the catechumens in their conversion and to receive them into the community of the faithful. The new rite of Christian Initiation stresses the importance of the role of the community, as stated in the opening paragraph of Nr.41:

> The people of God, represented by the local Church, should always understand and show that the initiation of adults is its concern and the business of all baptized. Therefore the community must always be ready to fulfil its apostolic vocation by giving help to those who need Christ... Hence, the community must help the candidates and catechumens throughout the whole period of initiation.[62]

This rite insists that "the whole community" should be present at the celebration of the different stages of the catechumenate. A program of religious education should be organized within the *umunna*. As those candidates for baptism and first communion are being given instructions, the rest within the community are strengthened. Concerning infant baptism, efforts should be made that the baptism takes place within the *Umunna* Christian Community. We shall cease to practice the old method, where the ceremony is between the priest and the mother of the child, including the proxy god-parents and the sleeping baby. Just as the traditional naming ceremony takes place within the family, so will the church initiation.

---

62 ***Rite of Christian Initiation for Adults***, <u>**ICEL**</u>, Washington, 1974, cf. Nrs. 4,19,20,21,23.

5.4.2. *Koinonia*

Liturgy is both a community act and worship. The specific practice that distinguishes the Church from a secular society of a well-meaning people, is to worship the Father in spirit and in truth, and to express this worship in our lives 'for others', so that others too may be drawn to sense the presence of the transcendent God and to worship Him in their lives. It is the mind of the Church that all participate actively in all acts of worship and especially in the sacramental life of the Church.

> Mother Church earnestly desires that all the faithful should be led to that full, conscious, and active participation in liturgical celebrations which is demanded by the very nature of the liturgy, and to which the Christian people, "a chosen race, a royal priesthood, a holy nation, a redeemed people" (1 Pet. 2:9, 4-5) have a right and obligation by reason of their baptism.[63]

The *umunna* offers a suitable place for conscious and active participation in the liturgical life of the Church. It offers every member the opportunity to participate in all forms of the community life. The principle in the *umunna* unit is that everyone is expected to work for the welfare of the whole community, as R. Banks affirms;

> One can only be an individual in a community and a community can only function properly when each individual is playing his own distinctive role properly in the community.[64]

No one is left out in the affairs of the *umunna*. In celebrating Church sacraments, we can learn much from the Igbo communitarian celebrations.

The place of the Eucharist in the church community can not be exhausted. Its importance in Christian Communities has been stressed in the AMECEA countries.[65] Sharing the Eucharist constitutes Christians as brothers and sisters; it also challenges us to be prophets. It makes Christians "denounce all unchristian ways, unjust systems and attitudes into which they have been woven, and in which they live – apparently culturally undisturbed".[66] The Eucharist is

---

63 A. Flannery, **Vatican II**, **"The Constitution on the Sacred Liturgy"**, **Sacrosanctum Concilium**, Nr. 14, (1988).

64 R. Banks, **Paul's Idea of Community: the Early House Churches in their Historical Setting**, (William E. Eerdmans Publishing Co., Grand Rapids, 1980), p. 70. The Igbo *umunna* members take their community contribution very seriously. The pride of the *umunna* is always at the mind of every member; everyone works and supports the less privileged, and tries to see that his own *umunna* is not any way ridiculed.

65 AMECEA Plenary study Conference, ***Building SCCs***, **AFER**, vol.21, 5(1979).

66 Kakuba-Kapia, ***A theology of fostering ecclesial Communities***, **Communities of God's People**, **AFER,** vol.33, 3(1991), p. 144.

the bread of life. And to be alive, recipients should be able to protest against structures that quietly tolerate and say nothing about the hungry men, women and children in their midst. In order to have a caring eucharistic community, the size of the community must be addressed. Looking at the nature and number of *umunna* units in a given parish, it would be difficult to make every unit an eucharistic center.[67] Provision should be made for four or more *umunna* units come together in an *Mkpuru* or *Ogbe* (Fig 4) to form an eucharistic center. Such eucharistic centers should be encouraged where the Blessed Sacrament can be reserved in the *Ogbe* Chapel for more frequent reception and adoration. Kakubi, the bishop of Mbarara, gives the green light to how the eucharistic center should be seen:

> Our aim was to set up eucharistic centers, where the Blessed Sacrament would be reserved. Before a center could become an eucharistic center, the community had to have a strong and secure building with a strong tabernacle. The Christians in the area should show signs of being worshipping Christian community, desirous of strengthening their Christian virtues through the frequent reception of the Eucharist.[68]

One may ask for the spiritual reason for installing the Blessed Sacrament in the Ogbe Chapels or eucharistic center. M.Lejeune's answers such question thus;

> For years we have been face to face with starving Christian groups, so food had somehow to be given to them. The conviction that the eucharistic Christ was needed in their midst became overwhelming. Why not install the Blessed Sacrament in our Communities, in our centers with a person authorized to distribute communion.[69]

The people should be encouraged to come for prayers, Bible sharing, saying the Rosary and eucharistic adoration. It is left for the community to decide the time for their meeting. They will be allowed to present their life situation to God and use their mode of expression and songs. The liturgy, which includes the conditions and modes of expression or activities peculiar to a local community, is informal, whereas formal liturgy entails rituals and formulas followed as a universal expression of the universal Christian community. It must be presided over at most by any ordained minister.

---

67 The eucharistic center should be differentiated from the eucharistic community. Every UCC should be a eucharistic community, for it is the life of the Church. The eucharistic center will be a place where the Eucharist can be celebrated or the Blessed Sacrament kept.

68 J.B. Kakuba, "**Christian Communities in Mbarara Diocese**", in: **AFER**, vol. 21, 5(1979), p. 301.

69 M. Lejeune, and R. Bouchard, "**Eucharist and Community**", **pastoral paper**, in: **SPEARHEAD**, **Nr. 28** (1973), p. 4.

The installation of the Blessed Sacrament in the center should not cloud the importance of the worshipping community that is actually expressed in the eucharistic celebration. Care must be taken that this does not turn the celebration of the memoria of the Risen Lord into only the reception of communion. Periodic eucharistic celebrations should be encouraged.

Both formal and informal liturgies are essential to the local community. The informal liturgy helps to hold together the local community, while the formal liturgy links the local community to the universal Church.[70]

The *Umunna* Christian Communities should become eucharistic communities, if they are to be authentic *loci* of pastoral and religious activities. The people's religiosity and their traditional practice of community worship should be tapped for the eucharistic celebration.

The personal and the essentially communitarian dimensions of worship must be reflected in the celebration. Just as traditional worship takes notice of the people's need, so will the Christian celebration correspond to the need of the community. Another aspect of Igbo worship that should be looked into is the communion sacrifice called *oriko*. Communion is so important in Igbo worship that communion with the living implies communion with the ancestors.

Anyone who is not in communion and solidarity with the *umunna*, is also denied the community of the ancestors.[71] The sense of communion inherent in *umunna* generates the invocation of benevolent spirits, and the desire to be in solidarity with them. There is a conviction that such spirits are God's agents. This sense of communion enriches the Catholic doctrine of the communion of the saints. The sense of communion for the Igbo is based on a blood relationship. Blood for the Igbo symbolizes life itself, as it did for the ancient Israelites (Gen. 9: 4; Lev. 17: 14; Deut. 12: 23). And every care, be it material or spiritual, is taken to protect this life.

(a) *Healing*: Healing ministries have taken a prominent position in Igboland. Apart from criticisms of the abuses in this ministry, one must acknowledge that it could become an important element in the building up of Christian communities, instead of becoming the occasion for a breakaway Church. Since sickness in Africa is often believed to be caused by some spiritual powers, a careful study is called for. Praying for the sick should be added to our routine liturgical celebrations. We recommend, at least once a week, a communal celebration of the healing Mass or Anointing of the Sick in an eucha-

---

70 Cf. M.F. Perrin-Jassy, "**Forming Christian Communities**" op. cit., pp. 27-33.

71 Cf. L.A. Ugbor, **Prayer in Igbo Traditional Religion: Its Meaning and Message for the Church in Igboland Today**, (unpublished Doctoral Dissertation, Rome, 1985), pp. 117-119.

ristic center, in preference to Extreme Unction for one person in his far-away homestead.

This will be an important contribution to the life of the Christian community. It will help the priest and the people to realize the significance of the change from Extreme Unction to Anointing of the Sick in the Second Vatican Council (SC 73). This sacrament is not only for those at the point of death, but also for the sick. The new rite of anointing the sick restores the emphasis on bringing the whole man to health again which is more understandable to the Igboman. Their traditional medicine is holistic. Both the new rite and the Igbo concept of healing accept that the minister, medical staff, family and friends of the sick have a complementary role to play. All Christians share in the healing ministry of Christ, which is a ministry of comfort and compassion.[72] In this case, the priest should not monopolize the ministry. The leaders of the community, the catechist those assigned to this ministry and the priest should all lay hands on the sick, while the whole community participates in praying for the sick. It is through such a ceremony that the community will be able to express concern for the sick in their midst and the afflicted will also see something of God's concern for them.

(b) *Training of leaders:* Since everyone will be prepared to help in working for the welfare of the community, it is pertinent to stress the importance of training the leaders to have true community spirit and the ability to build a *umunna* community in the Christian spirit of fellowship. There should be an on-going formation or training for the leaders. Care must be taken not to make this a mere external structure. The training should be able to bring about a change in attitude and an awareness that "we are the Church" together.[73] Training the leaders within the community by way of seminars and leadership courses will help the leaders not to separate themselves from their communities or to even think that they are entitled to a salary or a privileged position in the community.[74]

The evangelical concept of leadership is service to and by the community, that is, the Church as the People of God. The one who serves is part and parcel of that community. Different ministries and services demand specialized courses; for example, a special course for leaders would help them know the techniques of conducting meetings and the aim of the Christian Community.

---

72 Rite of Anointing and Pastoral care of the sick, <u>**ICEL**</u>, Washington, 1973, Nrs. 5-7, 32-35.

73 E. Van Huet, Religious Education and the Church; in: **The Community called Church**, <u>**SPEARHEAD**</u>, Nr. 60, Kenya, Gaba Publications 1979, p.71

74 This may even help American European Churches, whose lay theologians are managing parishes (see Mokambi of Zaire). The lay theologians should be sent by their own communities and they should return to their communities after training.

Van Huet suggests exercises in creative listening, in dialogue, group dynamics, role plays and photo-language, not only to equip leaders in their various tasks, but also to transform committees into communities.[75]

(c) *Ministries of Intercommunity:*[76] This entails the linking together of the different *Umunna* Christian Communities. Leaders (incorporating the above-mentioned secondary ecclesial personnel) of each *umunna*, catechists and the priest should belong to this category of ministry. It will give the UCCs a universal outlook and also enable them to gain a sort of cross pollination of ideas and experiences. We suggest that at some point in the year, there should be exchange of leaders to preside at different UCC meetings. This will create a broader outlook for the Church.

(d) *Theology of feasts:* Another way to stimulate an awareness of being one Christian community is to create occasions for large numbers of UCCs to meet. Each UCC could have a patron Saint (probably the name of the first Christian) and the feast of their Saint should attract all other members. This will unite the different communities and link them to the universal Church. Eucharistic celebration is appropriate at this feast, followed by other social activities.[77] Feasts and celebrations are very important in the life of the Igbo. An ordination to the priesthood or religious profession calls for festivity. Ash Wednesday, Palm Sunday, Easter, Christmas, Corpus Christi and the harvest thanksgiving are occasions that bring people of all works of life from the different *umunna* groups together.

> Deep within the people a sense of joy and festivity exists on account of the gift of life, the gratuitousness of people's existence; the life-cycle is characterized by joyful celebrations. Extraordinary generosity is shown when it comes to contributing to communal feasts, be it a wedding, a twin ceremony, or a burial.[78]

Africans celebrate practically everything. Therefore our liturgy should be permeated by a sense of celebration, "for the common Ancestor of the Christian family is being celebrated: his death, his resurrection, his life, his awareness and care for the poor and the sick, and his desire for a more human, authentic society".[79]

---

75 E. Van Huet, in: **Community called Church...** art.cit., pp.72-81.

76 B. Joinet, ***Practical steps towards building christian Communities***; **AMECEA DOCUMENTATION SERVICE**, 3\76\2, p. 7

77 M.F. Perrin-Jassy, ***Forming Christian Communities***, Pastoral Paper, **SPEARHEAD**, Nr.12, Gaba Publications, 1970, p.32.

78 J. Hetzen and J. Holmes-Siedle, ***Aspects of Christian Community building in Africa***, op.cit., p. 38.

79 Ibid. p. 39.

5.4.3. Diakonia

Jesus' words about service are part of the unforgettable tradition which stems from him. "He who is greatest among you shall be your servant" (Mtt. 23: 11). Jesus taught by example. His life was a life of service and he openly expressed that he came to serve, not to be served. His life challenges all offices in his Church to service, which is *diakonia*.[80]

Helping the sick, the aged in the *umunna* or neighbourhood, and caring for the poor has been a way of life for the traditional Igbo people. The *umunna* Christian community will see that this care does not stop at home or within a given *umunna* unit, but will be extended to other communities. Since the motivation has now changed from the blood-tie of the *umunna*, to a faith-tie and Christ's blood relationship, we all have become brothers and sisters in Christ, for we have the same Father. In actual fact, the sharing of joy and grief and the expression of mercy in work in UCCs will not be restricted to the *umunna*, but extended to the people beyond it. The members look after one another's needs. They see that the lonely, sick and impoverished of their neighbourhood experience the caring love of the Lord through his disciples. They are involved in the affairs of their localities, as they wish to put into practice the love they have received from Christ through one another.

The services should not be based merely in caring for the sick and poor, but must also include the question of examining and studying the causes of poverty, misery, sickness, as well as organizing common actions to change the structures of injustice and poverty. It is a pity that not much is done on the awareness of structural injustice within African countries in general and Nigeria in particular. The question of justice came up when the Symposium of Episcopal Conferences of Africa and Madagascar (SECAM) met in Yaounde, Cameroon, in 1981. There they issued an important address to all apostolic workers, on Justice and Evangelisation in Africa, because of "the urgency of these problems and gravity of the situation".[81]

In the SECAM's sixth resolution on justice, an appeal went out to all Christians and other men of good will in Africa, Madagascar and the Islands to strive to remedy all situations of injustice, oppression, discrimination or violation of human rights. One may say that this appeal ended in their documentation. There were no follow-ups to this appeal. In Nigeria today, the problem of the nullification of presidential election on June 12, 1994, is a case at hand. The case of the *Osu*-system in Igboland is a stumbling block to a real Chris-

---

80 Cf. G. Lohfink, **Jesus and Community**, (Paulist Press, New York, 1984), pp. 47, 118.

81 SECAM DOCUMENTS: ***Seeking Gospel Justice in Africa***, in: **SPEARHEAD**, Nr.69, Kenya, Gaba Publications, 1970, p.5.

tian Community. We may be seeing a better tomorrow with the use of *umunna* as a Christian community. In the *umunna*, the Church not only works for the poor, and the marginalized, but also with them. *Umunna* being a social, political and religious unit of the Igbo, will go beyond works of mercy and show real solidarity in the struggle for human development.

The awareness of the structural injustice within and outside *umunna* by members of the Christian community, will give the Church leaders no alternative than other to speak out for the children of God to be free from all domination, oppression and discrimination. Moltmann insists that;

> Only an ecclesial community that is united and unifying, free of dominion and oppression, and only a humanity that is whole, united and unifying, free from class domination and dictatorial oppression, can claim to respect the Trinitarian God. This is a world in which human beings are characterized by their social relationships, and not be power or possessions. This is a world in which human beings share everything in common, and share everything, except their personal characteristics.[82]

There should be mutual concern and mercy to those in need. Services and help among the community members is in obedience to Christ's command to follow him. The Apostles lived this life, for there was no one in need (Acts 4:34). It is a voluntary activity of the Christian community to serve.

The Igbo will not find *diakonia* difficult, for it is a part of *umunna* life. No one is left out in life or death. Therefore, Gichuhu says of traditional African sense of community *diakonia*:

> Members in an African community always showed concern for one another. If one of the community members suffered, then the rest felt very concerned and did everything possible to assist that member. If there was joy, it was also shared by all. The future of the Church depends on the development of values of this kind of concern for one another.[83]

The use of *umunna* as a Christian community is a creation of a basic *locus* of Christian life. As the sacraments are celebrated in the community, the *umunna* unit will become alive and more aware of itself as an evangelizing and evangelized community. This will help the group to transcend the ritual aspects of the sacraments in an effort to reach the inner significance of these signs of grace.

---

82 J. Moltmann, ***The Inviting Unity of the Triune God***, in: **CONCILIUM**, 177, 1(1985), pp. 50-58.

83 G.N. Gichuhu, "**The Spirituality of SCCs in Eastern Africa**", in: **SPEARHEAD, Nr. 85**, (Gaba Publications, Kenya, 1985), p. 55.

5.4.4. Ecumenism

Ecumenism, to put it simply, is a matter of ordinary people relating to one another in love. The Igbo, when he says *ebe nwa siri lo-uwa ya hiri* (no matter from where a child comes into this world, let him be alive), says it all. The spirit of *umunna* community calls for no distinction as to who is a Muslim, traditional religionist or Christian. The Church has a lot to gain with the use of *umunna*, for as theologians debate and argue about ecumenism, it is the people at the grassroots – in *umunna* – that are practicing ecumenism. But care must be taken, for sometimes Christians may be forced into unchristian sacrifices, in pretence that we all belong to the same *umunna.*

Ecumenicity can be better promoted better if it is rooted in the traditional communities and draws from a communitarian spirituality of the people. No wonder Kasenene says:

> The ecumenical challenge which faces the Church is to rediscover the African value of community which is manifested in natural communities and to use it as the starting point for ecumenicity activity.[84]

Love is the watchword in ecumenism; Jesus actually spelt this out when he said: "All men will know that you are my disciples if you love one another" (Jn 13:35). This instruction was followed by the early Church (Acts 2:42-47). Many people were attracted to the Church because of her unity and the communal life they practiced. *Umunna* is not lacking in this communal life. We find out that there are people of different denominations and religions in an *umunna*. This does not disturb the community life; love and care reigns in spite of the different denominations. Kinship, good neighbourliness and harmony are core values which are strongly emphasized in order to maintain a sense of community.

There exist strong and deep community ties in Igboland, which regulate all relationships, be they social, economic or political. For the Church to succeed in her bid for ecumenical movement, the Igbo spirit, experience and system of communality should be used as the natural starting point for initiatives towards Christian unity. One may notice that the main approach in the ecumenical movement in the Church today has been institutional ecumenicity, which has had limited success, in the sense that ecumenism has remained elitist.

(a) *Institutional ecumenicity:* The term "institution" always calls to mind rules and regulations, and organized patterns of behaviour, thought and cus-

---

84 P. Kasenene, ***Natural Communities in Ecumenical Activity***: **COMMUNITIES OF GOD'S PEOPLE**, in: **AFER,** vol.33, 3(1991), p. 150.

toms designed to meet certain basic needs of society.[85] Institutional ecumenicity simply means organized ecumenical activities and structures channelled into pursuing the ideals of ecumenism. Such organizations include the World Council of churches (WCCs) the AACC and a host of regional and national bodies. Naturally such establishments tend to be rigid, legalistic and bureaucratic. These hardly work because the concentration is on words, and not on the persons concerned. Cardinal Willebrand affirms that;

> The coming together of separated Churches can be brought only through the coming together of separated christians in areas where they live side by side. Ecumenical development is the work of real people in real places.[86]

Umunna then becomes a God-sent instrument for an ecumenical movement, since what the church authorities and theologians are saying is already being practiced. This shows that what the Church in Igboland needs is not institutional ecumenicity, but congregational ecumenicity.

(ii) *Congregational ecumenicity:* The way different denominations cooperate today, with the spirit of *umunna* (as opposed to the missionary era) is ecumenical. Feasts are celebrated together, irrespective of Church or religious affiliations; such feasts include marriages, death, birth and other local feasts. Jesus says: "For where two or three meet in my name, I shall be there with them" (Matt 18:20). In Igboland, feasts as mentioned above attract not only Christians, but also non-Christians. The openness of the Igbo society and its congregational ecumenism give room for accommodation and assimilation.

It is common to see an elder who is not a Christian breaking the kola-nut, (but realizing the presence of Christians); after calling all the spirits of the land and the ancestors he ends his prayer with "through Christ our Lord"; and all present will answer "Amen". One notices that the people are bound by both religious and natural links, so that the religious and social factors seem to make a perfect blend, promoting social cohesion. We have seen that *umunna*, the natural community in Igboland, unites members of different sexes, status and religious affiliations. Their sense of communalism is manifested in building houses; working in farms for the old and needy is *terminus a quo* for Christian ecumenical activity.

It is striking to note that many denominational differences melt away in *umunna* gatherings. The differences seem to be felt in their respective Church buildings and within the church premises, but at home, 'we are all one in love', they seem to say. This same spirit is manifested in urban areas. People living

---

85 E. Stewart, **SOCIOLOGY:** ***The Human Science***, New York, MacGraw-Hill Book Company, 1978, p.7.

86 AACC\AMECEA, ***Ecumenical Initiatives in East Africa***, Nairobi, 1982, p. v.

in the same yard, street and neighbourhood take interest in one another's affairs. They clean their yards and the streets and contribute to security, not minding their denominational differences. It is also a common practice to have neighbours participate in another's Churches, when a feast is called for, such as the Christian "Churching" of a new born baby. This is ecumenism in practice. The Igbo Church should use this spirituality manifested by the people as a basis for ecumenicity.

5.4.5. The Umunna Christian Community and Politics

This area may seem explosive, since many people think that the Church must keep out of politics. Those opposed to Church involvement in politics fail to understand that politics is the active way in which our whole secular life is organized; it concerns itself with health, labour, sport, finance, education, industry and commerce, communication, welfare services etc. To propose a *Umunna* Christian community means the Church has a political mission.

Nigeria is in a political crisis. She is experiencing social injustice. Where there is no justice, peace cannot prevail. The goal of a common good thrives only when there is peace. Canon 287 of the New Code obliges the clerics to uphold peace based on justice among people.[87] If the canon law lays the obligation on clerics to foster peace, then the Church in Nigeria has the duty to help in salvaging Nigeria out of its political distress. A look at the political situation in Nigeria today makes it a priority for the active involvement of the Church, and the *Umunna* christian Community will be the best ground to prepare herself for such a task. The simple people within *umunna* suffer or have suffered under colonial, civil and military regimes. It seems they are being told to look heavenward for consolation; but complacency is not the answer. Whether colonial rule, corrupt civilian rule or a military junta is standing on the neck of an Igboman, the effect is equally excruciating. The Church has to do something positive to remedy the situation. The first step is to make the people aware politically. In this case, the *Umunna* Christian community will prepare Christians and non-Christians to become actively aware their political obligation.

The *Umunna* Christian Community will be of great help to the Church to prepare the community against people trying to manipulate the *umunn*a for

87 Canon 287 states that: "Clerics are always to do their utmost to foster among people peace and harmony based on justice". **The Code of Canon Law**: prepared by *The Canon Law Society of Great Britain and Ireland*, London, Collins Liturgical Publications, 1983, p.49.

political ends. The Church should insist on the ohacratic mode of governance in *umunna*, where decisions are reached by a consensus that does not compromise the doctrine of the Church. The Church, by making use of *umunna*, will help herself to be more vocal where a discriminatory classism is concerned. We are witnesses to an uncritical Christian acceptance of a totally unchristian class structure such as the *osu* system in Igboland. Paul admonishes us: "There does not exist among you Jew or Greek, slave or freeman, male or female. All are one in Christ Jesus" (Gal.3:28).

The above statement portrays the difference between the Old Testament people who are clannish, the *umunna* that is based on common ancestorship, and Christianity that calls for global brotherhood. The words of Paul call for a classless society. But Christians, with the large parish structure, fall into this classism with terms: "first", 'second' and 'third' worlds, even some talk of the "fourth" world; upper, middle and lower class. In the large Igbo parishes we have *diala* and *os*u (freemen and slaves). This should not be the Christian spirit. The good News of Christ should be a liberating agent for the oppressed and the marginalized in our society. The use of *umunna* will actually help the Christians to see people for what they are and not for what they have. It will also help the Christians to see people as the children of God (*umunna*) brothers and sisters in Christ (*umunnam na Kristi*).

5.5. Conclusion

As a one-time parish priest, I am a firm believer in the parish and its durability and usefulness. The current structure of our parish does not help the deepening of the gospel in Igboland. The Igbo, as we have shown, prefer a less structured 'plant', one more charismatic, more communal, more in keeping with the *umunna* communities as had been manifested in the long tradition of the people. The appointment of Stephen and other deacons, the thirteenth-century Dominicans and Franciscans, for example, although very much "in union with Rome", operated with a very different spirituality and process, ministering more from charism than from office.[88]

Our parishes and the priests have such a lot on their hands administratively that it is difficult to reach everybody in the parish. The *Umunna* Christian Community, with the *umunna* spirit that leaves no one behind, will actually help the Church to reach everyone. Fraternity is the spirit of *umunna*. The parish ministry seems to be modelled on the pastoral Epistles, the letters of Ig-

88 W.J. Bausch, **"The Hands on Parish": *Reflections and suggestions for fostering community***, Connecticut, Twenty-third Publications, 1991.

natius of Antioch, and the example of Ambrose and Augustine. The *Umunna* Christian Community will be modeled on Jesus and his disciples in the synoptic, the community church of Paul, his Letters and Acts, and the example of Francis.

The *Umunna* Christian Community sees the Church more as a herald and communion. This is a pastoral option to achieve a deepening of faith in the Igbo context. There may be different reactions to this pastoral option. For some, it may be simply one of the novelties arising in ecclesiology, and as such, regarded as a passing fad.[89] And for others, it may yet boil down to another administrative measure invented by the church to run the parish. But from experience, we know that it is one of the best ways of bringing people back into the life of the Church. If the gospel is to have an impact in Igboland, it should be rooted on the basic community – *umunna*.

89 J. Hetsen and J. Holmes-Siedle, op. cit., p. vi.

General Conclusion

In this research, I set out to propose a framework for the formation of Small Christian Communities while maintaining the balance between the Igbo cutural set-up, called *umunna*, and the Church's life and faith, in order to make the gospel message meaningful and relevant for the majority of Igbo christians. Our conviction is that, if the Igbo Christian is offered the atmosphere or context within which faith and the ordinariness of life flow naturally from one to the other, that person could express the faith in an authentically Igbo manner. The Igbo is more at home with his *umunna* and for him to practice Christianity within it, is for him to be at home with Christianity. The anthropological study of the Igbo experience of community and of the different roles in traditional society shows that the Igbo has a natural basis for the phenomenon of the Small Christian Community.

Umunna, with its spirit of belonging, solidarity and communal life, is the basic community in Igboland. Apart from its literary or elaborate meanings, we found out that its spirit is transcendent. The tendency for an Igbo to be identified with a group is acquired from *umunna*. The Igbo finds fulfilment within a community. He recalls the spirit of *umunna* wherever he finds himself outside the natural community by forming similar units. This spirit of identifying with a group is life embracing, a vehicle for social integration and brotherhood, and also calls for communion. This is a primary group, where caring is at a personal level.

Because of the transcendental nature of the *umunna* spirit, its membership can allow those outside the blood and ancestorship. Though strangers are accepted and initiated into the *umunna*, it is after a long period of probation in the area and a proof of good neighbourliness. Such a spirit is God-sent for the enhancement of the Church in Igboland. This will help the Church to focus on a group of families, several of which make up *umunna*, composed of kindreds who live within a territory, and including foreign elements.

Umunna represents the social, political, economic, and religious life of the Igbo people. It is an existing political, social and religious structure found in Igboland. Within this structure, the leader plays the role of father, priest and protector, with the assistance of the elders of the community. His office is religiously guided, since he is representing both the living and the ancestors in the community. Authority in *umunna* is a shared one. Traditional democracy or what we call *ohacracy* is practiced. The people as a group have more power than the individual leader. In order to run the society more smoothly, the Igbo nation has various social structures of which *umunna* is an important one. The traditional Igbo society has no central political authority that welded all of Igboland into a political whole. Every *umunna*, as it were, is autonomous. We saw that because of this set-up, there was and still is a decentralization of power and authority. The social structure has some outstanding determinant factors which characterise the uniqueness of its ohacratic nature. These include individualism, self-regulation and representation. Our pre-occupation has been to examine the concept, structure, organisation and leadership as they help to deepen Christianity in Igboland.

Most of the traits within *umunna* have helped in the formation of Small Christian Communities in both Latin American and East African countries. These values are also seen within the early Christian Communities. Some of these values include the bond of love – whose essence lies in the fact that it is *a conditio sine qua non* for the members' unity; and community welfare, where each member acts freely and responsibly, respecting the dignity of the others and contributing positively and actively to the well-being of the whole community. The welfare of the community is the common concern of all its members, who are ready to share their time, talents and treasures together. In spite of the role of the elders, charismatic leadership is in vogue.

Authoritarian leadership is hard to find, since there is no leadership which feels destined for and capable of making all decisions and insists on making them without leaving room for participation of others. This type of leadership would help declericalize the pastoral ministry; and consequently, active participation of the whole community in the mission of the Church. The declericalization of the pastoral ministry would help to create lay ministries to meet some of the pastoral needs of the community. The Igbo innate community dimension and its shared leadership could be very useful elements in the construction of the *Umunna* Christian Community.

Inasmuch as we stress the small and manageable size of *umunna*, their authenticity as an *Umunna* Christian Community depends on their healthy connection and relationship with the larger Christian community on the parish, diocese, and universal levels. *Umunna* communities are smaller communities within a bigger one – the universal Church. A new image of the Church arises, namely, one of a communion of communities, giving a new value to the classical theology of the local church. We are aware that a change of mentality on the part of the clergy and the faithful is called for to achieve this. It will not be easy, as we mentioned, but some elements have been highlighted that could help in changing our traditional parish into a communion of communities. Some of the pastoral considerations we proposed include:- adult catechesis, communitarian catechumenate, and communally celebrated sacrament of the sick and leadership training courses. It is our contention that the Church has the function of acting as leaven for the natural communities through participation in their activities and giving Christian interpretations to everyday situations in the life of the people.

Umunna Christian Communities would offer the Igbo Christian the communitarian context in which to live his or her Christian faith. With the use of UCC, the Igbo Christian's different aspects of life would be centred on, and rotate around the gospel message. This, in a way, will make the important movements of life, such as birth, naming ceremonies, initiation, marriage, death or burial retain their communitarian and religious characters. The phenomenon of UCCs is the best way of bringing the gospel message to the grassroots level in Igboland. We know that this phenomenon tallies well with the early Church community in certain principles which could help in the growth of the faith in Igboland. It is also ad rem with the Igbo and African concept of community and therefore needs no new structures for implimentation. The use of *umunna* offers a privilege setting for evangelisation and incarnation of faith in Igboland. This position is affirmed by Hetsen as wrote: "A Church at grassroots level has the chance to incarnate itself in the local culture and will not only be a Church more and more self-reliant, born of all its members, but also a Church which realizes that it does not exist for itself but for the world, a Church which is aware that it is sent by the Father as his Son was".[1]

1 J. Hetsen and J. Holmes-Siedle, ***Aspects of Christian Community Building in Africa***, **SPEARHEAD**, Nr. 75, p,54.

Appendix I

(i).

Difference between the Parish and the Umunna Christian Community.

PARISH	**UMUNNA COMMUNITY.**
Membership: all live within a geographical territory	One is born in it and all know each other.
Size: The number is indefinite	Primary group, 30,40,100.
Basic attitude of members: Passive	Participation &solidarity.
Faith: Theoretical	Practical in real life situation.
Celebration: an obligation	Life of the community.
Sacraments: Non communitarian	All involved.
Charity: Institutionalized	Spontaiety in mutual help.
Leadership: Authoritarianism	Charismatic from the unit.
Structure: Uniformity	Plurality and variety.

(ii).

Functional system.

Since the *umunna* community is a natural one, people will be advised to meet more often than usual. In this case, Christian principles should be introduced. Prayer is a welcome exercise in Igboland, no matter who says it. Both Catholics and other Christian denominations and even traditional religionists participate in common prayers without discrimination.

When the UCC assembles, (a) there should be normal exchange of greetings after which the leader or one appointed should lead in the opening prayer; (b) a reader should be appointed to read a text from the bible; (c) some pertinent words should be picked out for meditation; (d) then there should be silence to allow God speak to each and every one; (e) then comes the sharing of thoughts about what has been read as it strikes any participant; the words or phrases that can be reflected are shared with a view of the people's everyday situation; (f) if there is any task for the community, it should then be discussed; (g) intercetory prayers and hymns follow. Here individuals and groups may present their intentions and all pray for them.

Figures (iii)

Fig. 1
(According to E. N. Nykaka)

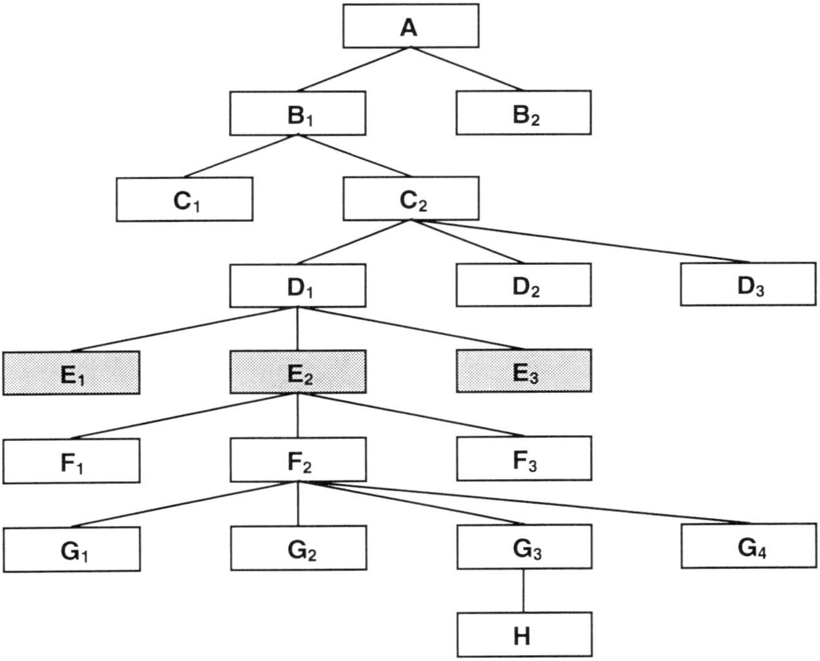

A = Town-State
B = Ebe or Ebo
C = Ogbe
D = Mkpuru
E = Umunna
F = Onumara
G = Ngwuru
H = Ama

Fig. 2
(According to F. L. Nzimiro)

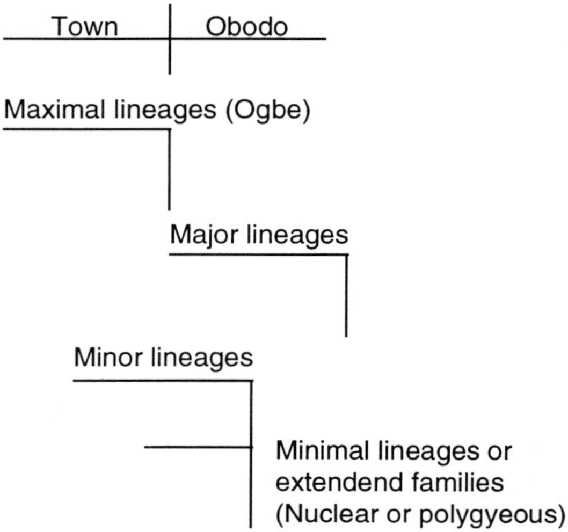

Fig. 3
(According to C. K. Meek)

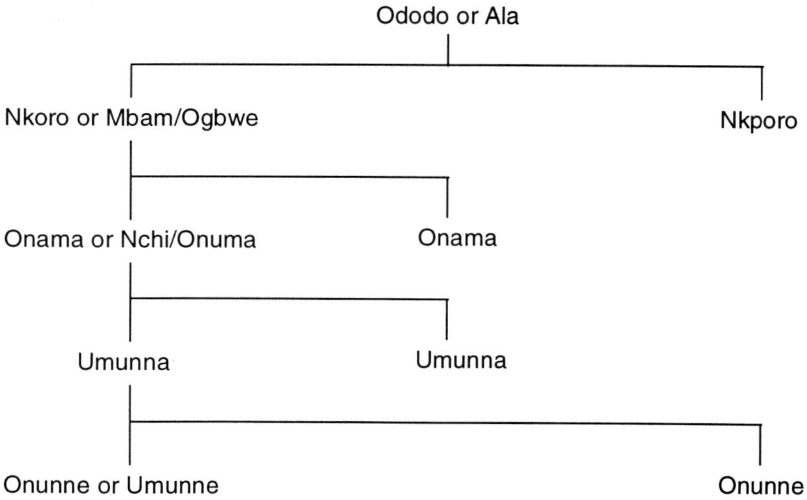

Fig. 4
(The writers town grouping)

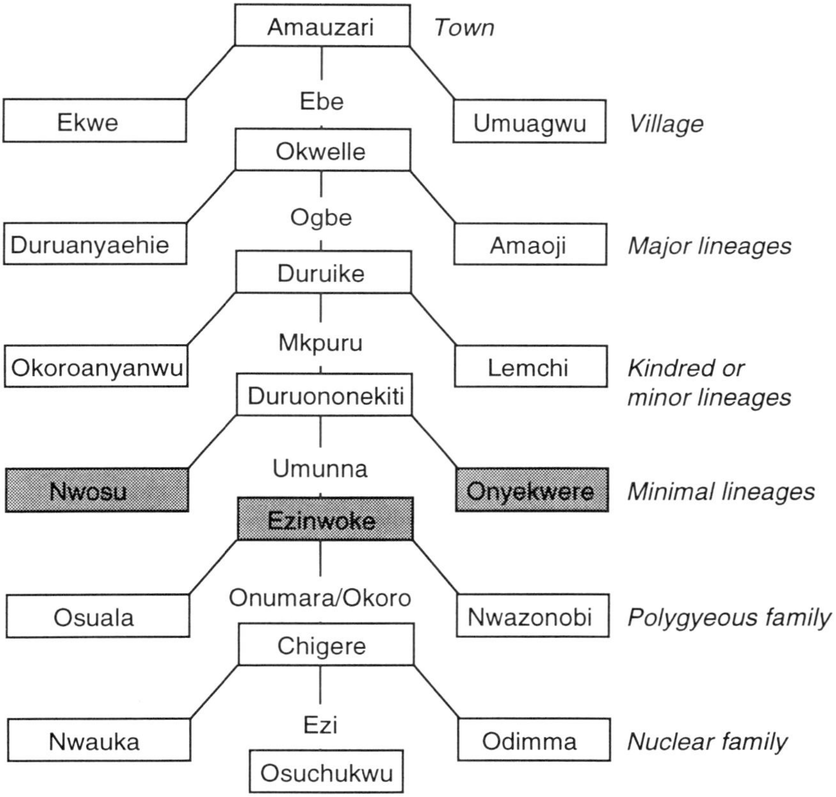

Fig. 5
(Secondary Ecclesial structures for a diocese)

DIOCESE	
RURAL	URBAN
CLAN (DEANERIES)	LOCAL GOVERNMENT AREA (DEANERIES)
TOWN OR GROUP OF VILLAGES (PARISH)	PARISH
SUBVILLAGE OR KINDRED (EUCHARISTIC CENTRE)	ZONES
UMUNNA (SMALL CHRISTIAN COMMUNITY)	GROUP OF YARDS OR QUARTERS (SCC)
FAMILY	FAMILY
A	**B**

Glossary

Ala	Earth Mother-goddess/ Land
Chukwu	God Almighty, (big God)
Ezi n'ulo	Family
Igbo/Ibo	One of the Ethnic groups in Nigeria
Mmanwu	Masquerade
Ndu	Life
Nmuo/agbara	Spirits
Nna	Father
Nnanna anyi ha	Our ancestors
Obi	An assembly or reception hall
Obi Ukwu	The big Obi
Obi Nnanyi	Our father's Obi
Obodo	Town
Ofor	A ritual staff of authority held by the head of the family.
Oha	People's assembly
Okenye	Elder
Okwara	First born son
Omenala/Omenani	Traditions, ordinances or customs inherited from theancestors
Osu	A person dedicated to deity
Ozo/Duru	Titles taken in Igboland
Uka Fada	The priest's Church
Ukwu	Big or great
Umu	Children
Umuada	Daughters married outside the umunna
Umunna	literally means children of the same father or those who can trace their relation to a common ancestor.

Bibliography

(A) ANTHROPOLOGICAL BOOKS

ABERNETHY, D.B., **The Political Dilemma of Popular Education**; California, Stanford University Press, 1969.

ACHEBE, A.C., **No Longer at Ease**; London, Heinemann, 1960.

–, **Arrow of God**; London, Heinemann, 1964.

–, **Things Fall Apart**; London, Heinemann, 1971.

AFIGBO, A.E., **The Warrant Chief's Indirect Rule in Southern Nigeria 1891-1927**; London, OUP, 1972.

AGU, C.C., **Secularization in Igboland: Socio-Religious Change and Its Challenges to the Church Among the Igbo**; Frankfurt, Verlag Peter Lang, Frankfurt, 1989.

ANENE, J.C., **Southern Nigeria in Transition, 1885-1906**; London, Cambridge University Press, 1966.

ANIGBO, O.A.C., **Commensality and Human Relationship among the Igbo**; Nsukka, University of Nigeria Press, 1987.

AZORJI, E.E., **Some Recurrent Problems of Christian Inculturation in Nigeria with Special Reference to the Igbo People**; unpublished Thesis, Rome, 1988.

BASDEN, G.T., **Niger Ibos**; London, Frank Cass., 1966.

BERRY, N., **Political Configurations: An Analysis of the Political System in Society**; New York, Goodyear Publishing Co.Inc., 1972.

BOORSTIN, D.J., **The Discoveries**; New York, Vintage Books, 1985.

BRADBURY, R.E., "The Benin Kingdom", in: Forde, D. and Kaberry, P.M., (eds.), **West African Kingdoms in the 19th Century**; London, Oxford University Press, 1954.

CASSIER, E., **Myth of the State**; London, Yale University Press, 1946.

CHAZAN, N., et alia., **Politics and Social in Contemporary Africa**; London, Macmillan, 1988.

COLEMAN, J.S., **Nigeria: Background to Nationalism**; Los Angeles, London, Berkeley, 1971.

CURTIN, P.D., **The Image of Africa: British Ideas and Action 1780-1850**; Madison, University of Wisconsin Press, 1964.

DAVIDSON, B., **The African Genius: An Introduction to African Social and Cultural History**; Boston, University Press, 1969.

EDEH, E., **Towards an Igbo Metaphysics**; Chicago, Chicago University, 1985.

EGDULIE, I., **The Hermeneutics of African Cultures**; Boston, Boston University, 1976.

EJIOFOR, L.U., **Igbo Kingdoms, Power and Control**; Nigeria, African Publications Ltd., 1982.

EKECHI, F.K., **Missionary Enterprise and Rivalry in Igboland 1857-1914**; Wisconsin, University of Wisconsin, 1969.

EVANS-PRITCHARD, E.E., **The Nuer**; London, Oxford University Press, 1960.

–, and FORTES, D., **African Political Systems**; London, Oxford University Press, 1940.

–, "The Kinship and Local Community among the Nuer", in: **African Systems of Kinship and Marriage**; London, PKI, 1987.

FIRTH, R., **Human Types**; London, 1958.

GAILEY, H.A., **The Road to Aba**; London, University Press, 1972.

GLUCKMAN, "Kinship and marriage among the Lozi of Northern Rhodesia and the Zulu", in: Radcliffe-Brown, A.R.and Forde, D., (eds.), **African Systems of Kinship and Marriage**; London, KPI, 1987.

GREEN, M.M., **Igbo Village Affairs, Chiefly with Reference to the Village of Umueke Agbaja**; London, Frank Cass and Co. Ltd., 1964.

HOMANS, G., **Human Group**; London, Routledge and Kegan Paul, 1958.

IROEGBU, P.O., **Communalism: A Theology of Justice for Contemporary African Political Communities**; A Doctoral Thesis, Louvain, 1989.

ISICHEI, E., **A History of the Igbo People**; London, Macmillan Press, 1976.

–, **Igbo Worlds: An Anthropology of Oral Histories and Historical Descriptions**; London, Macmillan Press, 1978.

–, **The Ibo People and the Europeans**; London, Faber and Faber, 1964.

IVAN, N.F., and BERNARDO, F.M., **The Family: Its Structure and Interaction**; New York, Orbis, 1973.

KALEM'IMANA, J.B., **Christianity and Socialism in Tanzania**; Doctoral Thesis, Madison, New Jersey, 1986.

KAUNDA, K.K., and MORRIS, C., **A Humanist in Africa**; London, University Press, 1966.

KIRWEN M.C., **African Widows**; New York, Maryknoll, 1979.

LEONARD, A.G., **The Lower Niger and Its Tribes**; London, Frank Cass, 1968.

MACIVER, R.M., **The Web of Government**; London, Faber and Faber, 1947.

MADU, R., **Hermeneutics: A Study of Traditional African Symbols, Proverbs and Myths on Human Destiny in the light of the Hermeneutic**

methodology of Paul Ricoeur; the Igbo Case; Doctoral Thesis, Louvain, 1990.

MAZRUI, A.A., **The Africans: The Triple Heritage**; Boston, University Press, 1986.

MBADIWE, K.O., **British and Axis Aims in Africa**; New York, 1942, pp.173-203.

MBAEFO, L.N., **The Reshaping of African Tradition**; Enugu, Spiritan Publications, 1988.

MEEK, C.K., **Law and Authority in a Nigerian Tribe**; London, OUP, 1950.

MILBRATH, L.W., **Political Participation: How and Why do People get Involved in Politics**; London, Rand McNally and Company, 1965.

MOREL, E.D., **Nigeria: Its Peoples and Its Problems**; London, Frank Cass, 1968.

MUNOYE, J., **The Only Son**; London, Heinemann, 1966.

NJAKA, E.N., **Igbo Political Culture**; Evanston, Northwestern University Press, 1974.

NNOLI, O., **Ethnic Politics in Nigeria**; Enugu, Fourth Dimension Publishers, 1980.

NORTH, P.J., **"People in Society"; An Introduction to Sociology**; England, Longman, 3(1986).

NSUGBE, O.P., **Ohaffia: A Matrilineal Ibo People**; London, Clarenden Press, 1974.

NYERERE, J.K., **Freedom and Socialism: Uhuru na Ujamaa; A Selection from Writings and Speeches**; 1965-1967, London, Oxford University Press, 1968.

NZEWUNWA, N., "Pre-Colonial Nigeria East of the Niger", in: R. Olaniyan, (ed.), **Nigerian History and Culture**; Lagos, Longman, 1985.

NZIMIRO, F.I., **Family and Kinship in Igboland: A Study in Acculturation Process**; Germany, University of Cologne, 1962.

–, **Studies in Ibo Political Systems: Chieftaincy and Politics in Four Niger States**; London, Frank Cass and Co. Ltd., 1972.

OBI, S.N.C., **The Igbo Law of Property**; London, Butterworths, 1963.

OJIKE, M., **My Africa**; New York, Day Press, 1946; repr. London, Blandford Press, 1955.

OJUKWU, E.O., **Because I am Involved**; Enugu, Spectrum books, 1989.

OKAFOR, D.O., **A Nigerian Village in two Worlds**, London, Faber and Faber Ltd., 1962.

OKONJO, I.K., **The Role of Women in Social Change Among the Igbo of Southern Nigeria living West of the River Niger**; Doctoral Thesis, Boston University, 1976.

ONYISI, E., **An Introduction to the Study of African Culture**; London, Heinemann, 1977.

ONWUBIKO, O., **Principal Elements of Igbo traditional Religion**; unpublished thesis presented for B.D. at Bigard Seminary Enugu, 1980.

ORIZU, A.A.N., **Without Bitterness**; New York, Creative Age Press Inc., 1944; repr. by Fourth Dimension Enugu, 1980.

OWNUEJEOGWU, M.A., **An Igbo Civilization, Nri Kingdom and Hegemony**; London, Ethiope Publishing Corp., 1981.

OZIGBO, I.R.A., **Roman Catholicism in South-Eastern Nigeria, 1885-1931: A Study in Colonial Evangelism**; Onitsha, Etukokwu Publishers, 1988.

PERHAM, M., **Native Administration in Nigeria**; London, Oxford University Press, 1937.

RADCLIFFE-BROWN, A.R., **Structure and Function in Primitive Society: Essays and Addresses**; London, KPI, 1979.

REINHOLD, N., **The Self and the Dramas of History**; New York, Charles Scribers, 1955.

RICHARD, A.I., "Some Types of Family Structure among the Central Bantu"; in: Radcliffe-Brown and Ford, D., (eds.), **African Systems of Kinship and Marriage**; London, KPI, 1987.

RUSSEL, B., **Political Ideals**; London, Unwin Books, 1963.

SALIMS, M.D., **"Tribesmen", Foundation of Modern Anthropology Series**; New Jersey, Prentice-Hall, 1968.

SCHAPERA, I., **Government and Politics in Tribal Societies;** London, Watt and Co., 1956.

SHEPPERSON, G., (ed.), **Horton Africanus 1886, African Countries and Peoples**; Edinburgh, University Press, 1969.

STEWART, E., **Sociology: The Human Science**; New York, MacGraw Hill Books Company, 1978.

TALBOT, P.A., **The People of Southern Nigeria**; vol.III, London, Frank Cass., 1969.

–, **The People of Southern Nigeria**; vol.IV, London, Oxford University Press, 1926.

UCHENDU, V.C., **The Igbo of South-East Nigeria**; New York, Holt, Rinehart and Winston, 1965.

UMEASIEGBU, E.M., **The Way we lived**; London, Heinemann, 1979.

WEBER, M., **Economy and Society: An Outline of Interpretation Sociology**; vol.2., Roth, G. and Wittich, C., (eds.), California, University of Californian Press, 1978.

WILSON, M., "Nyakyusa Kinship", in: Radcliffe-Brown, A.R., et alia., **African Systems of Kinship and Marriage**; London, KPI, 1987.

(A-b) ANTHROPOLOGICAL ARTICLES

AFIGBO, A., "The Indigenous Political System of the Igbo", in: **Tarikh**; vol.4, 2(1981).

ALLAN, G.A., "A Sociology of Friendship and Kinship", in: **Studies in Sociology**; 10., London, G.Allen and Unwin Ltd., 1979.

ARDENER, E.W., "Lineage and Locality among the Mba-ise Ibo", in: **Africa**; vol. xxix, 1959, pp.117-119.

AYANDELE, E.A., "The Missionary Impact on Modern Nigeria, 1842-1914: A Political and Social Analysis", in: **Ibadan History Series**; Nigeria, 1966.

–, "The Relationship Between the Church Missionary Society and the Royal Niger Company, 1886-1900", in: **JHSN**; vol. iv, 1968.

AZIKIWE, N., "Renascent Africa", in: **A Selection from the Speeches of Nnamdi Azikiwe**; Harris, P., (ed.), London, C.U.P., 1968.

–, "How shall We Educate the African?" in: **JAS**, 33(1934), pp.143-151.

BROWN, P., "Patterns of Authority in West Africa", in: **Africa**; vol.xxi, 4(1951).

BUBENDORF, J., "Bubendorf to Superior General", in: **APS**; B.191/v/xii, Onitsha, 10/3/1897.

ECHERUO, M.J.C., 1979 **Ahajoku Lecture**; Owerri, Information Press, "A matter of Identity" 1979.

EJIZU, C.I., "The Taxonomy, Provenance and Function of Ofo, a dominant Igbo Ritual and Political Symbol", in: **Anthropos**; 82(1987), 457-467.

JONES, G.I., "Dual Organization in Igbo Social Structure", in: **Africa**; vol.xix, 1949.

KASFIR, N., "Designs and Dilemmas: An Overview", in: Mah-Wood, P., (ed.), **Local Government in the third World; The experience of Tropical Africa**; New York, John Wiley, 1983.

NWOGA, D.I., 1984, **Ahajoku Lecture**, "Nka Na Nzere: The Focus of Igbo World-View", Owerri, Information Press.

NZIMIRO, F.I., "A Study of Mobility Among the Igbo of Southern Nigeria", in: **Kinship and Geographical Mobility**; London, Paadington, R., ed., Leiden, E.J. Brill, 1965.

OKIGBO, P.N.C., 1986, **Ahajoku Lecture**, "Towards a Reconstruction of the Political Economy of Igbo Civilization"; Owerri, Information Press.

OLISA, M.S.O., "Political Culture and Stability in Igbo Society", in: **CONCH**; vol. III, Nr. 2, 1971, pp. 16-27.

ONWUEJEOGWU, M.A., "The Igbo Culture Areas", in: Ogbalu, F.C., and Emenanjo, E.N., (eds.), **Igbo Language and Culture**; Ibadan, 1975.

ONWUSU, N., "Policy studies, Development and Political Anthropology", in: **Journal of modern African studies**; vol. 13, 3(1975).

OSUCHUKWU, P., "In diesen Tagen im Entlebuch getroffen", interview in: **Entlebucher Einzeiger**; Schweiz, 1990.

OTTENBERG, S., "Ibo receptivity to change", in: Bascom, W.R. and Herskovites, M.J., (eds.), **Community an Change in African culture**; vol. III., Chicago, University of Chicago Press, 1958.

PERHAM, M., "The British Problem in Africa", in: **Africa**, 29(1951).

SENG, C., "Gescheitertes Experiment mit der Demokratie", in: **Herkorr**; 38(1984).

SMOCK, D.R., "Changing Political Processes Among the Abaja Ibo", in: **Africa**; 38(1968).

WELBOURN, F.B., "Missionary stimulus and African response", in: V.Turner (ed.), **Colonialism in Africa, 1870-1960; Profiles of Change, African Society and Colonial Rule,** vol.3, Chicago University Press, 1971.

WOOD, J.B., "Report on the Investigations into the Niger Mission, January – March, 1880", in: **Archives des Peres Spiritans**; APS Bulletin General, Vol. xv and xvi, Paris.

(A-b-c) ANTHROPOLOGICAL DOCUMENTS

Legislative Council Sessional paper.

New Nigeria; "Census Figures Released", Nr. 8, 073, Lagos, 1992.

NIGERIA: "Annual Report Southern Provinces", Lagos, Government Printer, 1929.

United Nations, **Demographic Year-Book 1983**, New York, 1985

(B) THEOLOGICAL BOOKS

AMAFILI, L.E., **The Celebration of the Eucharist with an African Face: From Adaptation rooted in the Western World to Inculturation into the African/Igbo Sacrificial Setting**; vol. ii, a Doctoral dissertation presented for a Doctor in Theology, Katholieke Universiteit Leuven, Belgium, 1991.

ALVES, R., **Theology of Human Hope**; Washington D.C., Corpus Books, 1969.

ANUNOBI, T.O., **The Spirituality of Death**; Doctoral Thesis, Pontificia Universitas Gregoriana, Roma, 1975.

AQUINAS, T. (St.), **Summa Theologiae**; II – II, 6: 4, 2.

ARIAS, M., "Announcing the Kingdom: Discipleship as Evangelium", in: K. Aman, (ed.), **Border Religions of Faith: An Anthropology of Religion and Social change**; New York, Maryknoll, 1987, pp. 293 – 298.
ARINZE, A.F., **Sacrifice in Ibo religion**; Ibadan, University Press, 1970.
–, "The Christian as a Leader", **Lenten Pastoral**; Onitsha, Trinity Press, 1977.
ARNOLD, F.X., **Pastoraltheologische Durchblicke**; Freiburg, Herder, 1965.
AUGUSTINE, (St.), **The City of God**; 19: 20-24.
AZEVEDO, M.deC., **Basic Ecclesial Communities in Brazil: The Challenge of a New way of Being Church**; J. Drury, Trans., Washington D.C., Georgetown University Press, 1987.
–, **Inculturation and the Challenges of Modernity**; Rome, Gregorian University Press, 1982.
BAHR, W. and HURKA, H.P., Hrsg., **Basisgemeinden in Österreich**; Graz, Verlag Styria, 1989.
BANKS, R., **Paul's Idea of Community: The Early House Churches in their Historical Setting**; Grand Rapids, W.E. Erdmanns Publication Co., 1980.
BARCLAY, W., **The Letters to the Philippians, Colossians and Thessalonians**; Edinburgh, The St. Andrew's Press, 1979.
–, **New Testament Words**; London, SCM Press, 1977.
BARTH, K., **Dogmatic in Outline**; New York, Harper Torch Books, 1959.
BAUER, W., **A Greek-English Lexicon of the New Testament and other Christian Literature**; W.F. Arndt and F.W. Gingrich, trans., Chicago, University Press, 2(1979).
BAUS, K., and E. EWIG, "Die Reichskirche nach Konstantin dem Grossen, von Nikaia bis Chalkedon", **Band die Kirchengeschichte**; Band II/1, Freiburg, Herder, 1985, pp.348-369.
BAUSCH, W.J., "The Hands on Parish": **Reflections and Suggestions for Fostering Community**; Connecticut, Twenty-third Publications, 1991.
BEASLEY-MURRAY, G.R., **Baptism in the New Testament**; London, Macmillan, 1962, pp. 93-125.
BERKHOF, L., **Systematic Theology**; London, Banner of Truth, 1978.
BERNARDIN, J., "Evangelizing the Active Catholic", in: **Pentecost '87 Supplement; A National Satellite Celebration of Catholic Evangelization, Sunday, June 6**, 1987; Washington D.C., Paulist, National Catholic Evangelization Association,1987.
BERTSCH, L., "Laien Als Gemeindeleiter: Ein Afrikanisches Modell; Texte der Erdiözese Kinshasa", in: **Theologie der Dritten Welt**; Band 14, Freiburg, Herder, 1990.
BEST, E., **First Peter: New Century Bible**; London, Oliphants Press, 1971.

BIHLMEYER-TUECHLE, "Christian Antiquity", in: **Church History**; vol. 1, tran., V.E. Mills, Mary Land, The Newmann Press, 1958.
BOFF, L., **Church Charism and Power: Liberation Theology and the Institutional Church**; London, SCM Press, 1985.
–, **ECCLESIOGENESIS: The Base Communities – Reinvent the Church**; London, Collins Liturgical Publications, 1986.
–, **Eglise en Genese**; Paris, Desilee, 1978.
–, **Trinity and Society**; Kent, Burns and Oates, 1988.
BONHOEFFER, D., **Letters and Papers from Prison**; New York, Macmillan, 1967, pp.203-204.
BONINO, J.M., "Historical Praxis and Christian Identity", in: R.Gibellini (ed.), **Frontiers of Theology in Latin America**; New York, Maryknoll, Orbis Books, 1978.
BROWN, R.E., **The Churches Apostles left Behind**; New York, Paulist Publishers, 1984.
BRUNNER, E., **The Misunderstanding of the Church**; London, Lutterworth, 1952.
BUJO, B., "African Theology in Context"; in: **Christian Leadership in Africa Series**; J. O'Donohue, tran., Nairobi, St. Paul Publications, 1992.
BULMANN, R., **Theology of the New Testament**; vol.1, New York, Scribner's, 1961, pp. 306-314.
BURROWS, W.R., **New Ministries: The Global context**; New York, Maryknoll, 1980.
BYENG-HUN, P.L., **Leben aus der Communio mit Gott und Untereinander: Zur ekklesiologischen und praktischen Bedeutung des Communio – Prinzips für eine evangelisierende Pastoral**; Würzburg, Seelsorge/Echter Verlag, 1991.
CAMBRON, M.G., **Bible Doctrines: Beliefs that matter**; Grand Rapids, Baker Book House, 1974.
CERFAUX, L., **The Church in the Theology of St. Paul**; G. Webb and A. Walker (eds.), New York, 1959.
CLARK, D., **Basic Communities: Towards an Alternative Society**; London, SPCK, 1977
CLARK, S.B., **Building Christian Communities**; Indian, Ave Maria Press, Notre Dame, 1972.
COLLINS, R., **Models of Theological Reflections**, London, 1984.
CONGAR, Y., **Called to Life**, U.K., St. Paul Publications, 1988.
–, **The Mystery of the Church**; Baltimore, Helicon, 1960, pp. 97-117.
–, and O'Hanlon, D., (eds.), **Council Speeches of Vatican II**, New York, Paulist Press, 1964.
COX, H., **The Secular City**; New York, Macmillan, 1965.

CROCE, W. "The History of the Parish", in: H. Rahner, (ed.), **The Parish from Theology to practice**; Maryland, The Newmann Press, 1958.

CROSBY, M.H., **House of Disciples: Church, Economics and Justice in Matthew**; New York, Maryknoll, Orbis Books, 1988.

CULLMANN, O., **Christ and Time**; London, 1962.

DELESPESSE, M., **The Church community**; New York, Ave Maria Press, 1973.

De LUBAC, H., **CATHOLICISM: Christ and the Common Destiny of Man**; London, Burns and Oates, 1962.

DIFFERRAR ROY J., (ed.), **The Fathers of the Church**; "St. Cyprian Treatise", vol. 36, New York, Fathers of the Church INC., 1958.

DODD, C.H., **The Apostolic Preaching and its Developments**; London, Hodder, 2(1963).

DULLES, A., **Models of the Church**; New York, Doubleday, Image Books, 1987.

–, **The Reshaping of Catholicism: Current challenges in the Theology of the Church**; New York, San Francisco, Harper and Row, 1988.

–, **The Catholicity of the Church**; Oxford, Clarendon Press, 1985.

DUNN, J.D.G., **Jesus and the Spirit**; London, SCM Press, 1975.

EKWEKE, E.E., **Catholicism in Igboland and modern Evangelism**; unpublished Exercitatio practica, Enugu, 1988.

ELLIOT, J.H., **A Home for the Homeless: A Sociological Exegesis of first Peter; Its Situation and Strategy**; Philadelphia, Fortress, 1981.

EZEANYA, S.N., "Lord, Increase our Faith", **A Lenten pastoral**; Onitsha, Trinity Press, 1986.

EZEKWUGO, C.U.M., **Chi the true God in Igbo Religion**; Muvattupuzha, Mar Matthews Press, 1987.

FISCHER, J.A., **Die Apostolischen Vater: Schriften des Urchristentums**; Darmstadt, 1970.

FLEMINGTON, W.F., **The New Testament Doctrine of Baptism**; London, SPCK Press, 1948.

GATAMU, J.P.W., **Small Christian Communities in the Catholic Diocese of Nakuru**; Thesis presented for Licentiate in Catholic Higher Institute of Eastern Africa, Nairobi, 1986.

GOODWIN, L.J., **Ecclesiological Dimensions of Eucharistic Centers in the Diocese of Mbarara, in Uganda; An Inquiry into Christian Community Structure and Ministry**; Doctoral Thesis, Mimeo, Catholic University of America, Washington, D.C., 1984.

GOPPELT, L., **Apostolic and Post-Apostolic Times**; London, Black Press, 1970.

GRABOWSKI, J.S., **The Church: An Introduction to the Theology of St. Augustine**; St. Louis, E. Herder Book Co., 1957.
GRANT, R.A., **A Historical Introduction to the New Testament**; London, Collins, 1974.
GRAY, J., **The Biblical Doctrine of the Reign of God**; Edinburgh, T and T Clark, 1979.
GREMILLAN, J., ed., **Medellin Documents**; "The Gospel of Peace and Justice", New York, Maryknoll, Orbis Books, 1976.
GUTHRIE, D., **New Testament Theology**; England, Inter-Varsity Press, 1981.
GUTIERREZ, G., **The Power of the Poor in History**; New York, Maryknoll, 1983.
HAHN, F., **The Worship of the Early Church**; Philadelphia, Fortress, 1973.
HAIGHT, R.D., **An Alternative Vision: An Interpretation of Liberation theology**; New York, Paulist, 1984.
HAMER, J., **The Church is a Communion**; New York, Sheed and Ward, 1964.
HANLON, K.J., **PAUL: Pastor of Communities for Today**; United Kingdom, St. Paul Publications, 1991.
HUME, B., **Towards a Civilization of Love: Being Church in Today's World**; London, Holder and Stoughton, 1988.
ILOGU, E., **Christianity and Igbo Culture**; Netherlands, E.J. Brill, 1974.
ISICHEI, E., **Entirely for God: The life of Michael Iwenesi Tansi**; London, Macmillan Press, 1980.
PERRIN-JASSY, M.F., **Basic Community in the African Church**; New York, Maryknoll, Orbis Books, 1973.
–, **Forming Christian Communities: An Evaluation of Experiments in North Mara**; Tanzania, Eldoret, Gaba Publications, no date.
JORDAN, J.P., **Bishop Shanahan of Southern Nigeria**; Dublin, Enlo Press, 1971.
KAHLEFELD, H., "Community Life in the New Testament", in: H. Rahner, (ed.), **The Parish from Theology to Practice**; Maryland, The Newman Press, 1958.
KALLUVEETTIL, P., Declaration and Covenant, Rome, 1982.
KARRER, L., "Erfahrungen von Gemeinden Ohne Pfarrer am Ort: Einige Überlegungen und Anfrage aus praktisch-theologischer sicht", in: **Gemeinde Ohne Pfarrer am Ort**; Hrsg., Schweizerisches Pastoralsoziologisches Institute, Zürich, NZN Buchverlag, 1987, pp. 212-239.
KASPER, W., **Zukunft aus der Kraft des Konzils: Die außerordentliche Beschofssynode 1985**; Freiburg – Basil – Wien, Herder, 1986.
–, **Theology and Church**; London, SCM Press, 1989.

KASSEMANN, E., **The Testament of Jesus**; Philadelphia, Fortress Press, 1968.
KAVUNKAL, J., **To Gather them into One: Evangelization in India today a Process of Building Community**; India, Satprakashan Sanchar Kendra, 1985.
KEHL, M., **Die Kirche: Eine katholische Ekklesiologie**; Würzburg, Echter, 1992.
KENNY, J., **The Catholic Church in Tropical Africa 1445-1850**; Ibadan, University Press, 1983.
KLAUCK, H.J., **GEMEINDE. Amt, Sakrament Neuetestamentliche Perspektiven**; Würzburg, Echter, 1989.
KLEISSLER, T.A., LeBERT, M.A. and McGUINESS, M.C., **Small Christian Communities: A Vision of Hope**; New York/ Mahwah, Paulist, 1991.
KLOSTERMANN, F., **Kirche: Ereignis und Institution. Ueberlegung zur Herrschafts- und Institutionsproblematik in der Kirche**; Wien – Freiburg, Herder, 1976.
–, **Wie wird unsere Pfarrei eine Gemeinde?** Fuer alle Mitarbeiter in der Pfarrgemeinde; Wien, 1979.
KOCH, K., **Streifzüge durch Gottes Gegenwart**; Zürich, 1984.
KOREN, H.J., **The Spiritans: A History of the Congregation of the Holy Ghost**; Pittsburgh, Duguesue University, 1958.
Küng, H., **Council Speeches of Vatican II**; New York, Paulist Press, 1964.
–, **On Being a Christian**; trans., W. Collins Sons and Co. Ltd., London, Funt Paper Books, 1978.
–, **The Church**; New York, Image Books, 1976.
KUNNEL, W.G., **Promise and Fulfillment**; London, SCM Press, 1957.
LOHFINK, G., **Jesus and the Community**; New York, Paulist Press, 1984.
LONERGAN, B., **Method in Theology**; New York, Herder and Herder, 1972.
LOWRIE, W., **Art in the Early Church**; New York, Pantheon, 1947.
LUZBETAK, L.J., **The Church and Culture: New Perspective in Missiological Anthropology**; New York, Maryknoll, Orbis Books, 1989.
LYONNET, S. and SABOURIN, L., **Sin, Redemption and Sacrifice: A Biblical and Patristic Study**; Rome, Biblical Institute Press, 1978.
MAINER, G., "The Church in the Gospel of Matthew: Hermeneutical Analysis of the Current Debate", in: D.A. Carson, (ed.), **Biblical Interpretation and the Church**; Nashville, Thomas Nelson, 1985.
MALY, E., "Still a case for Infant Baptism?" in: M.J. Taylor, (ed.), **Readings in Contemporary sacramental Theology**; New York, Alba House, 1981.
MARINS, J. and TREVISAN, T., **BEC: Church from the Roots**; Bangare National Biblical Catechetical and Liturgical Center, Nairobi, 1981.

MARSH, H.G., **The Origin and Significance of the New Testament Baptism**; Manchester, MUP., 1941.

MBAEFO, L.N., **Towards a Mature African Christianity**; Enugu, Spiritan Publications, 1989.

MBITI, J., **African Religions and Philosophy**; Nairobi, Heineman, 1983.

McBRIEN, R.I., **Catholicism**; 2vols., Mineapolis, Winston Press, 1980.

McCARTHY, D.J., **Treaty and Covenant: A Study in Form in the Ancient Oriental Documents and in the Old Testament**; Rome, New Edition, 1978.

McINTYRE, J., **The Shape of Christology**; London, SCM Press, 1966.

MEEK, W.A., **The First Urban Christians: The Social World of the Apostle Paul**; London, Yale University Press, 1983.

MEEKS, M., **The Moral World of the first Christians**; Philadelphia, Westminister, 1986.

METUH, I.E., **The Gods in Retreat: Continuity and Change in African Religion**; Enugu, Fourth Dimension Publications (FDP), 1986.

–, **God and Man in African Religion**; London, Geoffrey Chapman, 1981.

MOLTMANN, J., **The Church in the power of the Spirit**; London, SCM Press, 1977.

MOWINCKEL, **The Psalms in Israel's Worship**; New York and Nashville, Albington-Collesbury, 1962.

MOZIA, M.I.C., **Solidarity in the Church and Solidarity Among the Igbos of Nigeria**; Ibadan, Claverianum Press, 1987.

MUHLER, H., **Una Persona Mystica**; vol. 3. Schöningh, Paderborn, 1968.

MUZOREWA, G.H., **The Origin and Development of African Theology**; New York, Maryknoll, Orbis Books, 1985.

NDINGI, R., **A New Missionary Era**; P. Flanegan, (ed.), New York, Maryknoll, Orbis Books, 1983.

NJOKU, S.U., **From Station to BCC: with Reference to Nguru Parish**; unpublished Thesis presented for M.A. Theology in CIWA, Port Harcourt, 1986.

NKWOKA, A.O., **New Testament Concept of Diakonia as a Paradigm for Interpreting Leadership Crisis in the Nigerian Churches**; unpublished Doctoral Thesis for Religious Study in Ife University, Ile-Ife, 1990.

NORTH, M., "The Laws in the Pentateuch: Their Assumptions and Meanings", in: **The Laws of the Pentateuch and Other Studies**; London, 1966.

NYAMITI, C., **Christ as our Ancestor: Christology from an African Perspective**; Zimbabwe, Mambo Press, 1984.

NZOMIWU, J.P.C., **The Moral Concept of Justice Among the Igbos**; A Doctoral Thesis, Academia Alfonsiana, Roma, 1977.

O'CONNOR, M.C., **The Family of the Church**; London, CTS., 1984.

–, and M. SANTER, **Church as Communion: An Agreed Statement by the Anglican Roman Catholic International Commission 1**; London, CTS., 1991.

O'GRADY, C., **The Church in the Theology of Karl Barth**; London, Geoffrey Chapman, 1968.

–, **The Church in Catholic Theology: Dialogue with Karl Barth**; London, Geoffrey Chapman, 1969.

O'HALLORAN, J., **Living cells: Building Basic Christian Community**; Dublin, Dominican Publication, 1980.

OBI, C.A., **A Hundred Year of the Catholic Church in Eastern Nigeria**; Onitsha, FEP Publishers, 1985.

ODIGBO, G., **Eucharistie im Afrikanischen Kontext: Ein Theologisch-pastoralliturgischer Beitrag zur Neugestaltung der Meßfeier bei den Igbo**; Als Lizentiatsarbeit vorgelegt dem Fachbereich katholische Theologie der Johannes Gutenberg-Universität, Mainz, 1987.

ODUYOYE, M.A., "The value of African Religious Beliefs and Practices for Christian Theology", in: Kofi Appiah-Kubi and Sergio Torres (eds.), **African Theology en Route**; New York, MaryKnoll, Orbis Books, 1979.

OLSEU, C.M., **The Base Church: Creating Community through Multiple Forms**; Atlanta, Ga., Forum House, 1973.

ORMEROLD, N., **Introducing Contemporary Theologies: The WHAT and the WHO of Theology today**; Australia, E.D. Dwyer, 1990.

OSUCHUKWU, P." Home-Sick for Paradise Lost": **The Place of Sacrifice in Traditional Ibo Religion and the Bible with Particular Reference to Amauzari Town**; Licentiate Thesis presented at the University of Fribourg, Schweiz, 1988, pp.33-35.

OSUJI, C.C., **The Concept of Salvation in Igbo Traditional Religion**; Pontificia Universitas, Roma, 1977.

PERRIN, N., **Jesus and the Language of the Kingdom**; London, SCM Press, 1976.

–, **Rediscovering the Teaching of Jesus**; London, SCM Press, 1967.

PETERS, W.G., **A Theology of Church Growth**; Michigan, Zondervan, 1981.

POBEE, J., **Towards African Theology**; Nashville, Albington- Collesbury, 1979.

PONCE, F., "Building Basic Communities: Communidades ecclesiales de base in the U.S. Experience", in: **Developing Basic Christian Communities**; A Handbook, National Federation of priests' Council, Chicago, 1979.

PRITCHARD, J.B., (ed.), **Ancient Near Eastern Texts Relating to the Old Testament**; Princeton, Princeton University Press, 1950.

PROVOST, J.H., "Code, Community, Ministry": **Canon Law society of America**; Washington D.C. 1983.
RAHNER, K., **Theology for Renewal**; New York, Sheed and Ward, 1964.
–, **The Shape of the Church to Come**; London, SPCK, 1975, pp. 120-125.
–, "The Concept of Mystery in Catholic Theology", in: **Theological Investigation**; vol.iv, London, Darton Lonman and Todd, 1966.
–, **Theology of Pastoral Action**; New York, Herder and Herder, 1968.
–, "Experience of the Spirit Source of Theology", in: **Theological Investigations**; vol. xvi, London, Darton, Longman and Todd, 1979.
–, "The Concept of Mystery in Catholic Theology"; vol. iv, London, Darton, Longman and Todd, 1966.
–, "Theology of the Parish", in: H. Rahner, (ed.), **The Parish from Theology to Practice**; Maryland, The Newman Press, 1958.
–, and METZ, J.B., **The Courage to Pray**; London, SPCK, 1980.
RANGER, T.O. and J. Weller, (eds.), **Themes in the Christian History of Central Africa**; London, Heinemann, 1975.
REISE, A., **Basisgemeinden und Befreiung in Lateinamerika**; Mainz, 1980.
ROBINSON, J.A.T., **The new Reformation**? Philadelphia, Westminister Press, 1965.
ROMERO, O., **Voice of the Voiceless**; New York, Maryknoll, Orbis Books, 1985.
ROWLAND, C., **Christian Origins**; London, SPCK, 1985.
RUSSEL, L.M., **House of Freedom: Authority in Feminist Theology**; Philadelphia, Westminister,1987.
SCHILLEBEECKX, E., **The Church with a Human Face**; London, SCM Press, 1989.
–, **Interim report on the books: "Jesus" and "Christ"**; New York, Maryknoll, 1982.
SCHINELLER, P., **A Hand Book on Inculturation**; New Jersey, Paulist Press, 1990.
SCHNACKENBURG, R., **The Church in the New Testament**; London, Burns and Oates, 1965.
–, **God's Rule and Kingdom**; New York, Herder and Herder, 1968.
SCHROTT, A., **Seelsorge im Wandel der Zeit**; Graz, 1949.
SCHüSSLER-FIORENZA, E., **In Memory of Her: A Feminist Theological Reconstruction of Christian Origins**; New York, Crossroad, 1983.
SCHWEIZER, E., **Church Order in the New Testament**; London, SCM Press, 1961.
SEGUNDO, J.L., **The Liberation of Theology**; New York, Maryknoll, 1988.
SHEAD, C.W., **How to Develop a Praying Church**; Nashville/New York, Abingdon Press, 1964.

SHERMAN, J., **MATTHEW: The Interpreter's Bible**; vol. 7, New York/Nashville, Abingdon- Collesburg, 1976.
SHORTER A., **Towards a Theology of Inculturation**; London, Geoffrey Chapman, 1988.
–, **African Culture and the Christian Church**; New York, Maryknoll, 1973.
–, **The Church in the African City**; London, Geoffrey Chapman, 1991.
–, **African Christian Theology**; London, Geoffrey Chapman, 1975.
–, "The Theology of Missions": in: **Theology Today Series**, Nr.37, Cork, The Mercier Press, 1972.
SMITH, D.M., **Johannine Christianity**; Columbia, University of South Carolina Press, 1984.
SOBRINO, J., **The True Church and the Poor**; New York, Maryknoll, Orbis Books,1974, pp.253 – 301.
SONG, C.S., **Theology from the Womb of Asia**; New York, Maryknoll, Orbis Books,1986.
TALBERT, C.H., "Once Again: The Plan of First Peter", in: **Perspective of First Peter**; Macon, Mercer University Press, 1986.
TENNEY, M.C., **The Reality of Resurrection**; New York, Harper, 1963.
UGBOR, L.A., **Prayer in Igbo Traditional Religion: Its Meaning and Message for the Church in Igboland Today**; Rome, 1985.
VINCENT, M.R., **A Critical and Exegetical Commentary on the Epistles to the Philippians and Philemon**; Edinburgh, T and T. Clark, 1955.
von HARNACK, A., **Das Wesen des Christentums**; Gütersloh, Siebenstern, 1977.
von RAD, G., **The Problem of Hexateuch**; New York, Maryknoll, 1966.
–, **Old Testament Theology**; vol. 1, London, SCM Press, 1985.
WHITCARE, R.A., **Johannine Polemic: The Role of Tradition and Theology**; California, Scholars Press, 1982.
WHITELEY, D.E.H., **The Theology of St. Paul**; Oxford, B. Blackwell, 1974.
WILLIS, J.R., (ed.), **The Teaching of the Church Fathers**; New York, Herder and Herder, 1966.
WINTER, G., **The New Creation as Metropolis**; New York, Macmillan, 1963.
WOLL, D.B., **Johannine Christianity in Conflict: Authority, Rank, and Succession in the Farewell Discourse**; California, Scholars Press, Chico, 1981.
ZIEGENFUSS, W., **Augustinus: Christliche Transzendenz in Gesellschaft und Geschichte**; Berlin, 1948.
ZIZIOULAS, J.D., **Being as Communio: Studies in Personhood and the Church**; New York, St. Vladimir's, Seminary Press, 1985.

(B-a) THEOLOGICAL ARTICLES

AJAYI, J.F.A. and AYANDELE, A.E., "Writing African Church history", in: N. Goodall, (ed.), **The B. Uppsala Report**, Geneva, (1969).

ALBERIGO, G., "The People of God (le Popolo Dio) in the experience of Faith", **Concilium**; 176, 6(1984).

ANGELO, D., **Revista Ecclesiastica Brasileira;** 17, (1957).

ANONYMUS, "NIGERIA: Die Kirche im Volksreichten Land Afrikas", **IFD**; Nr.3240, (1982).

BANS, K. and EWIG, E., "Die Reichskirche nach Konstantin dem Großen, von Nikaia bis Chalkedon", **Band die Kirchengeschichte**; BD. II/1, Freiburg, Herder, (1985), pp.348-369.

BARANSANARIYE, C., "Personal reflections on new ways of sharing in community", **SPEARHEAD**, Nr. 45, (1976).

BARREIRO, A., "Raizes da Consciencia eclesial das CEBs", **CONV.**; 17/158, (1982).

BERNARD, J., "Les Petites Communautes Chretiennes en Tanzanie", **SPIRITUS**; Nr.65, (1976).

BLOJOUS, J., "Development in Mission Thinking and Practice, 1959-1980", **AFER**; vol. 26, 6(1984).

BOFF, L., "Kleine Sakramentenlehre", Düsseldorf, 2(1978).

BOHR, D., "Evangelization: The Essential and Primary Mission of the Church", **Jurist**; 39, (1979), pp. 40-87.

BOKI di MPASI, L., "Towards the Pastoral Care of the African Family", **Lumen Vitae**, English Edition, 4(1980).

CENKNER, W., "The Emergence of an Indian Christian Theology", **Indian Missionary Review**; 57(1973).

CONZELMANN, H., "Die Mitte der Zeit", **Studien zur Theologie des Lukas**; 3(1960).

COPPO, S., "A Truly African Church", **SPEARHEAD**; Nr. 99, (1987).

COUSINS, E., "Models and Future of Theology", **Concilium**; 7, (1969), pp.78-91.

CROLLIUS, A.R., "Incarnation: Newness and Ongoing Process", in: Waliggo, J.M., et alia., (eds.), **Inculturation its Meaning and Urgency**; Nairobi, St Paul's Publications, (1986).

CROWTHER, A., "Crowther to Lang", **C.M.S. Archives**, G3, A 3/1886/18, Onitsha, (1886).

CULLMANN, O., PETER: Disciple, Apostle, Martyr, 2(1962).

DeJAIFVE, G., "L' ecclesiologia del Concilio II", in: G. Thils and A. Angel, et. alia, eds., L'ecclesiologia dal Vaticano I, al Vaticano II, Facolta Teologica Interregionale, Milano, Brescia: **Editrice la Scuola**, (1973).

DUSSEL, E., "A base na teologia da Libertaceo", **Concilium**; 104, 4(1975).
EDELE, A., "African Cities and Christian Communities", **SPEARHEAD**; Nr.72, (1982).
EKE, C.I., "Priestly and Religious Vocations", in: Obi, C.A., (ed.), **A Hundred Years of the Catholic Church in Eastern Nigeria**; Onitsha, FEP Publishers, 1985.
EKECHUKWU, A., "The Problem of Suffering in Igbo Traditional Religion", **AFER**, vol. 24, Eldoret, Gaba Publications, 2(1982).
FUERST, H., "Verlust der Familie – Gewinn einer neuen Familie", **Studia Historico -Ecclesiastica**; Rome, (1977), pp.17-47.
FUSSEL, K., "The Socio-Economic Conditioning of Church", **Concilium**, Edinburgh, (1981).
GICHUHU, G.N., "The Spirituality of the SCCs in Eastern Africa", **SPEARHEAD**; Nr.85, Eldoret, Gaba Publications, (1985).
GILBERT, J., and P. Grelot, "Covenant", in: L. Dufour, **Dictionary of Biblical Theology**; London, 1982.
GILMOUR, "Easter and Pentecost", **JBL**, 81(1962).
GREEN, R., "Religion and Morality in the African Traditional Setting", **Journal of Religion in Africa**, xiv, 1(1983).
GREGORY, A., "Communidades eclesiais de base: Utopia ou realidade", **Maringa Seminar**, Appendix 2.
GUINEY, J., "Comparing BCCs in South America and Africa", **AFER**, vol. 30, 3(1988).
GUTIERREZ, G., "L' Irruption du Pauvre dans la theologie de l' Amerique Latine", **CONVERGENCE**; 1 & 2(1981).
–, "The Irruption of the Poor in Latin America and the Christian Communities of the Common People", in: Torres, S. and Eagleson, J., eds., **The Changing of Basic Christian Communities**; New York, Maryknoll, (1981), pp.107-123.
HAFEY, P., "Personal Reflections on the New Way of Sharing in Community", **SPEARHEAD**; Nr. 45, (1976).
HAIGHT, R.D., "The 'Established' Church as Mission: The Relation of the Church to the Modern World", **Jurist**; 39, (1979), pp. 4-39.
HAMMAN, A., "La Trinite dans la Liturgie et la vie Chretienne", **Mysterium Salutis**; vol. 5, Paris, (1970), pp. 185 – 204.
HEALEY, J.G., "BCCs in Africa and Latin America", **AFER**; vol. 26, 4(1984).
–, "Our Stories as Fifth Gospel, **AFER**; vol. 30, 3(1988).
–, "Comment on the 1987 Synod of Bishops Topic on the Laity", **Tablet**; Sept. 12, (1987).
–, "BCCs in Africa and Latin America", **AFER**; vol. 26, 4(1984).

–, "Basic and Small Christian Communities", **ADS**; vol. 48, Nr. 284, Nairobi, (1984).

HEARNE, B., "Small Christian Communities: Let's Go Ahead", **AFER**; vol. 26, 5(1984).

–, (ed.), "The Community Called Church: An Experimental Source-book for Religious Education", vol. 5, **SPEARHEAD**; Nr. 60, (1979), pp. 16 – 24.

HEBBLETHWAITE, P., "Exit, 'the People of God", **Tablet**; 240 (Feb. 8,1986), pp.140-141.

HETSEN, J. and HOLMES-SIEDLE, J., "Aspects of Christian Community building in Africa", **SPEARHEAD**; Nr. 75, (1983).

HETSEN, J., "An Assembly of Brazilian Communities", **AFER**; vol. 23, 4(1981).

IDOWU, B., "The predicament of the African Church", in: Beata, C.G., (ed.), **Christianity in Tropical Africa**; London, Oxford University Press (OUP),(1968).

IRENAEUS, Adversus Haereses, v, 6, 1., **Sources Chretiennes**; 153, pp.72-81.

JOHN PAUL, II., "Opening Address at the Puebla Conference", in: J.Eagleson, and P. Scharper, (eds.), **Puebla and Beyond: Documentation and Commentary**; Maryknoll, New York, (1979).

–, "World Day of Peace Message", **L' Obsservatore Romano**; vol.17, Nrs.52-53, (1984).

JOINET, B., "Practical Steps Towards Building Christian Communities", **AFER**; vol.19, 2(1977).

KAKUBA-KAPIA, "A Theology of Fostering Ecclesial Communities", **AFER**; vol.33, 3(1991).

KAKUBA, J.B., "Christian Communities in Mbarara Diocese", **AFER**; vol. 21, 5(1979).

KALILOMBE, P.A., "The Theme's Biblical Background", **AFER**; vol. xvi, 1 & 2(1974).

–, "From Outstations to Small Christian Communities", **SPEARHEAD**; Nr. 82-83, (1984).

–, "An Overall view on building Christian Communities", **AFER**; vol.18, 5(1976).

KASENENE, P., "Natural Communities in Ecumenical Activity: Communities of God's People", **AFER**; vol. 33, 3(1991)

KASPER, W., "Kirche als Universal Sakrament", in: E. Klinger und K. Wittstadt, Hrsg., **Glaube in Proceß für Karl Rahner**; (1992).

KELLY, J., "The Evolution of SCCs", **AFER**; vol. 33, 3(1991).

KILIAN, S.J., "The Holy Spirit in Christ and Christians", **American Benedictine Review**; 20, (1969), pp. 99-121.

KILPATRICK, G.D., "Jesus, His Family and His Disciples", **Journal for the study of the New Testament**; 15, (1982).
KIRWEN, A.M., "A Theology for Village Apostolate in Tanzania", **AFER**; vol. 19, 2(1977).
KLAUCK, H.J., "Hausgemeinde und Hauskirche in frühen Christentum", **Stuttgarter Bibelstudien, (SBS)**; 103, Stuttgart, (1981).
–, "Die Hausgemeinde als Lebensform im Urchristentum", **Münchner Theologische Zeitschrift**; 32, (1981).
KOMONCHAK, J., "The Theological debate": Synod 1985-An Evaluation, **Concilium**; 188, T. and T. Clark, London, (1986), pp.110-117.
KONINGS, N., "Christian Communities, Nangina Parish, 1974-1979", **AFER**; vol. 23, 4(1981).
KYEYUNE, D., "Eucharistic Celebration as the Basis and Formation of Christian Life and Activities", **Ad usum Auditorum**; Nairobi, CHIEA, (1985).
–, "The Role of Liturgy in Pastoral Life of the Church", **ad usum auditorum**; Nairobi, CHIEA, (1985).
LABANIO, J.B., "A Community with a New Image", **International Review of Mission**; vol. Lxviii, 27(1979).
LABAYAN, J.X., "Basic Christian Communities", **AFER**; vol. 30, 2(1988).
LEHMANN, K., "GEMEINDE", **Christlicher Glaube in moderner Gesellschaft;** BD.29, Herder, Freiburg, (1982).
LEJEUNE, M. and BOUCHARD, R., "Eucharist and Community", **SPEARHEAD**; Nr. 28, Nairobi, Gaba Publications, (1973).
LEQUAT, M., "A Glimpse of Tomorrow's Church", **Lumen Vitae**; 2, (1972), pp. 185-219.
LORSCHEIDER, A., "BECs in Latin America", **AFER**; vol. 19, 3(1979).
LUMBASI, G.W., "Kinship and Small Christian Communities", **AFER**; vol. 26, 6(1984).
LWAMINDA, P., "The Theological Analysis of AMECEA – Documents in the Local Church with Special Emphasis on the Pastoral Option", unpubl. art., Nairobi, (1991).
MALINA, B.J., "Religion in the World of Paul", **Biblical Theology Bulletin**; 16, (1986).
–, "Jesus as Charismatic Leader", **Biblical Theology Bulletin**; 14(1984), pp.55-62.
MALULA, J., Mission de l'Eglisa a Kinshasa: **Options Pastorales**; Kinshasa, (1970).
–, Lettre du 14 Avril 1968.
–, Manuel du Mokambi wa Paroisse, Kinshasa, (1975).
–, Notes Pastorales, Nr.73, Kinshasa, (1973).

MANUS, C.U., "The Community of Love in Luke's Acts: A Sociological Exegesis of Acts 2:41-47 in African Context", **West African Journal of Ecclesial Studies, (WAJES)**, Vol. 2, 1(1990).

McCARTHY, D.J., "Three Covenants in Genesis", **CBQ**; 26, (1964).

McCAULEY, V.J., "On Going Formation Within the Parish", **AFER**; vol. 18, 1(1987).

McGARR, R., "A Village Catechesis", **SPEARHEAD**; Gaba Publication, Nr. 23, (1972).

MEEKS, W., "The Man from Heaven in Johannine Sectarianism", **Journal of Biblical Literature**, (JBL); 91, (1972).

MOLTMANN, J., "The Inviting Unity of the Triune God", **Concilium**, 177, 1(1985), pp.50-58.

MUSHETE, N., "The History of Theology in Africa", in: Appiah-Kubi and Torres, eds., **African Theology en Route**; New York, Maryknoll, (1983).

MUTISO-MBINDA, J., "African Background for Community Building", **AFER**; vol. 19, 6(1977).

–, "MINISTRY: Service in the Church and the World", **SPEARHEAD**; Nr. 61, Gaba Publications, 1980.

MWANA'A NZEKI, R.S.N., "Implementing AMECEA's Pastoral Priority", **AFER**; vol. 21, 5(1979).

MWOLEKA, C., "Ujamaa and Christian Communities", **SPEARHEAD**; Nr. 45, Nairobi, Gaba Publications, (1976).

–, "Small Christian Communities and Human promotion", **SPEARHEAD**; Nr. 45, Nairobi, Gaba Publications, (1976).

NAAB, J.T., "The Basic Christian Community in biblical perspective", **Incarnation Series**, Nr. 1, Owerri, Assumpta Press, n.d.

NJENGA, J., "Christian Community in Life Situation", **AFER**, 18, 5(1976).

–, "Christian Community in Life Situation", **AFER**; vol. 18, 5(1976).

NSABI, D.A., "SCCs in Kigoma Diocese", **AFER**; vol. 21, 5(1979).

NYAMITI, C., "African Tradition and the Christian God", **SPEARHEAD**; Nr. 49, (1977).

O'CONNELL, J., "The Church in Africa – Will its Success Continue?" in: Wilson, W.J., ed., **The Church in Africa**; New York, Maryknoll, (1967).

OKURE, T. et alia., 32 articles evaluating inculturation of Christianity in Africa, Gaba Publications, Eldoret, (1990).

OLIU, U.M., "How a People's Christian Community (Communidad Cristiana Popular) is Structured and how it Functions", **Concilium**; 176, (1984).

ONWU, N., "Igbo Religion: Its Present Situation", **African Marburgensia**; xviii, 2(1985).

OSADEBAY, D.C., "The Easter Reflection: The Missionary in West Africa", **West Africa**; (5th. April, 1947).

OTTENBERG, S., "Personal shrines at Afikpo", **Ethnology: An International journal of culture and social Anthropology**; vol. ix, University of Pittsburgh, 1970.

PAUL VI, "Address to the 4th. Plenary Assembly of the symposium of the Episcopal Conference of African and of Madagascar (SECAM)", **AFER**; (under the Title "Sign of Communion; A renewed faith Africanization"), vol. 18, 2(1978).

PER Frostin, "Liberation Theology in Tanzania and South Africa; a first World Interpretation", **Studia Theologica Lundensia**; 42(1988).

PERNIA, A.M., "The Ecclesiology of the Base Ecclesial Communities", **Studies in Philosophy and Theology**; vol. xv, Nr.2, Tacaytay City, Philippines, (1990).

PERRIN-JASSY, M.F., "Forming Christian Communities", **SPEARHEAD**; Nr.12, (1970).

PFLEGER, L., "Untersuchungen zur Geschichte des Pfarrinstitutes im Elaß", **Archiv für ecclesiastische Kirchengeschichte**; (1933).

PIXLEY, J., "The People of God in Biblical Tradition", **Concilium**, 176, Edingburgh, T. and T. Clark, (1984).

PROCKSCH, O., "HAGIOS", **TDNT**, vol. 1, 1981.

RAHNER, K., "Towards a Fundamental Theological Interpretation of Vatican II", **Theological studies**; vol. 40, 4(1979).

RAMIREZ, R., "Medellin and Puebla from a U.S. perspective", in: **Path from Puebla**, Washington D.C., U.S. Catholic Conference Inc., (1989).

RATZINGER, J., "Kommunion – Kommunität – Sendung", **Schauen auf den Durchbohrten**, Einsiedeln, 1984.

SAMMON, R., "Letter to J.G. Healey", **AFER**; vol. 30, 3(1988).

SALDANHA, J., "Theological Inculturation as a Missiological Problem"; **Indian Theological Studies**; 14, 4(1977).

SCHNACKENBERG, R., "Gottes Herrschaft und Reich", **Eine biblisch-theologische Studie**; Freiburg, Herder, (1963).

SCHNUERER, G., "Kirche und Kultur im Mittelalter", Paderborn, (1929).

SCHWEIZER, E., "The Matthean Church"; **NTS**; vol. 20, 1974.

SHOOLS, W., "Personal Reflections on the New Way of Sharing in Community", **SPEARHEAD**; Nr. 45, (1976).

STAF, M., "Liberation or Salvation?" **SERVICE**; Nrs. 5 & 6 (1974).

STANLEY, D.M., "Kingdom of Church: The Structural Development of Christianity in the New Testament", **Theological Studies**; xvi, 1955.

TIMIRA, A., "BCCs and the Participatory Church Theology", **AFER**; vol. 27, 6(1985).

TRILLING, W., "Das Wahre Israel", **Studien zur Theologie des Matthäusevangeliums**; (1959).

UZUKWU, E., "Christian Missions and an African Church", **AFER;** vol. 20, 2(1978).
van HUET, E., "Religious and AMECEA key Pastoral Priority", **AFER**; vol. 23, 5(1981).
–, "Religious Education and the Church", The Community called Church; **SPEARHEAD**; Nr.60, 1979.
VIA, D.O., "The Church in the Gospel of Matthew", **SJT**; vol. 11, 1958, pp.271-286.
VONCK, P., "Small is More than Beautiful", **AFER**; vol. 20, 6(1988).
WAGNER, A., "Kirche als Communio", **Anzeiger für die Seelsorge**, Heft 5, (1990) and Heft 6, (1990).
WEHRLE, P., "Der Katechismus in seiner theologischen und kirchlichen Bedeutung", **Informationen**; Erzb. Freiburg, (1986).
WEIGEL, G., "How is the Council Going", **America**; Nr.109, (1963).
ZAUNER, W., "Prinzip Gemeinde?" **Diakonia**; Heft 6, (1980).
ZORELL, (St.)., "Die Entwicklung des Parochialsystem bis zur Ende der Karolingerzeit", **Archiv für Katholische Kirchenrecht**; Lxxxii, (1902).

Ecclesiastical documents

FLANNERY, A., (ed.), **Vatican Council II**, The Conciliar and Post Conciliar Documents, New York, Costelo Publishing Company, 1987.
JOHN PAUL II, **Christifideles Laici**; London, CTS, 1988.
–, **Redemtoris Missio**, (The mission of Christ the Redeemer), London, CTS, 1991; **AAS**, 83, pp. 249-340.
–, **Address and Homilies at the Extraordinary General Assembly of the Synod of Bishops**, 1985; London, CTS, 1985.
Libertatis Nuntius; London, CTS, 1984.
PAUL VI, "Adhortatio Apostolica **Evangelii Nuntiandi** de Ad Episcopos, Sacerdotes et Christfideles totius Catholica Ecclesiae: de Evangelization in mundo huius temporis, 1975," in **AAS**, 68(1976), pp. 5-76.
PIUS XI, **Allocution to the Lenten preachers of Rome**; 1927.
PIUS XII, **Mystici Corporis**.
Rite of Anointing and Pastoral care of the sick; Washington, ICEL, 1973.
Rite of Christian Initiation for Adults; Washington, ICEL, 1974.
Synod Report: The final report and message to the people of God of the Extraordinary general Assembly of the Synod of Bishops Rome, 24 Nov.- 8 Dec., 1985, London, CTS, 1986.
SECAM DOCUMENTS: Seeking Gospel Justice in Africa, **SPEARHEAD,** Nr. 69, 1970.

The Code of Canon Law: The Canon Law Society Trust, London, Collins liturgical Publications, 1983.

Vatican Secretariat for Promoting Christian Unity, "Sects or New Religious Movements in the World: Pastoral Challenges"; United States Catholic Conference, 1986.

John Iheanyichukwu Obilor

The Doctrine of the Resurrection of the Dead and the Igbo Belief in the "Reincarnation"

A Systematico-Theological Study

Frankfurt/M., Berlin, Bern, New York, Paris, Wien, 1994. 261 pp.
Erfahrung und Theologie. Vol. 23. Editor in charge: Prof. Norbert Greinacher
ISBN 3-631-47295-1 pb. DM 79.--*

This systematic theological study in comparative religion aims at finding ways of making the mission of the Church more effective in Igboland of Nigeria. Three methods were used: the main is expository and analytic, the focus is anthropological and the end-vision is a doctrinal and pastoral dialogue. The result is an assertion that a traditional religious belief like the ịlọ-ụwa can be studied and evaluated theologically and offered healing by the Gospel message. Another result is an assertion that the Church must take inculturation seriously if it must witness to the cultures and peoples of Africa.

Contents: The Making of the Christian Belief in the Resurrection of the Dead · The Igbo and their Belief in "Reincarnation" · The Challenges of the Belief in ịlọ-ụwa ('Reincarnation') to Christianity in Igboland · The Relevance and Future of ịlọ-ụwa and the urgency for Inculturation

Peter Lang Europäischer Verlag der Wissenschaften
Frankfurt a.M. • Berlin • Bern • New York • Paris • Wien
Auslieferung: Verlag Peter Lang AG, Jupiterstr. 15, CH-3000 Bern 15
Telefon (004131) 9402121, Telefax (004131) 9402131
- Preisänderungen vorbehalten - *inklusive Mehrwertsteuer